HUNTER-GA

AMERIND STUDIES IN ARCHAEOLOGY

SERIES EDITOR **JOHN WARE**

Hunter-Gatherer Archaeology as Historical Process

Edited by **Kenneth E. Sassaman**
and **Donald H. Holly Jr.**

The University of Arizona Press
Tucson

 THE UNIVERSITY OF
ARIZONA PRESS

© 2011 The Arizona Board of Regents
First issued as a paperback edition 2013

www.uapress.arizona.edu

Library of Congress Cataloging-in-Publication Data
Hunter-gatherer archaeology as historical process / edited by
Kenneth E. Sassaman and Donald H. Holly, Jr.
p. cm. — (Amerind studies in archaeology)
Papers from a seminar held in 2008 at the Amerind Foundation
in Dragoon, Ariz.
Includes bibliographical references and index.
ISBN 978-0-8165-2925-4 (hard cover : acid-free paper)
ISBN 978-0-8165-3043-4 (paperback : acid-free paper)
1. Indians of North America—Antiquities—Congresses.
2. Indians of North America—Historiography—Congresses.
3. Hunting and gathering societies—North America—
History—Congresses. 4. Hunting and gathering
societies—North America—Historiography—Congresses.
5. Excavations (Archaeology)—North America—Congresses.
6. Archaeology and history—North America—Congresses.
7. Archaeology—North America—Philosophy—Congresses.
8. North America—Antiquities—Congresses. 9. North
America—Historiography—Congresses. I. Sassaman,
Kenneth E. II. Holly, Donald H., Jr. III. Amerind
Foundation.
E77.8.H8   2011
970.01—dc22   2010039354

Publication of this book is made possible in part by a grant
from the Amerind Foundation.

Manufactured in the United States of America on acid-free,
archival-quality paper and processed chlorine free.

18   17   16   15   14   13   7   6   5   4   3   2

In memory of
Donald H. Holly Sr.

Contents

Part III
The Structure of Historical Process

Hunter-Gatherer Archaeology as Historical Process

Transformative Hunter-Gatherer Archaeology in North America

Kenneth E. Sassaman and Donald H. Holly Jr.

Since the dawn of the discipline, anthropologists have looked to contemporary hunter-gatherers for clues to the beginnings of humanity, the essence of life before agriculture and the state, or as Alan Barnard (2004a:5) puts it, the last vestige of "natural man." Only recently have anthropologists come to grips with the deep and enduring connections between hunter-gatherers and their neighbors—from the farmers and herders with whom they often partner, to the nation-states in which they are encapsulated (Headland and Reid 1989; Wilmsen 1989). Over the last several decades ethnographic research has grown decidedly historical in orientation, with hunter-gatherers now understood as active agents in histories of intercultural connections (Trigger 1999). Unfortunately, as ethnographic study has become less evolutionary in its theoretical orientation, many archaeologists who study the premodern past have stopped paying attention. Given studies that leave little room for generalization and discourage analogical reasoning, archaeologists' benign neglect of recent literature is understandable but unfortunate, because the time before modern history was no less historical *in process* (Cobb 2005; Pauketat 2001a) than that which followed, even though *particular* histories of colonial encounters, genocide, and forced migrations were unique to the conditions of modernity. Indeed, archaeology offers a deep-time perspective and societal diversity well beyond the purview of ethnography and, therefore, has much to offer ongoing efforts to historicize "natural man," as well as the development of historical method and theory in anthropology at large.

Recent and ongoing archaeological research in North America is contributing to this effort. Discoveries of late make it difficult to generalize much at all about hunter-gatherers, that is, beyond the pale of subsistence. North America has always been noteworthy for its anomalously

complex hunter-gatherers of the Northwest Coast, and now archaeological inquiry throughout North America is revealing how wildly
divergent pathways to complexity can be. Elsewhere on the continent,
archaeologists have documented some of the signal accoutrements of
complex society (e.g., monuments), but in times and places of high
mobility, local group autonomy, and egalitarian structures. And where
archaeologists document the residues of the highly mobile foragers who
seem to fit the mold of "natural man," their particular histories involve
scales of social interaction and involvement with "others" that make
it hard to explain their existence without reference to regional, if not
continental or global, political economies.

Each author of this volume has made substantive contributions to
this corpus of newfound data, and many have been working on its implications for broader understanding of hunter-gatherer diversity. Field
research among this group of scholars spans the entire continent, from
subtropical Florida to the Canadian Subarctic, and from the Northwest
Plateau to southern California and the central Mississippi River valley.
Their research likewise spans all manner of temporal and formal variation among hunter-gatherer populations, and it encompasses an array of
method and theory. Nonetheless, this volume does not presume to be a
comprehensive account of hunter-gatherer archaeology in North America today. Indeed, there are many accomplished archaeologists who are
advancing knowledge about foragers through method and theory that
are not included in this volume, and irrespective of theoretical orientation, large areas of North America are unrepresented here. By design,
this volume includes contributions by archaeologists whose theoretical proclivities lean more toward "historical" paradigms, as opposed to
those we could gloss as "evolutionary." Our sense is that evolutionary
paradigms, such as those of behavioral ecology, evolutionary ecology, or
selectionism, have dominated discourse on hunter-gatherer variability
and change for at least three decades (e.g., Bettinger 1991; Binford 2001;
Kelly 1995). Archaeologists who draw theoretical inspiration from the
humanities and culture studies—as do most of the contributors of this
volume—have long been in the minority. This volume thus gives a bit
of collective voice to alternatives to the dominant paradigms.

A number of key points of agreement and articulation are evident
among the chapters of this volume. Foremost is the importance of

historical contingency in our understanding of hunter-gatherer variation and change. Whereas historical contingency is central to all sorts
of theories of change, including those inspired by organic evolution,
when the subjects of inquiry are hunter-gatherers, history is too often
swamped by variables that are portrayed as universal to organisms so
closely reliant on natural resources (i.e., the decision-making criteria of
optimal foraging models or the forces of selection).

In contrast, the sense of historical contingency promoted in this volume privileges actual lived experience in continuously shaping, reproducing, and transforming the contours of social and cultural difference.
From an archaeological perspective, this logic is encapsulated nicely by
an "emergent paradigm" that Pauketat (2001a) calls "historical processualism." Inspired by the theories of agency and practice, historical processualism is concerned with the dynamic interplay between the actions
people take and the structure that constrains and enables such actions.
It treats this interplay as recursive and generative of human history, as
in the Marxian notion that people make their own history, even if by
terms they themselves do not fully control (Marx and Engels 1963).
Moreover, when the cultural logic for motivating action makes reference to the past, humans actively manipulate the ontological structures
that inflect history. Fortunately, from an archaeological standpoint, historical production often involves material resources and consequences
that remain durable, if cryptic, as archaeological evidence. In this sense,
artifacts and other dimensions of materiality are less like the residues of
human behavior and more like the tools of social and cultural change:
mounds give materiality to mythology and serve as mnemonic devices
and as theaters for the performance of new histories; exotic raw materials index distant peoples and places and help to advance status claims
or identity and to assert genealogical precedence in emergent power
relationships.

Although not all contributors to this volume would point directly to
historical processualism as the framework for their research, all would
agree that there is nothing inherent in living off the land that precludes
hunter-gatherers from determining their own fates and interpreting
their own histories. Ironically, even modern social theory reveals a lingering bias in treating hunter-gatherers as being "back of history" (Wolf
1984:394) because of the ontological need to contrast the conditions of

modernity with what came before. It follows that most of the signature historical processes of the modern era (e.g., diaspora, coalescence, hybridity, genocide) are assumed to have little bearing on cultural variation and change among "primitives" (Cobb 2005). Contributors to this volume offer case material and theoretical justification to counter this entrenched way of thinking. They certainly agree that the generalizations about hunter-gatherers we learned as students cannot bear the weight of empirical evidence to the contrary, and that the conceptual baggage engendered by these generalizations derived from mid-twentieth-century ethnography continues to marginalize both hunter-gatherers as a subject worthy of study and, arguably, those of us who choose to study them.

We first convened as a group in a 2008 symposium at the Society for American Archaeology meeting in Vancouver, Canada. Our collective effort was rewarded with an invitation to reconvene at the Amerind Foundation in Dragoon, Arizona, where, over the course of three days, we discussed each others' papers and explored the intersections of our diverse perspectives. It is our hope that the synergy and synthesis enabled by the Amerind seminar, and now this book, will contribute to the agenda for hunter-gatherer archaeology in the twenty-first century. After three decades of overturning misconceptions about foragers in the modern era, it is up to archaeology to teach us about hunter-gatherers before they were canonized as "primitives" by anthropology (Kuper 1988).

We have structured this volume around three mutually dependent themes. Part I, Agents of History and Evolution, includes chapters on the agency of hunter-gatherer subjects in emergent patterns of social, demographic, and environmental change. Part II, The Sociality of Historical Practice, explores discursive actions that draw on perceptions of past human experience as proscriptions or interventions of social change. The chapters in Part III, The Structure of Historical Process, showcase specific long-term histories in the development of knowledge about historical processes in general. The volume is capped with an essay by seminar discussant H. Martin Wobst, an archaeologist who warned the profession about the pitfalls of uniformitarianism and analogy several years before revisionist thinking transformed hunter-gatherer studies in ethnography (Wobst 1978). The salience of his message for archaeological practice is as great as ever.

Agents of History and Evolution

A recalcitrant bias in anthropological conceptions of hunter-gatherers is that they are passive subjects whose fate is determined by the invisible hands of environment and demography (Yengoyan 2004). When afforded the privilege to act, by alternative theory, hunter-gatherers find ways to turn ecological imperative into political gain. Each of these perspectives has its limitations. The former describes an emergent condition familiar to evolutionary discourse, but it results in redundant and circular knowledge claims. The latter is a misapplication of agency or practice theory, which does not implicate methodological individuals but rather the interplay between structure and practice (Bourdieu 1977), an inherently social process. If, as Tim Ingold (1999) reasons, hunter-gatherers are distinct in their particular form of sociality, based on trust, then archaeology is challenged to determine when and how this follows from the intrinsic relationship between humans and their environment, which behavioral ecologists have suggested (Kelly 1995); and when and how the asserted sociality of a people follows from encapsulation by "others," as in the knowledge claims of political economists (e.g., Wilmsen 1989). Archaeologists have the related challenge of documenting the conditions under which this sort of sociality is transformed into institutions of mistrust and exclusion.

Authors of chapters in this section explore the intersections and contradictions of interpretive frameworks on hunter-gatherer diversity rooted in evolutionary paradigms, on the one hand, and historical or political-economy paradigms on the other, including agency or practice theory and phenomenology. Although theories in these contrastive paradigms are often characterized as diametrically opposed, evolution can be construed as historical narrative when situated in context, and both make observations of the particular to formulate (and test) generalized knowledge. It follows that some of the theoretical discord between evolutionary and historical paradigms may be more a matter of semantics than of epistemology.

In the lead chapter of this section, Anna Marie Prentiss carves out some shared conceptual space between evolution and history. Drawing on recent developments in macroevolutionary theory, Prentiss explores the historical contingency of emergent social inequality among hunter-gatherers of the Northwest Plateau. This case study serves to illustrate how the interplay between the genealogical and socioecological hierarchies of macroevolution bears similarity to the dynamic relationship between structure and practice in social process. As Prentiss demonstrates, the emergence of genealogical "cores" (like structure) is never simply the outcome of a predetermined process or product of human intention. Rather, historical twists and turns actualized in real lived experience leads to consequences—in this case institutionalized inequality—unanticipated by microevolutionary theory.

Through different theoretical lenses, Kathleen L. Hull makes much the same point in a study of demographic change in the Yosemite Valley of California. Demography is an oft-cited cause for culture change among hunter-gatherers, but it is commonly reduced to long-term population growth or decline due to environmental factors alone. Shifting the temporal unit of analysis to the human lifetime, Hull shows how demography provides an observational nexus that blends the experiential (practice) and the analytical (structure) in assessment of both short- and long-term change.

The enduring biases of cultural evolutionary typologies are exposed in modern perspectives on California shell mounds by Kent G. Lightfoot, Edward M. Luby, and Lisa Pesnichak. They argue that even as archaeologists began to appreciate that hunter-gatherers varied more than old typologies allowed, structural relationships were borrowed from existing types (e.g., chiefdoms) to make new types (e.g., complex hunter-gatherers) that, in effect, minimized actual variation. Thus, the shell mounds of San Francisco Bay were assumed to be like the villages of chiefdoms, while the application of fire to effect ecological change was likened to agricultural production. The actual histories of making and altering places across the California landscape defy both of these assumptions.

Cultural evolutionary bias permeates many of the metaphors and grand narratives of the popular imagination. In this sense, hunter-gatherers are renowned more by what they lack than by what they possess. In a case study from the Subarctic of eastern Canada, Donald Holly shows how this extends to the perceived inability of hunter-gatherers to succeed or fail on their own accord. This bias is accentuated in environments, such as the Subarctic, where the margin of error is considered to be so slim. Thus, instances of abandonment are read, a priori, as responses to environmental stress, and all cultural accoutrements are interpreted as features necessary for survival. In contrast, Holly makes the case that whether they were successful or not, all outcomes of hunter-gatherers were the result of the negotiations among people who operated within vast social contexts, including "others," and who understood their pasts and planned for their futures within historically situated world views.

The Sociality of Historical Practice

History is among Western civilization's more polysemous constructs. In the common usage, history is the chronicle of events that shaped the course and pace of change. Although it is filled with the concrete experiences of real persons, history is situated in objectified time, a sequence that is linear and irreversible, and is segmented into eras, epochs, genres, and periods. And although concrete histories can be abstracted into "whole" or "global" histories, as in Braudelian history (Braudel 1996), they are often written and interpreted in particularistic terms.

Alternatively, as an enduring subject of Western philosophical inquiry, history can be understood as the cultural production of the past (Pauketat 2001b). For westerners, this production has typically been a literary enterprise, the writing of narratives informed by historical facts and structured by the events, phases, and periods we abstract from observation. Historiography is the means we use to critically assess and contextualize knowledge claims about the past, to question entire genres of writing. The writing of "prehistory," for example, has been critically scrutinized for its role in reproducing the Western notion of progress, arguably its core ontological premise (Fabian 1983). Indeed, Western accounts of the past, ancient and modern, are a microcosm for the development of Western philosophy more generally (de Certeau 1988; Diamond 1974).

Just as the development of Western thought is revealed through historiographic inquiry, the consideration of how cultural engagements with the "past" among non-Western peoples is revealing of their own historical experiences (e.g., Sahlins 1995) might be profitable for us to pursue. Under what conditions, for instance, do humans mobilize historical consciousness in acts of cultural production? And, in the absence of writing, what sources are available for interpreting nonliterate acts of history-making? On the first question, a broad range of case material, anthropological and otherwise, would suggest that historical consciousness in non-Western cultures shares with Western experience a recognition of change predicated on encounters with "others" (e.g., Povinelli 2002). For westerners, encounters with the "primitive other" formed the basis for nineteenth-century evolutionism, a historical narrative of progress (Diamond 1974; Thomas 1989). Similarly, among non-Western peoples, encounters with the "others" often lead to the genesis or assertion of new cosmologies and new socialities aimed at unifying diversity, in some cases, and at resisting change, in others (e.g., Grinker 1994).

As to the second question, the North American archaeological record is rife with clues about the historical practices of ancient hunter-gatherers. Monuments, cemeteries, and portable heirlooms are among the more conspicuous material manifestations, while practices of traveling, migration, and alliance are reflected in patterns often glossed as settlement and exchange. Contributors to this theme have some of the latest data available on the cultural construction of history, identity, and social networks.

One of the most audacious acts of cultural production in ancient North America was the creation of Poverty Point in northeast Louisiana. In their size, grandeur, and engineering, the earthen mounds and rings of Poverty Point were unquestionably deliberate acts of interpretation and representation. Mound A, the second-largest mound north of Mexico, was assembled in a matter of months, in real human time. Tristram R. Kidder argues that this event materialized a cosmogonic myth known to us from ethnohistoric accounts of possible descendant communities. Whereas the myth and its materialization in form referenced existing "tradition" and thus appears nostalgic, it is useful to consider how the past was drawn upon to chart a new path for the future, to reinterpret and redirect the course of history.

This same theme is extended into deeper time in Asa R. Randall's analysis of the shell mounds of the middle St. Johns River valley of northeast Florida. Over several millennia, starting more than six thousand years ago, places of dwelling were transformed by depositional practices that, in some cases, recapitulated past practices and, in others, erased them. Discontinuities in the inhabitability of places and in the composition of regional populations inflected a long-term history that has been misinterpreted as "continuity" or "sustainability" by archaeologists who regard shell mounds as simply refuse heaps. When viewed as historical production, however, the shell mounds of Florida, like the mounds of Poverty Point, provide insight into discursive acts whose purpose was to mobilize society for structural change.

The focus shifts from cultural production of place to the structural linkages among places, and hence among people, in the regional alliances of the Eastern Subarctic. In her chapter, Moira McCaffrey turns our attention from monuments toward portable objects as embodiments of social practice. With data on the geological sources of flaked stone tools, McCaffrey reconstructs patterns of procurement that defy simplistic microeconomic predictions as well as the widespread belief that alliances of exchange were primarily safety nets against failure. Although networking no doubt averted risk for individuals and communities, the reproduction and transformation of alliances through lithic "exchange" operated at a much higher level of social reproduction. This pattern becomes evident in the emergence of elongated houses in the late prehistoric period, where social memory was created and renewed in ritual practice involving stone.

That hunter-gatherers are never merely victims of history but, instead, makers of history is exemplified in the study of Mountain Shoshone by Laura L. Scheiber and Judson Byrd Finley. Our modern understanding of encounters between the colonial juggernauts of Europe and hunter-gatherers worldwide formed the basis for "revisionist" ethnography, which substituted the political-economic processes of domination and resistance for the ecological imperative of theories from natural science. Scheiber and Finley illustrate how colonial encounters in the Yellowstone Mountains of western Wyoming encouraged certain factions of Shoshone to assert autonomy through mobility. The deep recesses and rough terrain of the Yellowstone Mountains offered not only refuge but a landscape of identity that distanced Shoshone—literally and figuratively—from the forces that would engulf them. This case builds on a series of similar studies that suggest that attributes of foragers once considered to be determined by environment alone (in this case mobility) are instead deliberate acts of resistance to oppressive (or at least unfamiliar) forces (Sassaman 2001). Studies such as these provide a basis for drawing inferences about historical production more generally.

The Structure of Historical Process

Many would say that the Achilles' heel of Boasian culture-history was its particularistic quality, but ironically, that was hardly Boas's goal. Mindful of the limitations of generalizable knowledge from nineteenth-century cultural evolutionism, Boas was deliberately empirical in his approach to inquiry, careful to build inference from observation. We subscribe to this doctrine of empiricism while acknowledging that emergent properties of concrete histories provide a basis for strong inference about broader historical processes. Hunter-gatherer (pre)history offers untapped potential for developing generalizations about migration, ethnogenesis, diasporas, and other processes that have hitherto been restricted to food-producing and modern societies.

Archaeologists working in the American Southwest have been assembling one of the more detailed accounts of large-scale human migration and cultural realignment in the pre-Columbian Americas. Abandonment of the Colorado Plateau by Ancient Puebloans and their resettlement to the far south involved not only diasporic movements but also coalescent societies whose integrated diversity begat the next generation of ancestral Pueblos (Cameron and Duff 2008; Lekson 1995). Similarly, archaeologists working the archaeological record of Cahokia and its Mississippian counterparts have been demonstrating how monumental events erupted from the coalescence of diverse peoples, gatherings that would eventually dissolve and reform in different locations repeatedly to shape the course of their own history (Alt 2006; Pauketat 2004).

Ancient hunter-gatherers are generally excluded from accounts of such historical processes, and for no good reason. We would imagine that among the hunter-gatherers of North America, instances of migration, group realignment, intergroup conflict, fissioning, diaspora, and coalescence were as frequent and spatially grand as those of later agricultural societies. Detailing the concrete histories of these "events" is requisite to investigating the historicism they entailed, but if studies of modern societies are any indication, what people inscribe through discursive historical practices often bears little direct relationship to lived experience. This itself is worthy of study and requires that we draw inferences with both Western and non-Western historicity in mind.

In broadening the scope of historical inquiry to include hunter-gatherers, we have to be especially vigilant about our use of the concepts of continuity, change, and tradition. We need to explore temporalities of human experience without imposing the linearity of Western history or historicism, which assumes an organic succession of human developments. We must develop methods for recognizing representations of culture in time frames that are nonlinear or cyclical. Likewise, we need to bear in mind that "tradition" does not depend on continuity in or the legacy of practice—people of diverse cultural dispositions draw on particular events or remnants of various pasts to assert identities that are oppositional to the "other" and to change.

Contributors to this section confront the patterns of continuity and change in long-term archaeological records. They address the role of events in influencing structure, continuities in structure when practice appears discontinuous, and the manner in which innovation is asserted as "tradition." The common goal of these chapters is to seek methods for drawing inferences about long-term and "whole" histories from detailed archaeological contexts.

The big picture of eastern North American is framed in a chapter by Kenneth E. Sassaman as a history of cultural encounters, ethnogenesis, coalescence, and diasporas. He focuses on processes of alterity—the cultural construction of the "other"—to suggest that emergent diversity among hunter-gatherer societies was a consequence of interaction, not isolation. Although none of the encounters leading to assertions of difference may have involved conditions as oppressive as those of European contact, if we relax the assumption that all indigenous people were like-minded, we can imagine processes of alterity that were as powerful in explaining emergent new cultural traditions and social formations as were the conditions of colonialism. History did not start with the arrival of Europeans.

A long-term perspective on the archaeological traditions of ancient New England enables Brian S. Robinson and Jennifer C. Ort to locate streams of ritual continuity in a patchwork of social boundaries and technological alternatives. New England has always proved challenging to archaeological interpretation because of the contrasting, oftentimes contentious perspectives of in situ, local evolutionary change versus the nonlocal stimuli of migration and diffusion. In the case material

Robinson and Ort review, sharply contrasting technologies share an emphasis on the importance of hunting rituals among northern hunters and gatherers. They amount to hunting technologies and social strategies that are not easily adopted or discarded but rather carry the weight of history that supersedes the costs and benefits of "practical" choices.

The final case study by Lynn H. Gamble delivers us to one of North America's most complex hunter-gatherer people, the Chumash of California. Recent research on the Chumash has centered on the causes of institutionalized inequality, with some researchers emphasizing the environmental changes that disrupted traditional practice and the technological and social innovations of adjustment to new conditions. Gamble has long been a proponent of the perspective that so much of what appears to be novel in the emergence of inequality has deep historical roots. The production and distribution of shell beads over a 7,000-year history is a strong case in point. In a review of the multiple and changing constituencies involved in the production, distribution, and consumption of shell beads, Gamble argues against a structural relationship between bead economies and social power. She identifies multiple transformations in the types and quantities of beads, their symbolic meaning, and their distribution to reveal changing contexts of gift giving, brokerage, transportation, conveyance, demand, genealogical ties, and alliance at multiple scales. Gamble further argues that such transformations had far greater impact on the political, economic, and social developments of the Chumash than did environmental changes, and thus warrant greater attention from archaeologists than they currently garner.

Conclusion

Hunter-gatherer studies are among the most dynamic specialties in anthropology, but the sea change that marks the past thirty years of critical analysis in ethnography has not affected archaeology as much as it should. Ironically, as the pursuit of knowledge about "primitive" peoples became historicized in ethnography, the anthropologists with greatest purchase on long-term histories became marginalized. This volume is intended to transcend the self-imposed dichotomies between primitives and moderns, and between those who study prehistory and those who study history. We hope to be able to contribute to the agenda for hunter-gatherer archaeology in years to come by offering substantive example and methodological innovation to the historical analysis of ancient times. If this volume is successful, the concept of hunter-gatherer will have lost most of its conceptual baggage and emerge in new guise as a subject that contributes to generalized knowledge about historical process among all manner of humanity.

Acknowledgments

On behalf of all contributors to this volume, the editors extend sincere thanks to the Amerind Foundation and its director, John Ware, for the opportunity to spend three days in Dragoon working as a group to advance this project, and for the opportunity to parlay this intensive and rewarding intellectual experience into a book. The entire Amerind staff deserves thanks too for making our visit so comfortable and productive. The editors also express gratitude to Allyson Carter, Scott De Herrera, Alan Schroder, and Pat Cattani of the University of Arizona Press for shepherding this project with great care. The senior editor acknowledges the Hyatt and Cici Brown Endowment for Florida Archaeology, Department of Anthropology, University of Florida, in its support of this project.

PART I

Agents of History and Evolution

Social Histories of Complex Hunter-Gatherers

Pacific Northwest Prehistory in a Macroevolutionary Framework

Anna Marie Prentiss

Why social change among hunter-gatherers? Today, in the early twenty-first century our discussions of hunter-gatherer sociality exhibit an incredibly high degree of sophistication in our knowledge of hunter-gatherer variability and our ability to parse that variability using modern and postmodern theoretical structures. Yet, in some ways we remain tangled in the same explanatory debates that plagued anthropologists a century ago.

We are asked to consider the chasm between hunter-gatherers as by-products of deterministic demoecological processes, whether associated with neoevolutionary theory (Binford 1968; White 1949) or human behavioral ecology (Kelly 1995), versus these same people as political actors less affected by environmental and demographic constraints (Clark and Blake 1989, 1994; Hayden 1994, 1995). Our debates reflect a deeper underlying tension between those who favor scientific explanation as law driven and deterministic versus those who assert an essential role for history and individual agency.

Consider the debate over adaptationist explanations in evolutionary biology. Gould and Lewontin (1979) castigate biologists for reliance on adaptationist "just so" stories rooted in deterministic "ultra-Darwinian" (Eldredge 1995) thinking. What if, they argue, historical events occur outside the predictions of scientific models, which have the effect of triggering new trends? Could not history be a significant contributor to the evolutionary process, at least as a provider of grist for the evolutionary mill? In contrast, many evolutionary scientists (e.g., Richerson and Boyd 2005) reject the role of nonadaptive explanations in favor of more deterministic Darwinian models, asserting that such processes (e.g., exaptations) are unlikely to have been important since they must have occurred less frequently than adaptive changes.

Ultimately, the tension in evolutionary biology reflects an even more fundamental rumbling between the sciences and humanities (Gould 2002). But archaeologists do not need to reject history to develop a scientific approach to culture change. It is well known that selection acts on variation; the source of variation certainly could come from adaptive processes, but it could also derive from historically unique events and actions, however rare (and I do not think they are insignificantly rare). Such historical "accidents" may be particularly important when it comes to truly significant changes, those that revolutionize the basic fabric of human societies.

Hunter-gatherer societies can be extremely conservative, substantially due to a common reliance on learning strategies emphasizing vertical transmission (e.g., parent to offspring) (Boyd and Richerson 1985; Shennan 2002). Consequently, evidence for major changes in the structure of hunter-gatherer socioeconomic strategies and political systems is rare in the archaeological record, and when change does occur, it seems to happen rapidly (Arnold 1993; Bar-Yosef and Meadow 1995; Chatters and Prentiss 2005; Prentiss and Chatters 2003a). Change in this context refers to the foundation-level organizing principles for integrating such things as mobility schedules, foraging tactics, labor management, and technological organization, what Rosenberg (1994, 2009) defines as a cultural "Bauplan," Prentiss and Chatters (2003a; Prentiss 2009) call a "Resource Management Strategy," or Bettinger (2009) terms a "Complex Adaptive Strategy." While change on this highest scale is apparently rare, lower-scale evolution (e.g., technology) is relatively constant. Under such highly conservative conditions (e.g., Savelle 2002), it seems a wonder that higher-order change could occur at all. Indeed, cultural extinction may have been more common in the past than radical change.

Institutionalized social inequality developed in the Pacific Northwest during the final two thousand years of the prehistoric period or, put differently, after eight thousand years of relatively egalitarian living. The emergence of the classic complex hunter-gatherer societies of the Northwest Coast and Interior stands as a major threshold event in North American prehistory and, consequently, has been the subject of much debate (Ames and Maschner 1999; Matson and Coupland 1995). Northwest Coast anthropologists and archaeologists have proposed deterministic explanations emphasizing the functional redistribution of wealth (Piddocke 1965), management of large groups (Ames 1985) and general impacts of population growth or packing (Binford 2001; Kelly 1995; Lohse and Sammons-Lohse 1986). Historical contingency and agency have also crept into explanatory arguments in the form of modeled relationships between ecological opportunities and actions of local factions and aspiring elites (Hayden 1994, 1995; Maschner and Patton 1996).

While these models have added important insight into many processes of culture change, many of them also suffer from the assumption that the adaptive value of an outcome explains its origin. Take, for example, status seeking by elites as at least a partial explanation for the emergence of complex society in the Pacific Northwest (Hayden 1994). As an evolutionary explanation this model presumes that the social structure is already in place that would permit such status-seeking strategies. But it cannot be in place because presumably it has not yet evolved. So either evolution is taking us in a predetermined direction or the evolutionary process relies upon individuals previously hardwired for specific outcomes. Since neither of these outcomes is likely correct (theoretically [Rose and Rose 2000] or empirically [e.g., Prentiss et al. 2007]), we must continue our search for alternative explanations.

Continuing this line of thought, I suggest that it is also worth asking whether adaptive innovation (whether agent defined or forced by systemic demands) was even necessary to develop complex social organization. We have a growing body of evidence to suggest that innovation, whether stimulated or not, was rarely the direct cause for major socioeconomic or political changes. Indeed, in contrast to earlier studies (e.g., Fitzhugh 2001; Rosenberg 1990), recent research by Chatters (2009), Zeder (2009a, 2009b), and Eldredge (2009) strongly implies that innovation often occurs largely independent of stimulus and rarely has any immediate direct impacts on broader patterns of organization. Rates of technological innovation (and loss) do appear correlated with numbers of innovators (Edinborough 2009; Henrich 2004). It appears increasingly likely that many of the cultural institutions we take for granted may have had their starts in problem solving associated with other contingencies. So, some forms of wild plant intensification began as unintended effects of alterations in hunting strategies (Bettinger 1999). Agriculture developed as an effect of domestication among other things (Richerson et al. 2001; Rindos 1984). And use of preexisting

knowledge and dormant technologies probably even reduced or elimi-
nated any need for significant research and development across these
transitions (e.g., Chatters 2009).

Most Pacific Northwest theorists have viewed social complexity to
be an innovation developed to solve problems associated with population packing, territorial circumscription, processing and distribution
of concentrated resources, and general self-betterment. But hereditary
inequality would not have benefited all (or at least not all equally),
which raises a problem for simple adaptationist explanations. In this
chapter I draw from macroevolutionary theory to argue that the evolution of hunter-gatherer cultures in North America's Pacific Northwest
occurred through a complex historical process that did not always require
stimulus-driven problem solving or elite machinations as the prime
movers. Indeed, some elements more likely developed as nonadaptive
"effects" or "spandrels" (Gould and Lewontin 1979) that in their initial forms offered no functional group or individual payoffs. Logically,
therefore, individual agents alone (e.g., "aggrandizers") could not necessarily have been the cause, but the consequence, thereby implicating a
more complex and interesting process behind the development of social
complexity in these societies.

A Macroevolutionary Perspective on Culture and History

Cultural evolution can be understood in Darwinian terms most simply
because humans inherit (by learning, imitation, and the like) and act
on cultural information. That information can form the basis for strategies allowing them to pursue food, learn resource configurations on
landscapes, and compete with one another socially. If such strategies
are successful in that the people realize socioeconomic payoffs in their
use, we can say they were "selected" in the sense of Skinner's (1981)
"selection by consequences" or Eldredge's (1995:34) "what worked better than what."

This view of cultural evolution does not presume that evolution
acts only on one scale (e.g., artifacts), but rather in a hierarchical form.
Consequently, we recognize cultural evolutionary processes acting on
scales ranging from artifacts to socioeconomic or political strategies.

Put more formally, and drawing from a broad literature in paleobiology and evolutionary anthropology (Boyd et al. 1997; Eldredge 1985, 2008, 2009; Holden and Shennan 2005; Mace and Holden 2005; Prentiss and Chatters 2003a; Rosenberg 1994, 2009; Spencer 1997, 2009; Zeder 2009b), we can envision culture minimally[1] in two complementary hierarchical frameworks: one, genealogical in nature, consisting of basic information units (e.g., "memes"), packages (integrated information), and cores (complex hierarchical systems held together by a central logic or "glue"); the other, socioecological, comprised of social units spanning individuals to families to various more complex socioculturally defined groups. This model assumes change could be stimulated and recorded on higher or lower scales with potential effects in either direction.

From a macroevolutionary perspective, cultural evolution is best viewed as a back-and-forth interaction between hierarchies or what Eldredge (2008) calls the "sloshing bucket." Action (human behavior and feedback—the cultural correlates of phenotypic variation and selection) within the socioecological hierarchy determines what gets recorded on the genealogical side (e.g., Durham 1979, 1990). Yet the genealogical hierarchy simultaneously defines any starting point for developments on the socioecological side (we act upon information). A major implication is that cultural evolution is an inherently historical process. The socioecological realm is where we recognize the action of individual agents, factions, and the like. This is where social theory makes its best contribution (e.g., Kidder, this vol.; Sassaman, this vol.). Oddly, this is also where we find human behavioral ecology with its emphasis on the microeconomics of human decision making (e.g., Cannon and Broughton 2010). While theorists from the two schools rarely converse, their disparate perspectives are essential to a complete understanding of the cultural evolutionary process because agency is subject to economic (and other) feedback (sometimes, selection) (Durham 1979). Or, as put by Clare Boothe Luce, "no good deed goes unpunished!"

Imagine selection or some cultural analogue of selection[2] such as the bias mechanisms of Boyd and Richerson (1985) targeting specific cultural characters that, under the classic Darwinian model, evolve because they offer payoffs (not necessarily reproductive) to their users. Now recall that evolution of one trait will often have impacts on others such that new traits or "effects" can emerge as by-products of evolution acting on the original character (e.g., Boyd and Richerson 1996). All other things being equal, the new traits are recorded in the genealogical hierarchy even if they are adaptively neutral. Here they may remain effectively dormant or they might be co-opted into use. If the latter occurs, the "effect" or "spandrel" could become a target of its own adaptive evolutionary process. In this new context we would term it an "exaptation" (Gould and Vrba 1982).

In recent years, social scientists, including a few archaeologists, have developed a range of evolutionary models drawing from these ideas. For example, De Block and Dewitte (2007) argue that new economic strategies could develop as effects of mating games whereby show-off behavior between sexes could accidentally trigger new forms of group-adaptive behavior (e.g., hunting in the Lower Paleolithic). Gamble (1996) asserts that as modern humans colonized new habitats during the Upper Paleolithic, old adaptive strategies were routinely co-opted to help solve new problems implicating exaptation. Catton (1998) suggests that mutualism between human groups evolved from labor diversification as an effect of altered social relationships. Bettinger (1999) and Rosenberg (2009) argue that historically contingent events such as introduction of new technologies (Bettinger 2009) could have unanticipated consequences on foraging strategies, sharing, labor arrangements, or ultimately even social status differentiation.

I want to highlight two important implications derived from this line of thinking. First, the source of variation necessary for cultural evolution is not necessarily always human innovation or conscious agency. While previous developments constrain future actions, they may also provide unexpected starting points for new ventures. Consequently, we may not be aware when the stage is set for new starts. If that is the case, then many of our institutions (like those associated with inequality) may have evolved from unintended beginnings. Second, we cannot escape the effects of contingent history, by which I mean events outside the bounds of our abilities to predict their occurrence with evolutionary theory. Climate, for example, has often played the arbiter for success and failure in many societies, particularly those living closest to the earth (as in most small-scale food producers and hunter-gatherers). I explore these thoughts further in the following case study.

The Evolution of Complex Hunter-Gatherer Societies in the Pacific Northwest

Classic complex societies of the Pacific Northwest developed through a historical process with unexpected twists and turns that just happened to lead to the emergence of ranked societies during the late prehistoric period. Put differently, the record implicates the late period societies as distinct entities with unique histories, not examples of unilinear global trends.

Collectors among Others

It is well known that the late prehistoric hunter-gatherers of British Columbia's coast and southern interior were organized in a pattern best described as winter-village collectors (Matson and Coupland 1995; Prentiss and Kuijt 2004). Subsistence economies centered on targeting and mass harvest of key marine species, including sea mammals ranging from harbor seals to whales, and fish such as herring and salmon. Terrestrial mammalian species varied in importance between ecological areas but generally included various species of bear, ungulates, and rodents. Plant foods, particularly berry and geophyte (root) species, have often been overlooked in Pacific Northwest prehistory (Lepofsky and Lyons 2003) but were often essential resources as well. These foods were harvested for both immediate and delayed consumption. Storage tactics included roasting, smoking, and drying, and subsequent collection and keeping in boxes, house rafters, cache pits, and specialized storage structures. Villages were generally placed optimal to key resources, and logistical mobility was employed to obtain more distant foods and other materials (Ames 2002). Seasonal abundance was used to create stored surpluses designed to buffer seasons of need as often occurred during winter and early spring. It was also put to use for social reasons (e.g., Hayden 1995).

Chatters and I have argued elsewhere (Chatters and Prentiss 2005; Prentiss and Chatters 2003a, 2003b) that the development of collector strategies throughout the region was the result of a distinctive historical process whereby collectors (collectors per Binford 1980) were only one of at least four equally viable strategies operating across the broader Pacific Northwest region during the Middle Holocene (ca. 4000–5000 BP).

Evidence from other parts of the broader region indicates the presence of sedentary and serial specialist forager-like strategies along with classic mobile foragers (Prentiss and Chatters 2003a). It is still not exactly clear how collecting first developed or exactly where. Currently, it seems most likely to have first emerged in relatively remote contexts such as the Queen Charlotte Islands (Haida Gwaii) where recent excavations provide evidence for an early and in situ shift from a residentially mobile, immediate-return strategy to one emphasizing greater residential stability and investment coupled with a possible delayed-return subsistence strategy (Christensen and Stafford 2005; Mackie and Acheson 2005).

Once present, a collector strategy was apparently favored by the colder and more seasonal conditions brought on by the Neoglacial climatic period after circa 4000 BP. These conditions permitted this strategy to spread widely throughout the region while other strategies apparently failed, as is so vividly attested in the archaeological record of the Plateau region of the Interior Pacific Northwest (Chatters 1995; Goodale et al. 2004; Prentiss and Chatters 2003a, 2003b; Prentiss and Kuijt 2004). As discussed by Holly (this vol.), "failure" is a complex issue requiring that we consider once again the dual roles of agency and feedback. Future Pacific Northwest investigators will need to explore these issues in reference to the question as to why some (e.g., on Haida Gwaii) made the jump to collector strategies while others simply ceased to exist as recognizable cultural entities.

Socioeconomically Complex Collectors

Once collecting had emerged and spread throughout the Northwest Coast and Interior Northwest regions (Chatters and Prentiss 2005; Prentiss and Chatters 2003a), some groups evidently began to experiment with more socioeconomically complex organizational forms featuring multifamily coresidential groups within larger house structures (Prentiss et al. 2005). Earliest evidence for this pattern could eventually come from the Prince Rupert Harbor area (Ames 2005a; Archer 2001; Coupland 1988) or Haida Gwaii (Mackie and Acheson 2005). Unfortunately, evidence firmly identifying these large "corporate" groups (e.g., Hayden and Cannon 1982) at early dates (ca. 2500–5000 BP) in these places is still too sparse to be considered reliable. Interior groups appear to have occasionally experimented with larger households in the range of circa 2500–3000 BP (e.g., Goodale et al. 2004), but these villages appear to have been short-lived and not part of any longer-term development. The large villages of the Middle Fraser Canyon area on the western Canadian Plateau developed after 2000 BP but may not have been an entirely independent development given the proximity to earlier house groups in the Lower Fraser Canyon and adjacent Fraser Valley (Prentiss et al. 2005).

The best evidence for early corporate group households marking the beginnings of a long-term tradition comes from the Scowlitz, or Qithyil, site in the Fraser Valley of southwestern British Columbia, at the juncture of the Harrison and Fraser rivers. Here, Lepofsky et al. (2000, 2009) documented at least one very large structure (House 3) with evidence for redundant hearth-associated activity areas potentially reflecting multiple family units. Given the rather sudden appearance of such large and complex structures in this particular context, it is tempting to suggest that the earliest corporate group structures were built large by new immigrants as conscious markers of group identity with their investment offering defensive payoffs in particular (e.g., Shennan 1993, 2002). However, there is little yet in the empirical record to support an immigration scenario. Neither is there adequate evidence to support the intrusion of radical new technologies as some form of trigger to rearranged resource procurement, food storage patterns, or social relations.

Lepofsky et al. (2005) point out that a warming climate and increasingly patchy resource conditions after 2500 BP favored the kind of concentrated settlement in evidence at Scowlitz. They also argue that the shift to these more dense population aggregates could have been triggered in situ by elites taking advantage of opportunity associated with an increasingly patchy foraging environment to produce surplus, benefit from trade, and attract followers from other less-well-off villages in the region. But this again begs the question as to the origin of the elites and the cultural structures permitting such behavior. Consequently, I have argued that socioeconomic reorganization could have occurred without immigration, elites, or new technologies; rather, such reorganization could have been associated with more basic adaptive changes in human demographics and labor organization, the result of actions taken by individuals and groups to solve immediate problems of resource management and, likely, defense (Prentiss 2009; Prentiss et al. 2005). Techniques for above-ground wooden houses had been explored a millennium earlier (Lepofsky et al. 2009). We do not know if this knowledge was retained intact via transmission and practice or if it had remained in some way dormant to be revived as needed (e.g., Chatters 2009).

But actions can take us down paths we did not expect. It is well known that big houses in the late prehistoric period typically marked the socioeconomic or political status of the inhabitants (e.g., Coupland and Banning 1996; Matson and Coupland 1995), even if those thoughts were not in the minds of the first builders (material wealth based inter-household ranking is not clearly evident in the earliest villages of the Fraser Valley and Canyon [Lenert 2007; Prentiss et al. 2007]). It was the creation of large houses that may have set the stage for the next drama in much the same way that shell heaps paved the way for the mounds of the St. Johns region of Florida (Randall, this vol.) and burned land-scapes locked collectors in north-central California into highly struc-tured land-use cycles (Lightfoot et al., this vol.).

Sociopolitically Complex Hunter-Gatherers

By the late prehistoric (post–2000 BP) and protohistoric periods of the Northwest Coast and portions of the interior Plateau, densely packed groups of socioeconomically complex collectors were also characterized by high degrees of sociopolitical complexity (Ames and Maschner 1999; Matson and Coupland 1995). Permanent villages were made up of inde-pendent houses whose members were organized into lineage groups and in some areas, clans, or sodalities. Many of these societies were strati-fied into broad classes that included chiefs or nobles, commoners, and slaves. Interhousehold and individual ranking was also evident. Indi-vidual and group status hierarchies were economically underwritten by a complex system of surplus production, exchange, and competitive generosity centered on feasting and potlatching (Ames 1995).

There is relatively limited evidence for status differentiation in the archaeological record of the central Northwest Coast prior to about 2750 BP, at which time the frequency of burials showing signs of status marking in the form of grave goods starts to rise coincident with fre-quency and size of house features (Burchell 2006). However, indicators of ascribed inequality such as cranial deformation are not evident until after circa 1800 BP (Burley and Knusel 1989). This follows a period

when major Fraser Valley villages like Scowlitz and Katz were temporarily abandoned, while the large Fraser Delta and Gulf Islands villages
of the later Marpole phase were emerging (Lepofsky et al. 2000, 2005;
Matson and Coupland 1995), and implies that cultural structures associated with status inequality underwent a rapid further evolution (e.g.,
Prentiss et al. 2007). While we still lack a detailed understanding of the
actual events associated with emergent ascribed inequality on the coast,
the process is becoming more obvious on the Plateau.

Data from the Middle Fraser Canyon support a similar history
(compared to the central Northwest Coast) though dating slightly later.
Villages with large houses appeared by circa 1800 BP, part of a cultural
tradition that may ultimately trace at least in some ways to the Fraser
valley as well, but have virtually no evidence for ascribed inequality.
Villages grew substantially (estimated at 400 percent by Prentiss et al.
2008) between 1800 and 1100 BP, and it is possible that by the latter date
new forms of intervillage relationships resembling polities (e.g., Hayden
and Ryder 1991) could have developed.

A period of subsistence stress likely occurred in the range of 1200–800
BP associated with village abandonments and likely emergent ascribed
inequality as marked by interhousehold distinctions and some burial
treatments (Prentiss et al. 2007, 2008; Schulting 1995). Marine fisheries
likely peaked in productivity at circa 1200 BP and then declined to sub-
average levels (Finney et al. 2002; Hay et al. 2007; Patterson et al. 2003;
Tunnicliffe et al. 2001). Salmon populations appear to have subsequently
fallen in the Columbia and Fraser drainages (Bochart 2005; Chatters et al.
1995; Prentiss et al. 2007). Mid-Fraser villages (e.g., the Bridge River site)
that were particularly dependent upon salmon were abandoned (Prentiss et al. 2008). Some others apparently persisted but quickly showed
signs of subsistence stress. At the Keatley Creek village there is evidence
that populations added more mammals into their diet and broadened
their range of plant foods. This process may have triggered local resource
depression, particularly in ungulates, but possibly in geophytes as well
(Kuijt and Prentiss 2004; Prentiss et al. 2007). Resource depression in
ungulates and decline in frequencies of salmon remains are now also
recognized at the Bridge River site at circa 1150–1300 BP. It is within this
context that we first see direct evidence of interhousehold inequality, followed by a short period of population growth in select houses.

The Northwest Coast and Plateau data suggest that major changes in social status arrangements occurred only during and after periods of economic stress (e.g., Arnold 1993). We can imagine a scenario whereby household heads, seeking to preserve their houses in the face of increasing intergroup competition and demographic crises (e.g., Ames 2006), likely engaged in tighter control of foraging landscapes, intensified select food resources, and when successful, held celebrations (direct evidence for feasts at the Bridge River and Keatley Creek sites occurs uniquely within these periods [Prentiss et al. 2003, 2009]). Feasts and other ceremonies may have served to signal success and potentially help recruit extended kin and even unaffiliated clients to make up for losses. I have argued elsewhere (Prentiss et al. 2007) that it is within this context that hereditary inequality developed, perhaps as house owners passed on their original rights to their offspring but not necessarily to the new members (e.g., Boone 1992). I do not think, however, this would have been possible without prior development of cultural traditions permitting variability in household size and quantity of household possessions, despite a prevalence of implicit rules reinforcing egalitarian behavior patterns.

Within this framework, incipient inequality was a nonadaptive effect of house group evolution. In some sense, the cultural trappings of inequality remained substantially "under the radar" since those first villages (e.g., Scowlitz) manifested only in such things as the ability of house groups to accumulate their own food and to celebrate their successes. But subsistence uncertainty and periodic demographic stress may have set the stage for new forms of competitive behavior and unequal payoffs. In villages where people were already accustomed to incipient household differences, ascribed inequality now evolved as neighboring house groups struggled for economic and demographic viability and, ultimately, status, through surplus production, control of resources, and display of rights and title. Inequality had crept in more like a "thief in the night" than a product of "research and development."

Discussion

Regional Prehistory

At 6000 BP, I am not sure any odds-maker would have predicted the emergence of sociopolitically complex societies in the Pacific Northwest region. Hunter-gatherer groups appear to have been small and mobile, relying upon a diversified immediate-return subsistence strategy. Occasional aggregations during peak fishing season (Ames 1998) helped to facilitate exchange of cultural information, and it is no surprise that the few artifacts imbued with style (e.g., leaf-shaped bifaces) showed little variation from Alaska to Oregon. Everything changed after circa 5000 BP. Today we recognize three distinctive transitions in Pacific Northwest prehistory: emergence of collectors, house groups, and hereditary status inequality. Not all of these occurred at the same time or the same place.

Collectors came about first, most likely on the northern coast, and apparently spread elsewhere from there after about 4000 BP. But collecting was only one of many, at that time, equally viable strategies operating around the region. The disparity in adaptive behavior at circa 4000–5000 BP virtually guarantees the importance of human agency as widely scattered groups of people explored different strategies during the mild conditions of this time. The fact that not all survived during an abrupt climatic downturn (Chatters 1995; Chatters and Prentiss 2005) also implicates group-level dynamics and historical contingency as a significant arbiter of future developments.

We still have a long way to go before we unravel the details associated with the development of the first house groups. However, it is clear that, as was the case for the emergent collector strategy, the socioeconomically complex collectors developed in localized contexts across the region, the result of human decision making within evolving landscapes. Such major shifts in socioeconomic strategies may even have required a significant degree of geographic or social isolation to prevent cultural swamping by larger regional populations. So, house groups developed independently in the Haida Gwaii and nearby Prince Rupert Harbor areas, the Fraser Valley, the Upper Columbia, and perhaps the West Coast of Vancouver Island at relatively early dates. Some were evidently successful and may have led to dispersals into other areas (e.g., McMillan 2003; Prentiss and Chatters 2003a, 2003b; Prentiss et al. 2005). Others were short-lived experiments that may have ultimately failed (Goodale et al. 2008).

The development of ascribed inequality was qualitatively different from the processes behind the emergence of new socioeconomic strategies.

It was probably not ultimately a result of economic strategizing but rather an unintended effect of other developments. Houses were built and populations grew, all the while maintaining a public veneer of egalitarianism. Yet, the walls of the growing houses helped to preserve the embedded code for the next threshold event. Inequality was not initially a strategy or a trend, but a historical development that came late in the region's prehistory; its foundation had been laid some time before its actual manifestation. Once the conditions were right, the fact was actualized not by psychologically predisposed aggrandizers but by ordinary persons, perhaps household heads seeking to preserve their houses and feed their families. Only then was the cultural package associated with inequality free to evolve further, perhaps through a fairly standard Darwinian competitive process. Now, success was measured in material goods accumulation and competitive generosity. Rights to corporeal and noncorporeal property were celebrated in monumental architecture and art. Sometimes, runaway sociopolitical competition led to local resource depression and economic collapse, as likely occurred at Keatley Creek (Prentiss et al. 2007). It is also possible that the cultural trappings of ascribed inequality, once in practice, were transmitted to other groups poised to make that jump. We know from the historical and ethnographic record that some groups, such as the Canyon Division Shuswap, did borrow such practices from their neighbors when context permitted (Teit 1909).

Evolutionary History

A recent attempt at modeling the region's cultural evolutionary history using ethnographic information (Jordan and Mace 2006) indicates that many groups have significantly nonrandom relationships between patterns of women's dress and adornment, house structures, and marriage rules, with the most significant division between those deriving from the north versus south. Far less significant relationships were found between such elements as potlatches, female rituals, and musical instruments. As pointed out by Jordan and Mace (2006:165), the former association makes considerable sense as dress signaled patterns of participation in marriage networks. Consequently, dress, as a status marker, should also have been associated with many features of structures. None of these cultural elements had strong nonrandom relationships to either language or distance between groups.

Historical linguistic analysis (e.g., Elmendorf 1965; Thompson and Kinkade 1990) suggests relatively ancient and independent origins for many of the major language groups on the Northwest Coast and Plateau, particularly Penutian (south coast), Salish (south-central coast, Plateau), Wakashan (central coast), Haida (north coast: Queen Charlotte Islands/Haida Gwaii), and Tlingit (north coast: southeastern Alaska). If dispersals leading to historical landscape associations generally happened prior to at least 2,000 years ago (and many much earlier), as is currently indicated by a variety of archaeological data (Fedje and Mackie 2005; McMillan 2003; Prentiss and Chatters 2003a), then evolution of ethnographically recorded practices linking marriage, adornment, and architecture likely postdate the establishment of those groups. Subregional similarities in these practices (Jordan and Mace 2006:figs. 10.2 and 10.6) imply that such traditions (e.g., cultural practices associated with ascribed inequality) evolved in localized contexts and were subsequently transmitted across linguistic boundaries postdating 2000 BP (this kind of transregional interaction is also supported by data on obsidian exchange [e.g., Carlson 1994]) But subregional diversity also implies subsequent further evolution in these core practices, some of which were undoubtedly further affected by developments in the region's colonial period.

Cultural evolutionary processes and contingent history collided in the evolution of the indigenous Pacific Northwest cultures. We can model the emergence and expansion of many technologies and socio-economic behaviors using very traditional evolutionary theory. As one reviewer put it, "ideas have to work in the real world." In many cases their economic underpinnings are easily explained with the basic tenets of human behavioral ecology. Yet we fall apart when asked to explain Middle Holocene cultural disparity or the rise of ascribed inequality in such simple terms. Indeed, the famous cultures of the Pacific Northwest could not have come into existence without the collector expansion favored only by cold conditions after 4000 BP. Had earlier warm conditions persisted, archaeologists today might be teaching a very different Pacific Northwest prehistory, perhaps one featuring a unique pattern of divergent immediate-return foragers occupying a variable but probably less-productive range of coastal and interior habitats. House groups came and went in Pacific Northwest prehistory, as in the Eayam phase on the central coast (Schaepe 1998) or the Upper Columbia I phase (Goodale et al. 2008), and there is no guarantee that other developments might have persisted into the recent historic period. Without the salmon bottlenecks of circa 2500 BP (e.g., Lepofsky et al. 2005), perhaps the resurgent architectural innovations of the central coast might not have occurred or been permitted to last long enough to reframe the nature of central and southern Northwest Coast cultures. And without those houses, competitive inequality may never have gained enough of a toehold to eventually bring worldwide prominence to the classic cultures of the region.

Conclusion

Ethnographic groups of the Pacific Northwest are not the result of a predetermined trend but the actualized result of a complex history affected by all of the processes considered in our discussion and undoubtedly more. This history offers lessons to future researchers interested in the subjects of hunter-gatherers and cultural evolution in general. Adaptive evolutionary process was certainly essential in the emergence of the region's cultures. As I have outlined, cultural microevolutionary processes, individual agency and innovation, interindividual transmission, and even selection acted in a concerted manner to affect the region's prehistory. How else could details of household architecture or women's dress have been spread between groups speaking mutually unintelligible languages? But in some cases, the forces of microevolution were clearly overridden by those of macroevolution, as during the Middle Holocene cultural disparity and subsequent spread of collectors where the dispersal of socioeconomic strategies was contingent on the actions and successes of populations, and individual success was likely more dependent on group membership than specific prowess. Yet ultimately, historical contingency may have trumped all as most dramatically illustrated in the nonadaptive and entirely unintentional emergence of cultural structures associated with inequality and their subsequent exaptive evolution and dispersal. Ultimately, the record of Pacific Northwest culture history denies a role for simple deterministic forces (especially genetic hardwiring) as the primary driving force behind an emergent inequality. However, in an evolutionary perspective acknowledging an important role for historical contingency, actions of the individual person still count, and that is something worth celebrating.

Acknowledgments

I thank Don Holly and Ken Sassaman for the invitation to join the Amerind seminar. My research at the Keatley Creek and Bridge River sites was generously supported by the National Science Foundation (Grants 0108795, 0313920, and 0713013), the Wenner-Gren Foundation, and the University of Montana. I thank all of the seminar participants for their thoughtful consideration of my research. In particular, I thank participants Kathleen Hull, Don Holly, T. R. Kidder, Kent Lightfoot, and Ken Sassaman. Beyond the Dragoon meetings, Kelly Dixon and two anonymous peer reviewers provided additional insightful comments on the paper.

Notes

1. Eldredge (2009) envisions a potentially far more complex scenario for industrialized societies incorporating a third cultural hierarchy targeting artifact makers and marketing and manufacturing entities.

2. Cultural transmission is not natural selection. However, it can act in an analogous manner in a cultural framework. For example, if there are systematic biases in transmission of certain cultural variants, some will likely persist in the long term and others will not. It is in this context that I use the phrase "analogue for selection."

3

Thinking Small

Hunter-Gatherer Demography and Culture Change

Kathleen L. Hull

As individuals living in the fast-paced, postindustrial world, we readily recognize both the substance of history and the incremental contributions of people to the process of local and global change. We comprehend and document dynamic departures from our collective past, and often recognize the significance of still-unfolding events to our impending futures. As analysts of a more distant past, however, we afford little of that same capacity and understanding to the people we study, and nowhere is this more evident than in the analysis of foraging societies. Hunter-gatherers have been reduced by their etic classification to little more than loci of responsive behavior rather than thoughtful agents whose actions facilitated or constituted the processes and patterns we seek to identify and explain. In the expediency of behavioral labels and variables, we lose sight of the fact that short-term lived experience and long-term culture change are intertwined and reinforcing—rather than mutually exclusive—processes in both ancient and modern societies.

History and process are built on perception and memory, and it is agency that underwrites them. Stability or change occurs in a contingent context defined by embodied practice. Therefore, the integration of agency in archaeological analysis of process requires that we take an emic perspective by considering the perception of both everyday and extraordinary dynamics by the actors as phenomena were unfolding. At the same time, however, a systematic approach and methodological rigor must be employed for such analysis to facilitate comparisons across time and space that lie at the heart of anthropology. Appreciation for pace, tempo, and duration within the span of an individual lifetime—rather than simply sequence over longer spans of time—is necessary to explore the dynamics of the short term, the routine of experience, and the contribution of perception in long-term change (Hull 2005,

2008). In addition, archaeologists must simultaneously incorporate and appreciate the significance of long-term processes playing out beyond the experience of an individual lifetime.

With a shift to the human lifetime as the fundamental temporal unit of analysis (Hull 2008), demography becomes a convenient foundation for an archaeology of foragers that blends the experiential and the analytical in a rigorous and meaningful assessment of short- and long-term change in small-scale societies. Demographic context (whether dynamic or static) as perceived by past people in such societies is rightly recognized as fundamental to experience and meaning making—and, thus, to history and cultural trajectory—we seek to understand. Demography is not simply a quantitative data point within a long-term trend to be viewed from the present but is instead appreciated as an unfolding process and a nexus for action in the past. Life within a small community speaks to relations of intimacy and enmity, stability and fluidity, both within and beyond the group, since small group size often necessitates links to others from outside. Starting from a demographic (i.e., "small-scale"), rather than the traditional economic (i.e., "hunter-gatherer"), analytical perspective also holds promise for bringing together concepts and cause as disparate as, for example, the "social relations of immediacy" that Ingold (1999) identifies as central to life in small-scale societies and the neoevolutionary views of cultural transmission (e.g., Shennan 2000).

It is indeed time to "think small," as a way of not only harmonizing the etic and the emic, but also of integrating the short and the long term—history and process—into systematic study of cultural change. With this goal in mind, this chapter provides an overview of previous deployment of demography in "hunter-gatherer" archaeology, considers new methods and models available to archaeologists that facilitate a "small-scale" approach that addresses agency and the perception of change within specific demographic milieus, and illustrates a perception-based demographic approach to the study of small-scale societies with a case study from the central Sierra Nevada of California.

Demography in Hunter-Gatherer Archaeology

Population size has often been identified among a few select variables worthy of attention by archaeologists who study hunter-gatherers, although demography is often just as quickly discarded once it has served a limited analytical purpose. In fact, despite decades of interest and research, archaeological treatment of demography has been restricted primarily to examination of population size within economic or ecological models that relate population growth, resources, technological innovation, and cultural complexity (e.g., Hassan 1978, 1979, 1981; Paine 1997a). In this, the macroeconomic models of Malthus (1976 [1798]) and Boserup (1965) have been particularly influential.

The Malthusian model posits that populations grow to the point at which capabilities for further resource extraction are exceeded. Population-resource equilibrium is obtained through either "positive" or "preventive" checks that come into play to stabilize the system (Malthus 1976 [1798]). Within Malthus's view, positive checks include such factors as starvation, war, and disease that decrease existing population, while preventive checks including late marriage and fertility control (e.g., abstinence or contraception) effectively curtail the growth of population prior to resource crisis. Population-resource equilibrium (homeostasis) at or below carrying capacity can also be achieved through the preventive check of technological change, but the source of such innovation is usually attributed to exogenous factors (e.g., diffusion) simply coincidental with, or fortuitously preceding, crisis. In contrast, Boserup (1965) concluded that population growth spurs technological innovation, effectively increasing resource potential within an area and allowing population to grow without the necessity of positive or preventive checks. While the Malthusian model is compatible with a biological, adaptational, or evolutionary approach to human foragers (Howell 1986:234), the anthropological significance of Boserup's model lies in the explicit recognition of a relationship between population, social structure, and cultural evolution (Howell 1986:235). Still, within this model culture change results from endogenous technological change driven by vital necessity (Hammel and Howell 1987:144) rather than social negotiation based on differing needs and priorities (e.g., Brumfiel 1992). Such technological change, in turn, spurs further population growth.

Following the macroeconomic trail of Malthus and Boserup, archaeologists tend to reduce demography to just population growth or decline predetermined by the natural environment (e.g., Hassan 1979, 1981) and often invoke population growth in global treatment of a few very broad research issues such as the development of agriculture (e.g., Cohen 1977) or colonization of continents (e.g., Steele 2009; Steele et al. 1998). When individual demographic decisions are considered at all, such action and decision making are essentialized under assertions or assumptions in support of ecological models (e.g., Hassan 1981:174; MacDonald 1998; Surovell 2000) rather than reflecting issues that also need to be addressed and explored. Such shortcomings are particularly evident in hunter-gatherer demography, and the potential perception of, and response to, demographic change is rarely dealt with in rigorous fashion and with fine-grained temporal methods necessary to support causal explanations with respect to population increase or decline (Hull 2005; see also Shennan 2000).

Lee (1986; see also Wood 1998) provided an economic perspective that combined the views of Boserup and Malthus regarding endogenous and exogenous technological development fostering or impinging upon population growth, respectively. In Lee's "phase" view of population growth or decline, he saw less unidirectionality or irreversibility in the dynamic between population and innovation. Population history is characterized by swift change that takes a relatively stable Malthusian population into "Boserup space" wherein population growth occurs in concert with internally driven technological innovation. The push or pull of innovation works together with absolute population size and factors such as surplus and wages (which would equate with "return" in typical arguments regarding hunter-gatherers) to determine if a population remains at equilibrium or experiences growth at any given time. Likewise, population decline could, in theory, result in a loss of technology.

Even Lee (1986) acknowledged, however, that models at such large scales are too abstract and decontextualized to provide reasonable interpretations for specific application. Furthermore, the reaction of demographers such as Lee to macro explanations, and the subsequent shift within the field of demography to more microeconomic assessments, may still fall short of a satisfactory basis for understanding or explaining demographic behavior in the past or present. As Hammel (1990:456) noted, microeconomic arguments "resting on individual-level behaviorist reasoning that assumes the exercise of a universal rationality little influenced by institutional context . . . have the same tenuous quality of connection to individual behavior as those of macroeconomic [analyses]." This sentiment was echoed by Wilson (1993:21) in his critique of neoevolutionary analysis of culture change, as he noted that "the driving force behind the neoevolutionary approach in archaeology lay in the exploration of the relationship between economics and political organization. The emphasis, of necessity, was on very large-scale processes [including] population trajectories through time."

It is in this intellectual context that anthropological demographers have recently broadened their views with respect to both culture and causation (Hammel 1990; see also Fricke 1997; Greenhalgh 1995; Kertzer 1995; Kertzer and Fricke 1997). Demographic behavior as measured in the aggregate represents uniquely personal decisions within an environment encompassing "not only [that which] is culturally perceived and exploited but also [environment] as socially distributed" (Hammel and Howell 1987:145). Archaeologists, however, have been slow or reluctant to undertake demographic interpretations that consider individual perception and action now advocated by many demographers as central to explanatory discussions. While efforts in archaeological demography of foragers incorporate standard demographic analysis methods (e.g., Paine 1997b; but see Ammerman [1989]; Petersen [1975] for critical review of work prior to 1980), the theoretical perspectives underlying much analysis remain rooted in abstract, macro-level phenomena. When theory is explicitly addressed, ecological approaches are almost universally applied (e.g., Hassan 1978, 1979, 1981; Paine 1997a) and, perhaps most troubling, the dominance of such views has not been challenged within archaeology even as demographers themselves are questioning deterministic approaches to population studies. That is, there appears to be a rather apathetic treatment of archaeological demographic theory, perhaps because of the perceived difficulty in addressing demographic issues with archaeological data. Even demographic variables beyond population size or growth rate—such as population structure (i.e., age and sex)— become descriptive footnotes rather than an axis for explanation rooted in intimate relationships, power dynamics, and cultural knowledge.

In his review of the potential contribution of anthropology to the field of demography, Hammel (1990) identified at least six ways *culture* has been described or might be invoked in demographic explanation. Although Hammel saw the value or applicability of nearly all perspectives, he concluded that any demographic anthropology or anthropological demography must be based on micro-level explanations of individual-level demographic behavior, preferably within a theory of culture as practice and utilizing emic frames of reference for data collection and analysis (Hammel 1990:457; cf. Kertzer 1995:47). Explicit in this view is the notion that interpretations must be considered within the particular contemporary or historic context (Hammel 1990:467; Kreager 1997). Although not specifically addressing archaeological demography, Hammel's (1990:457) further observations regarding the relevance of perception and time in both short- and long-term culture change introduce an important prerequisite to consideration of theory and scale in archaeological demography (see also Greenhalgh 1995:22).

Drawn from biology, life-history theory has also been recently advocated as an approach to demographic anthropology (e.g., Chisholm 1993; Hill and Hurtado 1996) and, thus, may ultimately find its way into archaeology interpretation. Life-history characteristics including age at first menarche or onset of menopause are, in fact, little more than factors constituting or affecting demographic behavior. In biological analyses, the goal is to recognize how these "constraints" dictate "behavior outcomes" (Hill and Hurtado 1996:8). Similarly, in anthropological application such factors are recognized to function directly to affect individual behavior and, thereby, to work indirectly on populations to shape culture (Hill and Hurtado 1996:7). In such analyses, contemporary "primitive" people follow modes of life that effectively represent the crucible in which all human demographic behavior was formed, and life-history analysis of foragers not only explains how these demographic traits came to be but also why human demographic characteristics unlike those of many other organisms evolved (e.g., patterns of mortality of postmenopausal females [see Hawkes et al. 1997]; but see Benton et al. 2006 on the complexities both underlying and resulting from individual life histories). Working within this hyperselectionist view, Hill and Hurtado (1996:16) argue that "social input is essentially biological in nature since it is composed of multiple behavioral adaptations of individual conspecifics."

The potential seduction of this use of life history in demographic archaeology seems clear given neo-Darwinian evolutionary approaches to the past (see Bird and O'Connell 2006), although the reductionist biological basis of this view may be too extreme for most anthropological archaeologists. In addition, biologists are still uncertain if life-history generalizations and explanations such as those possible for interspecies comparisons can be made at the intraspecies level of interest to archaeologists (see Chisholm 1993:5). Likewise, some scholars even dispute the relevance of such generalizations to anthropological explanation (e.g., Vayda 2001). In many ways, life-history theory appears to indicate only what is possible, rather than that necessarily observed in different contexts. Therefore, like macroeconomic and ecological perspectives, it too may have relevance to only macroscale issues. For example, age at first menarche may be related to environment (e.g., diet), but female fertility is ultimately directed by social factors such as marriage practices and sexual mores. In this sense, life-history constraints are similar to the concept of carrying capacity, in that biological capacity is culturally mediated.

Demography as Practice in Small-Scale Societies

Beyond archaeology, the field of demography encompasses an intriguing array of qualitative and quantitative data that remain a largely untapped resource in archaeological explanation of short- and long-term culture change. Lost in the traditional archaeological focus on population size in relation to resources are the nuances of population structure such as age, gender, nuptiality, fecundity, fertility, and mortality, as well as the life-history characteristics and consanguineal or affinal kin relations that underpin and are integral to human societies and practices. Instead, only population size is generally acknowledged or more thoroughly assessed. And even in this, there is no appreciation for the fundamental, one might even argue crucial, importance of population size to hunter-gatherer life—not simply in terms of growth or decline, but in the very *experience* of living in a small-scale world. Working in the enduring shadow of Julian Steward, archaeologists studying hunter-gatherers are too willing to limit the context of action to the natural environment, while ignoring the equally potent observations of anthropologists such as Radcliffe-Brown with respect to the importance of kinship and social relations (see Lee and Daly 1999a:8). Is this because such factors are seen as loci of stability rather than change? Or should we follow Ingold (1999) in exploring the idea that stasis requires its own form of intent and effort, and consider the roots of such commitment? The time is ripe to look for answers to important issues of forager life, practice, and change in the intimate social relations of such small groups.

Small, of course, is a relative term that may require redefinition in various contexts. For present purposes, the term refers to societies of less than approximately 500 individuals (see Kroeber 1955)—that is, societies in which it would be possible for all individuals not only to know of but also occasionally to interact with most others of the extended group. Since such interaction would have been mediated by age, gender, and other social factors, however, some individuals may have been recognized only by their relationships to others with whom one was more directly connected. Ethnographic data suggest fluidity in composition and distribution for such small-scale societies, perhaps including periodic aggregation or dispersal.

Archaeological study of hunter-gatherer groups has naturally focused on subsistence practices—and related gendered division of labor, productive technology, and residential mobility—rather than demographic and social scales other than the abstract "productive unit" in part because the subject of study is defined by economic pursuits and organization. As summarized by Lee and Daly (1999a), however, foraging groups share other important qualities including small population size, and the persistence and significance of such a fundamental characteristic is worthy of careful consideration. Demographic characteristics of foraging societies have much more profound implications than simply as a barometer of carrying capacity or an absolute figure of population size. Small size is just the visible result of low population growth rates that, in turn, relate primarily to female health and decision making in a specific cultural context. In addition, small group size and related demographic characteristics are accompanied by mutability of—and potential feedback from—kin, marriage, and intragroup dynamics that are significantly different than those of large-scale societies. Finally, small-scale group dynamics generally based on kinship are embedded within or draw upon broader social networks of intergroup relations (i.e., metapopulations; see also Wobst 1974 on "maximum bands") that may have no foundation in actual or fictive kin ties and may represent more than a risk-management strategy for survival in lean times (Hammel and Howell 1987).

At the same time, apparent stability in regional or even group population size in the short term may mask a much more dynamic picture of flux in the coming together and moving apart of individuals or households (Bird-David 1990). Hunter-gatherer societies, in particular, represent a constant potential for "reshuffling the deck" of individuals and relationships of social intimacy in everyday life that may find special resonance in, and contribute to an archaeological approach based on, Bourdieu's (1977, 1990) theory of practice (see also Pauketat 2001a). As discussed by Ingold (1999), it is the "social relations of immediacy" typical of small groups that produce social cohesion and define self in small-scale societies. Thus, it is reasonable to ask how such immediacy was maintained or transformed within the context of demographic fluctuation in either frequency or group constitution in small populations.

Shennan (2000) explored one direction for an archaeological demography that addresses the sociocultural consequences of small population size. His study concluded that fluctuating size typical of small groups could have had profound effects on the retention or loss of cultural traits when transmission was based on children learning from parents (see also Henrich 2004). Demographic shifts in both size and space would have altered opportunities for cultural transmission; therefore, drift rather than selection might play a greater role in the process of culture change (Bentley et al. 2004). By considering population size in terms of endogenous social resources rather than simply exogenous natural resources, Shennan (2000) concluded that "the single most important factor in understanding culture change is population dynamics." Although Shennan's focus on cultural transmission is not the path advocated here—given a preference for viewing culture as practice rather than "descent with modification"—it is certainly germane to a reappraisal of demography with respect to short- and long-term culture change. It also hints at how theoretical perspectives as disparate as an evolutionary framework and practice can be bridged when analysis focuses on demography beyond the economic (Shennan 2000:822).

Instead, the most promising avenue for work on the significance of demography to social relations and cultural change may be agent-based modeling such as that recently applied with much success to study of small agricultural societies of the ancient Southwest (e.g., Dean et al.

2000; Gaines and Gaines 1997; Kohler and Gumerman 2000; Kohler and Van der Leeuw 2007). Although computer simulations of hunter-gatherer populations were used as early as the 1970s (Dyke 1981; Wright 2000), recent archaeological simulation studies have been able to employ an agent-based approach that is much more useful for examining the types of decision making, interactions, and fluidity in group constitution that is of interest here. Going one step further than many archaeological studies to date, however, *individual* rather than *household* agents may be particularly important to such research. For example, studies such as those of Read (2003; Read and LeBlanc 2003) on demographic choices and population characteristics have revealed emergent properties. In Read's (2003) study, the emergent property was population stability in small-scale groups resulting from individual female decision making affecting birth spacing, unrelated to resource availability.

As Read's (2003) study suggests, agent-based modeling has the potential to recognize demography as fluid, cyclical, and perhaps even transformational with respect to characteristics beyond other demographic parameters. Various cultural practices including social relations of both production and consumption flow from and with demographic change, while we might also anticipate settlement shifts or other changes that have traditionally been attributed to economic rather than demographic factors (e.g., Gaines and Gaines 1997). Although Read (2003) framed his discussion in an evolutionary mode in which hunter-gatherers are the Ur-version of humanity and potentially "innate" or foundational aspects of social groups may be recognized, it may be more fruitful to simply focus on the dynamics of lived experience that studies such as this can reveal or serve as models against which archaeological data may be compared. Hammel (2005a, 2005b) provided nonarchaeological examples of such thought in his recent theoretical examination of the potential to mobilize power in small-scale societies through kin obligation—that is, duty derived from and exploited based on demographic relations alone. Through such methods, archaeologists may trace the implications for practice-based, rather than biological, foundations of social life. That is, we should consider the consequences of demographic conjuncture, perception, and decision making as both intentional and unintentional (i.e., emergent) processes relating to short-term lived experience and long-term cultural change.

Long-Term Demographic Change in the Central
Sierra Nevada

Recent archaeological study of long-term Native population trends in
Yosemite Valley in the central Sierra Nevada of California serves to illustrate demography as both a perceived process and a locus of action.
Ethnographic data for this region, and California more generally, suggest people were organized within tribelets, "village communities" that
existed as "sovereign though miniature political unit[s], which . . .
[were] land-owning and maintained . . . frontiers against unauthorized
trespass. The population size might run as low as 100, or as high as
500–600" (Kroeber 1955:307). Ethnohistoric data reveal that Yosemite
Valley and adjoining downstream portions of the Merced River canyon
served to define one such group, while the high cliffs and concomitant geographic boundedness of the valley itself allow this demographic
unit to be rendered archaeologically. This analysis does not assume that
geography acted as a barrier to population movement (i.e., a closed
population in the demographic sense), but it is assumed that population inflow and outflow were relatively stable.

As discussed in detail elsewhere (Hull 2002, 2005, 2009), large-scale
obsidian-hydration column sampling of 10 percent of the Casa Diablo
debitage recovered from 16 percent of the sites in Yosemite Valley was
undertaken to serve as the basis for a long-term demographic study of
Native occupation. The focus was on randomly selected habitation sites
recognized as such based on site constituents. This sampling strategy
avoided temporal bias in the obsidian hydration data, while also pre-
venting errors that would have resulted from including nonresidential
sites. Absolute dates were derived from obsidian hydration measure-
ments based on a temperature-dependent rate formula for Casa Diablo
obsidian developed for the Yosemite region (Hull 2001), a formula that
has been subsequently supported by association of additional radiocarbon and obsidian hydration dates (i.e., Hicks et al. 2006). The use of
obsidian hydration not only provided the substantial sample of dates
necessary to reveal short-term trends (discussed later in this chapter), it
also allowed this study to avoid many of the taphonomic concerns that
apply especially to use of radiocarbon dates in demographic studies (see
Surovell and Brantingham 2007; Surovell et al. 2009).

Two different proxy measures of population were established from the more than 2,900 obsidian hydration dates derived from 2,235 individual flakes (some flakes exhibited multiple hydration bands; Hull 2009:128). These proxies—debitage frequency and subsite frequency, respectively—were rendered via three-point averaging of raw frequency data within fifty-year increments (to reveal short-term patterns) and two-hundred-year increments (to identify long-term trends). The subsite proxy took site size rather than simply site frequency into account, by dividing large sites into smaller zones based on modal patterns of site area in Yosemite Valley (see Hull 2002). Different models of resource consumption for both mobile (i.e., lithic) and stationary (i.e., land) resources were considered to develop expectations regarding the relationship between resources and population. Briefly, use of lithic resources was unconstrained with respect to population size and, thus, was expected to increase in a linear fashion with population growth. In contrast, land (habitation space) was a finite resource within Yosemite Valley, so the relationship between occupied area and population would be logarithmic rather than linear (Hull 2002, 2009:132). Comparison of the two proxies verified these expectations and established initial confidence in the demographic basis of the two measures. These models also allowed the proxies to be quantitatively calibrated and compared, with results expressed as a percentage of the maximum population size witnessed in Yosemite Valley rather than as absolute numbers of people.

High positive correlation of the two proxies (r^2 = 0.839 for the fifty-year increment data; Hull 2009:129) and critical assessment of various factors other than demography that could potentially obscure or contribute to such patterns provided additional confidence in the results. The two potential confounding factors most germane to the debitage proxy would be shifts in production for exchange (i.e., surplus production of bifacial cores, bifaces, or finished tools) and technological or economic change resulting in significant shifts in the amount of obsidian reduced (e.g., core- versus flake-based reduction strategies, projectile point morphology, or the scale of procurement or processing activities undertaken with flake tools). Likewise, the potential contribution of shifting residential mobility strategies and diachronic trends in duration of site occupation to subsite proxy trends were considered. Shifts to use of toolstone other than obsidian were not a factor since nonobsidian materials make up less than 1 percent of lithic assemblages, while regional archaeological research has also not revealed other social or political changes that might influence obsidian tool production (Hull 2007; Hull and Moratto 1999).

With respect to the debitage proxy, detailed lithic technological studies over the past twenty-five years have provided no evidence of diachronic patterns in lithic reduction strategies or production for exchange. The use of multisite sampling for the demographic study also mitigated against possible errors deriving from site-specific idiosyncracies with respect to such practices. Similarly, although regional archaeological studies have documented diachronic changes in projectile point size and shifts between logistical and residential mobility strategies through time, there are no data supporting quantitative significance of such shifts to obsidian use within Yosemite (Hull 2002, 2009). Most important, however, there is no compelling reason why disparate factors of land and lithic consumption should covary as a result of any settlement or technological practices relevant to the region (see Hull 2002, 2005, 2009). Instead, shifts in settlement and technology germane to Yosemite would generally lead to disjunction between the two proxies rather than correlation. For example, increased residential mobility would lead to an increase in subsite frequency with a corresponding decrease in debitage production at any given site, but no such pattern was recognized in the proxy data for the period characterized by greater residential mobility. The use of two proxies rather than one was especially important in establishing the demographic basis of the trends revealed and ultimately discounting possible explanations other than population size as factors with demonstrative impact on the patterns observed (Hull 2002, 2005, 2009). The analysis suggested, however, that the debitage proxy was more robust, so this measure is relied upon for the current discussion.

The debitage population proxy revealed overlapping patterns of long-term processual and short-term cyclical change in Yosemite Native population size evident in the random sample of habitation sites spanning the last 5,500 years. Short-term cycles are evident in the 50-year-increment debitage proxy, with these data revealing a cyclical pattern of modest population growth and decline on the order of every 350 years. This pattern is especially evident in well-defined population oscillations between circa 2600 and 1300 BP (fig. 3.1), although such cycling

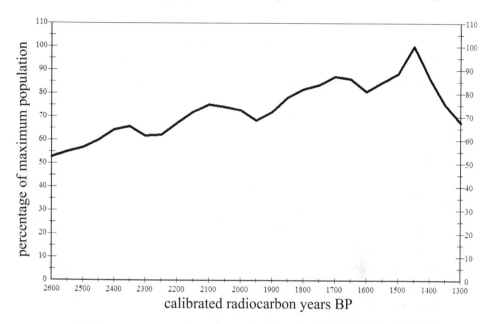

Figure 3.1. Population proxy data for 2600 to 1300 BP in Yosemite Valley based on 50-year increments, highlighting short-term population oscillations.

is clearly manifest for almost the entire 5,500-year span (fig. 3.2). Population growth rates during the episodes of increase indicate that the population would have doubled in only 180 years. Thus, population growth was likely perceptible during the lifespan of many individuals even within the posited small population inhabiting Yosemite Valley. Conversely, the cyclical declines represent a maximum loss that would halve in only 160 years. This latter trend would also be readily visible to individuals in the population. Cyclical population decline, though relatively dramatic on the scale of a lifetime or few generations, did not result in population as low or lower than the size at the time each cycle commenced (fig. 3.2). The only exception was after circa 1400 BP, although decline then was apparently due to unusual circumstances (discussed later in this chapter).

At the same time, the Yosemite archaeological data demonstrate that population size was growing incrementally over the long term, as highlighted by the two-hundred-year-increment data (fig. 3.3). Population peaked around fourteen hundred years ago at an estimated 1,000

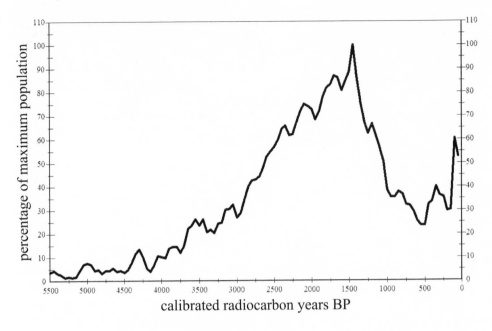

Figure 3.2. Population proxy data for Yosemite Valley based on 50-year increments for the last 5,500 years, revealing short-term cyclical patterning perceptible within a human lifetime.

persons, and plunged to a low of only 250 individuals or so around five hundred years ago (Hull 2002:254). This substantial decline appears to be related, at least in part, to prevailing environmental conditions at the time, including two extreme, long-term droughts between circa 1050 and 600 BP (Hull 2002:308). Examination of a subsequent decline around 200 BP (fig. 3.2) related to the infiltration of nonnative disease into Yosemite Valley (Hull 2002, 2009) also suggests that small population size itself was a potentially profound factor in group decision making. Thus, the collective data reveal shorter-term trends that may have been perceived by individuals over the course of a lifetime (fig. 3.2), while longer-term growth trends imperceptible to people unfolded in the background (fig. 3.3).[1]

Once again, the only exception is the significant decline between circa 1400 and 600 BP, which appears to have been recorded in Native oral tradition (see Hull 2002:305–312) and, thus, was clearly perceived by people at the time it was happening. It was a short-term experience to people

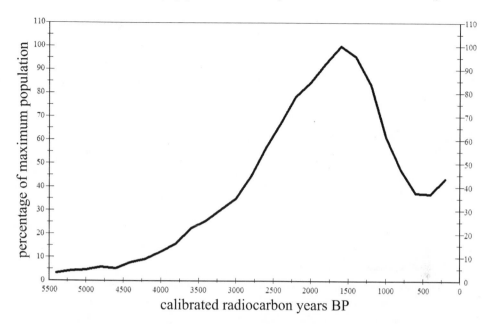

Figure 3.3. Population proxy data for Yosemite Valley based on 200-year increments for the last 5,500 years, revealing long-term trends beyond individual perception by people in the past.

at the time, while also persisting as a long-term process visible to archaeologists. The short-term cyclical trends speak to "relations of immediacy" as the decadal or generational demographic experience of people shifted, while the longer-term pattern of growth may reflect economic orientation or augmentation of the population through immigration, which may also have affected social relations. Thus, if we are to assess the everyday lived experience of past peoples, these observations suggest that we must use methods that permit such fine-grained demographic patterns to emerge, contrast such data on multiple temporal scales, and analyze the information as phenomena rooted in both economic *and* social factors. It is interesting that a similar periodicity of approximately 250- to 300-year population cycling is evident in Read's (2003) simulation for a small hunter-gatherer population (see also Lee 1974). This study modeled reproductive outcomes for the group given female decisions on energy invested in child care versus gathering. While Read (2003) focused on the emergent property of long-term population stability, it might be equally valid to explore the possibility of shorter-term cycles as an emergent phenomena in such groups. This is especially true given that the cyclical pattern is evident even under different scenarios within Read's (2003) simulation, with only the amplitude of fluctuations varying significantly with decisions.

It is difficult to know if the Yosemite results are indicative of the same or similar reproductive decisions that underpin Read's (2003) simulation, but the juxtaposition of fine-grained archaeological data and agent-based simulations suggests that the combination of such methods may point the way toward interpreting trends that transcended, but were nonetheless visible, during the lifetime of individuals. These methods provide for the examination of demographic data not as epiphenomena of environment or economy, but instead as social trends deriving from individual action and partly constitutive of the societies we seek to understand. While Read (2003) changed female decision making along only one axis (i.e., energy investment), I suspect that simulations incorporating multiple variables of social relations may be more revealing of emergent properties or long-term trends of relevance to archaeological interpretation. One can imagine the additional interpretive possibilities that would open up if agent-based simulations were run based on multiple social variables including marriage practices, definitions of incest (e.g., Read 2003), sex selection of offspring, changing ideals of family size, or consolidation of kin-based power.

A further approach would be to use such simulations to take "slices of time" from model data to get a sense of how age distribution, sex ratio, and kin ties and networks may have varied through time or within cycles. Thus, archaeologists might consider issues such as family support for child rearing or the rise of lineage-based social inequality, or assess how near or distant kin ties may have factored into population aggregation or dispersal. Using such methods, we might consider social circumstances potentially corresponding to archaeological or bioarchaeological data at a particular time and assess the contribution of such factors to the historical trajectory of short- and long-term patterns of cultural change or stability. Archaeological and bioarchaeological data might, in turn, serve to evaluate the relevance of simulation data and models to various temporal or spatial contexts, although the "simpler agents" of demographic agent-based models (i.e., largely encompassing a relatively small set of variables related to nuptiality, fertility, and mortality, the parameters of which are well-established based on cross-cultural studies and need not rely on assumptions of rationality) suggests such testing is less of a concern in this application than it might be in others (Ormerod and Rosewell 2009). As discussed elsewhere (Hull 2005), time-perspectivist layering of additional trends of technology, settlement, and other factors accessible in the archaeological record would serve to identify coincidence and conjuncture either revealing or prompting change.

Certainly, there are substantial methodological challenges to a perception-based approach to archaeological demography and "thinking small." The most obvious is the need for fine-grained temporal data or, as in the case of the Yosemite Valley demographic study, large-scale sampling with temporal control sufficient to allow data averaging techniques and, thus, interpolation (see Hull 2005:368). Obsidian hydration dating is a particularly cost-effective means to achieve this end, while also being useful for direct dating of artifacts that allows for the development of a proxy measure relatively uncommon in demographic reconstruction. Ceramic or shell bead data might also serve for those regions in which stylistic change was frequent and is firmly dated by absolute means. The cost of other absolute dating techniques (e.g., radiocarbon dating) and availability of archaeological materials suitable for such chronological methods might necessitate a more modest scale for such study in other regions lacking obsidian artifacts. The need to avoid temporal bias (e.g., Surovell and Brantingham 2007; but see Surovell et al. 2009) and focus exclusively on habitation sites also necessitates significant regional site sampling, likely including many previously unanalyzed deposits. In this case, the scale of the effort may call for an incremental approach to regional demographic analysis, instituting protocols for chronological sampling specifically suited to this research issue. The final challenge is defining a meaningful population. In the current example, this task was greatly facilitated by the extreme topography of Yosemite Valley, but such clear geographic cues may be rare in many other areas. Without such natural boundedness, it may be difficult to determine the appropriate geographic limits for archaeological sampling. As with the larger issue of appropriate sample size, it may be that initially modest analytical efforts might be a good starting point. As noted previously, the use of agent-based modeling in concert with archaeological, and perhaps bioarchaeological, data may be particularly helpful, as it can offer scenarios that are impossible to derive from archaeological sampling alone.

Discussion and Conclusion

Some might argue that the fast pace of today's postindustrial world has no analog in the world of hunter-gatherer societies past or present. Therefore, the reason people matter in the history of modern society is the expansive spatial and accompanying restricted temporal range that characterizes social processes in our world. In an ancient world characterized by the restricted spatial and expansive temporal, however, the importance of people to history may be equally significant, even if structurally different. In such contexts, all people and things were well-known, so change was likely readily perceived and, perhaps, just as easily acted upon. Whether such perception acted to reinforce stability or prompt change is the question that needs to be addressed. Ethnographic data, agent-based modeling, and archaeological case studies all indicate that "small-scale" is a meaningful axis for interpretation of cultural dynamics within ancient foraging societies. While "thinking small" need not completely replace the economic emphasis the "hunter-gatherer" label belies, the lack of appreciation for demography as perceived social process reflects a missed analytical opportunity.

As a condition subject to perception and individual action, demography—beyond carrying capacity or population size alone—should be on an equal footing with economy in archaeological analysis of foraging societies. In fact, by reframing our analytical perspective from "hunter-gatherer" to "small-scale" society, we are prompted to consider women and men not simply as "productive units," but rather as engaged individuals and active agents involved in a series of relationships that defined both self and society. We can consider perception and choice, emergent properties as well as intended consequences, implications of a fluid population to cultural transmission and information flow, and mechanisms for social cohesion such as ritual. Although the current study necessarily relied on a simulation based on a simple calculus of energy investment, the exploratory juxtaposition of archaeological and agent-based simulation points to the potential to both develop and interpret demographic information beyond human-resource interaction, considering various types of decision making as a basis for cultural change or stability. Simulations in the absence of archaeological data allow us to discuss only *potential* (see Riede and Bentley 2008), so acquisition of fine-grained demographic information must be placed on par with economic variables when incorporating simulations (see Shennan 2000). If demographic data are routinely developed as part of our research, we can "think small" in interpretation while thinking big (i.e., regionally) in the development of such data. Considering foraging peoples first as small-scale societies will allow archaeologists to get closer to the complex view of such groups that has emerged from ethnographic studies.

Such an analytical perspective also forces us to interrogate or critically examine the very concept of "hunter-gatherer" as the primary organizing principle in this work (see Barnard 2004a:4–5), following recent scholarship on extant hunter-gatherer societies (e.g., Ingold 1999) and studies tracing the rise of *hunter-gatherer* as a term and subject of research (e.g., Pluciennik 2004; Yengoyan 2004). Under the intellectual influence first of cultural ecology and later behavioral ecology, archaeologists, in particular, have lost sight of—or have simply chosen to ignore—myriad characteristics of such groups with significance to the organization of daily life. Despite the emergence of concepts like Ingold's social relations of immediacy, there has been no archaeological attempt to examine and test—let alone embrace—such concepts as organizing principles in analysis. On the other hand, even as evolutionary biologists are now considering developmental context as significant to the process of both the generation of and selection for variation (e.g., Oyama et al. 2001), archaeologists have yet to show equal concern for this locus of generation as opposed to selection. Such disciplinary self-reflection is especially relevant to examination of societies in the past—to a world in which most people (or *all* people, prior to about 10,000 years ago) made their living by foraging. It is time to think in more nuanced ways about such groups, to consider fundamental characteristics beyond subsistence and production, to commit to exploring multiple axes of short- or long-term cultural change, and, especially, to consider fluidity, feedback, cycles, and temporality within the span of an individual lifetime or a few generations as we pursue anthropological goals.

Note

1. Such long-term trends are similar in scale—and perhaps even in detail—to patterns hypothesized or observed archaeologically elsewhere in North America in both foraging and horticultural societies based on metapopulation data encompassing larger regions (e.g., Chatters 1995; Hill et al. 2004; Meltzer 1999; Schlanger 1988; Surovell et al. 2009; Yatsko 2000).

4

Evolutionary Typologies and Hunter-Gatherer Research

Rethinking the Mounded Landscapes of Central California

Kent G. Lightfoot, Edward M. Luby, and Lisa Pesnichak

Evolutionary perspectives continue to play a fundamental role in how archaeologists interpret hunter-gatherer economies and social organizations. For the last half century evolutionary typologies have been particularly influential in structuring our perceptions of foraging peoples in North America. Following the band-level description outlined by Service (1962:60–109), archaeologists in the 1960s perceived most hunter-gatherers as simple, diminutive, and highly nomadic. Fried (1960) fostered this perception by labeling most hunter-gatherer peoples as egalitarian, which in his evolutionary scheme relegated them to the simplest nonranked, nonstratified societies. The landmark publication of *Man the Hunter* (Lee and Devore 1968a) and Richard Lee's later work among the !Kung (Lee 1972, 1979) reinforced the belief that hunter-gatherers lived close to nature, maintaining simple technologies and rudimentary political organizations while pursuing their day-to-day quest for food and shelter by foraging for resources across the landscape.

With the growing recognition and interest in so-called complex hunter-gatherers in the 1970s and 1980s, archaeologists broadened their scope of research and theoretical approaches. Price and Brown (1985) defined complex hunter-gatherers as nonagrarian people with high population densities, facilities for food storage, relatively sedentary settlement systems, intensive harvesting practices, and hierarchically organized political and ritual systems. However, the advent of this new line of investigation did not diminish the influence of previous evolutionary thinking. Archaeologists differentiated affluent hunter-gatherers from mobile foragers by simply substituting many of the pertinent attributes used to distinguish bandlike societies from tribes, chiefdoms, and states. Many of the core characteristics of affluent hunter-gatherers, such as sedentary villages, ranked or socially stratified class structure, agrarian-like (protoagriculture) management practices, and simple chiefdom-level organizations, were taken almost directly from the evolutionary literature that discriminated simple from complex societies. As a consequence, many of the fundamental building blocks that we employ in the study of complex hunter-gatherers tend to be watered-down concepts derived specifically from complex agrarian societies.

The foregoing points are exemplified by hunter-gatherer studies in California. With the growing interest in affluent hunter-gatherers in the 1970s and 1980s, anthropologists began to rethink traditional models of California Indians. In making the case that Alfred Kroeber and other earlier anthropologists had underestimated the sophistication and complexity of Native California, these revisionists emphasized that its people were "analogous to many primitive agriculture societies elsewhere" (Bean and Lawton 1976:48). Some went on to note that California Indian "social systems were similar to those of peoples with presumably greater technological advantages: e.g., horticulturalists and some agriculturalists" (Bean 1976:99). The concepts introduced into California anthropology derived from the ethnographic and archaeological literature on primarily complex agrarian societies from outside the state. California Indian societies were characterized by sociopolitical hierarchies and distinct classes of people, including elite or chiefly families; religious and craft specialists; commoners, or the rank and file; poor-indigents; and even slaves, in some cases (see Bean 1976). Persuasive arguments were made that many of these chiefly, elite families tended to inherit their rank. Archaeological investigations of cemeteries played an important role in evaluating these class distinctions and the degree to which ascription defined status in California groups (Fredrickson 1974; King 1969; King 1970, 1974, 1978). The criteria employed in the mortuary analyses were derived from cemetery studies of agrarian chiefdom- or rank-level societies (later codified in such works as Peebles and Kus [1977]), which provided California archaeologists with a yardstick to evaluate how well their complex hunter-gatherers measured up to the "real deal."

Revisionist anthropologists also introduced various concepts about the built landscape that ultimately derived from evolutionary thinking about advanced tribes and chiefdoms. Important chiefs lived in central "towns" that served as political and ritual centers for the surrounding population. These sedentary or semi-sedentary settlements contained nondomestic architecture (dance or council houses) and centralized storage facilities, which were critical for the surplus-producing economy used to support the administrative elite (Bean 1976). Native Californians supposedly employed a range of protoagricultural (or quasi-agricultural or semi-agricultural) methods that provided the resource base for supporting complex societies and administrative elites. These resource management practices were argued to be directly akin to many of the cultivation techniques used by indigenous farmers (Bean and Lawton 1976:35–36; Heizer 1958; Ziegler 1968). These techniques included the systematic tending of local habitats by pruning, burning, weeding, digging, seed sowing, and possibly even irrigation. Some studies promoted the idea that California hunter-gatherers were just as complex and sophisticated as any other agrarian people in Native North America. The primary difference was that they cultivated a range of wild crops in contrast to domesticated cultigens, such as corn, beans, and squash (Anderson 2005).

Rethinking Hunter-Gatherer Research

We recognize that broad comparisons between complex hunter-gatherers and agrarian people worldwide can be extremely useful and insightful. The last three decades of hunter-gatherer research in California have been critical for revising and expanding upon previous concepts about hunter-gatherers that dated back to the days of Kroeberian ethnography. In using models derived from agrarian chiefdoms found elsewhere in North America, archaeologists have been able to demonstrate that California Indians are truly sophisticated and complex no matter what yardstick is employed. But it may be time to rethink once again the direction and purpose of hunter-gatherer studies in California.

A lingering problem with the legacy of evolutionary typologies is that complex hunter-gatherers are often perceived as passing through a transitional state between simpler band societies and more complex societal types. Understanding how and why these hunter-gatherer societies transformed into something else is often the ultimate question in many archaeological studies. That is, research focuses on the processes and causes involved in the transformation of affluent foragers

into fully developed agrarian societies. In this kind of study, protoagriculture is often viewed as an intermediary stage along an evolutionary
path between hunting-gathering and agriculture, with its cultivation
techniques transitional to the adoption of full-scale agriculture (see discussions in Smith 2001:23–25; Yen 1989). In viewing complex hunter-
gatherers as transitional in nature, there is a tendency for archaeologists
to place affluent foragers on a continuum with more advanced agrarian
societies. Research programs that examine the rise of agriculture and the
evolution of complex societies provide a strong impetus for employing
similar kinds of concepts, models, and criteria in studies of both complex hunter-gatherers and agrarian societies.

But what if some kinds of complex hunter-gatherer societies in North
America are fundamentally different from those of advanced agrarian
societies? What if some affluent foragers are characterized by social organizations, economies, labor systems, residential patterns, and landscape
uses that are distinctive from anything known among other complex
agrarian societies? More important, by continuing to derive analogies
from chiefdom-level agrarian societies to inform many of the concepts
and models used in the study of complex hunter-gatherers, are we not
risking the possibility of minimizing or neglecting these differences?

Our purpose in this chapter is to address these questions in an
archaeological case study of complex hunter-gatherers in California.
We believe the time is right for exploring not only the similarities of
California hunter-gatherers with other agrarian and foraging societies in North America, but also their fundamental differences. Otherwise we fear that deep-rooted differences between California complex
hunter-gatherers and fully developed agrarian societies will continue to
be played down or even ignored. Service (1962:60) and other evolutionary thinkers long ago recognized California Indians as an anomalous
case: hunter-gatherers who transcended band-level societies because of
great "natural abundance." But beyond noting that they are aberrations
in evolutionary schemes, little has been done to examine critically what
makes them different.

We focus in this chapter on the California Indians who built the
impressive shell mounds along the shorelines of the greater San Francisco Bay Area. Mounded landscapes produced by hunter-gatherers offer
an exceptional opportunity to examine some of the latent assumptions

underpinning archaeological interpretations influenced by evolutionary classifications. The construction of large-scale mounds tends to be equated with the concentrated use of space by societies typically associated with intensive habitations, sedentary lifeways, and the focused exploitation of local resources. Given these perceptions, it is not surprising that various attributes of chiefdoms derived from complex agrarian societies have been employed in the interpretation of California shell mounds. However, as exemplified by the chapters in this volume, we cannot assume the variable lifeways of hunter-gatherers will necessarily mimic the characteristics of chiefdom-level societies, even those who constructed substantial mounds. The people who built the mounded landscapes at Poverty Point in Louisiana and along the St. Johns River in Florida are truly unique in their cultural practices, uses of space, and histories. But what about the California shell mounds?

The Shell Mounds of the Greater San Francisco Bay

For more than a century, archaeologists have been fascinated by the imposing shell mounds of the San Francisco Bay Area (fig. 4.1). Hundreds of extensive mounds, comprising tons of shellfish remains (clam, mussel, oysters, etc.), dirt, ash, and rocks, have been recorded along the bay shore of San Francisco Bay, San Pablo Bay, the Carquinez Strait, and Suisun Bay of central California. Other striking "dirt mounds" have been described for the delta region at the terminus of the Sacramento and San Joaquin rivers. Some of the large mounds, such as Emeryville and West Berkeley, rose five to ten or more meters above the land surface and covered the equivalent of a couple of football fields. These imposing structures, now mostly destroyed due to urban development, contained hundreds or thousands of human burials along with diverse assemblages of artifacts, mammal, bird, and fish assemblages.

Archaeological investigations indicate that these places were used over extensive periods of time. The earliest basal deposits of many large mounds date between five thousand to three thousand years ago. Radiocarbon dates indicate distinct pulses of use and non-use that span thousands of years. The large mounds tend to be found in broader mound clusters comprising four to six sites, typically near sources of freshwater that enter the bay. It is thought that the oldest and largest mounds tend

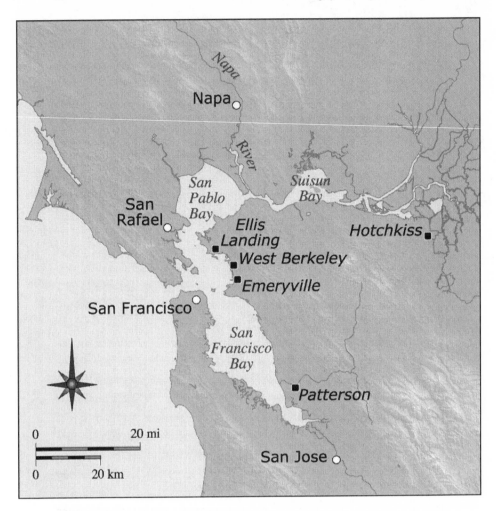

Figure 4.1. The greater San Francisco Bay Area, showing the location of key sites mentioned in the text.

to be found closest to the bay waters, ringed by other medium- and small-sized mounds. These site clusters are often associated with other kinds of sites, including petroglyphs, bedrock milling stations, lithic scatters, and nonmounded cemeteries (Lightfoot 1997; Lightfoot and Luby 2002; Luby et al. 2006).

Several interpretations have been proposed over the years to account for the creation of the great shell mounds. Archaeologists of the early twentieth century believed the mounds were "kitchen middens," essentially garbage dumps that accumulated over time from shellfish gathering and fishing activities. More recent investigations suggest that the mounds may have functioned as specialized cemeteries, as aggregation sites for feasting and mortuary ceremonies, or as full-service mounded villages (Leventhal 1993; Lightfoot 1997; Luby and Gruber 1999). The latter interpretation first surfaced during the 1943–1944 exhibition at the American Museum of Natural History in New York City that featured the archaeology of the San Francisco Bay area. Nels Nelson, one of the early pioneers in shell mound archaeology in California, directed the construction of a diorama depicting a village of tule houses built atop an impressive mound sited on a freshwater stream emptying into the bay. Populating the village were men, women, and children carrying out various domestic chores, while at the base of the mound men launched tule balsa boats into bay waters and women with burden baskets gathered foods (probably shellfish) from nearby bay flats for transportation up the mound.

It is this latter interpretation that most closely aligns with analogies drawn from chiefdom-level agrarian societies. Over the years since Nelson first proposed the mounded village model, there has been broad support for the idea that the large mounds served as sedentary or semi-sedentary villages. This popular perspective views the mound deposits as the consequence of people building up these places over many generations through the accumulation of residential activities centered in and near houses and adjacent food processing places, along with the burial of their dead in nearby spaces. The concept of the mounded village is analogous in structure and function to the classic tell structures of the Near East. In this model, families resided on the bay shore for hundreds or thousands of years, building up extensive, deep site deposits through their day-to-day practices of residential living, foodways, ritual, and mortuary observances.

It is not too far a stretch for some of us to view these California hunter-gatherer communities as maintaining tightly defined territories over many hundreds of years from which nearby resources were intensively tended, nurtured, and harvested. Lightfoot (1997:136) went so far as to argue that the large, centrally located mounds may have served as important sociopolitical and ceremonial centers for the surrounding mound clusters. With agrarian-like chiefdoms dancing in his head, he was imagining powerful chiefly elites and their retainers administrating these communities atop their imposing mounded architecture.

Ellis Landing Site

We evaluate the mounded village model using data newly derived from our ongoing geographic information system (GIS) analysis on the regional distribution of sites in the San Francisco Bay Area, along with a detailed study of the Ellis Landing site (CA-CCO-295). There are three reasons why Ellis Landing is an ideal candidate for this investigation. First, it was one of the largest prehistoric mounds constructed in the Bay Area (fig. 4.2). When Nels Nelson recorded it in 1906, the mound measured 140 by 75 m in size and about 5 m in height. Nelson later discovered that the archaeological deposits extended about four meters below ground surface. Second, Nelson directed a major excavation between 1906 and 1908 designed to collect samples from the center and margins of the site. The archaeological investigation proved to be timely as the mound was almost completely destroyed by commercial mining for shell and rich organic soils shortly after 1908. However, the field notes, photographs, artifacts, faunal remains, and soil samples from the excavation have been carefully curated for over a century in the Phoebe Hearst Museum of Anthropology on the University of California, Berkeley, campus. Much of our recent investigation is based on the reanalysis of these materials.

Third, in contrast to most other large mounds in the region, which had been seriously impacted by agricultural activities and urban expansion, Ellis Landing still had the top of its mounded structure intact when Nelson commenced his investigation. Situated in an isolated location surrounded by bay waters and marshland on the outskirts of the contemporary city of Richmond (fig. 4.3), the apex of Ellis Landing contained approximately fifteen surface depressions. In recording these surface features, each measuring about 3.5 m in diameter and 0.6 m deep, Nelson observed that they were probably the remains of house structures built on top of the mound. It appears the impetus for the mounded village concept originated with Nelson's work at Ellis Landing.

Nelson's field strategy involved the placement of a trench through a section of the above-ground mound, the excavation of a shaft to reach

Figure 4.2. Ellis Landing Mound in 1906; people in the foreground provide scale. (Courtesy of the Phoebe Hearst Museum of Anthropology and the Regents of the University of California; photograph by Nels Nelson; catalogue no. 15-10482)

buried basal deposits, and the opportunistic recording of graves exposed by the commercial mining of the mound. During the 1906 field season, Nelson and his team excavated a 33 m long by 1.8 m wide trench from the highest extant point on the mound to its edge along the marsh (fig. 4.4). The provenience of artifacts, faunal remains, burials, and sediment–constituent samples were meticulously recorded and collected during the trench excavation using a three-dimensional plotting system tied into a master stratigraphic profile. The fieldwork in 1907 consisted of a two-week salvage recovery of artifacts and graves unearthed during the mining of midden soils within a 50 by 18 m area. While men using teams of horses removed the mound deposits, Nelson did his best to

Figure 4.3. Ellis Landing Mound at high tide. Note the small shack on top of the mound. (Courtesy of the Phoebe Hearst Museum of Anthropology and the Regents of the University of California; photograph by Nels Nelson; catalogue no. 15-5229)

record burials and artifacts within a grid system of 1.5 by 1.5 m squares. The 1908 excavation involved the excavation of a 1.5 by 1.5 m shaft to a depth of about 4.2 m below the original 1906 ground surface using a hand-operated pump to dig below sea level. A total of 146 burials were recorded during the three years of fieldwork.

Evaluating the Mounded Village Model

We consider the following three issues in our evaluation of the mounded village model.

Community Structure. Our objective is to evaluate the degree of planning involved in the development of mound clusters over time. Are there patterned regularities in the regional placement, kinds of sites, and layouts of local communities? Our GIS investigation over the past few years indicates great variation in the spatial distribution of mound clusters across the San Francisco Bay Area landscape, as well as

Figure 4.4. Nels Nelson's trench excavation at the Ellis Landing Mound in 1906. (Courtesy of the Phoebe Hearst Museum of Anthropology and the Regents of the University of California; photograph by Nels Nelson; catalogue no. 15-5241)

considerable variation in the kinds and location of individual sites within specific mound clusters. Sites types associated with clusters, for example, include a variety of shell-associated sites, including shell mounds, shell middens, shell scatters, and "shell heaps" (Nelson's term), as well as earth mounds and nonmounded sites such as bedrock mortar sites, petroglyphs, and lithic scatters. Although temporal information is not yet available for all sites, clusters appear across the landscape in two forms: either as "contained" (or "tight") clusters or as "open" (or "dispersed") clusters, where clusters are defined as sites that are located in relative proximity to another and that are also linked by their presence in a similar physical landscape.

In general, the presence of water, either in drainages or along the bay shore, seems to be an important factor in the location of all clusters. "Contained" clusters are groups of geographically compact sites; most of the clusters identified in our analyses are contained clusters. Some contained clusters are located on the bay shore and consist of multiple site types, while others are situated along drainages in the nearby hills and consist mostly of single site types, such as petroglyphs or lithic scatters. "Open" clusters are groups of associated sites that are spread relatively far apart from one another but that, on a larger scale, still possess a spatial unity. Open clusters often span the shores of the bay or reach across several drainages in the hills and are arranged in a more linear fashion than sites associated with compact clusters. Open clusters are also less common than compact clusters, and the site types associated with open clusters seem to be less diverse than those associated with compact clusters. It is of interest that for open clusters situated along the bay shore, at least one of the associated sites is usually a large shell mound, with tidal flats also tending to be located nearby. Nevertheless, large shell mounds can be associated with both "contained" and "open" clusters, sometimes as part of a tight grouping of sites, and sometimes not.

Despite the identification of these cluster types, they are not uniformly distributed across the regional landscape, from the northern part of the San Francisco Bay Area through to the south. Furthermore, site types within these clusters do not recur in an easily recognized pattern across the region. Although temporal control will undoubtedly supply additional insight into community structure in the Bay Area, it appears that within a framework of broadly similar site types, communities of some complexity developed in highly variable and localized ways, without centralized building programs at mound clusters.

Village Organization. Another objective is to examine the spatial organization of the villages that supposedly formed the backbone of individual mounds. We began our investigation with a more basic question: what evidence exists that these mounded places functioned as villages? Our expectations are pretty straightforward: if the mounded places had been built up over time by multiple families residing on the sites, then we should find ample evidence of day-to-day domestic living in the deposits, including house structures and material culture resulting from myriad daily practices. However, the findings from previous shell mound excavations, as exemplified at Ellis Landing, are rather ambiguous.

An overview of excavated sites in the Bay Area indicates that house floors have been unearthed and reported, but the numbers are few (Lightfoot 1997:134–135). Nelson's excavations at Ellis Landing failed to detect any definitive house structures in the lower deposits of the mound. House features were identified only on the surface and in the uppermost levels of the mound deposit. Yet, other kinds of features, such as rock clusters, shellfish baking surfaces, and possible hearths, were recorded. Shell mound excavations also tend to yield low numbers of artifacts. From the beginning of shell mound archaeology in the San Francisco Bay Area, Kroeber (1936:133) and other anthropologists wondered how such huge edifices could have produced such "meagerness of content." As reported in Lightfoot (1997:132–133), the artifact densities for some of the best-known shell mound excavations were paltry: Emeryville (3 artifacts/m^3), West Berkeley (0.8 artifact/m^3), and the Stege Mound Complex (4–11 artifacts/m^3). The artifact density for Nelson's 1906 trench is no exception. Our calculations indicate that 0.3 artifacts were recovered for every cubic meter excavated.

Another problem with the mounded village interpretation is the insignificant amount of material that can be identified with day-to-day domestic activities. While there is much evidence for foodways practices (e.g., cooking features, food remains), other kinds of materials that might be associated with household activities, such as tool maintenance or craft production, are minimally present. A problematical pattern is the high proportion of formal tools or craft objects in relation to detritus from craft production. The majority of the formal artifacts include projectile points, bifaces, ground-stone artifacts (pestles, net weights, mortars), bone objects, and shell ornaments (mostly pendants and beads). In our analysis of the 428 lithic artifacts from the Ellis Landing excavation, 332 are ground-stone implements, 87 chipped stone artifacts, and 9 "other" lithics. Significantly, of the 87 chipped stone artifacts, only 17 may possibly be the detritus of chipped stone manufacture. These included 3 cores, 13 flakes, and one piece of shatter. To put this in perspective, there were more quartz crystals ($n = 31$) recovered from the shell mound than debitage from lithic manufacture.

In analyzing materials excavated more than a century ago, we recognize that these results may be skewed by biases in how Nelson and his team defined and recovered artifacts in the field. It is not clear from their journal notes if they would have recognized flakes and lithic or bone production debitage as "artifacts" worthy of collection and analysis. But the recovery of flakes and at least one piece of shatter suggests that they did make this distinction. To evaluate the degree of recovery bias at Ellis Landing, we are currently fine screening all extant soil samples from Nelson's excavation. Our purpose is to recover micro-remains from these samples that may have resulted from such daily practices as tool maintenance and craft manufacture. Although this task has not been completed yet, the results to 2010 indicate there is little evidence of debitage from tool production in the soil samples.

In evaluating the mounded village interpretation, it is important to consider the analytical challenges of working with archaeological remains from shell mounds. Lyman (1991), Ames (2005a), and others have documented the effects of sample size and sampling techniques in the interpretation of shell midden deposits on the Pacific Coast of North America. Archaeological deposits with high concentrations of shell tend to yield low artifact numbers and few recognizable features per unit of area excavated. They stress that unless sizeable areal excavations are undertaken, investigators may underestimate the diversity of archaeological remains, including house features, artifacts, and faunal remains. Lyman's (1991:3, 22) analysis of coastal Oregon shell middens suggests that archaeologists must excavate on the order of at least one hundred cubic meters to detect house features or to recover a sufficiently large sample of artifacts and faunal remains for detailed quantitative analysis.

We recognize that detecting relatively ephemeral house structures in midden deposits is notoriously difficult even in the best circumstances. Since the fieldwork at Ellis Landing took place more than a century ago using rather coarse-grained methods, we acknowledge the strong likelihood that Nelson and his crew may have missed some postmolds and house floors. Yet Nelson's excavation strategy did result in broad exposure of the site. His field notes indicate that his team excavated over twenty-nine hundred cubic meters of the mound from 1906 to 1908. Given the scale of this operation, we expect that at least some house structures would have been exposed and that a large enough sample of artifacts and faunal remains would have been recovered to make sense of the site.

In sum, there is not much evidence at this time to support the idea that Ellis Landing served primarily as a mounded village. Although data on foodways practices are plentiful at Ellis Landing given the cooking features and associated shellfish, fish, terrestrial mammal, and marine mammal assemblages, other kinds of domestic residue are scarce. Specifically, recognizable house structures are not found beyond the surface and upper deposits of the site. The number of artifacts is rather paltry, and of those, most are formal objects. There is little indication that much tool maintenance or craft manufacture took place on the site. This pattern is not unique to Ellis Landing but has been observed at other large shell mounds. These findings have fueled alternative interpretations that the shell mounds functioned as specialized cemeteries or places where people would have aggregated periodically for burial rituals, for feasts, and for mortuary observances and remembrances (Leventhal 1993; Luby and Gruber 1999).

Sociopolitical Hierarchies. A third objective is to evaluate whether large shell mounds, such as Ellis Landing, may have served as political and ceremonial centers for elite leaders, their families, and various retainers. The primary route for assessing the prehistoric social organization of the San Francisco Bay Area has been through the analysis of grave goods using expectations derived from chiefdom-level agrarian societies to evaluate evidence for social ranking (Fredrickson 1974; King 1970, 1974). Our analysis of the mortuary remains from Ellis Landing suggests a rather different perspective.

As mentioned earlier, Nelson excavated 146 "more or less" complete skeletons from the Ellis Landing mound; several additional sets of human remains had been removed by looters during excavations, for a total of 160. Based on these numbers, together with an estimate of the cubic footage of the entire mound, Nelson suggested that the site contained at least three thousand human remains, but he concluded that the mound more likely was associated with closer to ten thousand sets of remains. Whatever the total number of burials at the site, Ellis Landing certainly possessed an important mortuary function, at least for specific periods of time.

An ongoing analysis of published and unpublished archival material, as well as investigations of museum catalogs and databases, suggests that strikingly few burials are associated with grave goods at Ellis Landing. In fact, of the roughly 146 human remains excavated from the site, only 15 burials are associated with grave goods. Eighty catalog records of grave goods are associated with these 15 burials, consisting of roughly 250 objects, which range from several ground-stone items and many shell beads and ornaments to remarkable obsidian blades and sticks, bone tools, and a group of nearly 50 bone bird whistles from a multiple burial. Although the low number of grave goods may reflect bias in the methods of excavation, it also mirrors the results of other large mound excavations (Luby 2004).

Among the shell mounds of the San Francisco Bay Area, where many burials lack grave goods, it can be challenging to analyze burials through an interpretive framework that requires, from the outset, the presence of diverse assemblages of grave goods in order to evaluate social ranking. More to the point, efforts to identify rank may force the evidence into a framework where ranking is assumed to have existed, doing little to shed light on either mortuary behavior or sociopolitical hierarchies. Instead, it may be much more useful to expand the ways in which mortuary evidence is analyzed, to introduce interpretive frameworks that do not rely exclusively on the search for rank, and to move toward assessments that emphasize the totality of the mortuary behavior at a site, rather than those that focus on individual burials.

At Ellis Landing, two observations of the burials at the site may help in the attempt to move beyond some of these limitations. First, whether or not individual burials at Ellis Landing are associated with grave goods, almost all of the burials were found in a single stratum of the site, a stratum that can now be dated to the early Middle period, circa 500 BC to AD 300. On the other hand, only a few burials can be linked to the subsequent Late period, circa AD 900 to 1700. Elsewhere, based on an evaluation of long-term occupation patterns, Lightfoot and Luby (2002:276) observed that in this region of the San Francisco Bay Area, the Middle period was a "golden age" for shell mound communities, with a multitude of sites showing evidence of occupation. During the subsequent Late period, many of these same sites appear to have been abandoned, although some were later reoccupied (Lightfoot and Luby 2002).

Second, in the San Francisco Bay Area, researchers have not always been consistent in their use of the word "cemetery." The term has been applied variously to shell mounds, earthen mounds, and to nonmounded sites. However, within the body of theory that has developed around mortuary behavior, many would agree that a cemetery is defined as a bounded, discrete, permanent, and exclusive burial area (Luby 2004). At Ellis Landing, there is abundant evidence for subsistence activities, as outlined previously. While some of these activities could be associated with mortuary feasting, it seems highly unlikely that all were related to mortuary ritual, given the scope of shell deposition at the site, the pervasive evidence for food processing, and the fact that most burials are concentrated in one stratum. As a result, Ellis Landing and similar shell mounds cannot be considered "cemeteries," though their importance in mortuary terms can hardly be overstated.

Taken together, these observations suggest a different approach for using burials to examine sociopolitical hierarchies—one that does not rely exclusively on rank. At Ellis Landing, the use and function of the site likely changed over time. During the Middle period, for example, many burials were placed at the site, but not in a way that altered the site's function so drastically that it became a cemetery. Rather, perhaps Ellis Landing and similar shell mound sites represent a new kind of sociopolitical entity, a place where the dead were interred, venerated, and feasted, but also a place where routine food processing took place and people aggregated periodically. From this perspective, it would be hard to argue that during some periods, Ellis Landing, with its thousands of burials, was not a ceremonial center, or a symbolically important place in the landscape, and that because of the presence of these burials, it was also not important politically. It also seems likely that even as the function of the site changed over time—for example, from the Middle period to the Late period, when burial at the site became much less common—some site functions, especially concerning mortuary behavior, were retained or modified in interesting ways.

While it is important to learn whether shell mounds served as places for elite leaders and their families, it is unfortunate that years of investigation through the lens of rank in burials have not yielded a compelling snapshot of the situation. Certainly, however, if insight into sociopolitical hierarchies is the goal, examining the evidence concerning the burials at

Ellis Landing from a perspective that is not limited to rank is likely to be fruitful. The need to appreciate burials at shell mounds and to explore them from multiple frameworks is critically important. Assessments of shell mounds as places of food-related activities and mortuary ritual can then be supplemented with investigations of territoriality, analyses of the organizational behavior likely to be associated with accessing and managing food resources, and discussions of the place and meaning of shell mounds in the sociopolitical landscape.

A Reevaluation of the Shell Mounds

Our investigation of the shell mounds of the greater San Francisco Bay Area does not lend much support to the mounded village model. There is little evidence that the mound clusters were constructed using a regional master plan. The evidence for house structures and domestic residue from daily life is underwhelming. There is no indication of the building of various kinds of architectural elements of mounded landscapes that have become synonymous with chiefdom-level, agrarian societies in the American Midwest and Southeast: plaza complexes, elaborate mounds topped with elite or religious structures, and associated residential zones. While the creation of mounded landscapes in the heartland of America may have been planned and built over subsequent generations or exploded onto the scene in pulses of rapid (big-bang) building episodes, the tempo of mound construction appears to be different in California. We feel the shell mounds in the San Francisco Bay Area, as exemplified by Ellis Landing, are characterized by their own unique rhythms of history.

Ellis Landing appears to have been built up over time through different anthropogenic processes. The lower and earlier component of the mound consists of a "compact" stratum that was uniformly compressed and fine in texture, made up of crushed shell and finer sediment. A suite of radiocarbon dates span from BC 1700 to about AD 900. As noted previously, the vast majority of the burials are found in the lower component (Middle period). The upper component, which appears to date episodically between about AD 900 to 1700 (Late period), is composed of relatively coarse material, including deposits of whole or partial shellfish remains and lenses of ash, shell, and rocks. The upper component contains few burials but evidence of house structures: some appear in the stratigraphic profile while others are pit features recorded on the surface of the mound by Nelson.

Our current interpretation of Ellis Landing is that this place was re-used episodically by hunter-gatherers for almost thirty-five hundred years. During this extensive period, the mounded place may have served distinctive purposes and meanings to people, having been built up by diverse foraging groups who employed different kinds of mound-building practices. The earliest use suggests the place was repeatedly employed for burying people and for building up deposits that may have been associated with periodic mortuary ceremonies and feasting. It may have also served as a logistical base for the bulk collection and processing of bay resources, which could then be transported to other residential places in the nearby region. The use of mound appears to have transformed significantly after AD 900 with the construction of house structures and other features, but few associated burials.

What these findings all mean is still being considered. But it is clear that there is little evidence that Ellis Landing or any other large shell mound that we know of in the San Francisco Bay Area functioned in an analogous way to a Near Eastern tell structure. It appears that people repeatedly returned to the Ellis Landing site to exploit estuarine and nearby terrestrial resources and to bury their dead. Later groups continued to re-use the place but primarily as a place for collecting and processing bay resources and as a residential base that appears to have largely excluded burials near house structures. We are considering the possibility that the Ellis Landing site was created through the cumulative efforts of a diverse range of hunter-gatherer people whose uses, meanings, and intentions probably varied over time. Native peoples with distinctive cultural backgrounds and from diverse communities may have incorporated this area of the bay shore into their economic, political, and religious activities in unique ways over time.

Shell Mounds and the Management of the Regional Landscape

Our findings are stimulating us to consider new sociopolitical models, including the possibility that these sites served a critical integrative function for hunter-gatherer groups who spent much of their time dispersed across the regional landscape. As part of our reevaluation of the mounded landscapes of central California, we are rethinking how local hunter-gatherer groups managed landscapes on a regional scale. Our current work is focusing on the pyrodiversity practices of California Indians (see Lightfoot and Parrish [2009] for a detailed discussion). Recent findings from fire ecology studies indicate late Holocene fire regimes with "fire return intervals" at a frequency much greater than that possible from lightning strikes or natural fire occurrences alone (Carle 2008; Keeley 2002; Stephens and Fry 2005; Sugihara et al. 2006). In fact, a recent synthesis of this research suggests that 6 to 16 percent of California (excluding the southern deserts) was annually burned, resulting in the blackening of almost two to five million hectares of resource patches a year (Stephens et al. 2007). It is estimated that the emissions from these fires were so high in late prehistoric times that some parts of the state, such as the Great Central Valley, experienced hazy or smoggy conditions not unlike what we see today.

Based on these recent findings, we are considering the likelihood that local hunter-gatherer groups initiated small-scale, low-intensity burns of resource patches in some kind of staggered, multiyear rotation. These management practices would have enhanced the growth and diversity of economic plants, including roots, tubers, fruits, greens, nuts, and seeds, as well as provided forage that attracts birds and mammals. By burning patches in a staggered sequence over a number of years, hunter-gatherers could experience an ever-changing mosaic of resources as diverse stages of plant colonization and habitat successions unfolded in adjacent patches. These kinds of pyrodiversity practices would have encouraged the availability of varied and bountiful wild crops in specific resource patches across the region, in addition to other foods and raw materials exploited from specific riverine and coastal habitats, such as along the bay shore.

In exploring our so-called pyrodiversity collecting model—where California Indians were involved in a long-term tradition of pyrodiversity practices that created fine-grained, heterogenous mosaics of productive habitats—we are addressing some of the basic differences that may have set pyrodiversity collectors apart from indigenous farmers. These differences may have involved the employment of management strategies that enhanced resource diversity on a regional scale, methods of resource intensification that do not focus on a handful of crop staples, different rhythms in the structure and timing of labor, distinctive kinds of political and ritual organizations, and a much greater fluidity and movement of people across the landscape (Lightfoot and Parrish 2009). The upshot of our research on pyrodiversity practices is that some forms of complex hunter-gatherers may have developed distinctive kinds of relationships with regional landscapes from agrarian people or even other kinds of hunter-gatherers. Pyrodiversity collectors would have used the landscape differently over time depending on the nature of fire histories, the tempo of plant and animal colonization in burned parcels, habitat stand successions, and the differential ability to bulk collect specific kinds of resources. These relationships may have produced distinctive forms of histories, memories, and constructions of landscapes.

Regionally oriented pyrodiversity practices pose enormous organizational and logistical challenges for hunter-gatherers. On one hand, people needed to be relatively mobile and flexible in their ability to manage and monitor diverse resource patches across the region, as well as to bulk harvest specific resources when they became available throughout the annual cycle. On the other hand, local groups needed some way to coordinate and manage both information (when and where resources were available, which resource patches needed tending, etc.) and peoples' activities and movements across the region. Shell mounds would have provided ideal points of aggregation on the landscape, where groups could periodically come together for mortuary practices, ceremonies, feasting, and food gathering and processing. Even though these groups may have lived away from the mounds during some part of the annual cycle, they would probably have been brought back together on a regular basis as part the ceremonial scheduling of rites and observances dealing with the dead, as well as for fishing, gathering, and hunting along the bay shore. In terms of food-related resource procurement, the mere existence of a shell mound itself proves that shellfish beds were accessed; perhaps over time, these very important shellfish beds were also managed and controlled via shell mounds. Examining the issue of access to shellfish beds also raises the intriguing question of how newly emerging resources associated with fire-related activities were controlled and accessed by regularized meetings at the shell mounds.

Future work will address the relationship between the construction of shell mounds and the management of regional hunter-gatherer economies. Of course, pyrodiversity practices were not restricted to the greater San Francisco Bay Area, but appear to have been employed across much of Native California (Lightfoot and Parrish 2009). Yet mounded landscapes are not ubiquitous across ancient California. This observation suggests that other kinds of organizational strategies were probably employed elsewhere in the management and monitoring of both resources and people across the landscape. For example, Lynn Gamble's chapter (this vol.) on the Chumash emphasizes the important role that pyrodiversity practices played in southern California where extensive mounds were apparently not built. The management of the regional landscape by Chumash groups may have revolved around influential chiefs in coastal mainland villages (see also Gamble 2008). A similar kind of landscape management organization may have also centered around the development of large villages with multifamily houses in southern British Columbia during a period of increased fire activity associated with sustained warm weather and abnormally low precipitation (Lepofsky et al. 2005; see also Prentiss, this vol.).

Conclusion

In highlighting the legacy of evolutionary typologies in hunter-gatherer archaeology, we stress that evolutionary thinking, whether explicitly or implicitly, has affected our conceptualizations about hunter-gatherers, from the kinds of models that have been applied in archaeological research to perspectives on how hunter-gatherers relate to other kinds of advanced societies. It has been particularly influential in our thinking about complex hunter-gatherers. Many of the core concepts used in describing affluent hunter-gatherers, such as protoagriculture, sociopolitical hierarchies, ascription, sedentary or semi-sedentary village life, have been taken almost directly from evolutionary schemes that distinguish band-level societies from more-advanced tribal and chiefdom societies. The initial studies of complex hunter-gatherers in California employed many of the same concepts used to define chiefdoms in an attempt to show that Native Californians were just as complex and sophisticated as any indigenous agrarian people in North America. The upshot is that many of our models of complex hunter-gatherers have been created in the long shadow of agrarian chiefdoms.

The time is right to rethink complex hunter-gatherers. We raise the thorny question about whether we should view them as truly distinctive kinds of societies or on a continuum with agrarian societies. We may want to break down how we conceptualize hunter-gatherer and agrarian societies, recognizing that some complex hunter-gatherers may have more in common with particular agrarian groups than with other hunter-gatherers. In other cases, we may want to recognize fundamental differences between complex hunter-gatherer and agrarian societies with respect to social organizations, economies, and labor scheduling, among other dimensions. What we need to do is "think outside the box" in how we define hunter-gatherers, recognizing that there may be more variation within this category than between some hunter-gatherers and farming people. Understanding how and why these differences developed among complex hunter-gatherer societies is an important research program for the future of North American archaeology.

In light of the unrivaled cultural diversity in California, we also believe more effort needs to be placed on comparative analyses of California complex hunter-gatherers. Not only would this assist us in better understanding these groups, but such analyses would likely supply additional insight into and perhaps introduce more nuance and variability into a somewhat broadened concept of complex hunter-gatherer. However, while it is easy to state that such efforts should be made, we must be frank in recognizing that any comparative analyses will take place in a climate where the evolutionary approach has underpinned virtually all discussions in California for nearly thirty years, including some of our own. As insightful as the evolutionary approach has been in California, it may be challenging to step away from it.

We propose that California Indians followed a unique historical trajectory that was not heading down the road toward the adoption of agriculture. In this chapter, we have explored some ideas relating to shell mounds in the greater San Francisco Bay Area and the critical role they may have played in pyrodiversity economies. Rather than viewing these places as sedentary mounded villages or miniature chiefdom-level societies that were mysteriously "dropped from the Midwestern sky," it is best to consider not only their similarities with other complex societies but also their differences. Our analysis of Ellis Landing suggests it served various purposes over time, including as a burial place where feasting and mortuary observances took place; a logistical base where coastal resources were bulk collected and processed, possibly for transportation elsewhere; and a residential base in late prehistoric and early historic times. We are now experimenting with the idea that Ellis Landing and other shell mounds were incorporated into regional pyrodiversity economies. As a consequence, they may have been constructed for various purposes by assorted hunter-gatherer groups who employed different kinds of mound-building practices over many hundreds of years.

Acknowledgments

We appreciate the kind invitation of Ken Sassaman and Don Holly to participate in the original Society for American Archaeology symposium and in the subsequent Amerind Foundation seminar. Many of the ideas presented in this chapter benefited greatly from the excellent comments raised by all the participants of the Amerind Foundation symposium. We are especially indebted to Ken and Don for providing us with detailed post-symposium commentary. Our sincere thanks to Director John Ware for comments on the paper as well; we appreciate greatly his and the entire Amerind Foundation's staff for the hospitality and tender care we received in Arizona. Finally, we thank the Archaeology Program at the National Science Foundation for their support of our shell mound study.

5

When Foragers Fail

In the Eastern Subarctic, for Example

Donald H. Holly Jr.

As parents are apt to do, my father once told a neighbor that I was an archaeologist, to which the neighbor replied, "Has he read *Collapse*, by Jared Diamond? It's a wonderful book." And then, "Has your son written anything that I might enjoy reading?" Yes, I have; and no, not likely.

However intriguing and interesting Subarctic archaeology may be, I understand that it does not appeal to the general public in quite the same way as the collapse of ancient civilizations do. Their failure seems to strike a deeper chord. This is probably because these societies more closely resemble our own, and thus our tendency to see our future in their ruins. The effect is disconcerting, and after staring into the abyss the popular response seems to be to turn to books like *Collapse* for answers.

The answers one finds in *Collapse* and similar books often take the form of parables. Civilizations collapse because of human arrogance. We overharvest forests, raise salt tables, exhaust the land, tax our citizens to death, extend our empires too far, and stretch ourselves too thin—we are greedy and careless. Alternatively, we simply make mistakes. In such cases, ruins do not so much mock us as they are merely proof of our fallibility.

Yet the mistakes of civilizations—whether due to arrogance or simply poor judgment—are usually believed to be of our own making. Both popular and scholarly explanations for the collapse of ancient civilizations typically blame us; they blame people. People are given the power and agency to fail. And while it is true that explanations that involve environmental change are and have been popular for some time, it is uncommon for archaeologists to attribute the collapse of civilizations solely to environmental factors. Rather, the environment is frequently invoked as merely a sort of test or challenge that ancient people must overcome. That they often fail is irrelevant. What is important, to para-phrase Jared Diamond, is that societies *choose* to fail.

This is not the way that archaeologists have traditionally conceptu-alized and written about hunter-gatherer failure. In general, they have not been granted the freedom to fail. This is especially true for foragers inhabiting so-called marginal places, such as the boreal forests and rocky open country of the Eastern Subarctic. There, both failure and the suc-cessful efforts of hunter-gatherers to avoid it have been understood as a fundamentally different process from the way that ancient "civilizations" are thought to perish or persist. When Subarctic hunter-gatherers fail, it is attributed to the failure of the environment, but not to people's "choices." Success is understood similarly. The ability of hunter-gatherers to avert disaster is assumed to be self-evident—the result of an idealized, almost "natural" adaptation to one's environment. In neither case are hunter-gatherers really responsible for their fate. They choose nothing.

On the Failure and Survival of Hunter-Gatherers on the Island of Newfoundland and Elsewhere in the Eastern Subarctic

In 1966 Marshall Sahlins (1968) famously made the case for hunter-gatherer affluence at the Man the Hunter Symposium in Chicago. Countering negative stereotypes that were still popular at the time, Sahlins (see also 1972) asserted that hunting and gathering was a rela-tively easy and enjoyable way of making a living. Right or wrong, his argument was persuasive, and supported by the work of others, it soon replaced the notion that hunting and gathering was a difficult and mis-erable endeavor (Kaplan 2000). But June Helm, an anthropologist with extensive field experience in the Subarctic at the symposium, was imme-diately critical of the applicability of Sahlins's ideas to the region she knew best. Commenting on his paper she noted: "I do not think the thesis of confidence in the yield of tomorrow holds for the boreal forest peoples. Rather, my reading of northern Indian equanimity is that it is fatalistic rather than optimistic: If either the day or the morrow does not provide for itself, there is little one can do about it" (Helm 1968:89).

Helm's skepticism would have been shared by many archaeologists working in the Subarctic at the time. Writing about the interior of the

Labrador Peninsula, William Fitzhugh (1972a, 1973) suggested that hunter-gatherers of the region led a difficult and precarious life and would have suffered population crashes and even extinctions in "prehistory." Worse, failure was unavoidable—a consequence of having to depend on an impoverished resource base for one's livelihood (Fitzhugh 1972a, 1973:49–50; Samson 1975:76). A similar argument was advanced for the nearby island of Newfoundland. In what would become an influential article, Jim Tuck and Ralph Pastore (1985) suggested that hunter-gatherers on the island were likewise doomed owing to the inherent instability of the island's key food resources. While islanders might enjoy periods of prosperity, Tuck and Pastore reasoned that the hard times would have been particularly unforgiving. All that was needed was a hypothetical offshore breeze that kept harp seals out at sea or an ice storm that decimated caribou populations and people would have starved and disappeared. Tuck and Pastore cited gaps in the archaeological record—episodes when the island was devoid of people—to support their interpretation. To them, the gaps represented human extinctions.

Fitzhugh's and Tuck and Pastore's rather dismal view of hunters and gatherers' chances for long-term survival in the Subarctic is one that has been shared by many (Holly 2002a). Indeed, prior to intensive archaeological investigation, it was thought that vast areas of the Subarctic had not been occupied prior to the influx of Europeans, firearms, flour, and the incentive to obtain furs for trade. A number of scholars, for instance, suggested that the Hudson Bay Lowlands were too impoverished to support Native populations in "prehistory" (see Lytwyn 2002:28–39). A similar claim was made for the boreal forests north of Lake Superior. It was imagined as "a wasteland without permanent residents" (Hickerson 1966:8) prior to the arrival of fur traders. And on a map denoting archaeological cultures in North America circa 2500 BCE, James Griffin (1964:232) simply left much of the region blank. In time archaeologists would put Subarctic hunter-gatherers on the map, but tenuously at first. Most continued to read the archaeological record of the region as reflecting a homogenous and conservative culture, primarily oriented to the food quest (Dawson 1977, 1982, 1983, 1987; Maxwell 1980; Spaulding 1946; Wright 1972) and vulnerable to failure.

Archaeologists have since become more optimistic about hunters and gatherers' chances in the boreal forest. Archaeological investigations

in the Hudson Bay Lowlands have revealed evidence for human occupation preceding the arrival of Europeans (Julig 1988; Pilon 1990); assessments of the productivity of the interior of Labrador have brightened
(Fitzhugh 2006:50); and Tuck and Pastore's (1985) pessimistic take on
Newfoundland prehistory has been scrutinized. With regard to Newfoundland, Priscilla Renouf (1999a:415–16) has interpreted gaps in the
island's archaeological record as strategic evacuations rather than extinctions. She argues that islanders would not have been so vulnerable to collapse as Tuck and Pastore's model suggests (Renouf 1999a:405), thanks
to social institutions and strategies hunters and gatherers are known
to employ to buffer against resource shortfalls (i.e., Gould 1982; Halstead and O'Shea 1989; Jarvenpa 2004; Steegmann 1983; Stopp 2002;
Wiessner 1996). Accordingly, Renouf posits that when disaster struck in
antiquity, Newfoundland's foragers would have worked together, shared
food, and if necessary cut and run, but they would not have failed in the
catastrophic sense. For instance, Renouf (2003:6–7) and her colleagues
(Renouf et. al 2000) posit that different groups (Dorset Paleo-Eskimos
and "Recent Indian" Amerindians) living on the island would have
shared information regarding resource availability and established social
ties with each other to draw on in times of need. Conceptualized in this
way, Newfoundland's hunters and gatherers were well-equipped to cope
with sharp fluctuations in resource availability and to survive other environmental calamities (Renouf 1999a).

Discussion

Robert Braidwood (1960:148) once remarked that life prior to agriculture was hard, and that "men must have spent their waking moments
seeking their next meal, except when they could gorge following a great
kill." Clearly Braidwood thought of hunting and gathering as a miser-
able and irrational way of making a living. I suspect this is not, nor
has it been, the opinion of archaeologists working in the Subarctic for
quite some time. Actually, I imagine that most would take the opposite
position—that hunting and gathering was sensible and necessary, and
that the people who pursued this way of life knew what they were doing
and were very good at it. If anything, my impression is that archaeologists have taken the failure of foragers in this region as proof of how

challenging an environment the Subarctic is—*that even hunters and gatherers failed here!*—rather than as a statement on their shortcomings. Thus, archaeological interpretations of hunter-gatherer failure in the Eastern Subarctic can be read as parables about the poor environment, not poor choices.

Since Julian Steward's inspired ecological revolution in hunter-gatherer studies, hunting and gathering has been viewed as a completely rational endeavor, if not a noble pursuit. And the tables have correspondingly turned on farmers. No longer so championed, farmers now appear to live in a perpetual state of discontent, working long hours for little, prone to plagues and famine, and often hungry (Sahlins 1972:35–39). In contrast, hunter-gatherers are more-or-less happy, and certainly self-assured of their ability to survive and sustain themselves in their environment indefinitely. We admire their resourcefulness in unforgiving places and marvel at the ingenuity of social institutions that appear perfectly designed to mitigate against resource shortfalls; accurately assess and adapt to changes in the environment; and prevent people from hoarding, taking over, or even bragging. In short, hunter-gatherers seem largely immune to the problems that often brought down civilizations.

Of course, no one suggests that hunter-gatherers are naturally immune to disaster. Yet, the effectiveness of hunter-gatherer adaptations has sometimes been inflated to the point of near invincibility, to the effect that every cultural institution—from divination (Moore 1957) to infanticide (Steegmann 1983)—seems flawlessly designed to avoid starvation. In this way hunter-gatherer "adaptations" *are* naturalized. They are divorced from culture and history and seem to be merely the products of natural selection, or perhaps the cold calculus of survival, but they are not really made by "man." So whereas the people of ancient civilizations might exist in a state of discontent and be doomed to ruin, they are at least conceptualized as having the ability to will their way through history and thus, in a sense, determine their own fate. Hunter-gatherers are not. They are thought to be either invulnerable to failure or the victims of forces they could never hope to control. As a case in point, while we are used to thinking about the failure of the Norse in Greenland as partly due to their reluctance to adopt an Inuit way of living and an Inuit way of perceiving the resource landscape (Buckland et al. 1996:94; Diamond 2005; Fagan 2008:93–94; McGovern 1985,

1994; Outram 1999; cf. Dugmore et al. 2007), Inuit "adaptations" are rarely conceptualized in a similar way. We grant the Norse a culturally informed perception of the landscape but assume that the Inuit's perception was a natural twenty-twenty; we allow political and economic aspirations to cloud the Norse's judgment but imagine that the Inuit would have rationally dismissed such considerations in the better interest of survival.

On Strategy in Hunter-Gatherer Adaptation

The upshot of both "pessimistic" and "optimistic" perspectives on the fates of hunter-gatherers is that they dovetail into a kind of determinism where hunter-gatherers are denied the authorship and the ability to write their own—even if occasionally tragic—histories. I propose a different approach to thinking about hunter-gatherer success and failure, one that invokes the spirit of Braidwood's argument, but certainly not the message. Braidwood might have been wrong about hunting and gathering, but he gave people the agency to make poor decisions (to continue a life of feast and famine) and the ability to improve their lot ("invent" agriculture). Hunters and gatherers may be wise, but they are not infallible; and they are not infallible because, like other peoples, they have the ability to pursue strategies that resonate with traditional practice and accommodate social needs and desires, and that are informed by particular experiences and worldviews.

In a recent book on the foragers of South and Southeast Asia, Kathleen Morrison (2002a:22) argues that hunting and gathering in South Asia was more of a strategic decision than it was essential to survival. Echoing revisionist arguments for the Kalahari (Denbow 1984; Schrire 1980; Wilmsen 1989), Morrison points out that a wide spectrum of subsistence strategies was possible *and* realized in tropical and semitropical environments: farmers became foragers, foragers became farmers, and foragers remained foragers when presented with other opportunities. In short, people chose courses of action and ways of life that were socially relevant, desired, or at least sensible under the circumstances. Some opted to hunt and gather in part to trade fragrant woods, rubber, pepper, honey, game, medicinal plants, shells, and other products for rice, cloth, iron, and salt (Bowdler 2002; Endicott 1999; Fox 1969;

Hoffman 1984; Junker 2002; Morrison 2002b; Turnbull 1968), while others remained or were compelled to become foragers in the wake of devastating epidemics, under the threat of attack, or in the interest of achieving some measure of social, political, and economic autonomy (Bessire 2005; Endicott 1983, 1999; Rival 2002; Stearman 1984; Tucker 2003); but all had some ability to "choose" their adaptations—to make strategic decisions that, in turn, had ramifications for how they would live their lives. Thus Agta women hunt not only to satisfy their own needs but also their trading partners' appetites for forest meat (Estioko-Griffin and Griffin 1981:144), or people adopt a very strenuous mobile form of hunting and gathering to maintain their autonomy (Bessire 2005:1; Rival 2002), but tropical foragers do not hunt and gather in a particular way because it is essential to survival in their natural environment. Rather, they forage in particular ways for socially "strategic" reasons.

Hunting and gathering is clearly essential to survival in the Subarctic, but that does not mean that it could not also be strategic in the same sense that tropical hunting and gathering is. Indeed, the archaeological record suggests that a range of adaptive choices was possible and realized in the Subarctic. The last twenty years of archaeological research on the island of Newfoundland, for instance, has revealed rather stark differences in subsistence strategies, land-use patterns, and technology over time and between different groups of hunters and gatherers that have called New-foundland home (Erwin 2003; Holly 2002b; Pastore 1986; Rast et al. 2004; Renouf 2003; Schwarz 1994). This variation cannot be attributed simply to different environmental conditions. While hunter-gatherer lifeways on the island were influenced by climate change and constrained by dimensions of resource availability (such as seasonal fluctuations), different cultural traditions, social objectives, and historical circumstances appear to have played a critical role in the constitution of particular strategies too. This is evident in Paleo-Eskimo peoples' apparent interest in continuing a long tradition of maritime exploitation that was first forged in the Arctic and then actively maintained when they ventured south across the Strait of Belle Isle and settled the island of Newfoundland. And it is evident in later Amerindian peoples' (often referred to as "Recent Indians") different approach to similar environmental circumstances when they crossed the same strait and arrived on the island. In contrast to Paleo-Eskimos' more coastal-centered strategy, Recent Indian peoples adopted a more generalized subsistence strategy that included both terrestrial and coastal resources. Accordingly, within the parameters afforded by the environment, both groups were able to craft unique economies of hunting and gathering that resonated with "traditional" practice. Neither was narrowly determined by the environment.

Of course, strategies are subject to reinterpretation and adjustment. This can occur when environmental conditions change. When climatic conditions were highly variable and critical food resources were unpredictable for early Paleo-Eskimos, for instance, they adopted a subsistence and settlement strategy that was opportunistic and flexible; later, when conditions stabilized, Paleo-Eskimo peoples became increasingly sedentary and specialized in their subsistence efforts. Such adjustments suggest close correspondence between Paleo-Eskimo strategies and environmental change (Renouf 1993). Nonetheless, one can read these strategic shifts as variations on a theme rather than adaptations cut from entirely different cloth. To greater or lesser extent, Paleo-Eskimo peoples continued to focus on coastal resources when conditions changed, and this broad and long-standing commitment to the coast would seem to suggest that Paleo-Eskimo peoples saw the resource landscape in a culturally informed way (like the Norse did in Greenland).

In discussing the Natufians' transformation to agriculture, Bar-Yosef (1998) notes that not all hunter-gatherers of the Levant responded to the Younger Dryas in the same way. Some became more mobile; others remained sedentary and experimented with planting (Bar-Yosef 1998:173–174); and a few, such as the (Harifian) Natufians of the Negev and northern Sinai, disappeared (Bar-Yosef 1998:168). Such different fates may indicate that different groups of hunter-gatherers—like Paleo-Eskimos and Recent Indians on the island of Newfoundland—had different understandings of their environment and therefore would have responded to environmental change differently. This has implications for thinking about the failure of the Dorset on the island, a matter I will return to later.

In addition to the natural environment, strategies are also reinterpreted and restructured by changing social circumstances. There is some evidence to suggest, for example, that Dorset Paleo-Eskimos and Recent Indians gathered together into larger settlements and intensified subsistence efforts at times when they shared the same landscape (Holly 2005). Such efforts may reflect a desire for protection in the context of increased competition over resources (Erwin et al. 2005; Holly 2002b:94–95), or alternatively a means of divvying up resources in order to avoid it (Renouf 2003), but in either case the aims were strategic; that is, the social milieu served as an arena in which particular courses of action and "adaptation" were crafted.

In these and other ways, the strategies of boreal forest hunters and gatherers begin to resemble those of other peoples, such as the "strategic" foragers of the tropical forest. If they were capable of altering subsistence and settlement patterns to gather forest products for trade, then boreal forest foragers were so capable too. Indeed, historic documents offer ample evidence of Subarctic hunters and gatherers who reorganized their subsistence economies, settlement patterns, and social relations to participate in the fur trade (Abel 1993; Francis and Morantz 1983; Lytwyn 2002; Ray 1974; Reedy-Maschner and Maschner 1999). Likewise, as with tropical foragers who altered mobility patterns to avoid slave raiders or disgruntled trading partners, Subarctic foragers were able to employ similar strategies to avoid their enemies and debt collectors. The Beothuk Indians of Newfoundland, for example, relocated their main settlements to the interior of the island to avoid Europeans (Holly 2008; Marshall 1996); the Innu Indians of the Labrador Peninsula virtually abandoned the coast following the arrival of Inuit (Kaplan 1985; Loring 1992, 1997:208–209); and the Eastern Cree skillfully maneuvered between French and English trading posts to their economic advantage (Francis and Morantz 1983:25–40). And nor should we imagine that such strategic considerations would have been limited to the modern era. The quarrying and long-distance exchange of lithic raw materials throughout the Eastern Subarctic in antiquity (Denton 1998; Loring 2002; McCaffrey 1989a, this vol.; Stopp 2008:112–118) likely structured peoples' lifeways in the same ways that the procurement of rubber, tree resin, and honey did for tropical foragers. Hence, one could reasonably conclude that Subarctic hunter-gatherer "adaptations" have always been strategic.

Revisiting Failure on the Island of Newfoundland: The Case of the Dorset

If all hunter-gatherer adaptations are strategic, it stands to reason that some might be more-or-less vulnerable to failure than others. This point

was made by Fred Schwarz (1994) after considering variation in subsistence and settlement strategies among different groups of hunters
and gatherers on the island of Newfoundland and their different fates.
Schwarz noted that the Dorset Paleo-Eskimos, who were specialized harp
seal hunters, disappeared by CE 900, while contemporaneous Recent
Indian peoples, who were generalists, did not. Citing these dissimilar
outcomes, Schwarz recommended that archaeologists "perhaps pay less
attention to the *natural* instability of Newfoundland ecosystems than to
possible *cultural* sources of instability" (1994:67, emphasis in original).

Schwarz (1994:66) went on to conclude that the Recent Indians'
broad-based and generalized foraging strategy was more sustainable than
the Dorset Paleo-Eskimos' specialized maritime adaptation. And clearly
there is evidence to support his claim: Recent Indian peoples remained
on the island while the Dorset did not. But how should archaeologists
understand these different fates? Does the failure of the Dorset on the
island of Newfoundland speak to their inability to achieve an ecologi-
cally sustainable lifeway? Or was the Dorset's failure merely a "strategic"
blunder? I assume the latter—that Recent Indian people did not succeed
because they necessarily had a better understanding of island ecology,
but merely because under the circumstances they had a "better" adaptation (see also Bell and Renouf 2008:86–87). If the universal goal of
hunter-gatherers is not to arrive at some optimal and indefinitely sustainable adaptation to their natural environment but rather to survive
while pursuing a course of action that is socially, culturally, and historically meaningful and relevant, then hunter-gatherer failures must be
understood in the same ways that the "collapse" of ancient civilizations
are—as social phenomena.

As for the Dorset of Newfoundland, it has been suggested that a
warming spell might have precipitated their collapse (Bell and Renouf
2008; Hodgetts et. al 2003; Renouf 1993:206–207). The logic follows
that the Dorset were dependent on harp seal, an animal in turn dependent on pack ice, and therefore when the latter disappeared so did the
former (Bell and Renouf 2008). Presumably when this happened the
Dorset could have adopted a way of life akin to that practiced by Recent
Indians at the time and weathered the heat wave, but they did not. One
possibility is that the Dorset did indeed make an effort to become generalists but that they were prevented from doing so by Recent Indian

peoples who were already laying claim to the interior and portions of the coast and perhaps defending these areas with bows and arrows (Erwin et. al 2005). Analogous to a cruel case of musical chairs (Rosenberg 1998), Recent Indians may have simply been at the right place at the right time—more lucky than good. If this was indeed the situation, it is easy to imagine what would have happened to them if caribou had vanished instead of harp seals.

Another possibility is that the Dorset held steadfast to the coast, even as their "traditional" way of life proved increasingly untenable. It has been said that the Newfoundland Dorset were conservative (Erwin 2001:151; Harp 1969–1970:123, 1976:138), but this does not mean that they were ignorant. A common explanation for the collapse of civilizations is "failure to adapt." This occurs when people are unable or unwilling to reach the consensus necessary to change, and thus continue to pursue an unreasonable course of action (Janssen et al. 2003:722). If allowed to continue, the inevitable correction can be quite severe, as when the active suppression of small forest fires provides fuel for a larger conflagration—or when the strident efforts to continue a particular way of life leads to the demise of the Hohokam (Hegmon et al. 2008:314). In *Collapse*, Jared Diamond (2005) wonders how civilizations come to make poor choices. It is a good question, but my point is that we still let them do it. Yet if hunter-gatherers fail, it is more likely to be attributed to harp seals not showing up than to the Dorset remaining on the coast against their better judgment, hoping that they will.

Trevor Bell and Priscilla Renouf (2008) have recently suggested that the declining availability of harp seals in Newfoundland's waters may have caused the abandonment of the large Dorset settlement at Port au Choix, which in turn set off a rapid domino-like succession of failures at Dorset settlements elsewhere on the island (Renouf and Bell 2008). Citing its strategic location in the Strait of Belle Isle, they argue that Port au Choix served as an important gateway between Dorset communities on the island and those on the not-so-distant shores of Labrador (Bell and Renouf 2008:81–82). And thus when harp seals failed to materialize or proved inaccessible, the gateway closed, networks were severed, and the Dorset were compelled to abandon the island.

Social considerations, and not merely diminishing pack ice and harp seals, likely played a part in the demise of the Dorset at Port au Choix and elsewhere on the island too. While harp seals were clearly the economic engine that enabled the Dorset to flourish at Port au Choix, the Dorset's reluctance to relinquish social aspects of life there (established patterns of seasonal aggregation, ritual, trade, and deposition of the dead) when times got tough may have factored into their failure too. Port au Choix was clearly the epicenter of Dorset Paleo-Eskimo life on the island, if not beyond. The site of Phillip's Garden at Port au Choix has yielded nearly seventy semi-subterranean dwellings, numerous midden deposits, and tens of thousands of artifacts. At its peak and during the spring harp seal hunt, it was probably home to several hundred people (Bell and Renouf 2008:80). The site is also located near three Dorset burial sites (Anderson and Tuck 1974; Brown 1988; Renouf 1999b:48). Dorset burials are rare in the Eastern Arctic (Niels et al. 2003), which makes the several at Port au Choix not only unusual, but I suspect pretty special too. Accordingly, the site must have dominated the social and sacred landscape (see Renouf 2000:71), perhaps even to the point where the cultural significance of Port au Choix came to overshadow the banal fact that harp seals could be found there too. Thus when the ice disappeared and the harp seal followed suit, the Dorset may have held on, perhaps against better "ecological reason," in order to continue a particular kind of social life to which they had been accustomed and hoped to maintain. Indeed, at the end of Dorset's tenure at Port au Choix, there is evidence that they turned to birds and fish to help compensate for the loss of seals (Hodgetts et al. 2003). It was a strategy that would eventually prove unsuccessful, but at the time eating birds and fish may have seemed more palatable than abandoning their dead and traditions for a new way of life on unfamiliar shores. Indeed, if the seals were gone, why else stay?

Thus, the demise of the Dorset at Port au Choix and elsewhere on the island of Newfoundland probably had less to do with a changing environment, and more to do with the way the Dorset *chose* to respond to such changes. Indeed, that the Recent Indians survived the same ordeal would suggest that there were choices the Dorset could have made that would have enabled them to remain on the island, but they were not selected. Why not? While we have long recognized and admired hunters and gatherers' plasticity under challenging circumstances, we have paid far less attention to the cultural limits of this flexibility. We might question, for instance, the extent to which the Dorset were willing to change to a "Recent Indian" way of life in order to remain on the island—or if they were willing but were prevented from doing so by the Indians themselves. Maybe they were unwilling to change, and so sought a place on the other side of the Strait of Belle Isle where they could continue an appropriately "Dorset" way of life. Or perhaps they attempted to stay "Dorset" on the island and died trying. The archaeological record is rather mute on this point, but we can be assured that the story of the Dorset's demise is a social one—informed by the tenor of their relationships with Indian peoples, the nature of Paleo-Eskimo politics and decision-making processes, their commitment to a perceived "traditional" lifeway, and a particular way of seeing the resource landscape.

Conclusion

If to understand history is to understand "the undirected and creative negotiations of people whose dispositions were affected by their experiences (be they political, religious, gendered, technological, etc.)" (Pauketat 2001a:87), then hunter-gatherer history is poorly understood. By and large hunters and gatherers remain a people without history, and they remain so in part, due to a long-standing tendency to see hunter-gatherer lifeways as made by nature, not society. With regard to hunter-gatherer failure, this has made it difficult to imagine foragers failing at all, or when it occurs, to see it as the consequence of human choices.

That hunter-gatherers do indeed fail, however, is indicated by the disappearance of hunters and gatherers or their abandonment of the island of Newfoundland on at least two occasions (Tuck and Pastore 1985). If collapse is understood as a rapid decline in population or the sudden abandonment of a vast area, then the term is apt here. The island of Newfoundland is one of the largest islands in the world, encompassing an area (42,000 sq miles) greater than the states of Vermont, New Hampshire, Massachusetts, Rhode Island, Connecticut, New Jersey, and Delaware combined. At this scale, it is difficult to interpret a depopulated area of this size as anything other than failure. But this failure need not be conceptualized as the result of a poor environment or a Pompeii-like form of "natural" selection, as has often been advanced. Rather, if hunter-gatherer lifeways are strategic, then hunter-gatherers must be capable of the same sort of human-willed histories that we typically grant ancient civilizations—and that include the possibility of failing too.

Acknowledgments

I would like to thank Ken Sassaman for helping to organize this seminar and John Ware and the Amerind Foundation for hosting us at their beautiful facility in Dragoon, Arizona. This chapter has benefited from the constructive criticism and encouragement of two anonymous reviewers, John Erwin, and all of the Amerind seminar participants, especially Ken Sassaman, T. R. Kidder, Moira McCaffrey, Martin Wobst, Asa Randall, and Lynn Gamble.

PART II

The Sociality of Historical Practice

6

Transforming Hunter-Gatherer History at Poverty Point

Tristram R. Kidder

All archaeological sites are unique, but some stand out as being truly one of a kind. Some sites are exceptional for their size, particular architecture, or function they played, while other sites are exceptional because they represented at a particular point in time and space qualities that transcended their nominal function. Perhaps the best example of a sui generis site is Stonehenge (Renfrew 1997). Poverty Point (fig. 6.1), located in northeast Louisiana, is another example of a singular archaeological site. Poverty Point is set apart because of its size, relative scale, and complicated history of earthwork construction; moreover, it is unique because these characteristics are the product of a population that relied solely on hunting, fishing, and collecting for their subsistence.

Explanations for Poverty Point's remarkable qualities have focused on economic and environmental processes with little regard for the possibility that its inhabitants were active agents in their own development and transformation. Recent work provides new perspectives on the site's history. The people living at Poverty Point did not merely evolve; rather, they constituted themselves by employing specific social and historical practices, including earthwork construction, to inflect the course of their history. For them, earthwork building was a tangible deployment of myth and ritual to create social meaning and to mediate social interactions. Moreover, events and structure at Poverty Point had ramifications that extended across much of eastern North America. Understanding Poverty Point thus requires we concede that subsistence alone is not a suitable measure of how we view the history and organization of this remarkable settlement and, by extension, the histories of hunter-gatherers globally.

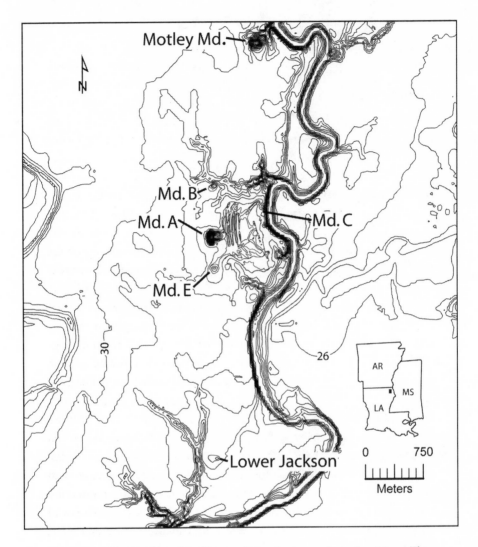

Figure 6.1. The locality of the Poverty Point site in northeast Louisiana. This map illustrates the area from Lower Jackson Mound in the south to Motley in the north. The inset shows the location of the site. The spatial resolution of this map precludes detailed representation of the topography of the main site area.

Archaeology of Poverty Point

Poverty Point is located in northeast Louisiana on the surface of Macon Ridge, a Pleistocene terrace five meters above the Mississippi River floodplain. Although some contemporary Late Archaic societies in the East were experimenting with low-level food production strategies, Poverty Point emerged within the context of a hunting, fishing, and gathering milieu. Radiocarbon dates place Poverty Point's occupation circa 3600–3100 cal years BP (Connolly 2006; Kidder et al. 2009:104–115; Ortmann 2007: 264–276). Poverty Point was for its time the largest pre-Columbian settlement north of the Rio Grande and was exceeded in size only by Cahokia. Contemporary habitation locations extend along the edge of Macon Ridge 2.5 km north and 3 km south of the site, with the area of intensive Poverty Point–era occupation covering approximately 200 ha. The boundaries of the community are marked at the north and south by earthen mounds. Contemporary communities nearby are all smaller than 12 ha. Elsewhere in the East, Late Archaic settlements almost never exceed 20 ha. Poverty Point is thus not only large in absolute terms but was built to a scale exceptional in its own time or, for that matter, at any time in North America's pre-Columbian past.

Poverty Point's monumental architecture is extravagant in the context of Native North America. With an estimated fill volume of 238,500 m³ (Kidder et al. 2009:116–117), Mound A is the second-largest earthen mound in the United States (fig. 6.2). It is roughly T-shaped with the western portion consisting of a cone ~207 m long and standing 21 m above the modern ground surface; the eastern portion of the mound is a flat platform 10 m tall and ~150 m long. Mound A is only the largest of five mounds at Poverty Point. The earthen architecture at Poverty Point also includes six semi-circular ridges, each 20–40 m wide and standing 1.5–3 m tall. The total volume of earth moved for mound building and ridge construction is estimated to be 665,163–764,555 m³. Adding the dirt necessary to fill gullies and level fields it is likely the total volume of earth moved at Poverty Point exceeded 1,000,000 m³.

Poverty Point's inhabitants depended on wood, bone, and stone for tools and implements. There is, however, no naturally occurring stone suitable for fashioning tools within 60 km of Poverty Point, thus requiring a long-distance trade network for procuring stone. Even so,

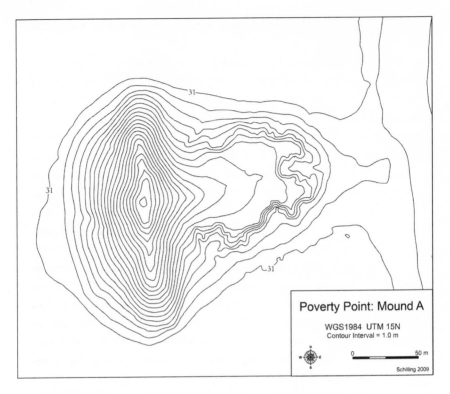

Figure 6.2. Contour map of Mound A at Poverty Point.

the extent of Poverty Point's lithic exchange system encompasses much of eastern North America and its scale (as measured by quantities of trade goods and distances they traveled) is well beyond any Archaic-era trade system in the East (Gibson 1994a, 1994b, 1994c; Webb 1982).

Poverty Point's location places the inhabitants of the site in an ideal setting for exploiting diverse and highly productive temperate upland and alluvial bottomland forest environments. Proximity to fish resources in the alluvial lands to the east coupled with abundant mast resources enhanced the site's physical location. The abundance and seasonal availability of edible biomass in this region make Poverty Point's location similar to those of "affluent foragers" living in temperate coastal environments (Jackson 1986; Kim and Grier 2006; Koyama and Uchiyama 2006). Multiple lines of evidence indicate Poverty Point was occupied year-round and was supported by a settlement system of residential bases and special function extraction locales (Gibson 1998b, 2000:205–206, 2006).

Readings of Poverty Point society range from early considerations that it was an indigenous population ruled by a theocratic elite derived from the north (Ford and Webb 1956) to North America's first chiefdom (Gibson 1974). Alternative interpretations focus on the absence of evidence for ranking and stress the corporate nature of the society (Gibson 2000; Kidder 1991). Gibson (2004) emphasizes that the site and its architecture were the products of a harmonious egalitarian society. Most interpretations of Poverty Point identify the origin of the people who built and occupied the site with an indigenous society evolved from deeply rooted local populations descended from those who built earlier Middle Archaic age mounds nearby. Alternatively, Jackson (1991) suggests Poverty Point was the product of periodic population aggregations coming together for trade fairs that provided opportunities for widely dispersed populations to exchange information, mates, and goods. Sassaman (2005a; Sassaman and Heckenberger 2004), however, argues Poverty Point is likely the result of larger demographic and social forces that brought together populations from a large area impelled by common social, ritual, and ideological needs.

Many perceptions of Poverty Point come from untested assumptions. One example is the notion that Poverty Point represents an unbroken temporal and demographic continuity reaching into the Middle Archaic. Another is that the site we see represents the unified vision of the founding population and is the product of a very short history. Yet another is that the mounds were constructed to serve a function in their final form. Recent work at the site allows us to reevaluate the history of the site. The key element in this revisionist history of Poverty Point is Mound A, the largest mound at the site and, until recently, one of the least known of all the monumental constructions.

Excavations at Mound A

Little effort has been devoted to understanding Mound A's role in Poverty Point's history. Ford and Webb (1956) argued the mound represented a bird effigy. Jackson and Crothers (Crothers 2004; Jackson 1991) suggest independently that it was built over a very long time through successive additions deposited by small work groups visiting the site intermittently or during periodic trade fairs.

Although Mound A was tested several times, the sum of the published information about it could be accommodated by a short paragraph (Haag 1990). Beginning in 2001 and continuing through 2006, colleagues and I excavated 89 cores and a 3 m wide by 10 m deep excavation on the south side of the mound (Kidder et al. 2009). In addition, in 2001 we placed test excavations in the four other mounds in the Poverty Point State Historic Site (Ortmann 2007).

Mound A was erected over a shallow, swampy depression. To build the mound, the vegetation was burned and immediately afterwards a thin layer of gray to grayish-white fine silt (Stage I) was deposited. Stage II, consisting of light-colored multi-hued sediments, was erected immediately afterwards. Once started, Stage II proceeded without interruption until the mound was completed. The western portion of the mound was begun first. The platform was built after the conical segment had been erected. The final construction event was a ramp that joined the cone to the platform. There was a brief hiatus after the completion of the cone and platform and before the erection of the ramp.

After its completion, Mound A was never used by the inhabitants for functions that left an obvious material signal. The mound's slopes and the fields immediately around the mound produced no evidence of artifact-producing activities. No structures, postholes, pits, living surfaces, hearths, or other features are found on or in the mound. The fill used to construct the mound was remarkably free of cultural debris. If the summit of the cone or the platform was used for any activities, the occupants of the site painstakingly cleaned up after themselves.

Mound fill accumulated so rapidly we cannot detect evidence of construction hiatuses or pauses. Despite analysis at the macro- and microscopic levels, there is no evidence to indicate mound construction surfaces were exposed to rainfall or were open long enough for insects, animals, or plants to disturb the soil (Kidder et al. 2009:56–90). Because of the absence of any weathering within the mound construction, or evidence of construction hiatuses, we conclude Mound A was built in a period of no more than three months and cannot falsify a hypothesis that it was built in a shorter span (Kidder et al. 2009:115–116). The impressive size of Mound A is not a source of contention; however, knowing the size of the finished monument without a detailed understanding of its construction history provides little information about how the society financed this project. The assessment of duration and intensity of construction is imperative to understanding various aspects of Poverty Point society, such as the size of the labor pool engaged in the project as well as the nature of labor relations and political authority among inhabitants of the site (Carr and Stewart 2004; Clark 2004; Gibson 1998b, 2004; Sassaman 2004a, 2005a). As the duration of construction events becomes more confined, labor efforts, the number of laborers, and the direction and organization of these individuals become increasingly monumental in scale (Galaty 1996).

Energetic calculations and corresponding population estimates for Mound A are shown in table 6.1. Previous evaluations of labor efforts at Poverty Point have yielded considerably lower numbers because the span of construction has generally been estimated to be in excess of forty years (Gibson 1987a, 1987b, 2004; Milner 2004). Table 6.1 reflects a variety of assumptions about the labor force and supporting population but all calculations imply a sizeable population residing at Poverty Point for at least a brief period of time. We do not subscribe to the notion that the site supported a permanent population of more than circa 1,500 persons; such a number would far exceed the known limits of population aggregation given the nature of political organization at the time (Kosse 1990, 1994). Instead, we envision that construction was the product of a modest to moderately large local permanent resident population drawing on extensive kinship and alliance networks from the regional cultural catchment. Note also that these calculations bear on the construction of Mound A only. They do not account for the building of the other mounds and ridges.

Mounds, Myth, and Ritual

Archaeological work in eastern North America over the last twenty years reveals that mound building, earthwork construction, and landscape transformation have a remarkable time depth and forces us to confront a hunter-gatherer legacy richer and more complex than previously imagined. Whereas the later Archaic was once seen as the province of unsophisticated hunter-gatherers eking out a precarious existence

Table 6.1. Energetic calculations and resulting population estimates for the construction of Mound A at Poverty Point

Excavation rate	Total person days[a]	30 days	60 days	90 days
2.6m³/1 person[b]	91,731	3,058	1,529	1,019
2.835m³/2 persons[c]	168,254	5,608	2,804	1,869
1.2m³/1 person[d]	198,750	6,625	3,313	2,208
1.1m³/1 person[e]	216,818	7,227	3,614	2,409

Total person days[a]	30 days	1:3 labor ratio[f]	1:2 labor ratio[g]	1:5 labor ratio[h]
91,731	3,058	9,173	6,115	15,288
168,254	5,608	16,825	11,217	28,042
198,750	6,625	19,875	13,250	33,125
216,818	7,227	21,682	14,455	36,136

Total person days[a]	60 days	1:3 labor ratio[f]	1:2 labor ratio[g]	1:5 labor ratio[h]
91,731	1,529	4,587	3,058	7,644
168,254	2,804	8,413	5,608	14,021
198,750	3,313	9,938	6,625	16,563
216,818	3,614	10,841	7,227	18,068

Total person days[a]	90 days	1:3 labor ratio[f]	1:2 labor ratio[g]	1:5 labor ratio[h]
91,731	1,019	3,058	2,038	5,096
168,254	1,869	5,608	3,739	9,347
198,750	2,208	6,625	4,417	11,042
216,818	2,409	7,227	4,818	12,045

[a] See Kidder et al. 2009:tables 11, 12.

[b] After Erasmus 1965:285; the volume of earth excavated by one laborer using a digging stick. Transport costs are not factored into this figure.

[c] After Erasmus 1965:table 1. The average volume of earth transported by two workers traveling 50 and 100 meters, respectively.

[d] After Muller 1997:273–274.

[e] After Gomez-Pompa et al. 1982:333.

[f] Data from Kelly 1995:213; approximate ratio of full-time foragers to total population of average hunter-gather band.

[g] Bernardini 2004:346.

[h] Muller 1997:274, fig. 6.10.

and living at the mercy of natural forces beyond their control, we now recognize a remarkable diversity of social forms and behaviors linked over large spaces and through time.

Mound building is usually studied to explore the function of the completed edifice. Mounds are generally seen as serving two distinct (but occasionally complementary) roles. The first is as a container for the dead. An extension of this function is the notion that burial mounds serve to demarcate space and to act as a marker for a group (or subgroup) claim to territorial identity (Buikstra and Charles 1999; Charles and Buikstra 1983; Charles et al. 1986). Alternatively, mounds serve as platforms for perishable architecture, usually the homes of elites or religious structures (Knight 2006). In both instances the mound was important because it served as the foundation for or container of, the social function being expressed. The problem with these traditional models is that there is no evidence Mound A contains burials or supported perishable structures. Knight (1986:678–679), however, argues that building mounds was an important symbolic act because it compelled the community or some subset of the community (e.g., clan, kin units) to operate as a group and thus served to simultaneously reinforce and express corporate unity.

Ford and Webb imply that Mound A was constructed to demonstrate power and authority by a theocratic elite. In a distinctly different context but in a similar vein, Milner (2004:305) notes mounds in general are "attractive to anyone who wants to make a powerful social and political statement." This position reflects a view that inequality is one of the diagnostics of the new social order exemplified by the mound builders (Milner 2004:301–307). In this instance, the mounds themselves reflect inequality of labor and access to the fruits of labor (but see Saunders 2004 for a critique of this thesis). Knight (2006:430) argues these functionalist arguments reduce mounds to "devices for legitimization of leadership by concentrating labor in public works . . . mounds were reminders of hierarchical power differences, and mound building reinforced important economic ties and social integration within the political unit."

In a twist on the functionalist argument, Hamilton (1999:348–349) suggests Archaic mounds were erected to "serve as an energy buffer" during times of "temporally fluctuating, unpredictable environments. . . .

Earthen and shell-and-earth mounds dating to the Archaic period represent archaeologically persistent, large-scale examples of investment in
non-reproductive behavior." In this argument the activities devoted to
the construction of mounds provide a way of "diverting energy into
[an] activity that does not contribute to the production of offspring."
While not denying symbolic or any other "unknowable rationale which
justifies the construction of earthen mounds, the cumulative effect [of
diverting energy from reproductive activities] . . . would have resulted
in increased survival in mound builders over time." Hamilton's argument suggests mounds are a form of bet-hedging whereby people build
mounds instead of producing children.

In fact, there is no evidence at present that episodes of mound
building in the lower Mississippi Valley were associated with episodes
of unusually fluctuating or uncertain environments. Indeed, mound
building in the Archaic appears to correspond most closely to times of
climatic stability relative to preceding and following periods (Kidder
2006; Kidder et al. 2008). Furthermore, this model assumes mound
building would have been an ongoing and energetically demanding task
that diverted excess energy from reproduction. While it is possible that
the Middle Archaic mound builders were constructing mounds over
long periods of time, this model does not hold for Mound A, which
would have been the energetically most demanding structure of all the
earthworks.

However, attention to mound function may be misplaced if by function we mean the end product and its use as a complete, unitary form.
Richards (2004:73) notes our perception of mounds "reflects our perspective on architecture so we tend to think about monuments, as we do
other buildings, by privileging their built form." Mound construction
may be a means to an end, but there is no reason to think that Mound
A at Poverty Point was erected to serve a purpose only in its final form.
Recent research on mounds has turned to understanding their symbolic
and iconic role. In this form, mound construction can be understood
"as a ritual practice, [and] that this ritual was communal in scale, and
that these practices were a form of world-renewal ceremony" (Knight
2006:430). In part, these notions come from disaffection with functionalist or adaptive explanations but also from a closer reading of ethnographic and ethnohistoric documents. These analyses have been pushed

farther back in time and have been adopted as one possible explanation for the mounds and earthworks at Poverty Point (Gibson 1998a, 2000, 2004; Knight 2006). While Knight is not "prepared to defend" claims that extend the antiquity of ethnographically derived explanations of mound symbolism back into the distant past, he acknowledges that "observations such as these hint at the possibility of a uniform symbolic core underlying the whole spectrum of earth mound building in the Southeast" (Knight 2006:431).

Jon Gibson posits the idea that Poverty Point peoples spoke a proto-Tunican or proto-Gulf language that connects them through time with historically documented groups living in the same area. If true, then this raises the "possibility that there had been one world outlook, one slate of cosmic explanations, and maybe even one set of heroic and epic stories." From this connection Gibson derives a hypothesis that situates the mounds and earthworks in a symbolic and iconic role; specifically, the earthworks were "magic" (Gibson 2000:185).

Gibson (2000:185–186) reads the layout of the mounds as a creation story. The ridges are open to the east where the sun rises, and thus these features are about life. A second "principle concerns protection." Geometric figures are held in mythology and lore to be "magical shields against an outside world filled with potentially disorderly beings and evil power." He notes that in Southeastern Indian mythology death and sickness come from the west while "social disharmony and witchcraft" come from the north. These are the "directions shielded by Poverty Point's rings and the partial square of its intersecting mound axes." Asserting Mound A and Motley were bird effigies, he argues "mound form itself may have symbolized the Earth Island." Thus the mounds and the ridges at Poverty Point are elements of a sacred geography that protects those within the earthworks from the forces outside of them and are also a metaphor for creation.

Given the structured deposition of sediments used in the building of Mound A, its location over a wetland, and its history of remarkably rapid construction, and the absence of other evidence for a clear function, I argue the mound was most likely built as a ritual feature whose significance lies, in part, in the act(s) of its creation. Specifically, I argue Mound A represents a ritualized recapitulation of creation similar to what is recorded in historic mythology (see also Gibson 2000:109).

Historic Indians of the Southeast emphasize two creation myths (Bushnell 1910; Grantham 2002; Hall 1997; Lankford 1987; Swanton 1907, 1917, 1929, 1931). Most common is the Emergence myth, in which humans were created within the earth from clay by a spirit and emerged from a precreated formlessness to populate the earth. In Choctaw mythology the ancestors emerged from a mound. The narrative of the myth varies; in one telling, this mound serves as the conduit for the emergence of only the Choctaw; in another, for a number of different tribal groups (Blitz 1993; Carleton 1996).

The other myth is Earth Diver. In this myth, animals who populated the formless, watery chaos of precreation agree that one of their members must seek something on which creation may rest. A member is elected (most commonly crawfish in the Southeast) and after a heroic struggle succeeds in capturing a speck of dirt from beneath the water. Once brought to the surface this speck expands to become the earth itself and while wet and still plastic is given shape by the beating wings of a bird. These two mythic forms generally have mutually exclusive distributions but overlap among the Choctaw and the Chitimacha (which may be the product of recent interactions). The temporal gap between historical myth and the construction of Mound A renders a specific interpretation disputable.

The myth of humans being created of and emerging from the earth symbolizes the creative force of the earth itself. The precreated world of Southeastern Emergence and Earth Diver mythology is subterranean (and often wet), without light, and formless, whereas the created world is defined by the opposite of these qualities. In these myths the seeming chaos of precreation is progressing toward a definite order present in the earth itself rather than something realized by the imposition of form from the outside. In Choctaw myth and history this latency is given physical form as the mound known as Nanih Waiya in Mississippi. Furthermore, the historic tribes specifically recognized this myth as an explanation for specific corporate claims to territory and as a means to "legitimate descent-based principles of corporate group formation" (Blitz 1993:34).

The construction of Mound A can be read as a symbolic representation of the story of creation. The dark, wet depression was burned and rapidly buried beneath the initial mound stage of light-colored silt. This silt entombs the low depression and seals the watery darkness of chaotic precreation from the created world of light and form. The vertically structured sequence of dark, light, and multicolored fills suggests the builders were simulating the tripartite world order encoded in mythological representations of American Indian cosmology. The color symbolism of dark pre-mound sediment and the light-colored Stage I is in keeping with historically recorded ideas about the colors of creation and their linkages to chaos (dark) and order (light) (Cobb and Drake 2008; DeBoer 2005). Above this stage was built, in remarkably rapid fashion, an original version of Nanih Waiya, the "Mother Mound."

Archaic hunter-gatherers are not credited with having complex ritual practices that structure social processes. In the Southeast, earthen mounds are frequently interpreted as symbols of social and political distinction. However, mounds and monuments were not simply platforms for social actions; instead they embody the foundations of community (Knight 2006). In historically recorded Indian mythology, the symbolism of humans being created of the earth and their emergence from earthen mounds represents the latent force immanent in the earth as a repository of all creation. This mythology, however, is history, both as recorded in the mounds themselves and in the way these physical objects were deployed to explain genealogical relationships (Blitz 1993). This lack of distinction between mounds as symbols and mounds as functional architecture reminds us also that the meanings of the built environment shift through time. We who inherit the landscape see the final (or what we take to be the final) product as we assume it was meant to be. The creation of the monument and its later interpretation may entail entirely different understandings (Richards 2004).

Ritual has recently been getting increasing attention as a means of interpreting the archaeological record (Fogelin 2007; Kyriakidis 2007a, 2007b). However, for the most part, hunter-gatherer studies have not been moving in the same direction (Jordan 2008). Archaeological emphasis on utilitarian and functional explanations has dominated, especially in hunter-gatherer studies, and thus ritual is considered an epiphenomenon. In archaeology, ritual often is a catchall term for "anything that defies a crudely utilitarian explanation" (Richards and Thomas 1984:189). One of the problems is that ritual itself is hard to fully define and has multiple meanings and analytic possibilities (Bell 1997); another is that ritual, religion, and other forms of social knowledge are often seen to be inaccessible to the archaeologist because they leave little or no material trace that can be effectively tested. Worse yet, ritual is often seen as a nonexplanation (Fogelin 2007; Kyriakidis 2007a; Richards and Thomas 1984).

Among the characteristics of ritual activities are actions that enhance and emphasize the status quo and that reinforce or reify existing social structures. Rituals are generally formal and emphasize tradition, rule-governance, invariance, and repetition (Bell 1997; Snoek 2006). In this sense rituals have been cited by archaeologists as forms of proscribed behaviors that provide stability over prolonged periods of time (Barrett et al. 1991:6–8; Bradley 1998:90).

However, rituals can create meaning out of an incomprehensible and socially challenging situation by bringing to bear traditional social structures to "embrace and subdue the new situation" (Bell 1997:77). For Sahlins (1981, 1995), the application of this cultural process, manifest most clearly as ritual, to new and potentially disruptive social situations is the very process of history itself. Ritual is perhaps one of the most obvious and visible (and potentially materially relevant) means whereby we see history being made in preliterate contexts. Ritual in this sense is an active agent of social transformation, challenging or altering existing structures and recasting them in a new light (Bell 1997; Bourdieu 1977; Pauketat 2001a). Ritual becomes a strategic mechanism for effecting the reshuffling of cultural rules and proscriptions. As noted by Bell (1997:79), "It is through ritual practice that culture molds consciousness in terms of underlying structures and patterns, while current realities simultaneously instigate transformations of those very structures and patterns as well."

Ritual is rarely completely inflexible and its alteration and evolution is often a means of accommodating change. One of the most critical means for doing so is by manipulating history. Ritual has "special time-binding properties" (Gosden and Lock 1998:4) whereby notions of the past are connected by physical expressions to places produced in the present as well as to features of the landscape derived from the distant past. Landscapes reflect ritual by (1) repeated use and maintenance of features with known antecedents; (2) undertaking actions (e.g., ceremonies, new constructions, maintenance of existing features) at ancient landscape features that give new meaning in contemporary contexts; and (3) inserting new features onto the landscape that by their location must be incorporated into the historical dialogue established by the landscape. Landscapes and their human manipulated contexts (including mounds, earthworks, monuments, and physical features given meaning through memory, legend, or mythology) are texts that record history and reflect how consciousness of the past is used to create and re-create social order.

Gosden and Lock (1998:4–5) suggest there are two types of historical consciousness, which they term "genealogical history" and "mythic history." The former "is an awareness that social relations are shaped by individual or collective action," whereas the latter views the "structure of human society as a product of superhuman forces, natural powers or presocial forces, which are different from human agency." History "operates in a time continuous with the present . . . whereas mythical structures refer back to a previous state of the world, where human beings either did not exist, or had no power, and where processes of cause and effect manifest themselves differently." Myth and history are linked forms of social memory, each with a role or function to play in the negotiation of social meaning. The notion that history is agentive while mythology is not suggests history transitions to myth as memory of human action becomes attenuated with the passage of time.

For eastern North America, however, this dichotomy between genealogical and mythological forms of historical consciousness must be carefully considered (Nabokov 2002). Myth and history are not conceived separately in an indigenous consciousness—the real and imagined, past and present, are not divisible. As Nabokov (2002:90) points out, in the American Indian deployment of an "inclusive and nonscientific sense of myth, anything old and everything new can—indeed *must*—be absorbed into its all knowing and omnipotent purview" (emphasis in original). In American Indian myth-history, the locus of agency is irrelevant because change does not require time-sequential cause-and-effect relationships. Australian dreamtime reflects a similar melding of mythological and historical modes of consciousness wherein the past and present are not divisible as Western notions of history demand (Berndt 1994; Guenther 1999; Taçon 1999). Linearity is not necessary because the past is always in the present giving it shape and meaning (Guenther

1999:429–430). Critically, however, whether in Australia, the Americas, or in Neolithic Europe, history and myth are inscribed on and in the landscape as a means of "retrieving memories and meanings . . . working together as social memory" (Gosden and Lock 1998:5).

Gosden and Lock point out the main mode of transmitting history (in their sense of the word) in preliterate societies is genealogy. The physical environment is a mnemonic device that records the role(s) of real people who lived in historical time (see also Basso 1996; Bradley 2000; Tilley 1997). Noting that kinship "is not a static charter, but a form of argument to be manipulated by those in the present," they observe "features of the landscape were not just physical things, but the manifestation of social relationships." They emphasize the role of ritual in developing and maintaining genealogical histories, especially focusing on the repetition of events and processes they feel would have maintained and perhaps reinforced peoples' "ties to a known past, [and] reinforced the potency of that past in the present or changed the nature of attachment to that past" (Gosden and Lock 1998:5–6).

Cobb and King (2005) make a similar argument for the long-term history of the Etowah site. They take the repetition of Mississippian mound building, most notably the repeated cycles of mound stage construction, surface use, destruction or dismantling, and burial, as a means of asserting the historicity of real individuals, thus reinforcing claims to hold power based on kinship to real ancestors.

The separation of history and myth is, in many instances, a false or needless dichotomy. Landscapes record mythology (Basso 1996; Kahn 1990, 1996; Malinowski 1922) and that mythology is history—it is as real as any Western time-sequent recording of events. If we recognize that history and myth are indivisible agents creating and making sense of social meaning, we also need to recognize the landscape (and objects themselves as a part of the social and physical landscape) is in itself an agent imbued with active properties that record histories and retain meaning and the power to alter the present and future.

Archaeological writing often portrays the landscape as an element acted on by human agency. Social meaning is expressed through acts of inscribing the landscape (e.g., building a mound or barrow) or by the human use of the landscape (built or otherwise). It is evident, however, that to many indigenous peoples, the landscape is a real thing with power to influence events and actions. For the Apache, "wisdom sits in places" (Basso 1996); geography and objects can be real actors in the social universe (Gosden 2005). The landscape is not a passive element waiting to be given meaning by human action. Mounds are mothers (Carleton 1996), mountains speak (Basso 1996), and stones move themselves (Kahn 1990). In the American Southeast, I would extend the argument to observe that even objects, especially hypertrophic artifact types (e.g., Johnson and Brookes 1989; Sassaman and Randall 2007), likely were imbued with real agentive properties much in the way the Trobriander's *vaygu'a* (valuables) were (Malinowski 1922; Ray 2004).

A New History of Poverty Point

In light of new data from Poverty Point it is possible to reframe the history of those who built the site (Kidder et al. 2009:103–138). The starting point for this history lies at the south end of the site area. The Lower Jackson Mound is located roughly 2.3 km south of Mound A (Clark 2004; Saunders et al. 2001). This earthwork was built just after circa 5000 cal BP. Lower Jackson and other Middle Archaic mounds were abandoned after circa 4800 cal BP, and throughout the lower Mississippi Valley, at least from the mouth of the Arkansas River south to the Gulf Coast, there is little evidence of significant occupation either in the valley proper or along its margins. We have no archaeological indicators that fit into this interval—no point styles, no artifact forms, and few settlements with dates. Poverty Point–affiliated sites in the lower Mississippi Valley are without stratigraphic precedent.

The absence of an obvious, locally derived founding population for Poverty Point is crucial because much of what we think we know about the site is based on the notion the initial occupants were a community with local antecedents. Gibson (2007) has been especially emphatic that Poverty Point is the creation of an indigenous population with deep roots.

The earliest well-defined archaeological context and first monumental architecture erected at Poverty Point was Mound B. The first stage was a low platform covered with 25–50 cm of very fine, light-colored silt containing abundant cane charcoal. A recently obtained accelerator mass spectrometry (AMS) date places the initial platform construction circa 3600–3400 cal BP. Three more stages were added before Mound B was capped and abandoned. Construction of the stages was rapid, and the mound was in use for a short time. We do not know what the mound's flat-topped stages were used for. At the south end of the modern site boundaries lies Mound E. This mound has resisted radiometric dating, but its construction sequence is a near perfect duplicate of Mound B, except in its lack of a final capping event (Kidder et al. 2004; Ortmann 2007).

Mounds B and E lie on a direct north-south axis that bisects Lower Jackson (Clark 2004; Gibson 2000). Mound B and Lower Jackson combine to form the foundational monuments and sacral axis for the community. By placing Mound B (and possibly Mound E) on a direct axis with Lower Jackson, the builders connected the foundation of Poverty Point directly to an ancestral monument, thus invoking legitimacy and marking a claim to territory. This linkage to the past enabled the builders of Mound B to evoke traditional, authoritative, and eternal values. Not surprisingly, the best-defined Middle Archaic context at Poverty Point is in the Mound B field, and there is a Poverty Point–age component adjacent to Lower Jackson. These mounds are the twin (triple, if we add Mound E) pillars of the coalescing Poverty Point community.

At the time Mound B was being built, Poverty Point was emerging as a community but no other mounds had been constructed. Radiocarbon dates associated with the preconstruction phase of activity indicate there was an episode of up to two hundred years (between ca. 3600 and 3400 cal BP) when Poverty Point was occupied but before there was any construction of features other than Mound B.

The preconstruction occupation was widespread across the site area. These deposits contain most of the material characteristics that define Poverty Point (Gibson 2007). One hallmark of Poverty Point's material culture is evident early on: there is remarkable variety among the formal tools and formal tool types. Scholars working at Poverty Point have always noted the diversity of formal tool types (Webb et al. 1963). Unlike contemporary sites in the Southeast, where the pattern is to have one or two formal point types (with a range of expected variation) at any one time (Coe 1964; Morse and Morse 1983:101–103), Poverty Point has dozens in nonburial contexts.

The chronostratigraphic relationships of various point types at Poverty Point are especially problematic because so much of our data depend on surface distributions. Gibson (2007) asserts point styles and tool types have been present in relatively constant numbers throughout the temporal sequence. Spatial variability in point styles and other artifact forms is explained by functional and/or gender-based differences in use and consumption (Webb 1970). Ortmann's (2007) analysis, however, indicates variations in frequencies of raw material types as well as the distribution of microliths and debitage classes (see also Connolly 2002; Menzel 2001).

The heterogeneity of materials in preconstruction contexts indicates that we can question whether Poverty Point was a unified community at the outset (Sassaman 2005a). This conclusion calls into doubt the concept that Poverty Point originated through the growth of an integrated local community with common ancestry. Based on variances in material culture, Poverty Point's founding inhabitants likely had different geographic, (possibly) linguistic, and social origins. This conclusion does not mean the populations who composed the Poverty Point community in its initial stages were drawn from far distant places or traced their origins to locations that provided much of the raw materials used for tool manufacture (cf. Gibson 2007). Yet, one thing seems certain: the people who made up this founding population had not resided at the site—or even very near it—prior to the construction of Mound B.

After a long period when no earthworks were built, there was a profound and rapid transformation circa 3400 cal BP. First, Mound B was capped and fell out of use. Second, a massive program of ridge building was undertaken in a short period of time. Gibson (2000:91–97) argues that the ridge system was built in less than two hundred years and perhaps as few as forty years. The construction of the lower portion of Mound C is synchronous with the ridges. Finally, the rest of Mound C, including a terminating cap, was constructed, while Mound A was built last and dates after circa 3264 cal BP. In addition to mound and ridge construction, the people living at Poverty Point undertook a labor-intensive program of landscape stabilization and repair. The scale of construction and labor pool required to achieve it is staggering when one considers the possibility Motley Mound was also erected during this interval. The net effect of this labor was the complete alteration of the Poverty Point landscape. This transformation built on the past—both literally and figuratively—while providing a complete break from what had come before.

Mound B was terminated by rapidly covering the final flat-topped stage with a conical earthen mantle, much of it constructed by packing together baskets and hide containers filled with dirt (Ford and Webb 1956:37–38) and covering these with fill. The absence of materials on its surface or in the area around the mound suggests that once capped, the mound was avoided as a locus for day-to-day activities. The burial of the flat-topped stages of Mound B removed this feature from the landscape of active social engagement. If this mound initially was built to define and celebrate the foundation of the community, its termination altered the cultural meaning of the once foundational monument from symbolically recording a historical event to memorializing the ancestral community.

Similarly, the rapid burial of the preconstruction occupation beneath the ridges was an act of erasure and historical reconfiguration (Cobb and King 2005). The original community plan was obliterated beneath a new residential form. As with any civic renewal, the old was cleansed and the new enshrined as apposite. The construction of the ridges buried the old community and forced upon the residents a new way of living—on ridges—that was a departure from the past. The new configuration constrained where within the site boundaries one could reside and structured social relations in new ways as there were physical boundaries, barriers, and structures one had to navigate simply to move around.

Capping Mound B transformed the history intrinsic to that monument, while the burial and reconfiguration of the preconstruction occupation altered—through erasure and addition—the history of the original society. The population did not relocate, however. The construction of the ridges used the past as a literal foundation for the new community and sanctioned the new community by symbolically incorporating the past into (or beneath and thus as the derivation of) the present. These actions emphasize how architecture and landscape at Poverty Point were ritualized to exploit the formal legitimacy provided by continuity between present and past.

Mound C, the only mound within the ridges, began as a series of surfaces rapidly covered with middenlike deposits that were then covered anew with an activity surface. Multiple activity surface–midden couplets were erected. It is not clear if Mound C was really a mound at this time or if it simply grew as the couplets accumulated. Alternating layers of light and dark sediment and texturally variant fills (Ortmann 2007:150–170) may have been manipulated to mimic world renewal or earth creation myths and imply a structured set of ritual behaviors (Charles et al. 2004; Van Nest 2006). These alternating layers were abruptly terminated by the erection of a low conical mound composed of heterogeneous sediments mixed with numerous whole and fragmentary artifacts.

But the most radical departure was the rapid construction of Mound A. If we accept that the foundational symbolic configuration of the site was formed by the Lower Jackson to Mound B axis, then the imposition of Mound A astride this axis redefines the meaning of the ancient founding order. Placing Mound A on this axis was more than simply a nod to the past as a means of legitimization. Mound A's emplacement on the sacral axis indicates the builders were engaging a dialogue with the past about the sacredness and relevance of the foundational axis. More to the point, the imposition of this monument on this axis suggests the builders were challenging the extant history and mythological charter of the original population by creating a new version of the story of creation. Mound A involved a vast labor force working as a community to create a different version or interpretation of the founding myth-history of Poverty Point. The scale of labor and the work force necessary to erect this mound argue that the community of laborers was composed of people who lived at Poverty Point as well as many drawn from a much wider region. This event likely incorporated social groups living throughout the region if not also from farther distances.

When it was built Mound A represented a novel interpretation of eastern North American cosmology. The transformations of Poverty Point after circa 3400 cal BP was about recreating community with a new, unified, and common cosmology, mythic charter, and history. In a series of actions these emplacements challenged the time-binding properties of the original ritualized landscape while asserting their own place in the temporal scheme of origins. The dramatic and remarkably rapid transformation of the Poverty Point landscape after circa 3400 cal BP suggests these activities were achieved through or mediated by ritual practices that created a context for social agents to alter or replace the founding cosmological charter. Building mounds and transforming them to monuments established a dialectic relationship where the past reverberated through the present and helped create or replicate ideals and cultural narratives that synthesized mythic and genealogical histories.

It is tempting to essentialize the construction of Mound A solely as an interpretation of mythology expressed in ritualized earth moving. There are, however, too many possible readings of these acts to limit them to one explanation. Building each earthwork was a discursive practice that by its action set the course of the future of Poverty Point while looking back at its past. These physical events and their manifestations helped to create community by inculcating a historically edited set of social values and memories. Through the building of monuments and the transformation of the built and natural landscapes, the inhabitants of Poverty Point were simultaneously making and transforming history. Once written, however, history is subject to interpretation. Future generations had to engage these monuments when negotiating the present and future directions of society.

Poverty Point's transformations were striking and had ramifications throughout eastern North America. Whereas before Poverty Point Archaic peoples were interacting over large areas through the circulation of physical objects of apparent prestige and which acted as containers that transmitted information, ideas, and notions of history—much like Kula items—this interaction ceased once Poverty Point developed. Poverty Point became a center of social and ritual gravity never before— and perhaps in North America never again—seen (Kidder and Sassaman 2009). The apparent flow of goods and objects into Poverty Point was not reciprocated outward in any materialized fashion. There is no Poverty Point material signal—objects traded or exchanged from Poverty Point—in the outlying regions that constituted the catchment of the site's interaction sphere. The historical, ritual, and mythic importance of Poverty Point, culminating in the building of Mound A, placed the site at the center of southeastern cosmology much like the Vatican became the center of Catholicism. Poverty Point's consolidation may have encouraged social transformations throughout the Southeast or midcontinent in a manner similar to Cahokia's emergence and fluorescence (Pauketat 2004) but at a scale appropriate to the Archaic.

The paradox of Poverty Point is that its history is backwards. Whereas in many other societies flamboyant ritual architecture and ostentatious displays appear early in their history, at Poverty Point the most visible processes come at the end. What happened at Poverty Point after 3400 cal BP represents an episode of consolidation, integration, and even termination. It was, however, remarkably rapid and dramatic. Ethnographic evidence suggests that episodes of ethnogenesis of this sort are often compelled by external forcing (Tuzin 2001), often warfare and demographic pressures that drive people with distinct backgrounds together. Alternatively, Poverty Point coalesced as a center of ritual significance. At Poverty Point both processes may have been at play over the course of history. One of the great unanswered questions is why people came together at Poverty Point in the first place and what sorts of social processes were influencing people's behaviors.

Poverty Point looks to be a planned community because its parts articulate so well. However, this unity is apparent because it represents a self-organizing phenomenon rather than because there was a master plan. The location of Mound A on the Mound B–Lower Jackson axis did not have to be planned because once that original axis was established anyone wishing to tap the political and ritual iconography of the landscape had to engage that axis. There was really only one place Mound A could go if it was to be the symbolic recapitulation of creation and the central node of community identity. Similarly, the ridges had to be where they were because that is where the former community had been located.

There is no evidence that the transformation of Poverty Point was driven by ranked political leaders; however, leaders would have been required to accomplish the multitude of logistical, not to mention ritual, tasks attendant on remaking the site. The duration of the transformations, which could credibly be within a single or at best a few generations, suggests it may have been initiated by charismatic prophet-like personalities (Pauketat 2008). A faint example exemplifying this possibility is seen among the Nuer, where the prophet Ngundeng constructed a large mound as a symbol of his power and renown. The emblematic value of this mound as a historical and political claim to Nuer identity was such that the British destroyed it to eliminate inspiration for future claims to Nuer social or political solidarity (Johnson 1994:88–101,

194–200). Alternatively, given the absence of obvious material culture ranking, it is possible that social order was organized and maintained through ritual processes that provided the structure for mobilizing and deploying labor. Ritual oligarchs who interpret the signs and symbols of religious structures are well known and can command the allegiances of large populations, often living in close quarters (Tuzin 2001).

Conclusion

Exceptional sites demand explanations that account for their uniqueness. We only dimly understand the place of Poverty Point in the social, political, and economic landscape of eastern North America at the end of the Archaic, but recent work suggests this role was more complex than anticipated. The history of the site indicates that the people who lived there used monumental architecture as one means of transforming their society. The mounds and earthworks at Poverty Point represent points of social insertion—wherein people consciously used material objects to translate legacies of the past into tools for framing the present and constraining the future. Because Poverty Point was so large and so outscaled relative to its contemporaries, I suspect these actions had ritual and social ramifications across the East.

This discussion emphasizes that people who practice a classically defined hunting-fishing-foraging lifestyle actively construct their social reality. Archaeologists have always had a hard time grappling with what drives social change and variability, and especially among those who study hunter-gatherers, the symbolic and social have tended to be considered epiphenomenal while the economic and material have been privileged. For this reason hunter-gatherers are inadvertently denied history. This study of Poverty Point shows these people had a history; moreover, the people composing this society actively engaged that history as they created and recreated their own society in the ongoing present.

There is a remarkable variability to the people we label hunter-gatherers. Traditional subsistence-based definitions fail to explain the range of social, economic, and political variability expressed in the archaeological record. The archaeology of the Archaic peoples of the southeastern United States shows they were not just more complex than some putatively common-unit society; they were in fact entirely different because they had a different history and because they constructed their present by an appeal to a socially construed past. I do not believe this conclusion renders the study of these societies "historicist"; instead, it suggests we should recognize that how the past is created, understood, and deployed as a means of creating and recreating the present is a universal aspect of every society, *and hunter-gatherers are no different.* Awareness of this fact means hunter-gatherers are not the original society; they are not now, nor have they ever been, the timeless evolutionary entity we have tried to make them.

Acknowledgments

I am very grateful to my collaborators at Poverty Point, most notably Anthony Ortmann, Lee Arco, and Katie Adelsberger. Our work at Poverty Point has been supported by the Louisiana Division of Archaeology and the Office of State Parks, Louisiana Department of Culture, Recreation, and Tourism. We owe considerable thanks to Dennis LaBatt and David Griffing who made our fieldwork possible. This work has benefited from suggestions by a number of colleagues, and I am indebted to Jon Gibson, Tim Schilling, Ken Sassaman, Tim Pauketat, Jane Buikstra, and David Anderson for comments and suggestions. Tim Schilling helped draft the figures.

7

Remapping Archaic Social Histories along the St. Johns River in Florida

Asa R. Randall

In what ways can hunter-gatherer landscape inhabitation be considered history? By history I mean lived experiences of contingent events as well as historical consciousness through which events are made meaningful (Pauketat 2001a; Rumsey 1994). Traditionally, landscape use is part of a core of attributes used by anthropologists to assess variation among hunter-gatherer communities in space and time (e.g., Binford 1980; Kelly 1995:111; Lee and Daly 1999a). It is also the primary means by which an ontological chasm is maintained between those communities who subsist by hunting and gathering and those who do not (Ingold 2000:56). This divide is as old as the invention of "hunter-gatherer" as a social category in the eighteenth century, when simply the idea of mobile and propertyless peoples provided an antithetical *other* for social theorists to ruminate on the origins of a civil society based on law, property, capital, and progress (Barnard 2004b; Pluciennik 2002). While anthropology has distanced itself from such representations, the effects of this intellectual heritage are still deeply manifest in the differential application of methods and theories today (Strassburg 2003). Hunter-gatherer landscape use is traditionally conceptualized within a natural history narrative, wherein actions and outcomes are structured by the physical distribution of social or economic resources (Bettinger 1991; Binford 1980; Keen 2006; Kelly 1995). Any modification of the environment in this view is incidental and inconsequential. In contrast, nonforager landscape use is routinely understood as social reproduction, through which communities construct, politicize, and inscribe their social and physical worlds. In so doing communities write and manipulate their own histories by variously referencing, destroying, or co-opting memories and materiality of the past (Barrett 1999; Meskell 2003). Devoid of their own agency and without the capacity or recourse to a past (mythical or otherwise), hunter-gatherers and the places they create still remain fixed as historically ignorant others.

Despite the continued reproduction of this dichotomy, there is an ever-accumulating database of ethnographic and archaeological evidence that demonstrates hunter-gatherers transform their worlds in historically constituted acts that subvert, affect, or make change meaningful (e.g., Jordan 2003; Morphy 1995). Among these are the communities who inhabited the middle St. Johns River valley of northeast Florida during the Archaic period (ca. 7300–3600 cal BP). The consequences of regional hunter-gatherer inhabitation are materialized as shell mounds, composed primarily of freshwater shellfish remains (fig. 7.1). Many of these places were inhabited some seven thousand years ago, and repeatedly occupied over the ensuing millennia. Consistent with traditional thought, local archaeologists coupled unilineal evolution with the presumption that shell mounds solely represent refuse deposition (Goggin 1952; Milanich 1994; Miller 1998). The location, seemingly mundane composition, and repeated occupation of mounds were thought to represent cultural continuity and redundancy in site use, ultimately enabled by the abundance of wetland resources. Quite to the contrary, recent investigations have revealed a much more complex (and interesting) story, the details of which implicate the active construction of places and manipulation of time by hunter-gatherers. In this contribution, I consider how Archaic communities negotiated social and ecological change by writing and contesting histories through the construction and maintenance of shell mounds. I focus on major transformations evident in the content, scale, and organization of depositional practices that include the construction of mortuary mounds, the replacement of small-scale settlements with platform mounds for the living, and the reorganization of mound complexes in the context of extraregional interactions. These practices intersect complex ecological processes and increasing scales of social connectivity. Such events and trends no doubt shaped the contours of structural reproduction. Yet, as I detail in the following sections, Archaic communities routinely mobilized the past as a means of accommodating or interfering with such change. These transformations in traditional practices resulted in a continuous reworking of relationships between people and places, the final outcome of which are the mounds we encounter today.

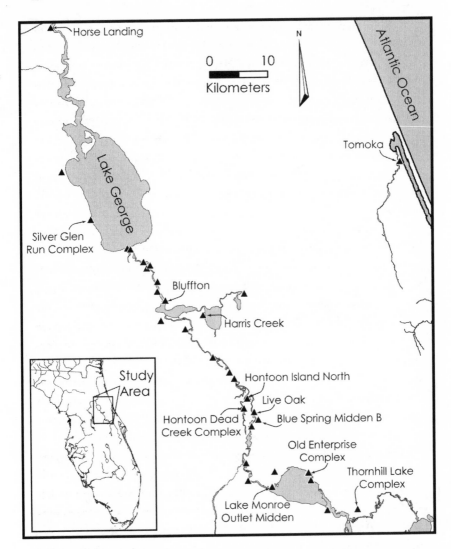

Figure 7.1. Distribution of Archaic period shell mounds and middens along the middle St. Johns River valley.

The Spatiality of Hunter-Gatherer Histories

It is my argument that the particulars of engagements in places distributed across landscapes are fundamental to the ongoing creation of hunter-gatherer social histories. This view requires shifting our analytical lens away from presuming that the spatial patterning of past practices reflects inevitable outcomes, to investigating how those patterns emerge as a contingent and relational process (Barrett 1999). Current perspectives on the relationship between hunter-gatherer society and space are operationalized under the trope of "mapping." While there have been many similar turns of phrase, the term "mapping" itself was canonized in Binford's (1980) "forager" subsistence-settlement pattern, wherein resources varying in space-time are "mapped onto" through mobility and group membership flux. The explanatory force of the trope rests on a posited direct, if dynamic, association between environment, the organization of subsistence practices, and population. As a result, hunter-gatherer lifeways are reduced to an algebra in which space and time are independent variables. Patterns of site location, architecture, social interaction, and even the construction of ceremonial facilities follow dependently (Binford 1990; Whallon 2006; Whitelaw 1983). Places remain analytically interchangeable, and the practices through which they were produced are reduced to best-cost solutions. Despite its prevalence, this notion of mapping as an objective response to resource distribution has been thoroughly assailed. In particular, "mapping" problematically reduces practices, worldviews, and experiences into totalizing ahistorical frameworks (de Certeau 1984:120–1; Ingold 2000). Not only does this perspective distance past agents from their own histories, it inserts foreign assumptions and categories upon what were once contingent cultural productions (Küchler 1993).

The notion of mapping can be recast if we reassess the linkage between hunter-gatherer landscape use and historical production. Landscapes inhabited by any society are not simply topologies upon which human action occurs (Thomas 1993). Instead, landscapes emerge as networks of meaning that are at once contingent and polysemous (Rodman 1992), yet are informed through systems of reference that naturalize the current social order. These systems structure and are structured by ongoing social reproduction embedded in different temporalities of everyday living, cosmological experience, and unforeseen events. Temporalities are informed by the material conditions of past practices and daily existence (Gosden 1994:17; Ingold 2000). The significance of places continuously arises through the interaction of humans and nonhuman agents (including ancestors or objects), such that the biographies of people and things become enmeshed through place (Gosden and Marshall 1999;

Munn 1996). The ways in which relationships are creatively reconstituted through practice in space emerge as *spatial narratives* (de Certeau 1984:129; Ingold 2000:219). Spatial narratives reflect a process of *remapping* in which biographies are generated through actions that reference other times and places. By default, such stories implicate acts of remembrance and recognition of a past as a means of interfering with or accommodating ongoing social process (Wobst 2000). Spatial stories are contingent acts, but are made meaningful through modes of historical consciousness embedded in cosmology and myth (Rumsey 1994).

Spatial stories do not reside solely in movement but are materialized in acts that alter the physicality of places and thus open up the conditions of living and memories of past places to contestation and manipulation (Pollard 2001). Such "depositional narratives" approximate what Connerton (1989) refers to as "inscriptive practices." On one hand, depositional narratives, and their effects, can be considered unintentional. All societies live out their lives in an ever-accumulating materiality that is an unintended consequence of practice (Barrett 1999:258). In the case of shell mounds, simply the act of depositing shellfish on the banks of the river would leave a visible trace. While such traces may have been incorporated by later inhabitants in nonreflexive ways, they also provided an accumulating historical resource that could be politicized and transformative in the context of novel scenarios (Joyce 2004). Depositional narratives can be brought from the nondiscursive to the discursive through collective practices that Connerton (1989) refers to as "commemorative ceremonies." Through commemorative practices, many possible perspectives are drawn together and asserted by modifying places, frequently by transposing seemingly mundane acts into highly public venues (Gosden and Lock 1998). By referencing either traditional practices or places, such events have the effect of reproducing unified or dominant social memories across diverse social fields, regardless of any true affiliation (Barrett 1999; Pauketat and Alt 2003). There are no more obvious inscriptive practices than the construction of monuments. Although monuments were once considered evidence for territoriality, recent discussions have emphasized the integrative nature of commemorative performances (Bradley 1998). Because of their durability, monuments are also likely to be continuously interpreted over the course of many generations by peoples with disparate historical consciousness and worldviews (Bradley 1998:42).

While depositional narratives may be about benevolently referencing a shared past, commemoration is also about forgetting, erasing images of the past and replacing them with new formulations between actors and landscape (Küchler 1993). In commemoration, historical production deploys the past in political economies of memory (Küchler 1993; Rumsey 1994:128). By creatively reconfiguring the sequence, structure, context, or tempo of inscriptive acts, actors can create depositional narratives that present new kinds of history. Such traditions verge on what de Certeau (1984) referred to as a "scriptural economy." For de Certeau, a scriptural economy is a process of historical production through which community identity is constructed by objectifying times, places, and *others* into an ordered and meaningful network. While his concern was with modern writing systems, it is applicable to hunter-gatherers if we consider that inscriptive practices such as movement between locales, the construction of sacred and mundane places, and the variable acquisition and deposition of objects are all historically situated acts through which landscapes are encultured.

If we allow then for depositional narratives as a primary means of history making, what are the appropriate methods and scales of analysis? I follow Pauketat and Alt's (2005:230) three principles: (1) document practical variability through time and across space; (2) construct genealogies of practices (their origin and context of deployment); and (3) tack between lines of evidence at multiple scales of analysis. The methodological process of tracing depositional narratives involves the same sorts of data archaeologists should be accustomed to: detailed chronology, adequate spatial scales, and arguably a deep experiential knowledge of the cultural materials being investigated. At the same time, it requires that we not impose rationality on either the structure or sequence of events, but instead investigate how practices were variously deployed in social settings (Walker and Lucero 2001).

Remapping the Archaic Period in the St. Johns Region

Prior to the twentieth century, the middle St. Johns River valley was inscribed with scores of shell-bearing sites, upwards of two per mile of river, that stood in stark relief to the extensive low-lying wetlands and terraces (Le Baron 1884). We know this because antiquarians such as Jeffries Wyman (1875) and C. B. Moore (1999) published detailed site descriptions. Unfortunately, the material record of Archaic inhabitation has been mostly mined away for road fill over the past century (fig. 7.2a). The sites that remain are but a small portion of those that once existed. Based on historic observations and archaeological excavations, there is some regularity to the structure and location of shell-bearing Archaic sites (Wheeler et al. 2000). The most prevalent form is the single shell ridge. These mounds are linear or crescentic in shape and typically measure 150 m long, 50 m wide, and upwards of 8 m high (fig. 7.2b). While many have asymmetrical apexes, others have flat platform summits. Most of these mounds date entirely to the preceramic Archaic Mount Taylor period and are situated away from contemporary river channels. A minority of mound complexes are composed of multiple shell ridges, often with sand mounds emplaced on or adjacent to the ridges (fig. 7.2a). These sites can measure over 300 m in length and 10 m in maximum height and tend to be located on large bodies of water. Finally, there are innumerable nonmounded middens, frequently referred to as shell fields, heaps, or nodes (fig 7.2b). Shell fields have been documented from Archaic and post-Archaic time periods and are found in many configurations and locations. Those occurring adjacent to mounds are often characterized by diverse material assemblages, suggestive of intensive living.

Despite regularities in form, location, and even subsistence, a detailed consideration of the histories of inhabitation indicates that the pattern we see today is but the final outcome of numerous overlapping and competing depositional narratives. It is impossible to fully detail in any isolated location how narratives were worked out in one given location due to destructive shell mining of many places. Indeed, the recursive nature of spatial stories along the St. Johns necessitates tacking between different localities at different times in the past. Collectively they provide a regional network to examine practical variations across space and through time.

Colonizing and Constructing Communities

If there is any similarity between Western and non-Western conceptions of mapping, it is that both are fundamentally colonizing processes in

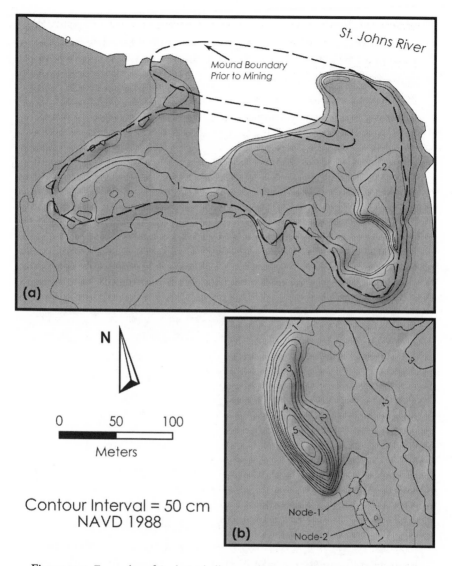

Figure 7.2. Examples of Archaic shell mounds in the middle St. Johns River valley: (a) now-mined multiridge mound complex (Hontoon Island North), (b) intact shell ridge (the Hontoon Dead Creek Mound). (NAVD 1988 is the North American Vertical Datum of 1988, the vertical control datum established for vertical control surveying in the United States.)

which preestablished traditions recursively impose order and are altered through experience (cf. de Certeau 1984:121). Such a colonizing process occurred at the outset of the preceramic Archaic period in the St. Johns region some seventy-three hundred years ago. Inhabitants rapidly rearranged the social and ancestral geography of the region as manifested in structured settlements, communal mortuary mounds, and platform mounds. This transformation occurred in the context of a dramatic reconfiguration of the environment, as large swaths of the river valley were inundated by sea level rise, rich wetlands developed, and shellfish were first exploited (Miller 1998). Despite the regional reconfiguration, the spatial stories materialized in this context of change referenced an earlier historical mode and created new domains for the incorporation of regional inhabitants across diverse social fields. In this section, I examine the significance of settlement and mortuary mound construction.

From the beginning of intensive regional occupation, communities reproduced structured settlements along river segments. Evidence for this practice comes from the Hontoon Dead Creek Complex (8VO214/8VO215), a multicomponent shell-bearing site located in the heart of Mount Taylor country (Randall 2007; Randall and Sassaman 2005). The complex is composed of three distinct loci, including an intact shell ridge (fig. 7.2b), a now-inundated and obscured shell midden that extends into the cypress swamp, and a series of shell midden heaps (referred to as "nodes") along the terrace edge. Much of the volume of the mound postdates the initial occupation of the landform by only a century or two (I discuss its significance in the succeeding section). The midden beneath the cypress swamp was inundated seven thousand years ago, but indicates the mound and associated shell nodes once fronted an open body of water, a pattern recognized at sites elsewhere (Wheeler et al. 2000).

Terrestrial evidence for early occupation is restricted to the non-mounded shell nodes, also known as the Hontoon Dead Creek Village (8VO215). A total of five equally spaced and structurally similar nodes were delimited through topographic mapping and close-interval soil cores. Radiocarbon assays and diagnostic artifacts indicate that there is a time-transgressive trend of Mount Taylor–aged deposits to the north, with successively younger Orange and Post-Archaic occupation occurring to the south. There is some limited evidence to suggest the presence of preceramic Archaic assemblages at the base of these southern, later nodes. Nodes 1 and 2 are the earliest and in closest proximity to the mound and notably the most spatially discrete (fig. 7.2b). Node 1 is the smallest and earliest, dating to seventy-three hundred years ago. The node is an oval dome measuring 13 m in diameter and rising 50 cm above the surrounding terrain. Node 1 is composed of dense, almost impenetrable concreted shell, which was initially laid down in small depositional episodes. Node 2 is evident on the surface as an elongated ridge with a flat summit that rises 40 cm above the surrounding terrain (fig. 7.2b). It measures 25 m long and 8 m wide along a north-south axis and is situated 20 m south of Node 1. A radiocarbon assay on marine shell from near the surface indicates that inhabitation of the locus began sometime before 6510 cal BP. Excavation targeted the contact between the eastern edge of the node and adjacent shell-free zone. In profile, Node 2 is composed of no fewer than eight shell strata, alternatively characterized by crushed and whole shell. Ostensibly, these register periods of use and abandonment. Crushed shell surfaces were created either by inhabitants walking or living upon the midden or, alternatively, by bioturbation. Because excavations were limited primarily to the shell deposits, it is unknown if shell-free residential spaces were present to the east of the midden. Soil probes did encounter organically enriched sediments in these zones, so it would not be unexpected if this were the case.

Collectively, the excavations suggest that once established as places to dwell, the structure and spatiality of early residential sites were reproduced over the course of many years, if not generations. It is currently impossible to know if Nodes 1 and 2 were inhabited serially or at the same time. Finally, the presence of similar nodes beneath the adjacent mound is implied by the presence of 7,000-year-old midden extending from beneath the cypress swamp into the core of the mound. Early Mount Taylor inhabitation apparently involved the establishment and reproduction of spatially structured residential middens that may have been organized in a linear settlement.

While we could ruminate on the significance of residential places from one site in isolation, the import of creating such landscape features in the context of mundane yet arguably communal domains is revealed when we consider the genealogies of coeval mortuary mound constructions elsewhere. The key datum point for this practice is the Harris Creek site (8VO24), which prior to its destruction was a multicomponent shell ridge complex. Excavations in the relict basal Mount Taylor component encountered at least 175 human interments in a mound constructed of sand and shell. This total reflects a small portion of those interments present prior to mining. Similar sequences are likely in mounds throughout the region (Aten 1999; Endonino 2003). Determining the chronology of the mortuary has been problematic. The original excavators dated charcoal from the mound fill. The assay intercepts clustered within a two-hundred-year span (ca. 6000–6200 cal BP), suggesting a relatively short use life (Aten 1999). Because of large sigmas, however, these dates place construction of the mortuary sometime between 5600 and 6900 cal BP. Recent dating of human bone from the mortuary layers by Tucker (2009) yielded a similar range between intercepts, but were much earlier and restricted in time, between 6480 and 7240 cal BP. This new information places mortuary construction roughly coeval with the regional onset of shellfishing and settlement inhabitation.

Aten's (1999) reconstructed sequence of monumental construction and maintenance demonstrates that the event of creating the mortuary involved co-opting a preexisting residential midden as a place of ancestral veneration. Across most of the site excavations encountered a basal shell midden (Layer 2) that matches the description of residential middens identified at the Hontoon Dead Creek Village (see fig. 7.3a for comparison). This midden was a linear ridge, approximately 15 m by 30 m in extent and 1 m high (fig. 7.3b). No mortuary features originate in this zone. Sometime after abandonment, the Layer 2 surface was the locus of human interment (Mortuary A), which included the deposition of white or brown sand on top of burials on the surface (fig. 7.3c). A number of grave pits were also dug, into which single and multiple bodies were covered with white sand. Above Layer 3 is a dense, organic and charcoal-impregnated "black zone" interpreted as a possible charnel house on the basis of associated post holes (fig. 7.3d). Mortuary A was succeeded by yet another mortuary layer, and then was subsequently the locus of large-scale, nonmortuary depositional events. In their early stages, mound-building practices were accretionary in nature, but nonetheless transformative and based in history. Much of the depositional activity during mortuary construction had the net effect of accentuating the preexisting nonmortuary basal midden. What is striking is that

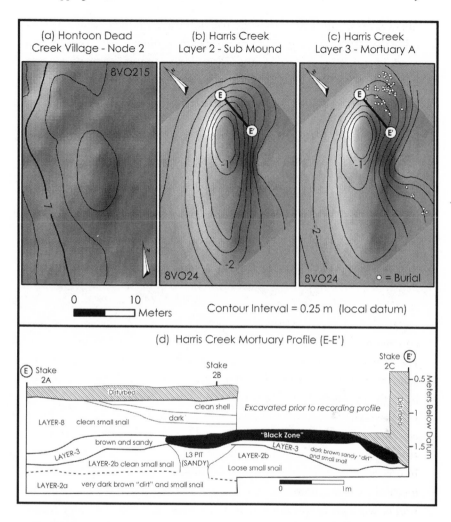

Figure 7.3. A hypothesized sequence of the transformation from domestic middens to mortuary mounds illustrated by a comparison of (a) the Hontoon Dead Creek Village, and (b–d) the Harris Creek Mound (redrawn from Aten 1999).

the premortuary midden at Harris Creek shares a number of structural similarities with Node 2 at 8VO215 (fig. 7.3a). Over the course of successive mortuaries and depositional events, this general configuration was reproduced. In this sense, depositional narratives generated social memories at burial mounds by referencing the spatiality and, arguably, the social relationships of settlements. At the same time, a structural link was established between the communal performance of venerating the dead and the act of capping or emplacing materials on places of prior everyday practice.

Such places were thus imbued with a new kind of history that was reproduced through depositional acts and the social bodies of practitioners. Yet whose histories were being reproduced? Do these events register moments of cultural integration, or were they more about creating social distance? Recent stable-isotope studies of Harris Creek burials indicate that those interred in the mound had distinct spatial stories of their own. As reconstructed by Tucker (2009), the majority of individuals interred at Harris Creek were born and spent their childhood years somewhere near the St. Johns, although a few individuals were from as far away as Lake Okeechobee to the south and Virginia or Tennessee to the north. Although individuals may have been mostly from the Florida peninsula, a finer-grained isotopic analysis suggests that spatial stories of individuals interred in the mound were referenced in burial treatments. Those individuals who spent their childhood years closest to Harris Creek tended to be interred as bundle burials after extended processing, while those individuals from farther afield were interred rapidly after death. The temporality of interment indicates that there was a political economy of memory that incorporated diverse ancestries from throughout the region in burial performance. Although these depositional narratives as mortuary ritual likely provided a context for differences to be negotiated (indeed differences were inscribed in the act of burial treatment), the mortuary program itself was largely integrative in that these potential differences in life were subverted by dominant commemorative and ancestral discourse at mound centers.

We cannot (and may never be able to) disentangle the reasons why settlements were replaced with mortuaries that referenced the spatiality of those prior places. Bradley (1998:49) does provide some possibilities. In discussing the Neolithic transformation of long houses to ritual long mounds, Bradley suggests that places may have been abandoned at the death of a member of the community or through some other traumatic event. Through time, these past places were referenced as metaphors for communal histories. Regardless, an enduring link was established at Harris Creek and other mortuaries at this time between capping places of prior practice (in this case with burials) during transformative social events through the deposition of shellfish remains and sand.

Replacing Histories

We have seen at Harris Creek that the significance of mortuary mounds arose in part from the transformation of residences to ancestral space. This pattern of replacing histories through depositional narratives that reconfigured preexisting traces extends to shell platform mounds variously constructed for communal ceremonies or residential spaces. Central to these revisions of place are hydrological perturbations associated with larger-scale climatic events (Mayewski et al. 2004) that may have reduced the stability of some locales and increased the economic viability of others. Equally pervasive was a vibrant exchange economy, in which new biographies were informed by objects and by others from outside the region. Variations in practice that emerge at these places register new temporalities of experience. In particular, the depositional narratives enacted appear to have been strategically deployed to make novel scenarios meaningful in ways that at once obscured and, in some cases, eradicated past places to make them newly relevant.

In the centuries postdating the mortuary at Harris Creek, residences continued at many mound sites but on a scale and intensity not seen before. In places such as the Mount Taylor–aged shell ridges at the Silver Glen Run (8LA1) and Hontoon Island North (8VO202), highly formalized settlements were reproduced above preexisting communal shell middens. Excavations on interior mined escarpments identified basal living surfaces that were replaced by alternating sequences of crushed and whole shell laid down programmatically after six thousand years ago. The inclusion of shellfish remains, ash, charcoal, paleofeces, and tool debris are all indicative of daily affairs. However, the structure and sequence of depositional events has implications for the significance of decidedly nondaily actions elsewhere. This situation is best observed at site 8LA1, where excavations exposed a deep cross section of the ridge (fig. 7.4a). The basal sequence is composed of concreted shell midden, some of which may have been deposited into pits in the underlying sand. These episodes were capped by a 10–20 cm thick lens of tan and brown sand. Although the ultimate geological origin of the sand is

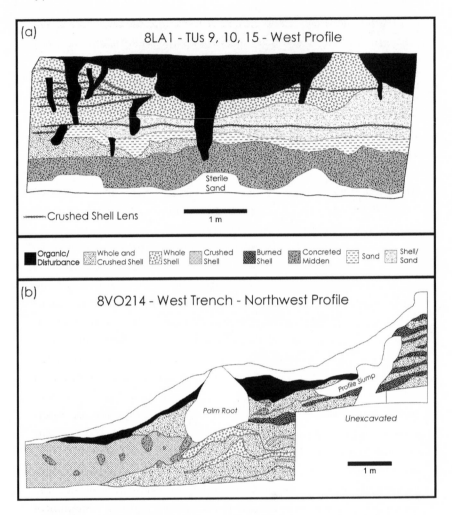

Figure 7.4. A comparison of (a) structured settlements, and (b) ritualized depositional episodes.

unknown, it had to have been transported and laid down upon the current surface, and may have extended across the entire site. Given the preexisting link between sand, death, and community renewal, it is not out of the realm of possibility that this event marked the "death" of the settlement, while at the same time opened the space up for new traditions. These new practices entailed the creation of new micro-mounds on the surface. The slope and inflection of these deposits is reminiscent of the household clusters identified at the Hontoon Dead Creek Village, although on a larger scale and with a significantly greater diversity in material culture and vertebrate fauna. Also different is the emergence of apparently prepared house floors as seen in the sand and shell deposits to the right of the profile (fig. 7.4a) and in the repeated deposition of shellfish remains to the left of the profile. These data collectively suggest that new settlements re-created in place were highly structured. Moreover, separating depositional episodes are lenses of crushed shell and charcoal that appear to represent burning events, possibly associated with either the renewal or abandonment of the settlement. The fact that these places were continually reproduced implies an underlying community biography that was spatially informed.

These inhabited settlements were presaged by earlier nonresidential platform mounds that mimic the configuration of places of daily living but were decidedly not mundane in character. Live Oak Mound (8VO41) and the Hontoon Dead Creek Mound (8VO214) are exemplars of this process (Sassaman 2003b, 2005b). Both sites share a similar configuration (i.e., a linear shell ridge) and are situated some 200 m from current river channels. At least in the case of the Hontoon Dead Creek Mound, sediment aggraded within an adjacent water body. Such patterns have been identified elsewhere, such as at the Old Enterprise Complex (8VO2601) to the south, where variance in surface waters allowed for the production of organic deposits that filled adjacent lagoons (McGee and Wheeler 1994). Unlike some of the largest mounds that are characterized by continued habitation adjacent to large bodies of water, the locations of these shell ridges may have been particularly susceptible to economic shortfalls (K. Sassaman, personal communication, 2008). Despite overall structural similarities to lived places, stratigraphic excavations within each ridge suggest that any spaces at the base of the mound were capped in massive mound-building events. This transformation is best seen at 8VO214 (fig. 7.4b). Unfortunately, excavations did not intercept basal deposits, although shell nodes at the adjacent Hontoon Dead Creek Village demonstrate early habitation did occur here. Whatever was beneath the Hontoon Dead Creek Mound, inhabitants eradicated any trace through the deposition of mounded deposits composed of clean shell, charcoal, and disaggregated concreted shell midden likely mined from a preexisting shell deposit. This expansion of the mound effectively created a platform apex. Successive depositional events above the mounded shell are characterized by couplets of mostly clean shell and burned and crushed shell. These couplets have analogues at sites such as 8LA1 and 8VO202. However, while couplets at other mounds were clearly the result of daily activity, those at 8VO214 were not. Although vertebrate faunal remains are present in some quantity at 8VO214, all the other debris of everyday life (tools, tool fragments, paleofeces) are missing. There is no evidence for mortuary activity occurring here within this time frame. Taken as a whole, however, the sequence at site 8VO214 points to at least one transformative event in which the very materiality of the surrounding communities (save for those at the associated Hontoon Dead Creek Village) were literally and figuratively mined as historical resources for the production of this new place. Any daily living in the vicinity was replaced with a new temporality of shellfish exploitation that made these places truly monumental. Radiocarbon assays bracketing the excavated couplets span 7150 to 6640 cal BP at two sigmas and indicate that deposition was rapid and chronologically early.

At places such as the Hontoon Dead Creek Mound, depositional practices appear to have been transposed from mundane acts and elevated to large-scale commemorative ceremonies aimed at renewing mound surfaces and, by extension, the social relationships involved in mound maintenance. At others, such as the shell ridge at 8LA1, extensive and long-reproduced communities were enabled only after spaces had been reconfigured. Further research will be necessary to detail the tempo of practices at either place, although a leading hypothesis is that the divergent social context of mound-top depositional narratives was the result of local ecological stability or vulnerability. In particular, practices played out at nonresidential mound sites likely occurred throughout the region at times of periodic resource abundance and likely as acts that incorporated others. Oyuela-Caycedo (2004) has described a similar process in the Amazon in which dances are performed during periods of resource abundance. These dances take the form of mythical narratives using ecological metaphors that bring outsiders into the local community as a process of difference recognition and subversion. If a similar process was afoot along the St. Johns, periodic collapses and abundance of symbolic and subsistence resources would have provided a powerful political economy of memory that at a minimum would have sedimented communal identities throughout the basin.

The Other Within

The ongoing construction of shell ridges and platforms and their shifting significance could be understood as a restricted regional process. However, depositional narratives also were deployed to interfere with large-scale social interactions. This is evident both in the construction of mortuary sand mounds at the terminus of the Mount Taylor period and in a revolution in mound construction at the beginning of the ceramic Archaic Orange period. In both cases, objects and individuals with nonlocal histories were folded into local frames of reference by imposing a master narrative upon them. Late Mount Taylor mortuary mounds (notably Bluffton [8VO23], Tomoka [8VO81], and Thornhill [8VO58–60]) share several structural and historical relationships (Endonino 2008; Piatek 1994). All are composed of mounded sand and shell that were erected upon preexisting shell middens as events. Unlike the earlier Harris Creek mortuary, these mortuaries do not appear to be open-access affairs. For example, the Bluffton mound was erected over a single individual (Sears 1960). The association of Mount Taylor burials with mounds at Tomoka is unknown due to a lack of preservation. At Thornhill, isolated individuals were identified by C. B. Moore in his excavations there as well. Linking Thornhill and Tomoka is the presence of objects of nonlocal origins, most notably bannerstones likely derived from Georgia and South Carolina. In the source area, bannerstones were circulated locally and along the Savannah River valley and not associated with mortuary practice (Sassaman and Randall 2007). However, in Florida these objects were either interred as caches or with individuals. The inclusion of foreign objects, which likely had distinct spatial stories of their own, was an interpretive act that recognized the "otherness" of the object and incorporated its biography through the material retelling of a larger ancestral narrative through large-scale depositional events (Randall and Sassaman 2010).

All of the diversity and intensity in monumentality comes to an end at forty-seven hundred years ago and, not coincidentally, coeval with the onset of local pottery production. Diagnostic artifacts of the Orange period are typically found situated away from shell ridges, even though Orange settlements were emplaced nearby. Radiocarbon dates from below near-surface mounded shell at the Hontoon Island North site indicate the site was capped and abandoned sometime after forty-eight years ago and apparently remained unoccupied until the later St. Johns period. Orange period ceramics are rarely recovered from the surfaces of shell ridges throughout the region, nor are they found in any great frequency upon sand mounds (Endonino 2008; Piatek 1994; Sears 1960). Nevertheless, evidence for Orange occupation is widespread throughout the region, with some researchers proposing an increase in regional population density (Miller 1998). Why were shell mounds sites avoided?

We can start with the observation that Orange period pottery has its origins a century earlier on the coast of Florida, and its introduction was likely facilitated by preexisting exchange networks (Sassaman 2004b). Although this process is currently modeled as an in situ evolutionary progression, pottery production in fact signals a complete and total restructuring of domains of practice, the scale of which is coming to light only now. For example, at the Blue Springs Midden B site (8VO43), Sassaman (2003b) documented the presence of a semi-circular Orange period compound, characterized by four crushed shell floors, measuring 4 to 6 m in diameter and spaced approximately 8 m apart. These clusters were oriented in an arc, approximately 34 m in diameter, facing the St. Johns River and adjacent to Blue Spring Run. This organization of space is arguably new to the region. However, circular villages and monuments are well documented in historically affiliated coastal groups. As a further contrast to Mount Taylor occupation, Orange compounds were routinely sited near, but noticeably away from, preexisting monuments, which were apparently avoided (Randall and Sassaman 2010). This pattern is evident at Bluffton (8VO22), the Hontoon Dead Creek Village, and the Silver Glen Run Complex. Finally, one other aspect shared by Orange residential spaces is the prevalence of plain wares. In contrast to the widespread evidence for Orange villages characterized by plain wares, incised and technologically distinct Orange pottery is largely restricted to four locations in the valley: the Silver Glen Run Complex, Harris Creek, Old Enterprise (8VO55), and Orange Mound (8ORI, not shown) (fig. 7.1). A similar spatial division between aggregation and residential contexts has been identified along the coast, a pattern that arguably represents a division between sacred and secular spaces (Sassaman 2003a; Saunders 2004). Along the St. Johns, large assemblages are situated some 20–30 km apart, a pattern which is entirely spatial, as incised and decorated pottery are coeval (Sassaman 2003a). As with community architecture and layout, the construction of monuments during the Orange period apparently involved the introduction and partial adoption of design principles, which also imposed a new ritual spatiality in which segments of the basin were segregated.

Recent excavations at the Silver Glen Run Complex are now providing a context for interpreting this emergent pattern. Prior to its destruction in 1923, Wyman described the site as a U-shaped amphitheater, upwards of 300 m long on a side, rising to a height of up to 8 m, with a deep valley between the ridges. In figure 7.5, I have superimposed Wyman's description (based in part on an unpublished sketch map he made) over the existing surface topography. The mound is scaled to the distribution of shell midden present at the site identified during subsurface testing, which is largely conformant with Wyman's description. If these dimensions are even close to correct, this mound is the largest in northeast Florida and dwarfs other coastal shell rings by a factor of two. Given that Wyman describes a cut bank at the mouth of the river as composed entirely of shell, it seems unlikely that resource depression was a factor in the reduction of mound building throughout the valley.

This transformation has recently been described as representing a "New World Order," through which the scale, situatedness, and temporality of depositional acts at mounds sites were recreated (Randall and Sassaman 2010). That is, a new master regional narrative was emplaced via the selective referencing of some elements of the past and the apparent neglect of others. Fundamentally an act of historical production, local and distant communities wove together new spatial narratives from multiple ancestral streams. Whether technology or potters themselves were introduced into the region, the *other* was integrated through hybrid village and monumental layouts that differentially incorporated elements of nonlocal settlement organization and monumental practice into a landscape already sedimented with enduring ancestral and mythic history. Much is still to be learned about this mode of historical production and the inherent spatial stories that were remapped onto the St. Johns during the Orange period. In the case of 8LA1, the amphitheater

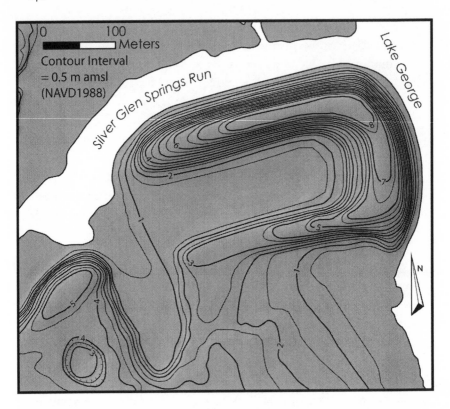

Figure 7.5. A reconstructed preceramic Archaic shell ridge (lower left) and an Orange period U-shaped shell mound at the Silver Glen Run complex (upper right).

was not constructed de novo. Not only was the Orange period mound situated in opposition to a large shell ridge to the west, but it appears Orange communities grafted a new monument on top of a preexisting Mount Taylor ceremonial mound in a way that referenced both coastal and interior ancestries. Moreover, there is some suggestive evidence for within-site differentiation in the production and disposal of pottery. Incised wares, found in great abundance, are largely restricted to the periphery of the mound's water-facing sides. In the location of the rear ridge, however, excavations uncovered only plain pottery. Yet even in these contexts, there is little to suggest that shell midden accumulated through acts of daily settlement. To the contrary, large pits (upwards of 2 m wide) were excavated and filled with clean, mounded shell. Future research will examine whether the two ridges actually represent the constructive efforts of two distinct ancestries.

Crafting Narratives across the Divide

When viewed through the lens of subsistence and repeated use of place, the practices that resulted in shell mounds of the middle St. Johns River could easily be mistaken for continuities. Indeed, there is little evidence for significant variations in subsistence throughout either the Mount Taylor or Orange period. Where shifts in settlement location are present, they rarely involved the wholesale abandonment of large swaths of territory. Yet, we must be circumspect when examining continuities, as they may be more apparent than real (Bradley 2003; Gosden and Lock 1998). As shown along the St. Johns, over the course of three thousand years, communities were variously reproduced through an ongoing historical production of biographical and ancestral depositional narratives. While altered through the recognition and incorporation of different kinds of events and others, the past as place and process was recursively referenced and drawn upon in creative ways.

The results of investigations into settlement and mortuary mound construction indicate that traditions of mundane and commemorative practice emerged in the context of new ecologies and social interactions. Such places of past practice rapidly emerged as central foci for return visits and local interaction as inhabitants returned annually from throughout the state. This potential diversity appears to have been negotiated through veneration of the dead in highly public acts. The primary inscriptive practice was not necessarily the interment of the deceased and construction of the mound. Instead, it was the striking replacement of settlements with sacred places emplaced and modeled on those structures. These central metaphors for referencing community and for reconstituting contemporary social relations were continuously reworked in depositional narratives throughout successive millennia. During times of considerable ecological and social upheaval, some settlements were abandoned, others became intensive loci of daily practice, and still others were maintained as monumental commemorative venues. Yet throughout, communities mobilized the past to write histories that either accommodated or interfered with contemporary concerns. In this frame of reference, traditions of ecological exploitation, residential spaces, commemoration of ancestral and mythic orders, and interactions with *others* emerge as the central historiographic method through which these hunter-gatherer communities were reproduced and transformed. In fact, this historiographic method would seem to be present in most societies, irrespective of their particular subsistence economy.

Acknowledgments

I would like to thank Ken Sassaman and Don Holly for inviting this contribution, as well as the Amerind Foundation for providing an immeasurably inspiring atmosphere in which to discuss hunter-gatherers. This chapter benefited greatly from the many hours of formal and informal discussions with colleagues during the seminar.

8

Ancient Social Landscapes in the Eastern Subarctic

Moira McCaffrey

> The exact experiences of people in the past may well elude us, but
> the ways in which they set up worlds that made sense to them is
> available to us through an appreciation of the sensory and social
> impacts of the objects that formed the fabric of past lives.
> —Gosden 2001:167

Hunter-gatherers of the Eastern Subarctic have long served as quint-
essential models for the reconstruction of early North American lifeways. Ethnographic accounts of their extensive seasonal rounds inform
hypotheses on Paleoindian band movements. Early twentieth-century
photographs are scrutinized to provide material culture inventories
and clues to hunting and processing techniques. Historic caribou-skin
coats appear prominently in museum displays. As painted canvases for
hunter's dreams, they highlight the symbolic and spiritual dimensions
of hunting success.

For the most part, interpretations of precontact life in this region
meld seamlessly with fur trade period accounts of the Cree, Innu, and
Naskapi who still occupy northern Quebec and Labrador. This essen-
tialist simplification is no doubt facilitated by the poor organic preservation and thin cultural deposits that characterize many archaeological
sites in the Eastern Subarctic. Stone tool assemblages, combined with
limited faunal remains and rare stratigraphic evidence, are usually all
that survive to document past lives and events.

Archaeologists are increasingly cognizant that modern hunter-gatherers
are not pristine survivals, but rather communities of people who have
been shaped by complex forces resulting from colonialism and global-
ization (Headland and Reid 1989; Jordan 2008:456; Wilmsen 1989).

Recently, Armitage (2004:52) remarked that Labrador "is, and always
has been, an imaginary place, a state of mind, as well as a fact of geography and nature." Citing disparities between the archaeological record
and the ethnographic portrait of peoples in the Eastern Subarctic, Holly
(2002a:15, this vol.) has argued in support of "the power of archaeology to unveil the historical and ethnographic complexities of subarctic
peoples and pasts."

In this chapter, I situate the artifacts most prevalent on northern
hunter-gatherer sites—lithic assemblages—within a socially and mean-
ingfully constituted landscape (Hodder 2002:322). My goal is to develop
a contextual understanding of lithic procurement, mobility, and interaction in the Eastern Subarctic that acknowledges the physical constraints of the northern environment while recognizing the capacity of
individuals and groups to imagine and constitute a cultural landscape
built not only on such constraints but also on choices, relationships,
and beliefs.

When the analysis of lithic assemblages in the Eastern Subarctic
is informed not only by constraints but by the histories and cultural
practices of the region's ethnohistoric and ethnographic people, new
readings of the archaeological record are possible, ones that challenge
entrenched evolutionary views and encourage an appreciation of the
complex social and ideological dimensions of hunter-gatherer movement and interaction. The Eastern Subarctic embodies one of the many
landscapes worldwide that became meaningful, and thus structured
practice through geographically expansive human experiences.

In this chapter, I present a case study from northern Quebec to illustrate this perspective. The data I bring to bear are drawn from a large
number of dated components excavated over the past thirty years in the
course of cultural resource management projects linked to hydroelectric
development.

The archaeologists involved in analyzing these sites have devoted
much effort to the study of lithic assemblages, including detailed iden-
tifications of the different lithic materials present on sites. Among the
intriguing results emerging from this research is the marked variation
evident in the stone types used for tool manufacture. From the earliest occupations, which date to about 4000 BP in the central interior,
site collections are dominated by a high percentage of widely available

quartz. Nevertheless, most sites also include varying amounts of fine-grained, high-quality cherts and quartzites. The most prevalent of these are visually distinctive and come from five sources that are widely separated in space. Often, two or more of these toolstone varieties co-occur with quartz.

To date, the presence on the same site of lithics from distant sources is accounted for by citing historic patterns of mobility and exchange. During the fur trade period, the Cree, Innu, and Naskapi followed seasonal rounds that involved long-distance travel on foot and snowshoes or by canoe. They tended trap lines and traveled to take advantage of gregarious and mobile animal species—for example, caribou in the interior, seals on the North Shore, and geese in the James Bay region. It follows that their ancestors may have obtained toolstone through embedded procurement practices within wide-ranging subsistence rounds. Furthermore, because high-quality lithic sources are restricted in number and location on the Eastern Subarctic landscape, we might assume that regular travel or special purpose trips to at least one of these sources must have been critical to ensure an adequate supply of toolstone.

Exchange mechanisms are also likely to have played an important role in dispersing different lithic materials. According to this view, toolstone would have been distributed down the line between groups living closer to sources and those farther removed. The close cultural and linguistic ties among the historic Cree, Innu, and Naskapi support this contention, as do many historic period accounts attesting to sharing as a basic feature of life in the North. In addition, archaeological evidence from across the broad Northeast has documented the movement of two of these lithics—Ramah chert and Mistassini quartzite—over extraordinary distances during specific time periods (Denton 1998; Loring 2002; McCaffrey 1989b).

Despite the usual microeconomic and ecological reasons for the acquisition of nonlocal lithic materials, the pervasive use of alternative media for many Subarctic tools lessens the likelihood that toolstone acquisition was merely a mundane concern. Many historic accounts and ethnographic collections in museums confirm the dominant position that bone and antler occupied in toolkits of the historic Cree, Innu, and Naskapi (Rogers 1967; Speck 1935; Turner 1894; VanStone 1982, 1985). Moreover, given the widespread availability of quartz, including fine crystalline varieties, and the fact that quartz tools and flaking debris dominate most assemblages of the region, is it at all tenable to assume that people had to go to great lengths to acquire specific lithic materials?

Explaining Toolstone Acquisition

The presence of raw materials from distant sources on archaeological sites has long attracted the attention of archaeologists as a means of inferring mobility patterns and exchange networks. The earliest models applied to hunter-gatherer data were drawn from studies of trade patterns in complex societies. Renfrew (1977) defined a number of important concepts including the Law of Monotonic Decrement, which states that when a commodity is available only in a highly circumscribed area, its distribution in space tends to fall off in frequency or abundance with distance from the source.

With data derived directly from ethnographic hunter-gatherers, processual archaeologists sought to relate stone tool variation to the organization of settlement and subsistence. For example, Binford's (1979) ethnoarchaeological work among the Nunamiut Inuit led him to propose that prehistoric raw material acquisition was a secondary pursuit integrated or "embedded" into the subsistence schedule. He (1979:260) concluded that "variability in the proportions of raw materials found at a given site are primarily a function of the scale of the habitat which was exploited from the site location. Exotic materials thus indicate the scale of the subsistence-settlement system." In other words, exotic lithics in assemblages are the by-products of mobility (Goodyear 1979).

Gould (1980; see also Gould and Saggers 1985) argued that Binford's explanation for lithic variability on archaeological sites overlooked the structural impingements of hunter-gatherer social relations. Analyzing the lithic procurement strategies of historic and contemporary Australian Aborigines, Gould identified "anomalies" that departed from utilitarian principles of mechanical efficiency or economy of effort. He (1980:156) concluded that "one must accept the premise that the presence of exotic lithic materials . . . is circumstantial evidence of social networks along which such materials flowed." In his view, these social networks were widely ramified kin networks that facilitated the sharing of food and access to basic resources. Gould and Saggers (1985:122–123) went a step further and proposed that "the tendency to establish long-distance ties in different directions characterizes hunter-gatherer societies that are subject to extreme uncertainties with respect to a key resource." This "righteous rocks" debate laid the groundwork for studies of hunter-gatherer lithic procurement and exchange that seek to explore the social while acknowledging the practical.

The approach adopted in this chapter uses complexity theory as a starting point and integrates elements drawn from both processual and postprocessual paradigms. Prominent in the natural sciences, complexity theory is rapidly gaining the attention of archaeologists (Bentley and Maschner 2003, 2008). One of the chief attractions lies in the centrality of a subtle role for individual agents and unique events "in constant dialectic with constraining and enabling structures of their social and environmental context" (Bintliff 2008:160). Central to complexity studies is "emergence," the idea that complex global patterns with new properties can emerge from local interactions (Barabási 2003; Bentley and Maschner 2003; Johnson 2002; Kauffman 1995; Lansing 2003; Miller and Page 2007; Watts 2003). Complexity theory offers a different way to think about the world and, in so doing, can help to destabilize entrenched ideas and illuminate new possibilities for inquiry.

Bruce Trigger (1991, 1998) proposed a framework for archaeological explanation that moves beyond both the ecological determinism of "New Archaeologists" and the historical particularism of postprocessualists, while working well within the complexity paradigm. It emphasizes the use of a broad base of explanation to construct and test alternate models to explain archaeological patterns. This approach places as much importance on internal constraints stemming from cultural traditions as on external ecological constraints. As Trigger (1998:8) has pointed out, "humans adapt to a symbolic world rather than to a real one . . . [but] this symbolic world has to correspond to the real one to a very considerable degree if a society [is] to survive." It follows that external constraints impose a certain "evolutionary" order upon the broad outlines of human history, but it is impossible to predict on the basis of general principles the specific details of actual human experience.

In contrast to the descriptive accounts originally generated by the cultural-historical paradigm, in this context the direct historical approach is used to explore worldview and related practices and the potential material signatures of these on the landscape. Recent work by Jordan (2003) has stressed the persistence through time of core ritual systems and has shown that significant insights can be gleaned from classic ethnographies and contemporary oral history accounts.

The Eastern Subarctic is known for a rich corpus of ethnohistoric and ethnographic literature, including missionaries' accounts, fur trade period records, adventurers' impressions, and in-depth studies by anthropologists. Often incorporating Cree, Innu, and Naskapi oral history accounts, these sources offer a wealth of insights into life in the Subarctic. Contained in these documents are descriptions of seasonal movements and group interactions, remarkable places and encounters, and beliefs and spiritual practices. As Pauketat (2007:203) concluded, "maybe, just maybe, archaeologists needed to think more about the ways and the contexts in which stories are told and the ways that memories of places, peoples, and things are created."

The Eastern Subarctic in Cultural-Historical Terms

The broad outlines of a culture history for the central interior of the Eastern Subarctic can be sketched thanks to a number of regional syntheses and the availability of over one hundred radiocarbon dates associated with sites in the La Grande River basin (fig. 8.1) (Administration Régionale Crie 1985; Archéotec 1985, 1992, 2009; Cérane 1983a, 1983b, 1984, 1995; Denton 1988, 1989, 1998; Denton et al. 1984; Ethnoscop 1995; McCaffrey 2006). For the purposes of this overview, the precontact chronology of occupation can be divided into an Early period (4000?–2000 BP) and a Recent period (2000–400 BP).

The Early period remains poorly documented (McCaffrey 2006). The oldest-known archaeological sites date to between 4000 and 2000 BP and are situated in the central (Caniapiscau, Laforge, La Grande-4) and western (Grande Baleine) parts of northern Quebec. In general, these sites are small, with evidence of single, wigwam-type dwellings. Assemblages are dominated by locally available quartz, but often contain high-quality lithic materials from distant sources. The cultural affiliations of these sites have not been firmly established. Denton (1988) suggested that early sites in the Caniapiscau region may represent late manifestations of the Maritime Archaic tradition, indicating an exploitation of the far

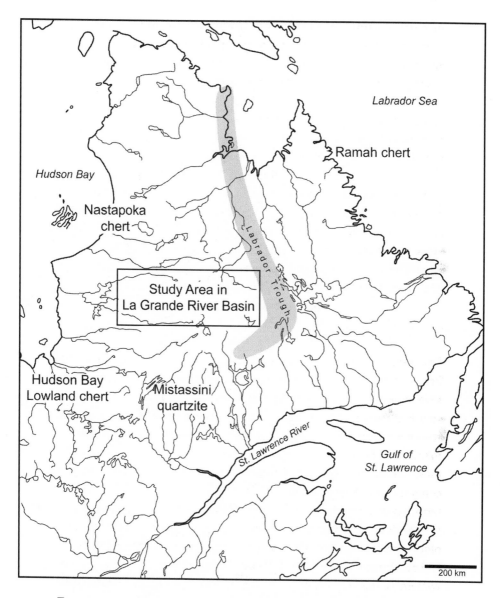

Figure 8.1. The Eastern Subarctic, showing the study area and the source locales of five distinctive toolstone varieties found on archaeological sites.

interior by groups from the Labrador coast and the Quebec North Shore. Early sites farther west in the Grande Baleine region contain ground stone gouges and side-notched projectile points that show affinities to Laurentian Archaic, as well as late Maritime Archaic, assemblages (Archéotec 1985; Cérane 1995; McCaffrey 2006). Occupations from this time period have not yet been identified in the western La Grande River region; however, recent research to the south on the Eastmain River has produced deeply buried sites and occupation dates approaching 5000 BP (David Denton, personal communication 2009; Archéotec 2009; Rousseau 2007).

A small number of sites date to 3200–2200 BP, a time span corresponding to the Intermediate period in Labrador and to post-Archaic sequences of the North Shore, Lac St. Jean, and Abitibi-Témiscamingue regions. These occupations are located primarily in the Caniapiscau, Schefferville, and western Labrador regions (Denton 1988; Denton and McCaffrey 1988; McCaffrey 1989a, 2006). Throughout the Quebec-Labrador peninsula, this time period is inadequately documented and poorly understood.

The availability of archaeological evidence increases dramatically for the period covering the last two thousand years. The presence of many dated sites from across the Eastern Subarctic attests to a continuous and more intensive period of occupation. Moreover, the Recent period bears witness to the first documented use of the western sector of the La Grande complex. By around 1300 BP, a veritable florescence of Eastern Subarctic interior adaptation is suggested by an increase in the number of sites, the distinctive patterns of lithic raw material use, and the appearance of pottery in numerous assemblages (McCaffrey and Dumais 1989).

Of particular interest during this period is evidence for the presence of long dwellings containing numerous aligned hearths or a single elongated hearth. Historic period accounts describe the construction of a special habitation designed to accommodate a large group of people following a successful hunt. The Algonquian name for these structures is the same across the Quebec-Labrador peninsula, although spelling of the term varies, with the most common forms being *saaputwaan* or *shaapuhtuwaan* in Cree and *shaputuan* in Innu (this latter spelling will be used in this chapter). Elongated houses were generally rectangular in shape, of variable length, with entranceways at opposite ends, and multiple aligned hearths or a single extended one situated on the long axis.

A number of sites in the Caniapiscau and Laforge regions show affinities to the Point Revenge complex on the Labrador coast (Loring 1992) and to some post-Archaic complexes on the Lower North Shore (Pintal 1989, 1998). Further west in the La Grande-3, La Grande-2, La Grande-1, and Grande Baleine regions, the presence of pottery on numerous sites, combined with a more intensive use of lithic materials from the region of Mistassini Lake, Hudson Bay, and James Bay point to closer ties with western and southern regions. Occupations from this time period relate directly to the ancestors of the Cree, Innu, and Naskapi peoples. Some of the most recent sites in this sequence, dating from the mid-sixteenth to the mid-seventeenth centuries, contain European trade goods.

The Lithic Landscape

Crucial to any understanding of lithic use patterns is the ability to identify "lithic types" among the tools and flakes in the archaeological collections and to attribute them to known geological formations (whether primary or secondary sources) with a fairly high degree of accuracy. Although this task can be monumental, it is facilitated by the geological history of the eastern Canadian Shield (Stockwell et al. 1970:44–45). Lithic materials with good fracture properties are neither uniformly available nor randomly distributed across the region. Consequently, although quartz and quartzites occur in many places, the five high-quality siliceous stones that appear most frequently on sites in the northern interior are concentrated in discrete geological deposits (fig. 8.1). Moreover, these lithic materials are generally quite distinctive both in their macroscopic and microscopic properties, thereby facilitating their identification following the "intrinsic characteristics" approach outlined by McElrath and Emerson (2000).

Ramah chert, which outcrops in the Torngat Mountains on the northern Labrador coast, can usually be distinguished by its color, ranging from light to dark gray, sugary grain, and striking translucent appearance. Ramah was clearly a much-coveted stone as it has been recovered from archaeological sites across the Eastern Subarctic and the broad Northeast, including the New England states (Loring 2002).

My fieldwork in the Labrador Trough, a geological formation extending from Ungava Bay to Wabush, led to the discovery of a suite of high-quality, primarily gray cherts (Birkett 1991; Denton and McCaffrey 1988;

McCaffrey 1989a, 1989b). Many varieties can be identified by the presence of vugs or pelloids, especially visible when flakes or tool edges are backlit. Thus far, Labrador Trough cherts show only limited use, appearing occasionally on sites in the central interior of Quebec-Labrador and also on the Middle North Shore.

Mistassini quartzite from the Mistassini and Albanel Lakes region of the boreal forest is a fine-grained stone that is generally snowy white in color with a distinctive slick luster. It was widely used across northern Quebec and has been recovered from sites much farther afield in the Northeast (Denton 1998; Martijn and Rogers 1969).

Nastapoka chert, which comes from the Hudson Bay coast, was also exploited by Paleo-Eskimo groups. It ranges from dark gray to mottled or striated in appearance, is generally opaque, and has a high luster (Chandler 1988; Desrosiers and Rahmani 2007). Within Aboriginal contexts, Nastapoka chert turns up on sites throughout the La Grande River region but does not appear to have traveled far beyond.

Finally, Hudson Bay Lowland chert, likely obtained from secondary deposits around the base of James Bay, has a wide range of colors including grays, browns, and pinks, although most varieties appear brown when backlit. Fossils are sometimes visible as is cortex, indicating an original nodular form (Julig 1994; Julig et al. 1992; Long et al. 2001). This material is present in small amounts on sites in northern Quebec, particularly those bordering James Bay, but rarely occurs beyond.

Distribution of Lithics at Sites in Northern Quebec

From a core study area encompassing the central and eastern La Grande complex, I selected for analysis a total of 63 components, all from single-component or well-sorted multicomponent sites that collectively span the full time range of regional occupation, from about 4000 BP to the contact period. A range of variables was recorded for each component including a description of habitation and hearth features, faunal remains, location of discarded tools, and notations on the presence of pottery and European trade goods. All stone tools and flakes were identified by raw material type based on visual sorting, complemented by thin-section analyses of selected samples. Tool and flake counts by lithic type were used to represent the quantity of different lithic materials, specifically quartz and the five fine-grained stone varieties previously described.

The decision to work with flake and tool counts rather than to record weights or variables related to lithic production stages merits further discussion. Existing studies (Denton et al. 1984; McCaffrey 1983) have demonstrated that different lithic materials were transported to sites in northern Quebec in a restricted number of forms, meaning that the reduction stages associated with these materials are fairly predictable. For example, locally available quartz and quartzite were almost always carried onto sites as blocks, block fragments, and cores, and occasionally as finished tools—especially in the case of higher-quality crystalline quartz. Consequently, unlike the debitage of other lithic materials, all stages of quartz reduction can generally be found on sites. There is little evidence of biface reduction, edge reworking, or resharpening (Chevrier 1986; Denton et al. 1984).

The finer-grained materials transported from distant sources, in particular, Ramah chert, Labrador Trough cherts, and Mistassini quartzite, appear to have been carried to sites as finished tools, bifacial blanks, biface preforms, or flakes struck from tabular pieces or cores. These observations are supported by the presence of large numbers of biface reduction flakes and the virtual absence of cores, chunks, or cortical flakes of these materials. In the case of Nastapoka chert and Hudson Bay Lowland chert, small nuclei and finished tools, mainly projectile points, scrapers, and the occasional small biface, are the most frequently encountered forms. This pattern is likely due to the small size of naturally occurring nodules and chunks.

In general, all of the fine-grained materials show evidence of conservation and curation (i.e., debitage is small and reflects the final stages of tool production, while tools are small and show heavy use, resharpening, and re-use after breakage). In some instances, it is clear that flakes were being struck from large bifaces for expedient purposes, while the original biface was subsequently carried away from the site (Denton et al. 1984; McCaffrey 1983). A small number of components show very liberal use of fine-grained lithic materials, indicated by the large size of flakes left on the sites as well as the discard of numerous complete and broken tools.

Lithic Distributions by Time Period

The sequence of calibrated radiocarbon dates was divided into periods according to perceived breaks, though these are not assumed to represent cultural discontinuities. Significant patterns in the presence and amount of specific lithic materials on sites are evident in a comparison of assemblages over time.

Assemblages dating to Period 1 (4000–2700 BP) are dominated by quartz but routinely contain small quantities of nonlocal toolstone. Patterned variation among all types suggests that people were entering the region from different directions and were not carrying large supplies of lithic material but rather were exploiting local quartz outcrops and preparing their tools on site. Lithic distributions indicate that most habitation features were wigwams with single hearths. Nevertheless, three sites had double hearths; two of these were situated in the Caniapiscau region and produced mixes of lithic materials from different sources.

Assemblages dating to Period 2 (2700–2000 BP) and the partially overlapping Period 3 (2300–1300 BP) are concentrated at sites in the Caniapiscau region, and in lesser numbers in Laforge. Of note on the sites spanning this long stretch of time is the consistent presence of Ramah chert, frequently accompanied by cherts from the Labrador Trough, suggesting strong contacts with the east. Nevertheless, western lithic materials co-occur with Ramah chert on a number of sites. Elongated hearths (distinctive features comprising one continuous linear hearth deposit) make an appearance for the first time, and it is likely that four sites contained elongated dwellings, or shaputuans. The most recent occupation consists of a dwelling with four aligned hearths.

Period 4 (1300–1000 BP) shows a strong presence of Nastapoka chert, including a number of sites in both Laforge and Caniapiscau, where this is the dominant lithic material. On this point, the tendency is to see associations with regions northwest, though once again other lithic materials make an appearance, with the exception of Hudson Bay Lowland chert. In fact, these two materials rarely co-occur on sites, while Mistassini quartzite is frequently associated with either Hudson Bay Lowland chert or Nastapoka chert. Hearth counts and flake distributions indicate that six of these sites were wigwams with single hearths, while four of them were larger dwellings, possibly elongated houses that each contained two aligned hearths.

Assemblages dating to Period 5 (1000–500 BP) are difficult to characterize because no obvious trends in lithic use are apparent. Notwithstanding the consistent presence of quartz and the quasi-absence of Ramah chert, sites tend to be dominated by Nastapoka chert, Labrador Trough cherts (in the case of two associated sites in Caniapiscau), or Mistassini quartzite. Once again, however, regardless of whether sites are in Caniapiscau or Laforge, a range of different materials co-occur on at least eight of the fourteen sites. Half of these sites are elongated houses, and two of these contain habitation features (one a remarkable 13 m long) encompassing four aligned hearths. Elongated hearths are present on a third of the sites. Finally, pottery makes an appearance on a site in the Laforge sector.

Period 6, which ranges from 800 to 500 BP and overlaps with the previous period, shows the beginning of a strong trend toward the presence of Mistassini quartzite frequently accompanied by Hudson Bay Lowland chert in greater quantities than previously seen. The two sites with the largest amounts of Mistassini quartzite also contain pottery. Half of the sites were elongated houses. The La Grande-3 region produced an exceptional site with thirty-three contemporaneous hearths, some of which were in wigwams and others in elongated houses.

The final grouping brings us into the contact period, with components ranging in age from about 600 to 300 BP. A fairly dramatic pattern is evident. For the first time, quartz drops in frequency and all fine-grained lithic materials co-occur on components. Nine of the eleven sites were elongated houses, some with three aligned hearths. One site contained a huge habitation 32 m in length with four aligned hearths. Trade goods appear on five of the sites and two of these also produced ceramics, in one case Huron pottery. A number of the sites with elongated hearths show a particularly interesting pattern (one which occurs sporadically in the previous two periods): projectile points and occasionally other tools appear to have been intentionally discarded in the hearth.

The Topography of Interaction

The data I have just presented suggest that a causal link between external constraints related to distance and effort, and observed patterns of lithic use, is not borne out. Rather, an exploration of economic and technological hypotheses, and a comparison of expected outcomes with actual patterns of lithic use evident in the component sample, produced a number of anomalies from anticipated trends. And these hold true regardless of assemblage size.

First, lithic patterns indicate that locally available quartz was by far the most popular lithic material on sites. Furthermore, quartz appears to have been used for the full range of tool types found in assemblages. Nevertheless, higher-quality lithic materials were generally also found on components, particularly after Period 1. However, these materials do not always originate from the closest of the five main sources, nor do they show distance decay in forms we would expect. In fact, high-quality Labrador Trough cherts, situated close to the study region, were virtually ignored. Most important, the patterns of lithic use cannot possibly be the result of a group traveling directly to each source area or the result of embedded procurement, as the distances involved are well beyond the range of even highly mobile groups. In other words, the complexity observed in the archaeological assemblages exceeds what one would expect if external constraints alone were dictating lithic procurement and use.

The presence of nonlocal, high-quality lithic materials on sites in the central interior of Quebec is clearly not related to a scarcity of locally available stone, nor to the consistent procurement of fine-grained stone from the closest source locale. Rather, a system involving both direct procurement and exchange was no doubt used to ensure a supply of specific toolstone as a matter of preference and choice. In the paragraphs that follow, I consider possible cultural, social, and spiritual practices that may have structured these choices.

Complex Social Networks

At the onset, when patterns of lithic procurement are considered in the context of habitation and hearth features—such as the presence of shaputuans containing multiple or elongated hearths—it becomes apparent that interaction increased across the study region about two thousand years ago at the start of the Recent period. A further jump in the number of these distinctive house and hearth features, combined with the presence on individual sites of lithics from across the peninsula, can be noted about thirteen hundred years ago, and then again seven hundred years ago, at which point the rise in site numbers suggests an actual population increase or a marked intensification in the use of the interior Eastern Subarctic. During this time period and into the proto-historic period, the largest habitation features frequently contain mixes of at least four fine-grained lithic materials, indicating connections with all parts of the Quebec-Labrador peninsula.

How then can we explain the complex patterns of lithic use apparent on sites in northern Quebec, as well as the appearance and increased numbers of elongated houses? Eastern Subarctic ethnohistory offers some clues. Mailhot's (1997) research on Innu history and genealogy contains detailed accounts and life histories provided by Innu people living on the Quebec North Shore and in Labrador. Based on this work, Mailhot developed the concept of "structured mobility" to describe the ancient pattern of Innu travel and interaction. She explains that the Innu place a high value on extensive knowledge of the land, but remarks that this mobility is not unrestricted, and individual move-ments are not random. Rather, they are patterned after complex social networks: "Their attention is drawn mainly to the horizontal axis of their genealogies, . . . members of the same generation. Because of their prodigious horizontal memory, they can retrace multitudes of remote genealogical connections—remote in geographical as well as genealogical terms. The Innu kinship system is the projection, so to speak, of their preoccupation with territory into the field of social relations" (Mailhot 1997:113–114).

I would like to suggest that sometime around 1300 BP, though possi-bly earlier, we see the emergence of a complex and wide-reaching social network similar to the one described by the Innu. A heuristic model based on concepts from complexity theory enables us to visualize this network as a vast web comprising hubs, clusters, and links that span the Eastern Subarctic and, in some places, reach beyond.

The static historic models that have dominated our understand-ing of hunter-gatherer social dynamics in the region—like the familiar depiction of northern bands by Speck (1931)—should be understood as "snapshots taken during an ongoing process" (Watts 2003:55). The same can be said of recent reincarnations drawn from central place theory, such as Whallon's (2006:266–277) heuristic model "constructed under the idealized assumptions of hexagonal packing of spatial units, or territories, over a perfect, uniform plane."

In contrast, the model I am proposing can be thought of as an organic structure, a "self-constituting system," which emerged, grew, and changed over time (Watts 2003:16). The "hubs" were most likely well-connected individuals—good hunters, shamans, healers—whether male or female, who traveled widely, who counted many people as their kin, and who were knowledgeable about the ways of humans, animals, and spirits. At various times, groups gathered around them to hunt together and to share. The development of elaborate food conservation techniques, documented for the Recent prehistoric and historic periods (Pintal 2003; Stopp 2002), would have facilitated the travel involved in such visits and the time invested in constructing large communal dwellings.

At present, it is not clear why such a network would have emerged around thirteen hundred years ago, though there are numerous factors that solely or in unison might have served as a "tipping point." Pollen records show a cooling period around this time, accompanied by a change in the forest fire regime. This change opened up the landscape and may have led to an increase in caribou numbers (Asselin and Payette 2005). The introduction of the bow and arrow might have changed and improved hunting techniques (Erwin et al. 2005). Archaeological evidence and oral history accounts indicate that Iroquois groups moved along the North Shore and penetrated the northern interior, while Paleo-Eskimo populations on both the western and eastern coasts of the peninsula expanded their territories southward. Aboriginal groups may have turned to the interior for safety and unimpeded hunting (Martijn 1990; Turner 1894). Finally, in the late fifteenth century, Europeans first arrived in the Gulf of St. Lawrence, releasing a ripple of change through populations in the region.

Culturally Motivated Procurement

While explanations for changes in lithic procurement remain open to debate, ethnographic sources can provide insights into practices that might underlie specific lithic choices and the distinctive house styles in which these toolstones are found. Until recently, survival in the Eastern Subarctic depended wholly on the success of the hunt. Not surprisingly, the worldview associated with the Cree, Innu, and Naskapi way of life—what Feit (1995:182) has termed a "culturally distinct science"—is a rich and complex web of knowledge, beliefs, and gestures. Hunting can be seen as a ritual cycle with three phases of rites: divination, which involves gathering information; capture and showing respect for animals killed; and sharing or reciprocity. The outcome of a hunting activity is never the result of chance. The hunter goes through a process of finding indications of possible encounters with animals. If the hunt is successful, an animal is given to a hunter, thereby fulfilling his anticipation (Feit 1973, 1995). These fundamental beliefs about hunting are documented back to the early historic period and no doubt had existed for thousands of years previous to this as part of a worldview shaped by shamanism.

Tanner's (1979) seminal research on the Mistassini Cree affords a particularly detailed and nuanced overview of hunting ideology. This work shows clearly how Eastern Subarctic hunters are guided by an intellectual tradition built on a complex interplay of "common sense thought" (i.e., practical knowledge and understanding that inform all decisions) and "motivated religious thought" (i.e., the rites, religious beliefs, and cosmological narratives that shape their worldview) (Tanner 1979:207). Where one approach ends and the other begins is not always obvious. Moreover, the two approaches to hunting and to life in general frequently operate in tandem, whereby various practical decisions and tasks are accompanied by a parallel process of ritual activities. As Brody (2000:267) explained, "these are societies where refusal of rigid boundaries between any categories—whether between humans and animals, men and women, or the natural and supernatural—has been integral to a way of being in the world. For hunter-gatherers, people's knowledge, health and even survival have depended on being able to move from one kind of reality to another."

Could the operation of such beliefs in the prehistoric period account for some of the lithic patterns observed in the sample of archaeological sites from northern Quebec? As information gathering was a critical part of divination and the interpretation of divinatory signs was a skill that had to be developed and nurtured, it stands to reason that individuals who

traveled widely and maintained far-reaching social networks might also
have been the best equipped to interpret "signs" and dreams. Whether
information about the activities of game animals came to them through
practical observation or via their ability to recognize and access messages
from the spirit world, those people who saw, heard, and experienced the
largest possible range of landscapes (physical, social, and spiritual) would
have been at the forefront of knowledge acquisition. And what better
way to know this world than to travel to its extremities and to have and
use stone materials that came from those boundaries? Perhaps some fine-
grained lithic materials traversed the peninsula in just this manner. In
fact, each of the lithic varieties under study can be interpreted as coming
from a different "boundary" of the Cree, Innu, and Naskapi world.

Procurement of Ramah chert, in particular, would have entailed
an arduous trip to a dangerous mountain range in northern Labrador,
situated in a region periodically occupied by Inuit. The locale itself is
visually impressive. The sheer cliffs of the Torngat Mountains are inter-
sected with gleaming Ramah chert beds, and one must climb through
a red, iron-stained creek in order to arrive at the quarry zone where the
chert is most accessible (Loring 2002:184).

An early historic period account may provide a written clue to the
deep significance of Ramah chert within Aboriginal belief systems.
In 1575, France's royal cartographer, André Thevet, wrote *La Cosmogra-
phie Universelle*, a book about the discovery and exploration of the "New
World," which included information gathered from Jacques Cartier and
other mariners. In it Thevet stated:

> Moreover in Canada and the neighboring countries are found jasper
> and chalcedony in great abundance. And there is a mountain there
> which the natives call *Quea*, which means [smoke[1]] (because from this
> mountain one sees ordinarily and continually smoke come forth),
> and it is some eight and one-half leagues distance from the *Hochelaga*
> River. In this mountain are found stones which occur naturally in the
> rock, gleaming with the color of the sky, which the savages call *Quan-
> hia*[2] and the natives of Newfoundland *Kyph* because of its brightness.
> (Schlesinger and Stabler 1986:52)

Thevet's mountain has never been identified. Nevertheless, the Aboriginal people he mentioned were almost certainly Innu and Beothuk,

therefore it is very tempting to speculate that he was, in fact, describing Ramah chert (McCaffrey 1989b:95). The connection with smoke, a spiritual substance that rises into the sky taking with it messages for the upper world, suggests that for Eastern Subarctic hunters, Ramah chert may have served as a vehicle through which the world of spirits became accessible to those skilled in this communication.

Mistassini quartzite also has striking optical properties. Although the stone can occur in a range of colors, much of the Mistassini quartzite recovered on archaeological sites is snow white with a brilliant sheen, suggesting that flintknappers specifically sought out stone with these characteristics. Once again, there exists an early written account to confirm its significance. In 1730, the Jesuit missionary Father Pierre Laure visited a cave at the source, which he named the "Ante de Marbre" (the marble antechamber):

> The most remarkable of all the curiosities to be seen in these woods, in the direction of Nemiskau, is a cave of white marble, which looks as if an artisan had carved and polished it. . . . [T]he savages think that it is a house of prayer and council, wherein the spirits assemble. Therefore all do not take the liberty of entering it; but the jugglers who are, as it were, their priests, go there in passing to consult their oracles. (Thwaites 1896–1901, 68:48; cited in Martijn and Rogers 1969:193–194)

Although the three remaining fine-grained lithic materials are not remarkable for either their color or translucent properties, they do originate in significant locations. Labrador Trough chert formations roughly follow the height of land where watersheds emerge and river basins abut. From the Trough, one can choose to travel major river routes east to the Labrador coast, north to Ungava Bay, west to James Bay, or south to the North Shore. Both Nastapoka chert and Hudson Bay Lowland chert come from coastal boundaries that could conceivably have been seen as places situated between land and sea. They may also have been sites of cultural encounter—the former material was well known to Inuit knappers, while the latter was used by Algonquian groups on the western James Bay coast.

Archaeologists working farther afield have speculated that, in some instances, the movement of distinctive materials and the concomitant assumption of long-distance travel by individuals may reflect the operation of shamanistic beliefs (e.g., Saunders 1999). Perhaps specific stone sources in the Eastern Subarctic—whether located amid mountainous cliffs, near caves, or within tidal ranges on the seacoast—were thought to be situated at spiritual boundaries. Did individuals acquire knowledge, status, and ultimately, power by traveling to these sources and bringing back stone from realms that were both physically dangerous and spiritually charged? Were these localities that evoked entire worlds of meaning and prompted transformations (Basso 1996:5)? Of significance is the observation by Mailhot (1997:177) that "in the speech of the Sheshatshit [Innu] people the idea of 'knowing' is closely related to that of 'seeing.' To say, 'I know this person or that place,' one says literally 'I have seen this person or that place.'"

Sharing with Neighbors, Spirits, and Ancestors

Contemporary descriptions of elongated houses suggest that an important reason for their construction was to facilitate processing the meat, hides, and antlers of large numbers of caribou. Cree trapper Fred Georgekish (1979:20–22) explained that when people were out caribou hunting, "this was the type of house they constructed because it could hold 40 caribou on the racks. The three hearths were convenient for drying the meat. Sometimes, during a long caribou hunt, the women would follow the men's trail and they would erect this type of structure near the kill so the carcasses would not be carried any great distance." Georgekish also indicated that elongated houses, some large enough to hold ten families, were built when many people wanted to stay together or needed to hold meetings.

Historic accounts imply that one of the main reasons for building a shaputuan was in order to hold a feast, thereby formalizing "the ideological expression of the proper final disposition of game" (Tanner 1979:153). The "ceremonialized group-sharing of food" was an integral part of Cree, Innu, and Naskapi life (Tanner 1979:170). One type of feast in particular—the *makusaanu* (in Cree), or *makushan* (in Innu)—is directly associated with hunting. The makushan involves the preparation, sharing, and eating of animal fat, often but not exclusively from caribou and usually but not always within a shaputuan. The cooking methods used are designed to preserve the animal fat in a solid state or to allow it to be collected and served separately. Bone marrow extracted from the long bones of caribou and turned into solid cakes was particularly prized both as a delicacy and as a substance imbued with symbolic potency (Tanner 1979:168).

Sharing and gift-giving in the Eastern Subarctic extended well beyond consumables, reflecting the basic interdependence of individuals and hunting groups. As Henriksen (1973:27) observed, "the children are taught to give away things they value to other children who want them." The result of this upbringing is evident in the following account from the 1920s:

> What in fact takes place is a redistribution that leads to a leveling of supplies. It starts with people visiting one another in their spare time soon after a camp has been established, and openly examining their hosts' supply of goods. Even if the visitor's own supply is not exhausted, he can make demands on other people's goods. If he sees that his host has more of a particular item than he, he will not hesitate to ask for some of it. Consequently, within a short time every household has about the same amount of each article. (Henriksen 1973:33)

At the conclusion of a successful hunt, sharing also took place between members of the hunting group and the spirits of those who had assisted them, be they animal masters, spirit helpers, or ancestors. This was manifest by burning offerings of food and other materials (Henriksen 2009:115–118). Tanner (1979:161) was not able to obtain from his informants a clear idea of who was intended to receive the offerings thrown into the fire, though the generally agreed purpose was to improve hunting success in the future. "Specific persons or spirits who received the offerings were usually spoken of as *cumusum* ('your grandfather') a general term of respect applied to several spirits . . . the bear, *Mistaapew*, the spirit of the 'outside' (*wiiwiitimiskew*), the master of the animal that was being eaten, and the spirit of the old man who no longer went hunting but lived in Mistassini Post" (Tanner 1979:161).

Within this worldview all things (winds, water, animals, stones) were thought to be alive and to have a spirit. While among the Montagnais (Innu) in 1634, the Jesuit Father Paul Le Jeune (Thwaites 1896–1901,

6:175–177) described this belief as follows: they "persuade themselves that not only men and other animals, but also all other things, are endowed with souls, and that all the souls are immortal; they imagine the souls as shadows of the animate objects. . . . Hence this is the reason that they say the souls drink and eat, and therefore they give them food when any one dies, throwing the best meat they have into the fire." Turner (1894) observed the same phenomenon while living among the Naskapi in Kujjuuak (formerly Fort Chimo) in the late nineteenth century.

As noted earlier, projectile points were recovered from some of the hearths in elongated houses in the study region. Were stone tools put in hearths as offerings to animal spirits in gratitude for a successful hunt? We might even ponder whether tools of specific materials were placed in fires as offerings or gifts for deceased hunters who came from regions associated with certain varieties of stone. Ancestral hunters may have required these tools to carry on their hunting activities, as suggested by the following response given to Father Le Jeune when he questioned why objects were placed in graves with the deceased. "They hunt for the souls of Beavers, Porcupines, Moose, and other animals, using the soul of the snowshoes to walk upon the soul of the snow, which is in yonder country; in short, they make use of the souls of all things, as we here use the things themselves" (Thwaites 1896–1901, 6:179).

Although these ideas will have to remain speculative for the time being, ethnohistorical accounts provide compelling analogies to explain the apparently intentional placement of still-usable lithic tools in hearths.

Conclusion

There is little doubt that the unique and challenging Eastern Subarctic environment has always played an important role in shaping the possibilities, choices, outlooks, and outcomes of the hunter-gatherer societies who lived there. Yet, historical and contemporary accounts show us that woven through the cycles of resource availability and seasonal movements are the threads that bind these people together— a common language and shared names for places on the land; kinship ties and hunting partnerships; knowledge of how to find, harvest, and best use animal and plant resources; an understanding of the universe and spirit world; and a shared sense of belonging to a distinct people and place.

We have seen that during the Recent prehistoric period the use of elongated houses increased and was associated with the co-occurrence of lithic materials from divergent parts of the Quebec-Labrador peninsula. Moreover, in some instances, stone tools appear to have been discarded or intentionally placed in hearths. This pattern suggests that with the emergence of an extensive social network came practices that did more than serve as a "safety net" and as a means to exchange information for people living in an "ambiguous" environment. As Jordan (2003:xiii) has argued, "Artefacts deposited at sites store up, as residues of communication, the symbolism that the place, image or artefact has carried on the wider mobile round. Places derive their meanings from their context in the landscape—more importantly, from their context in the biographies of communities inhabiting those landscapes." The Eastern Subarctic was a landscape where high levels of personal autonomy were required and large distances might separate groups for long periods of the year. The data presented in this chapter suggest that elongated houses emerged as "places" where social memory was created and renewed, where the living, ancestors, and spirits came together and reenacted the core elements of a shared ideology. I would argue that the patterns of lithic materials observed during the Recent period give archaeological visibility to this social network and to the beliefs that held it together.

Acknowledgments

The research presented in this chapter was made possible through the efforts of archaeologists who directed major survey, excavation, and analysis projects in northern Quebec, particularly David Denton, Daniel Chevrier, and Jocelyn Seguin. I have also benefited from discussions with José Mailhot and Jean-Yves Pintal, who have always been willing to share insights and ideas. Roger Martin and Marc Trudeau provided critical assistance in designing the database and graphs used in a larger study. Finally, I would like to thank editors Ken Sassaman and Don Holly, as well as the other volume contributors, who participated in the Amerind Foundation seminar and provided valuable feedback and comments on earlier drafts of this chapter.

Notes

1. In Thevet's book, this word is "woman" rather than "smoke." However, as Schlesinger and Stabler (1986:52) explain, "here is a clear case of a misreading of Thevet's manuscript by the typographer. *Quea*, according to the Cartier-Ramusio vocabulary, means smoke (*fumée*), which the typographer misread as *femme*, or woman. This was an easy mistake to make, since the acute accent mark was usually used only over a final "e" by Thevet and most French Renaissance writers."

2. *Quenhia* (sky) appears in the Cartier-Ramusio vocabulary.

9

Mobility as Resistance

Colonialism among Nomadic Hunter-Gatherers in the American West

Laura L. Scheiber and Judson Byrd Finley

> Here we found a few Snake Indians comprising 6 men, 7 women,
> and 8 or 10 children who were the only Inhabitants of this lonely
> and secluded spot. They were all neatly clothed in dressed deer
> and Sheep skins of the best quality and seemed to be perfectly
> contented and happy. They were rather surprised at our approach
> and retreated to the heights where they might have a view of us
> without apprehending any danger.
> —Russell 1955[1914]:26, as recorded in 1835

On the Road

In this chapter, we discuss material and social effects of colonialism among mobile hunter-gatherers living in the northwestern Plains and central Rocky Mountains, highlighting recent research in the Greater Yellowstone Ecosystem (GYE). As the title of this chapter suggests, our research has led us to explore the juncture of two major themes in contemporary archaeology: one is the study of mobility among hunter-gatherers, and the other is the study of colonialism and resistance. These major structural metaphors function not just within the discipline of anthropology but more broadly as symbols of the western frontier in American mythology and history.

Although archaeologists increasingly study the material and social impacts of colonialism among indigenous populations (Cusick 1998; Lightfoot 2005; Lyons and Papadopoulos 2002; Scheiber and Mitchell 2010; Stein 2005), work on colonial period hunter-gatherers (especially highly mobile ones) is more likely to come from ethnohistorians and cultural anthropologists. When we first conceived of the title, we considered our work to be unique in this regard. However, in 1993 Timothy Cress-well published a paper in *Transactions of the British Institute of Geographers* with the same name (Mobility as Resistance). In his article, Cress-well draws attention to the way that author Jack Kerouac uses mobility as a symbol of counter-culture resistance to 1950s America in the novel *On the Road*. Although distant in some ways from an archaeological study of nineteenth-century mobile hunter-gatherers, we find that these concepts from cultural geography are particularly salient for our study, and we have incorporated them in our analysis.

The setting for this study is the Absaroka Mountains, an area of generally high elevation in western Wyoming with numerous moun-tain ranges and broad desert basins that was the last colonial frontier of the conterminous United States. Indigenous nineteenth-century occupants—variously called Mountain Shoshone, Sheepeaters, and Snakes—are often portrayed as faceless hunter-gatherers who have been relegated to a minor role in the annals of history. Eyewitness and other written depictions of indigenous Mountain Shoshone are uninforma-tive, and they leave persistent, inaccurate images of contact period Native life (Hughes 2000), with labels such as destitute and harm-less (Norris 1881:35), and shy, secretive, and solitary (Irving 1910:237). Archaeological evidence from postcontact campsites reveals a very dif-ferent story. The sites are few in number but contain the material record of nineteenth-century domestic life, otherwise untold in local and global histories (Wylie 1993).

We view the central Rocky Mountains and the Greater Yellowstone Ecosystem as one of the last potential Native strongholds in the heart of the American West. We question whether mountains and mountain mobility became a means of resistance to colonialism and postcolonial reservation life and consider whether changes in mobility may relate to the development of ethnic band divisions following the intensification of sheep hunting in the mountains and buffalo hunting in the basins and plains sometime in the eighteenth and nineteenth centuries. We view postcontact changes in mobility as a response to American settlement during the early nineteenth century having specific, measurable material manifestations. We investigate multiscalar forms of resistance, ranging from broad patterns of land use and resource procurement to campsite spatial layouts and technological choices (Scheiber and Finley 2010).

In this chapter, we consider three material data sets. First, we model the landscape in which and through which these people traveled in a geographic information system (GIS) to illustrate the limitations to mobility in this environment. Next we focus on both obsidian and ceramic sourcing studies as direct evidence for changes in mobility strategies. We suggest that Mountain Shoshone mobility was not reduced but simply changed during postcontact times. Shoshone Indians continued (and continue) to use the mountains in new and traditional ways to satisfy both subsistence and ceremonial pursuits.

Structural Metaphors

Mobility is one of the primary and distinguishing characteristics of hunter-gatherer societies (Kelly 1995; Lee and Daly 1999b), although some hunter-gatherers are and were more sedentary than others (see examples from the West Coast and the Southeast by Lightfoot, Sassaman, Randall, and Kidder, this vol.). Settlement pattern research and studies of foraging strategies remain a dominant research topic in contemporary archaeology (Barnard 2004a; Binford 2001; Shennan 2003). Considering mobility within the realm of a wider hunter-gatherer social geography has also gained scholarly attention during the last several decades (Bird-David 1990; Conkey 2001; Ingold 1999; Ingold et al. 1991). Despite years of debate as to a definitive hunter-gatherer as well as a series of revisionist analyses of the role of outsiders in forming their identities (Miracle and Fisher 1991; Wilmsen 1989), many agree that some degree of movement remains key.

One of the oft-quoted characteristics of mobile groups is that they "vote with their feet" in order to resolve conflict (Lee 2006), that is, they move somewhere else in opposition to stress. We think researchers actually admire the ability of hunter-gatherers to do this, and in some ways they bestow our own American ideals of the symbolic value of mobility to these groups. The concept of mobility is influential as an American hallmark. It is a valued commodity closely connected with equally symbol-laden concepts of freedom and choice. The irony of this parallel is that research giving priority to economic values such as caloric return rates strips nomadic people of inherently active choices in deciding how and why to move from place to place. Indeed, if we accept Wendrich and Barnard's (2008:5) definition of mobility as "the capacity and need for movement from place to place," then we are forced to consider what happens when the need to move is constrained by external forces. This leads us to consider the role of resistance in mobility studies.

Equally valuable to the field of anthropology is the study of resistance and domination, especially in archaeological studies of social inequality and colonialism. Resistance to colonial oppression is seen as a key indigenous response, and studies of Native resistance have remained common since the early 1990s (Deagan 1990; Ferguson 1991; Mills 2002; Paynter and McGuire 1991; Prince 2002). Archaeologists acknowledge a variety of material manifestations of resistance, ranging from tool types and pottery decorations to architectural design and community organization. Recently, Silliman (2009) advocated an approach that emphasizes "residence over resistance" based in part on his work on the Eastern Pequot Reservation in Connecticut. A refocus on residence emphasizes survival and agency in day-to-day actions. That is, resistance is experienced through residing in traditional homelands. We argue that archaeologists also value resistance as a core American principle, harkening back to the first American colonies and the overthrow of British colonial control.

Although archaeologists have studied resistance particularly by sedentary societies, ethnographers of contemporary hunter-gatherers have considered hunter-gatherer resistance vis-à-vis interactions with their neighbors for the last several decades. Hunter-gatherers throughout the world experienced much more interaction with other groups (hunter-gatherers, farmers, pastoralists, nation-states) than anthropologists traditionally acknowledged. In some areas, foraging and farming coexisted for over a thousand years (Layton 2001; Zvelebil 1998). Just because hunter-gatherer societies came into contact with others, they did not then become the others themselves, in part because of social organization and value systems based on egalitarianism and sharing (Barnard 2004a). Some groups believe that sharing is why the environment continues to give food to people (Bird-David 1990). We could say that some hunter-gatherers resist giving up their mobility because of an underlying ethos of movement (Sassaman 2001).

Frontiers, Resistance, and Ethnogenesis

As important as the concepts of mobility and resistance have been within their respective spheres of archaeology, linkages between them have not necessarily been forthcoming (but see Sassaman 2001). Very few archaeological studies of New World mobile hunter-gatherers in colonial contexts exist (but see Harrison 2002; Harrison and Williamson 2004; Murray 2004; Paterson 2008; Schrire 1995 for examples from Australia and South Africa). Perhaps this gap exists because the topic has been so well studied by ethnohistorians and ethnographers (Sahlins 1972). Or perhaps culture change sustained by these groups makes them less likely to be selected as models of nomadism by archaeologists focused on finding so-called pristine societies with broad cross-cultural comparability.

The concept of pristine, unaltered, or unaffected societies is particularly problematic and has been explored in some detail within the context of hunter-gatherer revisionism. All groups are affected by contact with others (Headland and Reid 1989; Layton 2001; Spielmann and Eder 1994). Still, the notion that culture change associated with colonialism forever damages an original condition remains tacit in anthropological literature. These societies, especially in North America, are thus poor candidates for studying hunter-gatherers globally, or so the argument follows. Additionally, nomadic people often leave behind ephemeral sites that are particularly difficult to identify in archaeological contexts, so that the available data about their daily lives are limited.

Mobility is also a key concept in American mythology, imperialism, and Manifest Destiny. Frederick Jackson Turner (1962[1920]) coined the term "frontier hypothesis" to discuss the western advancement of American settlement, which continues to influence historical frontier research today. The frontier hypothesis states that the character of American society was heavily influenced by what happened in frontiers at the borders of civilization. According to Turner, frontiers are zones where the disaffected go to pursue alternative activities, sometimes changing their cultural ways of life in pursuit of new practices. Cusick (2000:48) defines a cultural borderland as a corridor between two expanding states, and a periphery as settlement on the edge of society. Frontier research in archaeology has been applied to both cultural borderlands and peripheries (Aron 2006; DeAtley and Findlow 1984; Donnan and Wilson 1994; Green and Perlman 1985; Klein 1997; Lightfoot and Martinez 1995; Rice 1998; Staski 2004; Usman 2004).

The concept of the American frontier, which encapsulates both traditions of mobility and resistance, is nowhere more present than in the

American West. Nomadic Indian occupants of the plains and mountains who found themselves living on French, Spanish, British, and American frontiers were able to resist some colonial powers and pressures in ways that Native peoples on the coasts or more populated areas, for example, could not. This ability was in part a product of their mobile lifestyles, made more mobile by the introduction of the horse in the early 1700s.

Early anthropological studies assumed that culture change was inevitable in contact situations, but archaeologists have demonstrated that indigenous people resisted colonial domination in social, economic, political, and material realms, in both active and passive ways (Ferguson 1992; Jackson and Castillo 1995; Paynter and McGuire 1991; Scham 2001). Resistance to outside pressures and residence in the frontier may have contributed to processes of ethnogenesis as hunter-gatherer groups forged new identities in association with migration to new places.

Most inhabitants of the plains and mountains underwent significant cultural transformations between the seventeenth and nineteenth centuries, sometimes bringing together formerly disparate bands and clans to forge new identities and sometimes specializing in specific resources as a means of establishing unique cultural strategies. Early ethnographers working in the twentieth century tend to portray these nomads in a timeless past that we know does not reflect the active and complex social changes that occurred in the centuries prior to written accounts. Our study adds data from everyday experiences at actual sites abandoned by people who witnessed this change. These materials and locations tell stories independent of the ones remembered one hundred years later. This research also contributes to a growing archaeological literature on culture change and colonialism in nineteenth-century Native America (Lightfoot 1995; Mitchell and Scheiber 2010; Silliman 2009), one that tries to break down artificial divisions between prehistory and history.

Mountain Shoshone in the Greater Yellowstone Ecosystem

The length of indigenous occupations of the Greater Yellowstone Ecosystem and by whom are debated topics involving contributions from historians, anthropologists, and archaeologists. Historically, the Shoshone

Figure 9.1. A Shoshone encampment in the foothills of the Wind River Mountains in Wyoming, 1870. (Photograph by William Henry Jackson; Library of Congress, LC-USZ62-115466)

were one of a few tribes that claimed rights to the GYE and are one of only two tribes permanently settled on reservations in the area (Shimkin 1986; Trenholm and Carley 1964). The creation of the Eastern or Wind River Shoshone is a historic phenomenon that is in part a product of the intense sociopolitical reorganizations and ethnogenetic negotiations surrounding contact between Indians and Europeans in the late eighteenth and early nineteenth centuries (fig. 9.1) (Stamm 1999). Several bands came together to form the Wind River Reservation in 1868, including people who regularly occupied the mountains, basins, and plains of western Wyoming and adjacent states. We could call these groups Plains and Mountain Shoshone, realizing that these terms are more convenient and geographical than solidified and separate band designations. Prior to that time, Plains Shoshone (i.e., Buffalo Eaters, or *Kukundika*) bands were horse nomads actively engaged in trade with American settlers. The Mountain Shoshone (i.e., Sheepeaters, or *Tukudika*) bands occupied the remote reaches of the Absaroka and Wind River Mountains taking a more reserved and guarded approach to social interactions with fur trappers, explorers, and immigrants (Hultkrantz 1961). We do not know to what extent these band divisions existed prior to the late eighteenth century, but we believe those social distinctions became more pronounced as contact intensified.

Mountain Shoshone archaeology is central to this study. We consider Mountain Shoshone history and ethnicity to be intermeshed with identities gained from living in a high-altitude mountain landscape. Mountains are symbolic loci of social identity but are also key to resistance and may have had dual effects on indigenous people. The Rocky Mountains are a natural fortress and were one of the last Native North American strongholds. Not until the last two decades of the nineteenth century and into the twentieth century was this area permanently settled by ranchers, due to what was conceived as an inhospitable environment. For instance, the town of Cody, Wyoming, was not incorporated until 1902.

Prior to that time, trappers, fur traders, lumberjacks, and cowboys (from many Indian and European nations) started moving into northwestern Wyoming and adjacent areas. In fact, the mythology of western expansion is gold cast by stories such as Sacagawea (herself a Lemhi Mountain Shoshone) leading the Lewis and Clark expedition through the Rocky Mountains. Native and Euroamerican encroachment into mountain territories undoubtedly affected the indigenous inhabitants. Circumscription to mountainous environments may have changed subsistence strategies that included intensified use of preexisting resources such as bighorn sheep, lithics, and clays. At the same time, resistance based on mountain isolation may have made possible syncretic use of aboriginal and introduced technologies in a way that allowed maintenance and persistence of social identities. The relationships between these social issues and materiality of daily lived experiences are the focus of our archaeological research.

Sites across the region dating between about AD 1300 and 1800 provide evidence for a well-defined set of material attributes that includes tri-notched and triangular projectile points, a distinct form of Shoshone knife, Intermountain Ware ceramics, steatite vessels, sheep and antelope traps, cribbed log structures, conical pole lodges (often called wicki-ups), and Dinwoody rock art (Larson and Kornfeld 1994). One unique facet of Mountain Shoshone archaeology is extensive wooden and stone hunting features used to trap and kill bighorn sheep (fig. 9.2). Most features date to circa AD 1800 (Frison 1987, 1991; Frison et al. 1990) and may be an indicator of intensification of high-altitude resources. Nowhere are these attributes better expressed than in the mountainous reaches of the GYE where they have been attributed to the Sheepeaters or Mountain Shoshone (Dominick 1964). While Julian Steward (1938) was among the first to associate Shoshone ethnic divisions with staple food resources, Swedish ethnographer Åke Hultkrantz (1957, 1979) was responsible for embedding the notion of Sheepeaters into the common knowledge and lore of Yellowstone National Park and the area's indigenous occupants. Hultkrantz writes that all Shoshone bands were involved in some way in the fur trade, which effectively ended in the 1840s. Yellowstone National Park was established in 1872, and the story of Indian occupations in and around the park was effectively countered by the narrative of a mythical untamed wilderness that was unmodified by prior human occupations (Nabokov and Loendorf 2004). This narrative is not unique to Yellowstone, but was one of the means for nineteenth-century governmental officials and conservationists to "naturalize" places in order to convince a skeptical American public that saving the forests should be a national concern during a time of unchecked industrial expansion (Reiger 2001)(see Hull, this vol., for comparisons in Yosemite National Park).

The extent to which a unique Mountain Shoshone identity existed prior to contact is debatable. Some archaeologists argue that a distinct Mountain Shoshone lifeway focused on bighorn sheep hunting and other montane resources existed for millennia (Francis and Loendorf 2002; Holmer 1994; Husted 1995; Loendorf and Stone 2006; Nabokov and Loendorf 2004; Swanson and Bryan 1964), while others argue for a relatively recent genesis (Butler 1978; Wright 1978). Regardless of the timing of occupation, the Rocky Mountains are a key source of social identity. Although many modern Americans value mountains for their stunning beauty and pristine isolation, the wilderness reality dictates a special set of subsistence and settlement strategies that lend themselves

Figure 9.2. A sheep-trap catch pen at Indian Ridge in Wyoming. (Photograph by Laura L. Scheiber)

to the development of a unique social identity of "mountain people" (Foster 1988; Keefe 2000; Nagel 1998).

Exploring Mountain Landscapes

One of our hypotheses is that people identified as Snakes, Shoshones, and Sheepeaters in early American literature used mountains as places of refuge and safety from others. Some early travelers and writers describe these people as renegades and outlaws, driven to the mountains by militaristic lowlanders (Clayton 1926; Nabokov and Loendorf 2004; Sheridan 1882). Although we do not think "renegade" is the most appropriate term, we do see merit in the idea that people either retreated or more accurately *chose* to remove themselves from certain situations and contacts by occupying high-altitude places:

> Notwithstanding the savage and almost inaccessible nature of these mountains, they have their inhabitants. As one of the [Bonneville] party was out hunting, he came upon the track of a man in a lonely valley. Following it up, he reached the brow of a cliff, whence he beheld three . . . running across the valley below him. He fired his gun to call their attention, hoping to induce them to turn back. They only fled the faster, and disappeared among the rocks. (Irving 1837:192–193)

At elevations between 7,000 and 12,000 feet above sea level, the rugged terrain of the Absaroka Mountains in the eastern GYE structures the nature of Native mobility. Because of the rough terrain and remote nature of this area in the eyes of contemporary wilderness travelers, we view the mountains as central to resistance to colonial pressures. To date only a handful of postcontact archaeological sites have been positively identified. This is in part due to the imprecise nature of dating the sites. If metal or glass are not identified in assemblages, these sites are rendered invisible on the historic landscape, and categorized as Late Prehistoric. But we know not all people had access to nor chose to use European-manufactured goods even after they were present in local areas. This is a chronological and temporal issue that will require further consideration.

Similarly, conducting archaeological research in the mountains to locate additional sites is difficult, due to field logistics and site visibility.

Many sites are buried under several hundred years of pine needles. One consequence of the federal fire suppression policy, increased drought conditions, and pine beetle infestation of mature tree stands is that lightening strikes are likely to burn several thousand hectares of forest every summer. The fires expose archaeological sites in the mountains that we did not know existed before. We are targeting both burned and unburned parts of the forest for further survey, guided by assumptions about the ways people would have moved in and through these areas in the past. We can document more sites with new technological advances for spatializing landscapes.

Our research is based on the assumption that people favor certain factors of the natural environment in their settlement choices. We model the human landscape in a GIS environment as a tool to refine our approach to archaeological survey. With GIS we can calculate various least-cost travel corridors that incorporate many data sets. Human mobility, particularly foot travel with families and households, is particularly constrained by slope. Particular drainages are key travel routes, and few mountain passes exist even today. Thus identifying these pathways is critical for predicting the location of potential contact period archaeological sites. We are using the spatial distribution of known sites in the area as a basis for finding similar, undocumented sites. These are important starting points for accessing wilderness land-use strategies and to construct archaeological survey designs. We start with natural and geological features such as bedrock, slope, precipitation, and sheep habitat to develop predictions of likely site locations (Nicholson et al. 2008).

In 1837, while camping with a group of Sheepeaters in our study area, Osborne Russell recorded that "One of them drew a map of the country around us on a white Elk Skin with a piece of charcoal after which he explained the direction of the different passes, streams, Etc." (Russell 1955[1914]:27). This act reminds us that we should also consider additional, perhaps more emic assessments of land use. For instance, anthropologist D. B. Shimkin recorded Shoshone place names and traditional medicinal and food resource maps when he conducted fieldwork among the Wind River Shoshones in 1937 and 1938. Shimkin (1947) shows trails that ran through the area under investigation, still important when he recorded them in the middle of the twentieth century. In the next stage, we may also consider other factors, which we might call "viewsheds of resistance." Spatially modeling resistance may include variables such as surveillance, interstitial spaces of invisibility, wind patterns, and sound patterns. We hope to incorporate these other kinds of data into our GIS model as well.

Obsidian Source Analysis

In the culture contact literature, the introduction and adoption of European-manufactured materials by Native people have received much attention. With the availability of metal arrowheads and firearms, in addition to horses, people experimented with new hunting practices and new technologies, and sometimes new forms of interpersonal conflict. Native peoples continued to use stone tools even after other materials were available (Cobb 2003; Rodríguez-Alegría 2008), and this is true in western Wyoming through the nineteenth century. When Osborne Russell encountered unmounted Shoshones in what is now Yellowstone Park in 1835, they were using obsidian-pointed arrows, bows decorated with quills (not beads), and stone pots. The Shoshones traded animal furs for awls, axes, kettles, tobacco, and ammunition (Russell 1955[1914]:26). Although they were not using the objects associated with contact, the fact that they were carrying furs for trade suggests that they were already affected by it.

With all of the rubric and focus on stone-to-steel transitions, understanding how access to traditional stone sources may have changed is key to considering issues of mobility and resistance (Scheiber and Finley 2011; Silliman 2003, 2005). Obsidian is a common lithic raw material type in the study area that provides important insights regarding diachronic changes in mobility or exchange (Eerkens et al. 2008; Lyons et al. 2001). Chemically distinct obsidian sources are available in southeastern Idaho, northeastern Idaho, Jackson Hole (Wyoming), and Yellowstone National Park. In another study, we assembled a data set of nearly 2,300 sourced obsidian artifacts from western Wyoming, eastern Idaho, and southwestern Montana, including more than 170 obsidian artifacts from four postcontact sites (fig. 9.3).

The purpose of the study is to examine diachronic patterns in regional obsidian source use, testing the idea that source use changed from precontact (i.e., Paleoindian, Archaic, and Late Prehistoric) to postcontact (i.e., Protohistoric and Historic) periods. The analysis identified eighteen

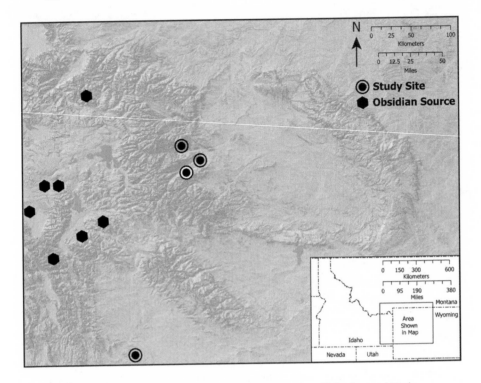

Figure 9.3. Archaeological sites and obsidian sources. (Scheiber and Finley 2010)

chemically distinct obsidian sources dating to the last 12,000 years. We classified the data set according to region, source area, and age. We applied the Shannon diversity index (Beals et al. 2000) to analyze regional temporal variation (Scheiber and Finley 2010).

We hypothesize that high-diversity measures equate to increased mobility or exchange. By this, we mean that more obsidian sources reflected in the artifacts at a site indicate that people were more highly mobile or were more frequently engaged in trading with outsiders. Conversely, reduced diversity for any period indicates a change in mobility patterns or exchange with neighboring areas. For the purposes of this chapter, we focus on the Late Prehistoric to Historic period transitions in northwest Wyoming (the Greater Yellowstone area) and southwest Wyoming (the Wyoming Basin), traditional homelands of the Mountain Shoshone and Plains Shoshone, respectively.

Distinct patterns emerge in the data set, with both regions showing the highest diversity during the Late Prehistoric period (AD 500–1700) but a sharp decline in source diversity during the Historic period. During the contact period, Yellowstone obsidian from northwestern Wyoming rarely occurs in Wyoming Basin sites to the south. Instead obsidian from eastern Idaho (i.e., Malad and Bear Gulch) and Jackson Hole are most common. On the other hand, obsidian from southeastern Idaho is rare in GYE archaeological sites, which are dominated by Yellowstone and northeastern Idaho sources. Variation in northeastern Idaho and Jackson Hole sources drives the diversity measure as northeastern Idaho sources drop from historic Wyoming Basin assemblages and Jackson Hole sources drop from historic GYE assemblages. Because of ethnographic regional associations between Shoshone bands, we argue that pre- to postcontact changes of obsidian source utilization reflect changing mobility patterns and exchange between the two regions that may ultimately reflect the formation of distinct Mountain and Plains Shoshone social identities. This change in the material record is a historic phenomenon and is one that we argue is the direct result of culture contact and colonialism in the central Rocky Mountains. People chose to restrict their movements to local procurement areas. This pattern runs counter to assumptions that Plains inhabitants became more mobile after the arrival of horses. We believe that the impact of the horse on historic settlement patterns is another mobility trope that needs to be investigated rather than assumed. We also suspect that some of the designated Late Prehistoric sites in fact date to the very early part of the Historic period, when the newly mounted Shoshone dominated Plains trade relations (Secoy 1953). The sites thus designated as Historic may actually represent a territorial retreat or retraction in response to highly organized mounted and armed indigenous neighbors such as the Blackfoot.

Ceramic Source Analysis

The continued use of clay ceramic vessels and stone bowls offers additional insight into cooking strategies at a time when metal pots would have become more readily available. Sheepeaters were carrying stone bowls when they met Francois Larocque in 1805 and Osborne Russell in 1835 (Russell 1955[1914]; Wood and Thiessen 1985). So far, linking quarries to stone (steatite) vessels has not been possible (Adams 2006). Although we do not have written eyewitness accounts of pottery use, Intermountain Ware ceramics are recorded at archaeological sites of the region. Archaeologists working at Shoshone sites in the adjacent Great Basin have successfully studied patterns of mobility in prehistoric contexts based on ceramic sourcing (Eerkens 2003).

Intermountain Ware ceramics are found at regional Shoshone occupation sites, yet little is known about Wyoming ceramics in particular (Haspel 1984; Marceau 1982). Our geochemical analysis of ceramic clay provides an important, complementary analysis to the obsidian research. We initiated a pilot study to identify compositional variability in raw materials used to form ceramics from Shoshone sites in western Wyoming. We examined fifty sherds from four sites, one in the Wyoming Basin and three in the GYE, in order to begin understanding the variability in clay use and whether ceramic vessels were made locally or in distant places (Ferguson and Glascock 2007). All sites date to the terminal Late Prehistoric or early Historic periods within the last 500 years (AD 1500–1800s).

As with obsidian source use, geochemical analysis of ceramics provides important insights regarding pre- and postcontact changes in mobility. The Wyoming Basin and the GYE are suitable for this approach because of their distinctly different geology. The Wyoming Basin is largely a Tertiary sedimentary environment while the GYE is dominantly an extrusive, igneous landscape (Love and Christiansen 1985). Thus, following the logic of the obsidian analysis, we would expect greater ceramic clay source diversity during the Late Prehistoric, precontact period and reduced diversity during the Historic, postcontact period.

Our initial instrumental neutron activation analysis shows very promising results. Eight chemically distinct compositional groups were identified with only two sherds unassigned to specific groups. Little overlap exists between sites or regions, again suggesting local production with little exchange. While this current sample of sites and ceramic sherds is still small, the preliminary results are intriguing and with obsidian artifacts indicate that the Wyoming Basin and GYE were socially distinct areas during the early contact period. Future work with the ceramic study requires addition of more sites and ceramic samples in order to refine regional diachronic patterns that may indicate broader patterns of regional interaction, mobility, and ethnogenesis of distinct mountains and plains social identities.

Conclusions

In this chapter, we showed how archaeological sites and artifacts could reveal new information about colonial hunter-gatherer lifeways. Likewise, a focus on colonial period historical contexts can tell us about hunter-gather variability more broadly. By asking if nomadic hunter-gatherers of the central Rocky Mountains were employing the time-honored practice of "voting with their feet" as a means of expressing resistance to external colonial pressures, we try to link two dominant traditions of archaeological practice. We ask if mobility can be structure and resistance simultaneously. Indigenous inhabitants of the Rockies made active choices that included restrictions and modifications in mobility strategies, in clear response to the presence of outsiders. Concrete examples from human landscape use, obsidian procurement, and ceramic production trace changes in movement strategies, undoubtedly impacted by new people, diseases, and pressures in the area.

We contend that the concepts of mobility and resistance have additional meanings on the American western frontier that are enmeshed in our own American value system. While we acknowledge the symbolic capital surrounding our research, we hope to show how archaeological data can further reveal the underlying structural metaphors too often implicit in the study of western indigenous colonial practices.

Acknowledgments

We would like to thank Kenneth Sassaman and Donald Holly for inviting us to participate in this volume. We also thank the Shoshone National Forest, Indiana University, Northwest College, the Wyoming Bureau of Land Management, and the George C. Frison Institute. Chris Clerc, Maureen Boyle, and two anonymous reviewers provided additional feedback. Obsidian source analysis from our research sites was performed at the University of California Berkeley Archaeological X-Ray Fluorescence Laboratory and the Geochemical Research Laboratory in Portola Valley, California. Ceramic sourcing is part of collaborative research with Jeffrey Ferguson and Michael Glascock at the Archaeometry Laboratory of the Research Reactor Center at the University of Missouri. This project was partially supported by Indiana University's New Frontiers in the Arts and Humanities Program, funded by the Lilly Endowment and administered by the Office of the Vice Provost for Research; by a Grant-in-Aid of Research from the Vice Provost for Research at Indiana University; and by the National Science Foundation (Award #0714926).

PART III

The Structure of Historical Process

10

History and Alterity in the Eastern Archaic

Kenneth E. Sassaman

> There was a measure of acknowledgement that communities in
> modern societies had historically come to form parts of larger
> totalities or wholes, but the societies and cultures of primitives—
> savages and barbarians—were thought to have formed "back of
> history," and were seen as existing and persisting outside the flow of
> historical change. Thus they could be understood still as distinctive,
> separable, bounded, isolated—one people, one society, one culture.
> —Wolf 1984:394

Eric Wolf's urge to archaeologists to rethink their concept of culture is as apt today as it was twenty-five years ago (Kohl 2008). Wolf suggested that archaeologists deconstruct the static, bounded units implicit to the taxonomies of culture history and investigate how people related themselves to one another through the construction of social identity. This was an especially tough challenge for archaeologists whose perceptions of cultural variation remained anchored to the intellectual construct of organic evolution. For them, the bounded, static units of culture history were seen as outcomes of diversification processes akin to speciation, that is, outcomes of geographic isolation and niche specialization. The histories of global interaction Wolf so eloquently scripted in his 1982 book, *Europe and the People without History*, offered guidance on methods for rethinking ancient cultures, but few archaeologists regarded this account as anything more than the story of modernity, conditions that did not apply to people such as hunters and gatherers, whose cultures were construed as products of nature and evolution, not history.

In this chapter, I characterize the Archaic hunter-gatherer past of eastern North America with a model that privileges group interactions as the primary cause for cultural diversity and change. In place of the static and bounded entities of archaeological "cultures," I consider how archaeologists are able to reconstruct the shared social fields of "relationships within which cultural sets are put together and dismantled" (Wolf 1984:397). I differ from Wolf in his Marxian emphasis on social relations of production, but agree with his notion that the processes by which social fields are formed and transformed reside in the mutual constitution of everyday experience and idealized culture, or what Kroeber (1952:152–166) called "reality culture" and "value culture," and modern theorists refer to as "agency" and "structure."

Social fields of relationships in archaeological time can be inferred from patterns of technological diffusion or subsistence change (Kohl 2008), but analytical proxies for social fields are also located in the discursive practices of "value culture." For instance, ritualized practices such as mortuary ceremonialism, crafting, and monument construction are among the more accessible contexts for observing culture in idealized form. In the archaeological record of eastern North America, hunter-gatherers engaged socially in ritual with material consequences that are preserved for us to view, however indirectly. The intentions of such practices will not likely be known to us, but in their materialization, ritual and other discursive acts became symbolic expressions of social fields of relationships. Given the markedly varied social contexts of Archaic ritual in eastern North America, it is hard to imagine that the only measure of distinction in social fields was the symbolic understanding or who was and was not kin, as in Wolf's (1982) kin-ordered mode of production. We may instead consider how social fields were multidimensional and included formations that enabled the spread of ideas and practices across people of diverse culture, as well as the persistence-through-change of "traditions" that lasted millennia. Accordingly, we may find it useful to consider that the processes accounting for cultural variation and change among ancient hunter-gatherers were not fundamentally different from those of modernity (Cobb 2005).

The modern concept of "alterity" bears relevance to a revised history of ancient hunter-gatherer cultures. In its most general connotation, alterity is the conceptualization of "otherness" that is essential to human self-awareness. As a social process, the cultural construction of the "other" entails both the distinction between one and another "people," as well as exchanging one's perception for that of the "other" (cf. mimesis; Taussig 1993). These are two sides of the same coin in determining the contours of social affiliation, and they operate at scales ranging from the local community to global populations. When temporalized, the cultural production of the "other" draws on the distinction between the past and present to assign rank or value (Bloch 1977; Fabian 1983). Encounters with the primitive "other," for instance, were the basis for a Western historical consciousness that viewed the ancient past as inferior to the present and the future (de Certeau 1988). In this sense, cultural production of the "primitive" was the cultural production of evolutionary history (Fabian 1983).

Hunter-gatherers of ancient times are not apart from these sorts of processes so long as we allow that the diversity we see among them is indeed a product of interactions, not isolation. We must also allow that observed cultural diversity goes well beyond slight differences in choices of food or tools or places to dwell, to include the sorts of dispositional contradictions of intercultural encounters (e.g., Sahlins 1985), along with the ensuing processes of diaspora, coalescence, and ethnogenesis we know from modernity. My case material from the Eastern Archaic of North America (ca. 10,000–3000 radiocarbon years BP) lends itself to this exploration in its enormous cultural diversity through time and space (Sassaman 2010). In promoting the idea that this diversity is best understood in the contexts of social fields of interaction, it is useful to begin with a critical look at the long-standing assumption that all Archaic cultures descended from a single ancestral line.

One, Two, or More Ancestral Lines?

Modeled as organic evolution, the family tree of Native North America has typically been drawn as if it were biologically and culturally rooted in one ancestral root, Clovis (fig. 10.1). The single-ancestry model is a familiar theme because it recapitulates the broad sweep of macroevolution—it is what we expect of any biological history of considerable duration, especially under changing environmental conditions. Thus, post-Pleistocene adaptation to global warming and sea-level change, especially during the mid-Holocene, is the dominant theme for explaining late Paleoindian and Archaic prehistory. The theme features

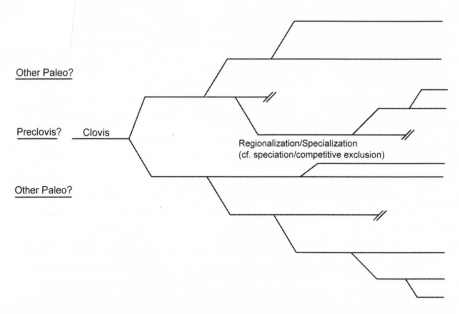

Other Paleo?

Preclovis?   Clovis

Regionalization/Specialization
(cf. speciation/competitive exclusion)

Other Paleo?

Figure 10.1. An organic evolutionary model of cultural diversification in eastern North America based on the assumption of one ancestral line (Clovis) and increased diversity of Archaic cultures over time through processes akin to speciation.

diversification and adaptive radiation under ameliorating climate, marked by increased regional specialization, cultural and geographical circumscription, and population packing. Human mobility, notably large-scale migration, decreased over time, and there are few or no convergences of lines that diverged in the ancient past.

The appropriateness of an organic evolutionary model for explaining cultural diversity has been debated since the middle twentieth century, when Darwinian theory gained traction in anthropology. Debate has turned on the difference between processes accounting for biological variation and those contributing to cultural variation. In a now-classic repudiation of organic evolutionary models of culture, Kroeber (1948:260) drew a distinction between the "Tree of Life" and the "Tree of Culture." Organic evolution resulted in diversification of species the way branches diverge on a tree, becoming increasingly distant from a common trunk (ancestor), with distal branches (species) incapable of reversing their pattern of growth or converging with counterparts to form coalescent branches. The Tree of Culture, in contrast, involves branches that diverge in isolation from others but also converge and coalesce into new forms and, in some cases, seemingly reverse the direction of change.

The processes Kroeber believed to be unique to culture change are now known to have parallels in "reticulate" evolution and methods for modeling convergences are now common in the field of cladistics (Lipo et al. 2006; Mace et al. 2005; O'Brien and Lyman 2003). Irrespective of these recent advances, actual historical relationships among late prehistoric and ethnohistoric communities in eastern North America lend empirical proof to a reticulate model of cultural variation and change. These histories are rife with instances of fissioning, migrations, encounters, coalescence, and other measures of ethnogenesis (e.g., Blitz and Lorenz 2006; Galloway 1998; Moore 1994). We have good reason to suspect that these same sorts of events and consequences inflected the histories of ancient eastern North America.

Figure 10.2 illustrates one possible form a reticulate or ethnogenetic model for Paleoindian and Archaic phylogenies might take. It is not intended to represent the actual historical relationships of particular peoples but merely to enable discussion of the modes of intercultural transmission at a grand scale. The most unorthodox feature of this model is its assertion of at least two separate ancestral roots for Archaic peoples, one traceable to the Paleoindian populations of eastern North America (Ancestry I), the other to the later influxes of populations whose affinity to Paleoindians is uncertain (Ancestry II).

Ancestry I

Descendant from Clovis and its late Pleistocene affines, Ancestry I is manifested across the continent in traditions involving highly formalized lanceolate, side-notched, and corner-notched bifaces and unifacial toolkits dominated by hafted scrapers. These include Plano, Dalton, the side-notched horizon, the corner-notched horizon, notably Kirk, and lesser traditions through the ninth millennium BP.

It goes without saying that the immediate descendants of Clovis culture experienced relatively severe changes in environment at the close of the Pleistocene. The multigenerational lineage signified by the manufacture of classic Clovis points drew to a close at circa 12,900 calendar

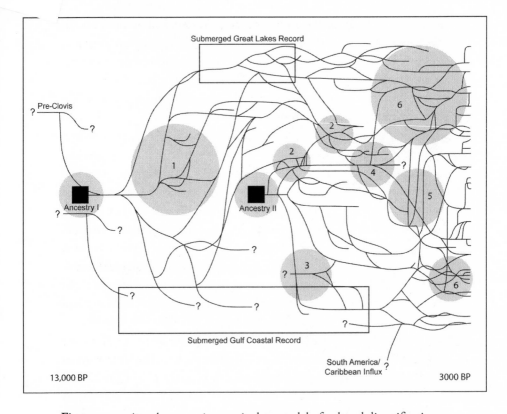

Figure 10.2. An ethnogenetic or reticulate model of cultural diversification in eastern North America based on the assumption of at least two distinct ancestral lines (Ancestries I and II) and increased diversity of Archaic cultures over time through processes akin to the ethnogeneses, diasporas, and coalescences of modernity. The model mimics both temporal (horizontal axis) and spatial (vertical axis) dimensions of Archaic history. Shaded circles exemplify particular sorts of historical processes: (1) the time-transgressive northward movement of descendants of Ancestry I at the onset of the Holocene; (2) the convergence of populations of distinct ancestry in midcontinent; (3) the convergence of populations of distinct ancestry near the Gulf Coast, begetting the region's first mound-building traditions; (4) diasporic movements of descendants of Ancestry II; (5) the rapid expansion of populations along the Eastern Seaboard; and (6) the convergence of diverse, widespread, cultural influences in the mortuary traditions of the North and the Poverty Point phenomenon of the South.

years ago, the onset of the Younger Dryas (Waters and Stafford 2007), coincident with the extinction of late megafauna that is the hallmark, although not necessarily the staple, of the Clovis hunting economy (Mead and Meltzer 1985).

Changes evident in the emergence of certain post-Clovis traditions implicate a considerable amount of population displacement and structural realignments of ancestral social fields (Koldehoff and Walthall 2004, 2009; Walthall 1998). Driving these changes at the close of the Pleistocene was the common, if not pervasive, efforts of people to maintain the status quo by following the time-transgressive changes wrought by postglacial warming. Presumably this occurred along both a latitudinal gradient (from south to north), as well as an altitudinal gradient (from low to high elevations). The large-scale result was the temporal attenuation of a hunting economy involving a lithic technology for dispatching game and processing hides within an environment of marked seasonality that was on the wane first in lower latitudes and at lower elevations.

The record of early Holocene populations to the north and along the Appalachian Summit reflects the persistence of Clovis ancestry. Most obvious is the persistence of lanceolate point technology in the Northeast and Great Lakes region well after the onset of the Younger Dryas and the end of Clovis. At present water levels, the Great Lakes cover much of the land that was available for settlement in the early Holocene (Lovis 2009:742; Shott 1999). The same applies to vast areas of the Gulf of Mexico and lesser portions of the Atlantic Seaboard (Faught 2002). Both of these extreme locations, to the far north and subtropical south, supported Archaic hunter-gatherers who almost certainly descended from Clovis well into the mid-Holocene.

In contrast, large interior regions of the lower to middle latitudes of the Eastern Woodlands appear to have been abandoned at about 8500 BP (Anderson 1996:163–165). When these regions were reoccupied some six or seven centuries later, the cultural expressions were so different from what came before as to suggest a complete replacement of one people by another. Given the prior abandonment of these regions by populations of Ancestry I, this process was not so much a replacement as it was an opportunity for displaced people to emplace themselves in unoccupied, uncontested land. In figure 10.2, I refer to these immigrant people as Ancestry II.

Ancestry II

Ancestry II signals the immigration of people into the lower Midwest and the mid-South and portions of the South Atlantic slope after circa 8500 BP. The immediate geographical origin of these interlopers is unknown, but they came to settle large stretches of major rivers in the Midwest and the mid-South to beget what is glossed as the Shell Mound Archaic.

The concept of Shell Mound Archaic has undergone considerable change since its inception in the 1930s by Works Progress Administration archaeologists who excavated thick shell deposits in Kentucky, Tennessee, and northern Alabama (e.g., Webb 1939, 1974; Webb and DeJarnette 1942). In the trait-listing methods of culture history, the Shell Mound Archaic was portrayed as a singular, unitary phenomenon. Modern study of the Shell Mound Archaic (e.g., Crothers 1999; Hensley 1994; Marquardt and Watson 1983, 2005) reveals consideration diversity in the form and function of sites, and there is little to recommend that the freshwater shellfish deposits across the entire mid-South—let alone farther afield, where the moniker was sometimes applied (e.g., Crusoe and DePratter 1976)—was the work of a single "people." Nonetheless, shell-bearing sites situated between the Ohio and Tennessee rivers are among the oldest in the eastern United States (Dye 1996), and the region as a whole encompasses an advanced level of sustained settlement, with some stratified sequences spanning at least four millennia.

Although the Shell Mound Archaic indeed embodies much greater variation than the architects of the construct imagined, compared to the Archaic archaeological records in surrounding areas, it stands together in sharp contrast. The procurement and deposition of freshwater shellfish is the signature feature. Human interments in shell are very common (Claassen 1992) and generally co-occur with domestic refuse, leading some to suggest that burial was merely incidental to habitation (Milner and Jefferies 1998). Burial goods include items with no precedent in early Holocene assemblages. Notable among them are tubular stone weights for spear-throwers (complete examples of which have been found in graves [Webb 1974]), otherwise known as bannerstones (Sassaman

1996). Marine shell beads and cups adorn some graves, mostly those of children (Claassen 1996), and instances of trophy-taking and other forms of mutilation among adults are not uncommon (Smith 1996). No singular trait, mortuary or otherwise, distinguishes the Shell Mound Archaic from its counterparts outside the mid-South and lower Midwest, but as a constellation of cultural practices, it is without precedence in the greater East.

Convergences of Ancestries I and II

The convergences of lines in figure 10.2 that unite Ancestries I and II exemplify the coalescence or syncretisms of Kroeber's Tree of Culture and, through analogy, the reticulate evolutionary processes of biology. That is, they signify the sort of horizontal or synchronous transmission of information (in this case cultural, through discursive and nondiscursive practice) that is precipitated by encounter.

Working from the hypothesis that an immigrant wave of Ancestry II moved into the largely vacated mid-South and was surrounded on the east, north, and south by people they could not possibly have recognized as "kin," the opportunities for encounter and ethnogenesis between hitherto separate peoples were many. We can be certain that interactions soon developed between Shell Mound Archaic people and their neighbors to the north and south, for it is from these directions that materials such as copper and marine shell arrived (Winters 1968). Interactions with neighbors to the east, in the Appalachians and beyond, are not so apparent, but circumstantial evidence for regular interactions indeed exists. Interactions no doubt varied from sustained to intermittent, and from friendly to hostile. Under many circumstances interactions did not blend or homogenize cultural differences; rather, interactions often accentuated differences, and in many cases led to entirely new formations and cultural dispositions (ethnogenesis). Once the historical "events" of immigration and encounter took place and processes of ethnogenesis and other cultural changes ensued, lineages of human experience did not map onto discrete, spatially contained social collectives, or if they did, it was not because of isolation, but the asserted difference and separation that is found in traditions of resistance (Sassaman 2001; Scheiber and Finley, this vol.). This point is hardly trivial because it suggests that even the most geographically remote and discrete cultural formations of Archaic history can be explained only in the historical contexts of encounters and interactions with "others."

One of the hotbeds of ethnogenesis was the northern geographical seam between presumptive populations of Ancestries I and II (Emerson and McElrath 2001). Variation in bone pins (Jefferies 1997), bannerstones (Burdin 2004), and bifaces show that the Ohio River was as much an enduring seam of cultural differences as it was the threshold of interaction. Some interactions ostensibly were violent, with instances of interpersonal strife registered in bone occurring pervasively, albeit infrequently, among humans interred at sites in the valley (Schmidt et al. 2010). By circa 5500 BP, cemeteries north of the Ohio River showed marked variation in treatment of the dead (e.g., Jefferies and Butler 1982) and the inclusion of items, such as bannerstones, whose ancestry traces to the Shell Mound Archaic (Hassen and Farnsworth 1987). The Great Lakes were infilling at this same time, reaching higher-than-present levels in what is known as the Nipissing Stage (ca. 5000–4000 BP). Some of the displaced populations likely moved south, perhaps obliging existing social alliances that facilitated the southward movement of copper. Likewise, small, intermittent influxes of immigrants from south of the Ohio River provided the necessary raw material of ethnogenesis in forming coalescent communities of diverse cultural disposition (e.g., Emerson and McElrath 2001; McElrath et al. 2009:359). That not all resident groups south of the Ohio River embraced these changes is apparent among persistent and entrenched communities of Shell Mound Archaic postdating 5000 BP. One of the latest sites in the region, Read, reveals the first major shift in mortuary practice in many centuries: the spatial separation of dogs and humans (Hensley 1994). At least one diasporic event dating roughly to this time (ca. 3500 BP) can be inferred from the site unit intrusion of the Riverton culture in Illinois (Winters 1969) and perhaps signals the final effort in the area to maintain autonomy and reinvent tradition.

The other major zone of intercultural exchange and ethnogenesis is the Gulf Coastal Plain south of the middle Tennessee River. Connections between the Shell Mound Archaic and Gulf coastal people are implicated in the importation of marine gastropod shell, although the means by which this occurred and the brokers involved are uncertain (Marquardt 1985). By about 5500 BP, another manner of interaction becomes evident in what Johnson and Brookes (1989) call the Benton

Interaction Sphere. The production and exchange of oversized Benton bifaces and other craft goods appears to be tied to mortuary ritual, and underlying the geographic expansion of this ritual practice were probable small-scale relocations of middle Tennessee River valley groups to river drainages of the Gulf Coastal Plain (e.g., Bense 1987). Arguably, the entire Benton tradition was the ethnogenetic consequence of interactions between regional populations that included coastal denizens of Ancestry I. Once again, the inundated record predating 4200 BP limits any significant examination of this proposition. Later examples of Benton-like incursion into the Atlantic Coastal Plain provide other examples of ethnogenesis, most notably the emergence of the Stallings culture of the middle Savannah River valley (Sassaman 2006).

Migrations

A final significant feature of note in the ethnogenetic or reticulate model of figure 10.2 is the repeated instances of population displacement and resettlement. The circumstances and reasons for human displacement are no doubt many. Already we have touched on adjustments associated with time-transgressive environmental change, exchange alliances, coalescence, conflict, and cultural resistance. We can generalize some such movements as "diasporic" inasmuch as they represent the forced or voluntary migration from an established "homeland" of people of common cultural identity who resettled, often in dispersed fashion, in locations far afield. The Shell Mound Archaic diaspora mentioned earlier provides examples in the Lamoka Lake (Ritchie 1969) and Riverton (Winters 1969) cultures, as well as the antecedents of Stallings culture with affinity to Benton (Sassaman 2006).

Other population movements in figure 10.2 exemplify the sorts of processes that draw people of distinctive cultural heritage together either permanently or temporarily into multicultural collectives. It goes without saying that these ethnogenetic or coalescent outcomes require the relocation of at least one community to the location of another. Often, perhaps nearly always, this is predicated on existing social alliances that would predetermine the emergent structure of coalescence, including genealogical ranking or some manner of order among constituent units. The so-called Broadpoint Dispersal of the Atlantic Seaboard is a likely candidate for this sort of process.

Ultimately, much of what I have outlined in the foregoing paragraphs, symbolized in figure 10.2, has archaeological correlates that are testable. However, I do not think it is advisable, or perhaps even feasible, to trace any given line in figure 10.2 through archaeologically constructed time with reference to material culture alone. Discursive acts of interpreting the world and representing one's existence—the stuff of ritual (i.e., "value culture")—are perhaps better sources of data on histories of ethnogenesis, coalescence, and diaspora, than are the mundane details of concrete history. In the balance of this chapter, I consider briefly three areas of such practice.

Making Histories, Making Communities

If human perception of a past that is different from the present is predicated on encounters with people who are unfamiliar, then the historicism of Eastern Archaic people must have been enormously complex. In the subsections that follow, I introduce three archaeological entrées into historical practice among Archaic communities. In (1) burying their dead, (2) crafting and gifting objects, and (3) building and using monuments, Archaic peoples referenced other times, places, and peoples.

Theory suited to the challenge of comparative method such as this is embodied in the recent literature on "memory" (e.g., Van Dyke and Alcock 2003). What this literature shows, through empirical illustration, is that memory making entails far more than the social autobiography of past events and their consequences. Collective consciousness of the relationship between the past and the present is influenced as much by the mode of transmission of historical knowledge as by the content of experience. Following Connerton (1989:3), a community must share memories of the past at some level for it to be integrated in a fashion that is reproduced over time and space. When constructed of people of distinct ancestry and history, social memory is liable to be politicized.

Conceptual tools of historical anthropology offer some utility for modeling the historicism of Archaic communities, multicultural and otherwise. Of relevance for our purposes is the distinction between "diasporic" and "coalescent" culture that is informing recent analyses of ancient Puebloan community formation (e.g., Cameron and Duff 2008; Clark et al. 2008; Mills 2008). The contrast between the two traces to difference in concrete historical experience and the relationship of communities to place. Diasporic communities share a common history but not a common place (at least not in locations of resettlement), whereas coalescent communities share a place but not a common history (Clark et al. 2008). In the latter contexts we can expect that assertions of social memory depend greatly on a sharp demarcation between specific pasts and the present and hence the subversion of diverse social memories to a new social order (Connerton 1989:7). Diasporic communities, in contrast, strive to preserve "tradition" in the face of challenges from without that not only forced displacement and resettlement but also "assimilation" when backed by coercion. In this sense, many contemporary hunter-gatherer peoples are diasporic insofar as they use mobility as a form of cultural resistance (Sassaman 2001; Scheiber and Finley, this vol.).

To the diasporic-coalescent dichotomy we can add the cultural milieu of staged colonization, as in the Paleoindian expansion models proffered by Anderson (1990) and Dincauze (1993). Before the influx of people of Ancestry II, Paleoindians and their immediate descendants experienced histories of colonization or "frontier expansion" (including the time-transgressive patterns noted earlier) without infringing on the landscapes of "others." Cultural differentiation among them is of course expected and highly relevant to emergent communities, but even more relevant are the variety of discursive practices that linked together widely dispersed places and people, lending a temporality to landscape (sensu Ingold 1993) that subverted processes of cultural differentiation to a shared sense of history. Unlike diasporic communities, those of colonial processes are typically able to assert physical ties to "homeland" through repeated transfers of objects or persons.

We can now turn briefly to examples of discursive practices that reference the past to assert, reproduce, and transform Archaic communities. The three basic models of community (diasporic, coalescent, and colonial) previously outlined are not intended to serve as pigeonholes in which to insert specific instances of historicism, but instead to simplify comparisons for purposes of developing inferences about historical practices in general. As I indicated at the outset of this chapter, the lingering separation between those with and without history that continues to bedevil hunter-gatherer archaeology is erased when we allow that Archaic peoples were just as active in "writing" their own histories as were Europeans in modernity. Despite vast differences in concrete histories between the two, they both had to constantly accommodate encounters with the unknown "other" in communities of ever-changing composition, structure, and integration.

Mortuary Traditions

If disposal of the dead is dissociated from the material conditions of life, as Alfred Kroeber (1927) once suggested, then we may find in mortuary practices of the Eastern Archaic some of the best evidence for root metaphors of culture. In this regard, two major mortuary programs are evident: those that separated the dead from places of mortal living, and those that conflated the two. These differences have deep ramifications for cultural dispositions beyond death. The former implies that time was materialized through sequential place-making, much in the way that Australian Dreaming or similar nonwestern landscapes are temporalized as life cycles. The latter disposition—keeping the deceased with the living—sediments all time in one place, enabling claims to ancestry that require formalized and tangible warrants on place. It can also denote a severing of ties to other places and with it other times and other people.

The mortuary practices of Ancestry I vary in multiple ways but almost always involve the creation of dedicated places for the dead (i.e., cemeteries), and they often involve cremation of human remains and sometimes the burning of objects interred in graves. Commonly, objects of foreign provenance are involved and sometimes these objects take on exaggerated proportions. The Sloan Dalton cemetery of northeast Arkansas exemplifies all these qualities (Morse 1997). Other mortuary contexts of Paleoindian age involve isolated graves in remote locations. For instance, isolated ridge- or hilltop graves with burned objects are found across the Great Lakes region (Deller and Ellis 1984; Mason and Irwin 1960). And somewhat later are the cremation cemeteries of early Holocene age south of the Great Lakes in Indiana and Ohio (Schmidt et al. 2008; Tomak 1979). Although we cannot assert with authority that the various Archaic mortuary cults of the Northeast and Great Lakes drew directly from Ancestry I, they are indeed dedicated spaces apart from habitation, and they commonly involve cremations and elaborate grave goods, sometimes also burned (Dincauze 1968; Pleger 2000; Robinson 2006). The Windover Pond site (Doran 2002) and other pond cemeteries in Florida provide a limited view into what form mortuary traditions took among southern coastal populations of Ancestry I. Despite the lack of cremations and burned grave goods, Florida's pond cemeteries appear to have been places used exclusively for human interment.

In contrast, the numerous burial populations of the Shell Mound Archaic (Ancestry II) have been retrieved from deposits that are arguably the output of everyday living. The cultural significance of this manner of burial placement has been a rigorously debated topic in recent years (cf. Claassen 1992; Milner and Jefferies 1998), but whether shell mounds of the mid-South are classified as "cemeteries" or simply "trash heaps" says more about the underlying ontologies of modern archaeologists than it does the sensibilities of Archaic people. No matter, Shell Mound Archaic mortuary traditions are vastly different from what came before and what surrounded them. Besides existing in places inferred to be habitation sites, Shell Mound Archaic burials only rarely involve cremation, and in the Green River valley, the locale of the largest burial populations exhumed, cremation simply was not practiced.

Syncretisms of diverse mortuary programs begin to appear in the Archaic record at about 5500 BP in vastly different places. One example just to the north of the Ohio River is the Black Earth site in southern Illinois (Jefferies and Butler 1982), where a combination of burial styles signals one possible microconfluence of Ancestries I and II. Burials at Koster, hilltop bluff cemeteries, and the Bullseye site, all in Illinois, not only show a great deal of interpersonal variations, often clustered in two forms, but also tremendous intersite variation, not all of which can be attributed to change through time (Charles and Buikstra 1983; Hassen and Farnsworth 1987). The Ervin site of the Duck River in Tennessee also shows an array of mortuary treatments, notably the combination of primary and secondary interments, including cremation (Hofman 1986). Dating to the Benton phase, this array exemplifies possible convergence of traditions between Ancestries I and II that were oriented toward the south, in alignment with Benton exchange patterns.

Crafting

A second domain of historicism is found in the crafting and gifting of objects. These are biographical processes that encompass vast social spheres through circulations and enchainments (sensu Chapman 2000). We have a good sense of how the gifting of objects creates, reproduces, and transforms social bodies. But other sorts of discursive practices entail assertions of difference and separation, while others enjoin the past as resistance to change. The forms objects take, raw materials of choice, contexts of making, use lives, and patterns of deposition all have potential historical referents in assertions of identity and difference. One example is the production, gifting, and deposition of oversized bifaces.

Dalton sites of the central Mississippi valley include locations where unusually large and exotic lanceolate blades were cached (Morse 1997:17; Walthall and Koldehoff 1998). These blades measure up to 38 cm in length and exhibit remarkable workmanship on high-quality raw material. Most often they are isolated finds, but at least six caches of up to nine large blades each have been recorded in the southern half of this region (Walthall and Koldehoff 1998:260).

Late Middle Archaic Benton points are generally large, well-crafted items often made from blue-gray Fort Payne chert of the middle Tennessee River area of northwest Alabama. Occasional examples up to 26 cm in length have been recovered in caches and mortuary contexts in the greater region, particularly in northeast Mississippi, where Johnson and Brookes (1989) documented some 13 caches along the Tombigbee River.

A mortuary context for Benton caches is demonstrated at a number of sites in the mid-South, including those of shell-bearing sites on the Tennessee (Webb and DeJarnette 1942), Harpeth (Dowd 1989:103), and Duck rivers (Hofman 1986). Benton mortuary complexes apart from shell middens are known too (e.g., Deter-Wolf 2004; Parker 1974). When accompanying cremations, Benton caches were sometimes burned and heat-fractured (e.g., Hofman 1986; Parker 1974). Clusters of heat-fractured Benton points have also been recovered from presumably nonmortuary contexts (e.g., Alexander 1983:72). At least one cache from northern Alabama consists of intentionally fractured, but not burned, bipointed and notched blades, apparently nonmortuary (Fundaburke and Foreman 1957:123).

Situated in the larger context of Shell Mound Archaic sites, Benton biface caches evoke many of the signature attributes of Ancestry I mortuary practices, including cremation or thermal destruction of the bifaces themselves. As we have already noted, the Benton Interaction Sphere transcended the southern boundary of the Shell Mound Archaic in northern Alabama to connect with communities to the south, some of which most likely relocated from the north over the preceding centuries. Thus, like the Dalton biface caches at cemeteries, Benton points were deposited in graves at locations far from their points of origin, linking through mortuary deposition the living and the dead and, presumably, locations of dwelling with ancestral land. Insofar as the mortuary programs involved more than one burial treatment, acts of interment and ritual deposition integrated participation across ethnic and cultural boundaries.

The production and use of bannerstones provides another entrée into intercultural encounters. Most discussions of bannerstones have centered on formal variation, function, and contexts of deposition. Less consideration has been given to the organization of production and conduits of exchange. Among the major "centers" of surplus production are Mount Johnson Island in the lower Susquehanna River of Pennsylvania (Baer 1921); the lower Great Lakes area of southern Michigan, northeast Indiana, and northwest Ohio (Bowen 1994); and the upper to middle Savannah River valley of Georgia and South Carolina (Sassaman and Randall 2007). All three examples of bannerstone production and exchange exist outside the core area of the Shell Mound Archaic, the ancestral source of bannerstones in the East. None of these extralocal locales involves the use of bannerstones in mortuary contexts after hypertrophic forms appear after 4200 BP. However, with both the hypertrophic bannerstones and the oversized bifaces discussed earlier, we can hypothesize that exaggerated forms signal attempts on the part of toolmakers to assert unambiguous identities (see Sassaman and Randall 2007).

Monumentality

The final example of historicism is found in Archaic monuments. There is perhaps no better example of what Connerton (1989:37) meant by conserving "recollections by referring them to the material milieu that surrounds us" than the construction and use of monuments. These are large vessels of time and space, vivid reminders of the past, stages on which commemorative performance happens, and enduring evidence of permanence and stability.

Discoveries of late lay to rest any doubt that hunter-gatherers of eastern North America built monuments, but we remain saddled with the bias that such constructions were the work of a single, local people or the de facto result of fixed living. In some cases, monuments were thrown up rather quickly, in "big bang" fashion to borrow from Pauketat (2004). Arguably, these acts of cultural assertions involved the coming together of people of different experience and knowledge, perhaps even different language. The actual conditions drawing people together implicates shared beliefs that we will likely never know. However, in the act of making monuments and memories, participants fabricated the structure that explains their place in the panoply of diversity.

The assertion of new cultural identity through monumental acts is perhaps best exemplified by the Poverty Point complex of northeast Louisiana (Kidder, this vol.). In its particular configuration, Poverty Point is without precedent. However, elements of deep ancestry are evident in the mathematics and engineering of the complex (Clark 2004; Sassaman and Heckenberger 2004). Likewise, Poverty Point is a highly localized phenomenon, replicated nowhere else. And yet, its massive inventory of nonlocal goods reveals its cosmopolitan qualities. Indeed, Poverty Point is rife with contradiction: when viewed at the scale of northeast Louisiana, it seems parochial and synchronic; when set into the larger context, it appears continental and diachronic. It is in this latter sense that I regard Poverty Point to be a historical atlas, embodying in earthen form all the time and space of its constituent subjects (Sassaman 2005a).

That the genesis of Poverty Point was a multicultural affair, a coming together of diverse cultural streams, is highly controversial and seemingly without on-site empirical support (Gibson 2007). However, I would suggest that Poverty Point's apparent sameness and localized form belies the diversity of its monumental foundations. Kidder (this vol.) has provided strong evidence that the largest mound at Poverty Point was erected virtually instantaneously. Moreover, it was constructed according to a grammar that arguably symbolized a cosmogonic myth that sequenced and perhaps ranked diverse parts of a whole. In this orchestrated act, the diverse were subsumed by an emergent new corporate structure (a "people"), and in this context of mimesis (becoming the "other"), individual biographies were masked or forgotten.

Who were these diverse peoples? The answer is unclear, but we can hypothesize that they involved coastal groups who supplied soapstone by way of South Atlantic Slope suppliers, as well as groups from the north who supplied literally tons of nonlocal cherts and ferrous minerals. Notably, populations of Shell Mound Archaic traditions (Ancestry II) left no evidence of participation in Poverty Point's genesis.

It appears self-evident that Poverty Point was one of the Archaic Period's most elaborate and emphatic acts of cultural representation, and evidence for its "eventful" construction substantiates this claim. That it entailed the coming together of diverse people will remain unsubstantiated so long as we insist that this purported multiculturalism be expressed in the mundane residues of life (Gibson 2007). In making reference to other times and places, the construction of mounds at Poverty Point did not require the permanent relocation of foreign peoples to northeast Louisiana, nor were participating ethnic groups destined to leave their unique marks on the land. If the construction of Poverty Point was strictly the corporate act of local people who interacted with one another routinely and had no basis for contesting identity and ancestry, one is left to ponder who this elaborate act of representation was intended to inform. Coming as it did at the end of the Archaic period, on the eve of large-scale demographic realignments, much of it precipitated by massive flooding in the South (Kidder 2006), I would suggest that the construction of Poverty Point was the asserting of a new social order that drew from millennia of intense, multifaceted interactions among people of enormous diversity.

Another major venue of monument construction is the middle St. Johns valley of northeast Florida, the subject of Randall's chapter in this volume. The first mounds in the middle St. Johns River valley were capping events dating to circa 6000 BP, coincident, in some cases, with the abandonment of linear "villages." Specialized mortuary facilities went up at some sites (Aten 1999; Endonino 2008), but repeated mounding events subsequent to capping appear to have occurred with some regularity, in seemingly rhythmic fashion, at sites with no obvious traces of burial or even habitation. Mounding continued for centuries and a subtradition of conical earth mounds appeared at about 5000 years ago, coincident with the influx of foreign items. Then, some five centuries later, mounding took on larger and more formalized significance. At four locales along the river, spaced about 20–30 km apart, linear shell ridges dating to the sixth millennium were incorporated into massive, U-shaped "amphitheaters." These were about fifteen times the size of the earlier shell mounds and presented a spatial structure never before seen in the valley. This quick transformation of the landscape coincided with the influx of the region's first pottery, whose spatial patterning at amphitheaters suggests some manner of dual social organization or at least a dichotomy between domestic and non-domestic uses.

The mounding traditions of the St. Johns have been characterized as continuous and, it would appear, indicative of the stability of an aquatic life on the river (Milanich 1994; Miller 1998). However, commemorative acts and reenactments do not simply imply continuity with the past, they claim it as rationale (Connerton 1989:45). Each of the inflection points in the history of mound building in the St. Johns signals either a radical change in the local availability of aquatic resources (i.e., channel switching in the braided river system) or influx of "foreign" peoples. The seeming continuity masks a repeatedly contested landscape in which certain communities drew on the past, through repeated commemoration, to make claims of ancestry that may or may not have been concrete. As in the case of Poverty Point, the material culture assemblages encased in and below St. Johns mounds belie radical cultural changes that can be revealed only at larger scales of observation.

In this regard, the diverse concrete histories leading to ethnogenesis in the middle St. Johns extend consideration of at least two major ancestral trunks (Ancestry I and II) to a third potential source. James Ford (1969), among others of his era, believed that so-called Formative developments in the Americas (such as construction of mounds) were precipitated by the arrival of interlopers from the Caribbean and South America. Whereas the method of controlled comparisons Ford employed is today insufficient to substantiate such a claim, the reinterpretation of monumental acts as crucibles of mimesis and cultural integration underscores the need to resuscitate efforts to investigate the possibility of concrete connections across the waters.

Conclusion

Everyday Archaic life experiences were punctuated with intercultural encounters, displacements, emplacements, ethnogenesis, resistance movements, diasporas, and coalescences. We ought not to assume that these ancient populations were more isolated and self-contained than modern ones, or that the conditions of encounters and history-making in ancient times were so radically different than those of modernity (Cobb 2005). But to treat prehistory as if it were history is not merely to allow that events happened and persons lived in the ancient past. We know that to be true. A historically informed prehistory is one in which real persons or social bodies made history through materialized acts of alterity. Many of the ritual practices among Archaic hunter-gatherers are particularly revealing of historical production because they involved persons and things whose biographies trace to other times and places (Sassaman 2005a). It is easy to misread these sorts of symbolic resources as the works of "one" people, for the mimetic capacity of alterity (i.e., to absorb the "power" of the "other" through imitation [Taussig 1993]) obscures, indeed masks, cultural plurality. In cases where monument construction or other ritual practices erupted in an elaboration of everyday life (e.g., Bradley 2005), it is worth investigating the extent to which this transformation was attended by events of intercultural encounter. Accordingly, the various mortuary cults, monumental acts, and traditions of crafting and caching long regarded as the works of a single people need to be reexamined as multicultural historical processes.

I have proposed a model for the Eastern Archaic that rejects the untested assumption that all constituent populations trace ancestry to a common ancestor and the ancillary assumption that all such people were like-minded and thus given to the same interpretations of intercultural experience. The model awaits empirical substantiation in the concrete histories of actual experience, but the real value of the model is its foregrounding of processes of historical production for which we have strong analogy in global experiences of modernity. In this sense, the archaeology of ancient hunter-gatherers has more to contribute to general theory in anthropology than merely recapitulating the classic Western benchmark for primitiveness.

Acknowledgments

My thanks to Don Holly for instigating the Society for American Archaeology symposium that led to our Amerind seminar and this book. Thanks also go to John

Ware and the Amerind Foundation for generous support of this project. Revisions of an earlier draft of this chapter were enabled by the constructive comments of my fellow Amerind participants, notably Brian Robinson, T. R. Kidder, Kent Lightfoot, Don Holly, Anna Prentiss, and Asa Randall, and by Tom Emerson and an anonymous reviewer. Any lingering shortcomings of logic or empirical substantiation remain with me alone. For a monographic treatment of the subject of this chapter, see Sassaman (2010).

11

Paleoindian and Archaic Period Traditions

Particular Explanations from New England

Brian S. Robinson and Jennifer C. Ort

Anthropology may be characterized, in part, as the endless balancing of general theory and processes with historically particular explanation (Trigger 2006:30; Kroeber 1935). One variation on the theme uses "survivalist" (materialist) and "transcendent" (symbolic) interpretations (Foster 1990:6), recognizing that the search for cross-cultural processes often focuses on necessary factors of survival but that the range of responses incorporates systems of meaning and technologies that are developed and maintained in varied historical contexts. In this chapter, we focus on two scales of cultural process that inform each other: broad archaeological traditions and particular historical events. We look at a case of strongly contrasting technological patterns spanning the Paleoindian and Middle Archaic periods in New England, exploring the realm of "technological style," or the cultural components of technology (Lechtman 1977:3). The two broad traditions are the Atlantic Slope macrotradition (Dincauze 1976:140), having a highly visible sequence of projectile point styles, and the Gulf of Maine Archaic tradition, lacking flaked stone projectile points (Robinson 1992). The problem in its most reduced form may be called "The Case of the Missing Projectile Points." Like any good mystery plot, it thickens with historical detail, in this case drawn from the Bull Brook Paleoindian site and Early Archaic period cremation cemeteries in New England.

Stone projectile points are among the most used and abused of artifacts for many good reasons. They are durable, abundant, and highly stylized and in some cases are the only diagnostic element of cultural assemblages. This last characteristic makes them dangerously visible, attracting attention that may be archaeologically understandable but also distracting. They are quintessentially killing tools, incorporating attributes of efficiency (Ahler and Geib 2000; Torrence 1989) with the symbolism of life and death (Bradley 1991; Loring 2002:184). The meaning of their presence and absence is a culture history problem, especially in the Middle Archaic period of New England (ca. 8000 to 6000 radiocarbon years BP), where two broadly contrasting traditions border abruptly with each other as neighbors (fig. 11.1). It is a case study in interpreting large-scale archaeological patterns, weighing factors of cultural tradition and adaptation.

Nested theoretically in the structure of historical process (Pauketat 2001a), we employ the overall approach described by Trigger (2006:33) and others in which high-level theories serve as important "controlling models" but with only general or imprecise predictive power because they are so distant from particular circumstances. Particular histories are the product of specific interactions and thus may be defined and tested with greater precision, but subject to high-level controlling models, historical understanding, and available evidence. Similarly, larger-scale historical generalizations (like traditions) may be broadly applicable but strongly selected and may have little predictive power outside their narrowly defined domain. The isolation of widespread aspects of technology or ritual (or any other factor) in time and space emphasizes continuity of separate cultural subsystems, defined as archaeological horizons and traditions, recognizing that cultures are open systems and that different subsystems overlap and interact in different ways (Clarke 1978:250; Kowalewski 1995:148; Willey and Phillips 1958:32, 37). Broad explanatory domains (e.g., ecological, social, ritual) are integrated in specific cultural contexts, but may sometimes be distinguished and weighed against each other to identify multiple factors that influenced the past.

Hunting technologies need to be physically adequate. But beyond that requirement, many hunter-gatherer societies also have beliefs about appropriate ways of killing, honoring, processing, and disposing of animals to assure the success of future hunts and the survival of the group. Cultural appropriateness is the stuff of tradition, initiating distinct causal chains that incorporate but transcend the physical necessities of survival (Feit 1973:116; Trigger 2006:526). Widespread Subarctic traditions, among others, provide examples of pervasive hunting ritual (e.g., Feit 1973; Tanner 1979). Although these modern traditions could be directly descended from Paleoindian and Early Archaic predecessors, we do not call on the direct historical approach for support. Rather, we

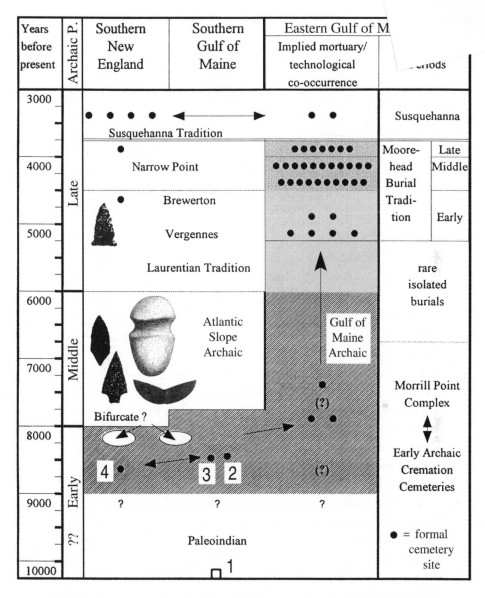

Figure 11.1. A culture history chart, showing the major boundary (the heavy vertical line) between the biface-dominated Atlantic Slope Archaic macrotradition and the bifaceless Gulf of Maine Archaic tradition. Temporal–spatial positions of sites discussed in the text are (1) Bull Brook, (2) Morrill Point Mound, (3) Table Land, and (4) Wapanucket.

apply the archaeological equivalent, using particularly lucid archaeological cases situated near the temporal origins of our reputed traditions. The particular cases incorporate the trappings of hunting and death in socially and ritually structured contexts, providing archaeologically visible signatures of organized events. The large-scale historical traditions provide a contextual stage on which the particular cases have greater meaning. Have we put the right historical details on the right stage? That is a problem with all archaeology. We provide a plausible cultural explanation for very large and contrasting technological patterns that applies to macrotraditions in the context of neighbors.

Projectile Point Function and Northeast Environments

An obvious explanation for the absence of flaked stone points in the Gulf of Maine Archaic tradition is that they were made of perishable organic materials. Bone and antler are more durable than stone for projectile points, especially in very cold weather, but stone points are more lethal (Ellis 1997:40, 58; Knecht 1997:206). Guthrie (1983:277) notes that caribou antler was the dominant material for projectile points during Paleolithic times from France to eastern Beringia (often combined with microblade inserts). Although bone and stone were widely used for projectile points on both large and small animals, an important cross-cultural observation is that stone points were used almost exclusively on large game "such as deer, elk, caribou, moose, bison, and so on" (Ellis 1997:40). Material availability influenced material selection, such as in parts of the Amazon basin where stone is absent (Ellis 1997:54), but this is not a problem in the Gulf of Maine region. Raw material characteristics are necessary factors in the consideration of tool manufacture, but only occasionally adequate to explain the range of cultural variation (Knecht 1997:207; McGhee 1977).

The sharpest boundary between the Atlantic Slope and Gulf of Maine Archaic traditions occurs roughly at the Kennebec River in central Maine during the Middle Archaic period (ca. 8000–6000 radiocarbon years BP). At this time, the Neville and Stark complexes of the Atlantic Slope macrotradition extend to the Androscoggin River in southwestern Maine (figs. 11.1 and 11.2; Dincauze 1976; Pollock et al.

2008:109; Robinson 1992; Sanger 2006:231). This boundary region corresponds to a geographic zone of relatively rapid environmental change. Much remains to be learned about specific cultural patterns in the broader region, but renewed cultural differences through time at the mid-Maine boundary, with occasional interruptions (such as the Susquehanna tradition intrusion, Bourque 1992:45; Sanger 2006:235) testify to the importance of the boundary area. At the time of European arrival the Kennebec River marked the northeastern extent of corn agriculture, with hunter-gatherer economies to the east (Bourque 1989:262). The Kennebec drainage is loosely associated with a variety of important environmental and geographic contrasts, including vegetation zones, wetland habitats, coastal configuration, and upland lake patterns. It has been used as a convenient boundary for the Maritime Peninsula and the Far Northeast (fig. 11.2).

The Kennebec River crosscuts a modern vegetation tension zone (where a large number of plant species reach their range limits) in southwestern Maine, defining the ecotone between central hardwood forest to the south and the spruce-fir-northern hardwood forest (fig. 11.2). The forest boundary is well defined in the north-central United States, interrupted by the Appalachian Mountains and strongly expressed in Maine (McMahon 1990:28), where it is constrained by upland topography and marine climate, stabilizing it to some degree (Gaudreau 1988:231–232; Schauffler and Jacobson 2002:237). The hook-shaped tension zone includes the "range boundaries of 67 species (28 percent of the state's woody flora)" (McMahon 1990:33) roughly correlated in the past with the 20 percent oak pollen isopol, a significant cultural boundary zone in the Northeast (Dincauze and Mulholland 1977). Six out of eight species of oak, butternut, and shagbark hickory are restricted to the southwestern part of the state (Sidell 1999:196).

The broad boundary distinguishes the Mast Forest Archaic of the south (after nut- and fruit-bearing plants) from the Lake Forest Archaic of the more interior Great Lakes region and the Maritime Archaic of the Far Northeast (Snow 1980:190–233; Tuck 1978:29). Among the major resource differences associated with terrestrial vegetation, the southern mast forest supports larger numbers of white-tailed deer, in contrast to moose, beaver, and caribou on the Maritime Peninsula (Robinson 2001:72; Sanger 2006:235: Tuck 1978:30), with black bear spanning both

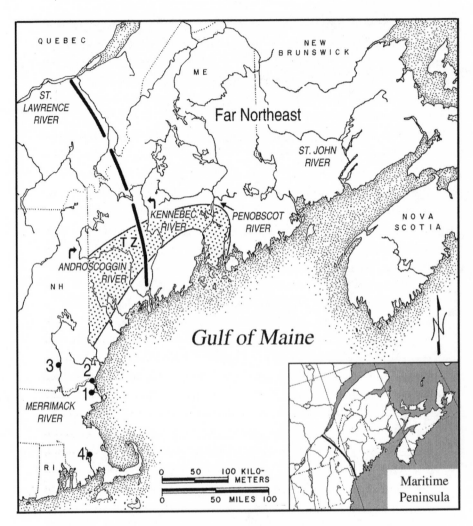

Figure 11.2. The approximate boundary (dark line) of the Far Northeast and
the Maritime Peninsula (to right) as distinguished from the broader Northeast. The stippled zone in southwestern Maine (TZ) is a vegetation tension
zone (McMahon 1990:101). Site locations discussed in the text are (1) Bull
Brook, (2) Morrill Point Mound, (3) Table Land, and (4) Wapanucket.

areas. The distribution of white-tailed deer and other mast forest animals
is associated with greater use of broad interior landscapes, while central
and eastern Maine are noted for occupation in proximity to water, for
access to moose, beaver, fish, and transportation (Sanger et al. 2007:440).

The Middle Archaic period was generally warmer and dryer with lower water levels than at present, although calcined faunal remains from this period often suggest a wetland focus (Sanger et al. 2007:441; Spiess and Mosher 2006:390). All faunal remains from the early Holocene are burned or calcined, acknowledging that the occurrence of burned bone is subject to both natural and cultural factors (Sanger 2003; Spiess 1992:164, 176). The small faunal samples from western Maine during this time include white-tailed deer in the Middle Archaic period (Spiess and Mosher 2006:390). Faunal samples from the upper Penobscot often have little deer, with much greater proportions of beaver (Spiess 1992:176). White-tailed deer are consistently important on coastal sites of the Late Archaic period Moorehead phase, east to the Penobscot and beyond (Bourque 1995:86; Spiess and Lewis 2001; Spiess and Mosher 2006:396). The coastal distribution reflects vegetation patterns for the Late Archaic period, but also shows that simple correlations of culture and environment at the Kennebec River are not sustained at close range.

If the discussion were limited to the most strongly contrasting technological patterns of the Middle Archaic period, the distribution of Atlantic Slope biface tradition approximates the greater abundance of white-tailed deer while the Gulf of Maine Archaic has greater association with wetland species. If increased focus on wetlands represented a focus on small-bodied animals, then stone projectile points may have been less important, given the strong association of stone points with large game (Ellis 1997:40). However, environments east of the Kennebec supported moose, caribou, and bear associated with well-developed biface technologies throughout the second half of the Holocene epoch. The most recent analysis of Gulf of Maine Archaic and Neville–Stark faunal samples in Maine does not show strong contrasts between them (Spiess and Mosher 2006:399). Moreover, the Gulf of Maine Archaic tradition originated in the Early Archaic period when both technological and ritual patterns were more widely spread throughout southern New England, disassociated with the sharp vegetation boundaries emphasized for the Kennebec cultural boundary (fig. 11.1).

Biface Traditions of the Southeast

The long succession of diagnostic projectile point styles in eastern North America provided an important tool for chronology building in the Archaic period (Broyles 1971; Coe 1964; Dincauze 1976:140). Points are abundant and widely recognized, and although it has long been recognized that "one culture–one point style" constructs are inadequate (Fitzhugh 1972b:3), projectile points often served as the chosen implement of identity (Robinson 2006:345). The lack of these point styles in the Far Northeast was for decades interpreted as a possible population hiatus (no points–no people), until deeply stratified sites revealed a different technological tradition (Petersen and Putnam 1992; Sanger 1996).

In the Southeast, earlier styles seem to transform into later ones, from fluted points, to unfluted Dalton points, to notched varieties with concave bases, and so on (Anderson 1995:11, 15; Broyles 1971:45; Coe 1964:63–68; Kowalewski 1995:159) and are associated with ground stone tool forms such as bannerstones and grooved axes introduced at equally wide scales (Cross 1999:63; Sassaman 1996). Certainly the styles and frequencies are not uniform over the entire Southeast and into Maine. Rather, the pattern is more like a series of broad spatial-temporal lenses, suggesting stylistic signaling at macroregional scales (Kowalewski 1995:160). Concordant changes in point styles "remain unexplained, but at least the fact that they do change in concert means there was a flow of information on a subcontinental scale" (Kowalewski 1995:159). The macroscale pattern of projectile point styles is, in effect, a tradition of broad stylistic horizons, although it is emphasized that this perception of broad similarity does not contradict diversity in other domains (Sassaman 1996). The marked emphasis on concurrent style changes from Paleoindian through Middle Archaic times provides a basis for enquiry into other social or ritual functions that would support continuity. Caches of oversized bifaces in the Late Archaic period provide a focus for social interaction (Jefferies 1996:228). Here we look more closely at a well-defined social event of the Paleoindian period, early in the tradition of broad stylistic continuity.

Paleoindian Origins and Social Context of Projectile Point Production at the Bull Brook Site

Paleoindian technology as a whole is often characterized by extremely fine workmanship and technological signatures (e.g., fluting and parallel flaking). Plains Paleoindian projectile points have been described as "exceptionally and unnecessarily well-made" (Bamforth and Hicks 2008:136). The extreme care taken in production has been explained variably as "symbolic of the power invested in them" (Bradley 1991:379) or the critical efficiency of specific technofunctional attributes (Ahler and Geib 2000:799, 804). The issue of extreme emphasis placed on projectile points has also been raised for the present (Why do some archaeologists focus so much on projectile points?), but we make the case that it is a valid question during Paleoindian and Eastern Archaic times as well.

The conditions for technological function are to some degree testable in the present if they can be successfully replicated. Social factors need to be explored in the spatial and temporal arrangements of archaeological cultures, in this case the ring-shaped settlement plan of the Bull Brook site in Ipswich, Massachusetts. Recent investigation of settlement and activity patterning at Bull Brook revealed distinct patterns supporting the proposition that the site represents a single event, the largest and most highly organized social event from the Pleistocene of North America, with thirty-six activity loci arranged in an oval pattern measuring 170 m by 135 m (Robinson et al. 2009).

The Bull Brook site was salvaged by seven avocational archaeologists from gravel pit operations between 1950 and 1959. The history of research provides a dramatic account of the interplay between archaeological evidence and theoretical models of the time. The excavators included four Vaccaro brothers and William Eldridge, the principal record keeper. They consulted regularly with Douglas Byers (1954, 1955, 1956, 1959) of the Robert S. Peabody Museum and Douglas Jordan (1960), a Harvard graduate student. By 1959, they had produced a site plan showing a large circular arrangement of house-sized artifact concentrations that they interpreted as a camp circle. Archaeologists in the 1950s rejected the proposition that a Paleoindian site the size of Bull Brook could represent one occupation (Byers 1959:428; Jordan 1960:132; Robinson and Eldridge 2005). Settlement pattern archaeology was in its infancy at this time (Trigger 2006:21). Two decades later, archaeologists reconsidered the "single occupation hypothesis" (Curran 1984; Grimes 1979; Spiess 1984) and multiple explanations for other large Northeastern Paleoindian sites were explored (Curran 1999; Dincauze 1993; Ellis and Deller 2000; Spiess et al. 1998). Recent analysis of the settlement

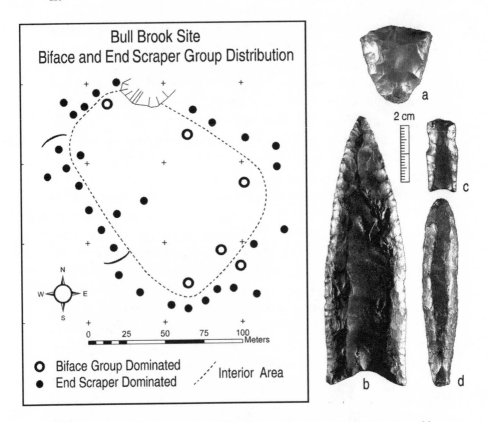

Figure 11.3. The ring-shaped Bull Brook site plan, showing loci dominated by biface group artifacts (b, bifaces; c, drills; and d, flake shavers) and end scrapers (a). The brackets show a linear segment of the outer ring referred to in the text. (Photographs are courtesy of the Peabody Essex Museum [a, c, d] and the Robert S. Peabody Museum [b]; the map is from Robinson et al. 2009)

pattern and artifact distributions support the interpretation of a single occupation in a large camp circle with strongly differentiated concentric activity patterning representing inner and outer rings of activity (fig. 11.3; Robinson et al. 2009).

Eight loci are situated distinctly on the inside of the more continuous ring of 28 loci, allowing separation of the large artifact assemblage (totaling 2,500 specimens of seven standardized tool forms, into two groups). Statistical analysis of the two groups demonstrated that four of the seven tool forms were strongly contrasted between the interior and exterior groups. Bifaces, drills, and flake shavers (here called the biface group), were concentrated on the interior (fig. 11.3). End scrapers were concentrated on the exterior.

Focusing on the most highly contrasting sets of artifacts, six loci (shown as black rings on fig. 11.3) have distinctly higher proportions of bifaces, flake shavers, and drills. These six loci produced 17 percent of all artifacts, but 34 percent ($n = 97$) of the bifaces, 64 percent ($n = 44$) of the drills, and 63 percent ($n = 79$) of the flake shavers. With recent analysis of 36,475 flakes by Ort, building on Jordan's investigation of flute flakes, these six loci also produced 89 percent ($n = 108/122$) of the flute flakes, suggesting that flute removal was the single-most-concentrated activity associated with the interior loci. The six loci produced only 5 percent ($n = 61$) of the end scrapers. Five of the six loci dominated by the biface group of artifacts were interior loci.

The recent analysis also supports the interpretation that the large aggregation at Bull Brook was probably associated with a caribou drive, perhaps at the scale of a maximum band (Wobst 1974:152). This is based, in part, on the working model that Jeffreys Ledge, a fishing bank now located fifty meters below sea level, was a large maritime island during the Younger Dryas cold period, providing a predictable caribou migration route to the interior past the Bull Brook site (Pelletier and Robinson 2005). Three loci at Bull Brook produced diagnostic foot bones of caribou, from over one thousand fragments of shattered calcined bone (Spiess et al. 1998). Interpretation of Bull Brook as a communal caribou hunt does not limit the range of subsistence practices at other times of the year (Spiess 1979:131). Although the model remains to be tested, the probability that Bull Brook represents a communal caribou drive provides substantial context with which to interpret the spatial patterns at Bull Brook.

Planning for large gatherings puts extra stress on social and subsistence activities, including coordinating labor for the hunt, processing large amounts of meat, feasting, hide processing and manufacture, and disposal practices, among other activities, in order to ensure a successful hunt (Binford 1991; Halperin 1980:392). Large-group planning is often associated with heightened spatial organization (Whitelaw 1991:158). Gender roles are often well developed among Arctic and Subarctic cultures that focus on large mammal hunting, particularly at communal hunts involving a variety of tasks (Frink 2005:92; Halperin 1980:392; Waguespack 2005:671). Ritual practices are important parts of these highly charged endeavors. For example, pleasing the spirit of the animals may have strong economic and religious motives, initiating rites, reinforcing taboos, and elaborating ritual performance and equipment (Feit 1973:116; McCaffrey, this vol.; Tanner 1979:140, 153; Trigger 2006:526).

The separation of biface production from end scraper use, among other tools, is well known at Northeastern Paleoindian sites (Curran 1984:14, 31) with evidence of zonal separation at Parkhill in Ontario (Ellis and Deller 2000:226, 246) and Debert in Nova Scotia (MacDonald 1968:133). Bull Brook adds more strongly developed concentric organization, larger sample sizes, and specialized tool forms to the understanding of this activity pattern. For Parkhill and Debert, gender roles were suggested as one probable source of explanation for the separation of activities (Ellis and Deller 2000:232; MacDonald 1968:133). In the context of a probable caribou drive site with a large number of families hunting and processing a large number of animals, Bull Brook adds to evidence of gender activities. The strong separation of projectile point production from abundant hide-processing tools and other activities is interpreted, at least in part, to represent a separation of gender roles, with male hunting preparations and other activities situated in a smaller number of concentrations on the interior, and female production and processing activities concentrated in the larger number of activity areas in the major circle of loci. The emphasis placed on projectile point production represents a disparity in preservation when the end product of technical expertise is made of stone, compared to a wide variety of perishable products such as winter clothing, shelter, and other hunting gear (Gero 1991:167; Waguespack 2005:673). At Bull Brook, the spatial separation and high degree of organization enhance the visibility of male and female activities, subject to more intensive analysis of use wear and spatial relationships at multiple Paleoindian sites.

Returning to the social context of projectile point production as a more general topic, the Bull Brook site provides evidence that projectile point production was segregated, probably with other utilitarian and ritual aspects of hunting preparation. The removal of the flute is the single-most-segregated activity identified at the site, with 89 percent of flute flakes in 17 percent of the loci. It is suggested that flute removal probably occurred within male-dominated activity areas and, minimally, in a specialized social context of production. Although ritual activities were undoubtedly part of hunting preparations, the spatial evidence at Bull Brook does not specifically designate ritual context for fluting. Rather, the extraordinarily wide distribution of fluting on multiple styles of points in North and South America (Morrow and Morrow 1999) suggests to some archaeologists that "a stronger force must have been driving the fluting process; something more than the advantages gained in projectile penetration or the strength of haft bonding" (Ahler and Geib 2000:803). With regard to Folsom fluted points, Bradley (1991:378) suggests that because "the fluting of an already thin preform was a risky business, the success or failure of the attempt may have been considered a prognostication of the success of an upcoming event such as a hunt."

Divination, pleasing the animals, and shamanism are variations among hunting rituals (Speck 1935:34; Tanner 1979:110, 136). Favoring the efficient technofunctional explanation for Folsom points, Ahler and Geib (2000:800) suggest that the "fluting shaman" viewpoint is now in the minority, in part based on the "clear lack of evidence for spatial restriction of fluting behavior. Byproducts from fluting confirm that fluting events occurred in virtually every non-kill Folsom site yet found."

Bull Brook provides new information on the context of fluting for Eastern fluted-point cultures. At this largest and most highly organized Paleoindian settlement currently known, fluting is the single-most-restricted technological practice associated with the inner ring of loci. There is no need for a "fluting shaman," although the role is plausible. For our present problem with the Atlantic Slope Archaic macrotradition, it is sufficient to say that at Bull Brook, projectile point production, including horizon-wide attributes of lithic technology, was part of specialized social and perhaps ritual aspects of hunting preparations. This conclusion is derived from the unusual visibility afforded by a large and well-organized communal hunting event, combined with regional- and continental-scale observations on style, activity patterning, and ritual caching of bifaces (Bamforth 2002:68; Deller and Ellis 2001:280). Taken in the context of technological style, the extremely precise reduction techniques characteristic of broad Paleoindian technologies (Bradley 1991) represent a complex chain of activities that are specific to stone technology, not simply an elaborate product (Dobres and Hoffman 1999:3). Although these precise reduction techniques are less prevalent in the Archaic period, the focus on specific lithic styles that change concurrently over large areas represents a similar technological and cultural focus, remembering that the Paleoindian tradition is the apparent predecessor of the Atlantic Slope Archaic macrotradition. The potential importance of the social and ritual context of projectile point production at this scale is emphasized by the striking contrast with the adjacent Gulf of Maine Archaic tradition during the Middle Archaic period.

Bone, Stone, and Ritual Contexts in the Far Northeast

The abundant stone projectile points, elaborate bannerstones, and full-grooved axes of the Atlantic Slope Archaic are largely absent east of the Kennebec River in the Middle Archaic period (fig. 11.1). Flaked stone projectile points are absent in the Gulf of Maine Archaic tradition, but there is no shortage of distinctive stone tools including the Early Archaic period development of elaborate polished full-channeled gouges, long finely made stone rods, and a wide occurrence of cores and unifaces made of quartz or other materials (Forrest 1999; Petersen and Putnam 1992; Robinson 1992; Sanger 1996). Added to these technological differences, the Gulf of Maine Archaic tradition is associated with formal cemeteries from the time of its origin (8600 BP) continuing intermittently for five thousand years, and culminating in the Late Archaic period florescence of the Moorehead Burial tradition (Red Paint burials) (Bourque 1995; Moorehead 1922; Robinson 1996; Sanger 1973). Thus there is a concordance of technological and mortuary patterning through the Middle Archaic period, with continuity in the mortuary elaboration through the Late Archaic period.

With poor organic preservation in the Northeast, we can only say that apparent bone projectile point tips and shafts have been recovered from cremations (Robbins 1968:60, 62; Robinson 2006:fig. 4d), providing a plausible substitute for flaked stone points, but not in any quantified manner. Nor would the presence of bone points explain in a meaningful way why stone was not used. Early Archaic period cremation cemeteries provide a window on ritual and technological development that includes rare assemblages of bone tools (Robinson 2006). Three cremation cemeteries in southern New England are dated between 8600 to 8400 BP, all excavated by avocational archaeologists. The Table Land site (Robinson 1996:99), Morrill Point Mound (Robinson 1992:81), and Wapanucket Feature 206 (Robbins 1968; Robinson 2001, 2006) produced artifact assemblages including early adzes, gouges, and long stone rods or whetstones characteristic of the Gulf of Maine Archaic tradition.

Detailed analysis of the cremations revealed a significant component of cremated bone tools (table 11.1), including cut bone-shaft fragments of mammal and bird, a bone gouge bit, a needle, a probable projectile point midshaft, and large quantities of turtle-shell fragments with scraped interiors. Four cremation deposits produced a minimum of thirteen different worked bone artifacts and a range of animal species including deer, bear, bobcat, and great auk. There is a sufficient quantity of cremated bone tools at all three cemeteries to identify a pattern in which bone artifacts are included with human remains *at the time of cremation*, while stone tools are excluded (Robinson 2006). Stone tools are added to the graves unburned, in secondary burials at formal cemeteries. If this pattern is representative, it means that bone tools are properly associated with primary death rituals at the time of cremation, with stone treated differently.

The dichotomous treatment of bone tools and stone tools associated with the cremation ceremony has two important implications. First, although the sample size is now small, the pattern is readily testable if other samples become available. Second, the cremations are the earliest evidence of rituals associated with a technology in which flaked stone points are largely excluded from occupation sites. At the Morrill Point Mound site, projectile points of elaborated or nonlocal forms are sometimes included in burial contexts but not yet recognized in occupation sites (Robinson 1992:93).

Specialized treatment of bone in hunting practices is widely associated with Inuit and Algonquian people of the Subarctic and Arctic, associated with tool manufacture and disposal (Feit 1973; McCaffrey, this vol.; Tanner 1979). Among the Thule culture of arctic Canada, projectile points for hunting caribou are made from caribou antler, while those for hunting sea mammals are usually made from ivory or sea mammal bone, with later Inuit mythology and practices providing suitable

Table 11.1. An analysis of cremations from the Early Archaic period at the Table Land and Morrill Point Mound sites

Burial area	Sample number	Count and weight (grams)	Bone totals[a]		Unmodified animal				Modified bone, scraped or cut					Minimum number of bone artifacts	Animal taxa, non-human
					Mammal or bird		Turtle		Turtle		Mammal or bird		Percent modified of total bone		
			1/4 in.	1/16 in.	1/4 in.	1/16 in.	1/4 in.	1/16 in.	1/4 in.	1/16 in.	1/4 in.	1/16 in.			
Table Land Burial Site															
Clyde Berry[b]	MHS: 4256	Count	482	1193	10	2	5	3	3	2	10			4	beaver, turtle
Sample		Weight	243	52.6	4.51	0.06	1.36	0.16	0.38	0.09	7.56		2.72%		
Morrill Point Mound															
CB101 area[b]	CBS: H, I, J, K, L, BB	Count	178	3669	6	28	3	61	8	8	3	7		5	bobcat, deer, great auk, gull-like bird, turtle
		Weight	75	93.6	3.33	1.77	0.79	2.17	1.42	0.34	3.8	0.31	3.48%		
CB103 area[b]	CBS: O, Q, R, S, T, U, AA, CC	Count	115	347	1	4	1	6		2				1	deer, turtle
		Weight	49.4	28	0.34	0.27	0.14	0.48		0.12			0.16%		
CB104[b]	CBS: P	Count	128	375		3	4	4	4		2			3	turtle
		Weight	56.9	30.4		0.28	0.77	0.23	1.07		1.41		2.84%		
N36E9 scatter	CBS: M, N	Count	11	14											
		Weight	4.66	1.96									0%		
Near CB101 and CB104	CBS: Z	Count	46	407	1	6	2	4	1						turtle
		Weight	20.7	13.6	0.41	0.25	1.07	0.24	0.41				1.20%		
Total for 18 sq. meter area		Count	478	4812	8	41	10	75	13	10	5	7		9	
		Weight	207	168	4.08	2.57	2.77	3.12	2.9	0.46	5.21	0.31	2.38%		

Source: Adapted from Robinson 2006:fig. 5. The analysis emphasizes the proportion of unmodified animal bone and modified or worked bone artifacts.

[a] Human bone dominates all samples and is included with "bone totals."

[b] Separate cremation deposits.

explanations (McGhee 1977). Frank Speck recorded an ethnographic case of specialized animal-bone use among the Innu or Naskapi of sub-arctic Canada: "Another object of special utility having religious associations is the bone skinning tool. . . . Ordinarily they are made from the leg bone of the bear. . . . It is a definite teaching among these hunters that the slain beaver feels satisfaction in having its pelt removed with the leg-bone skinning tool. And so it becomes a religious obligation for the righteous-minded hunter to skin the beaver with such a tool" (Speck 1935:216–217).

The tenacity with which such obligations may be maintained is reflected in fundamental human–animal relationships, since the soul of the hunted animal survives and directly influences the success of future hunts (Feit 1973:116; Speck 1935:76; Tanner 1979:136). Although specific practices will vary, beliefs associated with increasing hunting success may serve as powerful motivations. The specialized inclusion of bone tools from different animal species in Early Archaic period cremations, accompanied by a practice of replicating bone tool forms in ground stone (Robinson 2006:351) may be forerunners of the elaborate use of animal symbolism during the Late Archaic period mortuary traditions of the Far Northeast (Tuck 1976) and perhaps that of Algonquian hunters and gatherers into recent times. Part of the problem of such large-scale patterns is deciding whether they are meaningful and worthy of scrutiny, or so commonplace as to be taken for granted. Tenacious meaningful patterns may be commonplace, with identification facilitated when they are manifested in multiple contexts.

Summary

New England archaeology encompasses boundaries between horizon-scale ritual and social traditions. Especially well-structured social occasions such as the aggregation at Bull Brook and Early Archaic period cremation cemeteries provide windows on hunting and social rituals near the beginning of long traditions that span the Archaic period. The small number of cremation burials that were analyzed may or may not be representative. However, in specific cultural contexts, a small number of cases may indeed represent strongly held ritual beliefs that are viewed as critical to survival and social relations. The cases presented in this chapter are potentially homologous cultural cases near the origin of widespread and strongly contrasting archaeological traditions.

The original problem of this chapter was to explain a broad but narrowly defined contrast in technological traditions, first recognized at the scale of macrotraditions. The presence and the absence of flaked stone projectile points are both directly associated with hunting technology. The particular cases provide views of the problem from specific cultural contexts in which the greater combination of subsistence, social context, and ritual can be brought to bear.

At Bull Brook, technological operations requiring skilled stone working represent the single-most-restricted activity associated with specialized activity areas lining the interior of the circular settlement pattern. In the Early Archaic period cremation cemeteries, there is an apparent dichotomy between bone and stone in the context of death rituals, suggesting that a similar dichotomy might apply in the context of hunting rituals. Quite literally, in this interpretation, the presence and absence of one of archaeology's traditional indicators of identity, projectile points, represents alternative cultural solutions to the problem of hunting animals appropriately, supporting substantially different technologies for thousands of years. The particular cases, the broad macroregional traditions, and regional environmental factors all require further testing. It is certainly the combination of scales and contexts that makes the problems more meaningful, in the richly cross-connected patterns of culture history.

Acknowledgments

Research on both the Bull Brook site and the Early Archaic period cremation cemeteries cited in this chapter is part of long-term projects incorporating Robinson's dissertation research at Brown University, collaboration with the late James B. Petersen, Frederick H. West, and William Eldridge, among many others. Recent work was conducted at the University of Maine, the University of Montreal, and the Peabody Essex Museum. Research on Bull Brook was supported by Frederick H. West and National Science Foundation grant No. BCS 0352918. The Amerind Foundation seminar provided the opportunity to assimilate these projects with the ideas of other participants, in the richly cross-connected patterns of culture history research. Special thanks for invitations, discussant comments, and advice go to Don Holly, Tristram Kidder, John Ware, Moira McCaffrey, David Sanger, Ken Sassaman, Laura Schieber, Ann Surprenant, Martin Wobst, and anonymous reviewers, among others, none of whom are responsible for shortcomings.

Structural Transformation and Innovation in Emergent Political Economies of Southern California

Lynn H. Gamble

The Chumash populations of southern California differed from many societies discussed in this volume in that they lacked monumental architecture. Instead of building mounds, large plazas, and other public spaces, they invested time and energy into the production, distribution, and use of shell beads that were traded over a wide region. Beads were made and used in the Santa Barbara Channel region continuously for over seven thousand years, making them one of the longest-running media of Chumash material culture. Perhaps it is no coincidence that current evidence suggests there were no major population replacements or other significant population shifts on the northern Santa Barbara Channel Islands and the adjacent mainland for at least the last ten thousand years (Glassow et al. 2007). Recent research on California Indian mitochondrial DNA lineages suggests "an ancient presence of Chumashan peoples in the Santa Barbara Channel" (Johnson and Lorenz 2006:33) (fig. 12.1). Recent linguistic evidence suggests that the Chumashan language family is an isolate that appears to have great antiquity in California, supporting the DNA data (Johnson and Lorenz 2006). This is not to say that the people in the region were culturally static throughout this history, as change among the populations of the Santa Barbara Channel region is well documented (e.g., Erlandson 1994; Gamble et al. 2001; Glassow 1993; Glassow et al. 2007; Kennett 2005; King 1990). Nevertheless, this unique example of continuity among biological populations provides researchers the opportunity to examine in situ cultural development in a historical context.

My primary area of concern in this chapter is the complex history of shell beads and how variation in the production, form, and distribution of shell beads informs us about changes in their meaning, value, and power. A number of researchers working in the Santa Barbara Chan-

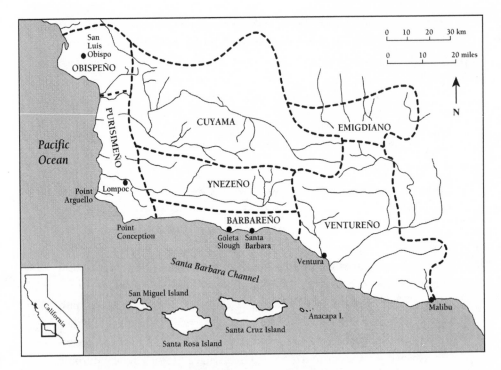

Figure 12.1. Chumash linguistic groups and modern place-names in the Santa Barbara Channel area.

nel region have focused on the production of beads and, to a lesser extent, their distribution, use, and social contexts (Arnold 1992, 2001a, 2001b; Arnold and Munns 1994; King 1976, 1990). The emphasis has tended to be on the economic nature of beads and how beads served to minimize risk in the region. It has been suggested that intervillage exchange crosscut three environmental settings—the Island, the Mainland, and the Inland—in the Santa Barbara Channel area and that the dependence on beads developed in part so that the people of the region were able to ensure that they had adequate food supplies throughout the year, including inhabitants of ecological zones with relatively limited resources (King 1976). There is strong evidence for this hypothesis, but Chumash-produced shell beads have been found far beyond the confines of the historically documented Chumash territory. In fact, shell beads have always been about making, reproducing, and transforming social alliances and as such, many constituencies were involved:

the producers, the distributors, and the consumers, including those who removed beads from circulation through burial. Multiple and dynamic options for alliances through bead production, exchange, and use always existed. Once systems of bead production and exchange were in place, any disruption of the network would have the potential of disrupting the entire economy in ways that perhaps eclipse, or at least rival, the effects of climatic changes such as El Niño–Southern Oscillation (ENSO) events and other environmental crises.

The main thrust of this chapter is not about the subsistence economy, which was organized at the household level, but about the political economy. Although the political economy intersects the sphere of the subsistence economy, it encompasses the exchange of services and goods within a complex network of interconnected families. As such, beads are about making and reproducing entire networks of affiliation and interaction, not simply individual communities and households. It is this network of relationships, both within and outside the Chumash region, that I am concerned with here. The social life of beads as they journeyed through multiple hands and were interpreted and reinterpreted in different cultural contexts is explored. Although the economic significance of beads is considered, I move beyond ecological models to address the complex history of shell beads and how transformations in this history reflect the lives of people who participated in the production, distribution, and consumption of beads.

The Chumash Example

The inhabitants of the Santa Barbara Channel region exhibited a number of characteristics at the time of European contact that are associated with complex hunter-gatherer societies (Ames and Maschner 1999; Gamble 2008). They lived in relatively large sedentary settlements, some with hundreds or even thousands of inhabitants, supported by relatively large quantities of stored food, including acorns, seeds, and dried fish, some of which could be stored for several years. They managed their environment, as did other California Indians (see Lightfoot et al., this vol.), through the use of fire to promote the growth of seed-bearing plants, discourage the growth of less desirable plants, and create habitats that were more favorable to deer and other wildlife (Timbrook et al. 1982).

They developed specialized technology, such as the plank canoe, that intensified fishing, hunting, gathering, and trade practices. They used shell beads as currency, which facilitated exchange, and had a social hierarchy with permanent leadership positions (Gamble 2008).

The population of the Chumash peoples at historic contact is estimated to have been between eighteen and twenty thousand people (Cook 1976:37–38; Johnson 1998:i). The Chumash inhabited large villages and towns along the Santa Barbara Channel coast, living in houses that were clustered next to the shoreline in places where freshwater was available in nearby streams and springs. Many settlements were near lagoons, such as those located around the Goleta Slough (fig. 12.1), where the population exceeded two thousand people in 1769. Sandy beaches, which were usually adjacent to communities, served as ideal landing spots for watercraft. Most villages south of Point Conception had at least a few plank canoes, and several larger settlements had between ten and sixteen canoes each. There is evidence for a settlement hierarchy during the Late period, with the larger towns having some authority over smaller settlements (Gamble 2008; Johnson 1988).

Information on the social organization of the Chumash peoples derives primarily from mission register documents, ethnohistoric accounts, and ethnographic data. Postmarital residence patterns were primarily matrilocal, although patrilocal and less commonly bilocal and neolocal residence patterns have been recorded (Harrington 1942:30–31; Johnson 1988). Chumash chiefs were often polygynous and tended towards patrilocal residence. According to ethnographic accounts, chiefs, members of their family, and other highly ranked individuals were required to be members of the 'antap society, a group of specialists who performed dances and rituals at public ceremonies (Blackburn 1976:236–238). The parents of children being initiated into the society paid relatively large quantities of shell-bead money as a type of membership fee. Evidence suggests that the 'antap organization also operated at a regional level to integrate chiefs and other wealthy individuals from a wide area (Blackburn 1975; Hudson and Underhay 1978:29; Hudson et al. 1981). Ethnographic data indicate that members of the 'antap society exclusively used large deer tibia whistles (Hudson and Blackburn 1986:354). That these items are found in archaeological contexts dating to the late Middle period led Corbett (1999) to suggest that the 'antap society existed for hundreds of years in the region. Although we have a rough idea of the population density of the Chumash in 1769, we lack detailed information on changes in settlement locations and population densities over the previous seven thousand years. Most scholars of the Santa Barbara Channel region agree that by at least one thousand years ago, large settlements were permanently established on the coast, especially where boats could land.

Shell Beads and Economic Structure

Shell beads were used in the Santa Barbara region fairly continuously for over seven thousand years. More than twenty-two species of shell have been identified, and most of these species were formed into a number of different types of beads. Just as pottery styles and other types of objects change over time, so did shell-bead styles. The changes in the morphology, hole size, diameter, and final finishing of beads are some of the variables that are used to identify types and to distinguish different chronological periods. A number of important changes in the use of shell beads took place over the millennia, the most important of which was the appearance of cupped beads at the onset of the Late period. These were made from the thick callus of the shell of the *Olivella biplicata* and have been identified as money beads by King (1990), an interpretation that is widely accepted by researchers working in the region (Glassow et al. 2007). It has been suggested that at about the same time cupped beads first appeared, the scale of shell-bead production increased significantly (Arnold and Munns 1994) and shell-bead making had become a specialized craft on the northern Channel Islands (Arnold 1987; Gamble 2008; King 1976).

Two types of craft specialization were associated with the production of shell beads. The first is the manufacture of the beads themselves; the second is the production of the stone drills used to make the perforations in the beads (King 1976). Bead making did not appear to be an "attached" specialization in the sense that administrators controlled the production of the specialists (Arnold and Munns 1994; Brumfiel and Earle 1987; Costin 2001). Although Arnold and Munns propose that bead makers most likely were not monitored in their daily activities, they suggest that the trade of beads probably was controlled by canoe owners who manipulated exchanges throughout the channel region (Arnold and Munns 1994:487). I have recently questioned this latter proposition, as the controlled release of shell beads has not been empirically documented (Gamble 2008). Instead I propose that beads were freely produced and exchanged based on the principles of supply and demand, and that the value of shell beads was maintained as a result of periodic destruction of beads and ornaments, most commonly seen in the accompaniment of shell beads with burials, but also through destruction at ceremonies. The labor investment in the making of shell beads was enormous. Milliken and his colleagues (2007:110) estimate that "each shaped bead, cut from the hard wall of *Olivella*, *Haliotis*, or clamshell, represented almost an hour of production activity." The manufacture of a cupped bead from the thicker and harder portion of the callus of the *Olivella biplicata* was even more time consuming.

Sources of Shell Beads in California

Shell beads were used all over California (Bennyhoff and Hughes 1987), with the earliest examples, *Olivella biplicata* spire-lopped beads, dating to approximately eleven thousand years ago (Fitzgerald et al. 2005). Although several regions have been identified as sources of many shell-bead types, the northern Santa Barbara Channel Islands exhibit the most extensive evidence of shell-bead manufacturing and have been referred to as a "mint" for certain types of shell beads found throughout California (see Hughes and Milliken 2007 for a discussion of this issue). Central California has been recognized as a source of *Saxidomus* shell beads. Although shell-bead detritus has been documented in the region, shell-bead manufacturing has not been observed at the scale of that seen on the northern Santa Barbara Channel Islands, leading some to believe that many bead types were made on the these islands. A method for sourcing *Olivella* shell, one of the most common materials used to make shell beads in the region, using isotopic signatures, has proven to be promising (Eerkens et al. 2005). Jelmer Eerkens and his colleagues analyzed ten *Olivella* beads found in sites in central California and the Owens Valley from various time periods; all ten appeared to have been harvested from the warmer waters south of Point Conception, indicating that most were probably produced in the Santa Barbara Channel region.

Changes in Shell Beads and Their Use

Chester King (1990) systematically recorded artifacts from burial lots in the Santa Barbara Channel region from both the mainland and northern Channel Islands, documenting thousands of shell beads, in addition to stone and bone beads. He identified and quantified many different types of shell beads using burial lot seriation to illustrate how beads, ornaments, and other artifacts changed over seven thousand years (King 1990). On the basis of bead-making refuse from southern California sites, King (1990:xiv) proposed that one important change in bead production was a shift from relatively unspecialized shell-bead making during the Early and early Middle periods to localized specialization that began later in the Middle period and continued throughout the Late period. He suggested that this reflects increased integration of California societies as regions became more economically interdependent.

Olivella biplicata beads that were probably produced on the northern Channel Islands have been found well beyond California, including the Great Basin, Colorado Plateau, Columbian Plateau, and Southwest (Chester King, personal communication 2009; King 1990; Jernigan 1978). Jernigan suggested that in the Anasazi area *Olivella biplicata* saucer beads were used from Basketmaker II through Pueblo IV (300 BC–AD 1600), and that *Olivella biplicata* wall disc, saucer, and probably even cupped beads were used by the Hohokam between about AD 550–1450. Although we know that there was long-distance export of beads produced in the Santa Barbara region, detailed analyses of the types and distribution of shell beads in western North America has not been completed.

Early Period. King found that during the Early period (5500–600 BC), there were relatively few types of beads compared with the number of types found during later periods. He identified three major types of shell beads in use at this time. *Olivella biplicata* spire-removed beads, which were relatively easy to make, were found throughout California and the Great Basin, although there is no evidence that these were made in the area historically occupied by the Chumash. Clam disc–cylinder beads were another fairly common bead type that was used in the Early period; most were used in the region historically occupied by the Chumash (King 1990:108–109). In the early part of the Early period, these beads were highly variable in shape and found associated with many burials. Toward the end of the Early period, Phase z (Ez, 600–200 BC), these types of beads changed to more standardized shapes and were associated with fewer burials. King interprets this pattern as a shift from more egalitarian societies to societies where political leaders controlled wealth. Overall, there were fewer changes in beads throughout the Early period than in the following two later periods.

Middle Period. The Middle period dates from approximately 600 BC to AD 1150, according to King. Relatively few burials from the Middle period contain beads compared with the Early period. Moreover, generally less wealth was buried during the Middle period than the Early period, despite the fact that greater amounts of beads were manufactured in the Santa Barbara Channel region during the Middle period (King 1990:154). King attributed this to "a shift to a more centrally organized society with inheritance of political and economic powers" (King 1990:154). Two shell artifact types, *Olivella biplicata* wall discs or saucers and *Megathura crenulata* ring ornaments, appear in the Middle period and are common for more than a millennium (Middle period, Phase 2a–Middle period, Phase 5c) in the Santa Barbara Channel region, in central California (Bennyhoff and Hughes 1987), in the San Joaquin Valley, and farther to the east, including parts of Nevada and Arizona (King 1990:153–154).

Four *Olivella* saucer beads from central California (types G1, G2a, and G2b, which were in use between M2a and M5c) were sourced by Eerkens and colleagues (2005:1509) and had isotopic values indicating that they were from southern California. The sourcing of type G2b is significant because they were common in central California; in fact the largest documented bead lot ever found in California consisted of approximately 30,000 *Olivella* type G2b saucer beads. These were associated with a 30-year-old male burial that was dated to AD 388 from a site in the Livermore Valley in central California (Milliken et al. 2007:116). Most of these beads, along with thousands of other *Olivella* saucer beads, were probably traded from the Santa Barbara Channel region to the San Francisco Bay area. Only a few years after this interment, however, saucer beads were no longer found as burial accompaniments in the region. They were replaced by rough-edged full saddle *Olivella* beads (Milliken et al. 2007:116), a type not found in the Santa Barbara

Channel region and believed to be made locally in the Bay Area. It is difficult to know why groups in the Bay Area suddenly stopped importing beads from the Santa Barbara Channel region, even though the *Olivella* saucers continued to be made and used in the region. Notwithstanding, the advent of the *Olivella* saucer beads in the Channel area and their wide use both within and outside the region during the early Middle period indicates a significant period of interregional interaction.

It is relevant that prior to the use of saucer beads in Middle period, Phase 1 (M1), large, showy bone and clamshell beads, ornaments, and pendants with punctate and incised designs were common. The bone beads and ornaments were made from large mammals that did not live on the Channel Islands, indicating these were probably made on the mainland. These conspicuous beads and ornaments were less important after the *Olivella* saucers and *Megathura* ornaments were introduced. King has suggested that the large bone and clamshell beads and ornaments, which are not found outside of the Santa Barbara Channel region, were probably not used as currency, but instead were indicators of political position. Later in the Middle period, large bone tubes with appliquéd shell beads appear (fig. 12.2). One burial at Mescalitan Island (CA-SBA-46) had four or five of these around their waist in a belt-like fashion (King 1990:140). These bone tubes probably also were used as signifiers of rank.

Late Period. The Late period as defined by King (1990) dates from AD 1150 to 1804. The beginning of the Late period is marked by a new shell-bead type, cupped beads made from the thick portion of the callus of *Olivella biplicata* shells. These cupped beads effectively replaced the *Olivella biplicata* wall disc or saucer beads by the end of Late period, Phase 1a (AD 1250), and became the most common type of bead used until Spanish colonization, when their use stopped abruptly. The production of other types of shell beads, however, was not discontinued, despite the influx of glass beads brought by the Spanish and other European colonists. Because cupped beads were made from the thick portion of the *Olivella* shell, they were much more time consuming to manufacture than *Olivella biplicata* wall beads and many other types of shell beads. Cupped beads were prevalent throughout the Chumash region during the Late period and have been identified as money beads on the basis of their distribution in cemeteries and other contexts. They also have been

Figure 12.2. A large deer-bone tube with appliquéd shell beads from Burton Mound, CA-SBA-28. (Courtesy of the Santa Barbara Museum of Natural History; image no. NA-CA-28-1C-2; photograph by Lynn H. Gamble)

found throughout central California, the Great Basin, and southern California (King 1990:157; King and Gamble 2008). The one cupped bead from a site in eastern California (INY-5207) that Eerkens and colleagues (2005) sourced was probably from the Santa Barbara Channel region.

After European contact, the Chumash populations continued to make, use, and exchange shell beads even though European glass beads were introduced (Gamble and Zepeda 2002; King 1990). Wall disc beads from *Olivella* shells (*Olivella* rough disc beads) became more common again, although their edges usually were not fully ground. Eventually, the perforations of wall disc beads were drilled with iron needles that were introduced by the Spanish.

The Significance of the Plank Canoe in Exchange

The distribution of shell beads from the northern Channel Islands to the mainland was dependent on watercraft for transportation. Watercraft also facilitated exchange between settlements on the mainland coast, where, at least during the Late period, the highest population densities existed. The most seaworthy type of watercraft in the Santa Barbara Channel was the sewn wooden plank canoe (*tomol*), a common sight when Europeans first visited the region. These boats were important in the conveyance of beads, as well as other items made on the Channel Islands, such as large and heavy steatite *ollas* and *comals* (flat, pan-shaped vessel) used for cooking and ceremonial feasting, mortars, and other items. Canoes were also instrumental in the intensification of fishing practices that allowed the Chumash greater access to large deepwater fish. Ethnographic evidence indicates that the plank canoe was the most expensive item made by the Chumash, surpassing the cost of houses, sweat lodges, and other objects or structures (Hudson et al. 1978). Only very wealthy individuals could afford to build and own a canoe; some historic evidence indicates that it was primarily chiefs who owned plank canoes (see Gamble 2002).

Arnold (1992, 1995) argued that social ranking developed around AD 1200–1300 in the Santa Barbara Channel region and has explained its origin from the perspective of environmental degradation, political opportunism, and the manipulation of labor by rising elites. More recently, Arnold (2001a, 2001b) suggested that the control of exchange between the mainland and the Channel Islands by canoe owners on both sides of the Santa Barbara Channel was a fundamental component in the rise of hereditary leadership among the Chumash and that a small group of leaders, including canoe owners and traders, seized opportunities that most likely resulted from resource imbalances to gain economic and political advantages. Chumash chiefs and other wealthy individuals had the means to control the distribution of both the manufactured goods that were exported from the Channel Islands and the food and other materials that were imported to the islands. However, there is no clear empirical evidence that boat owners actually restricted access to watercraft or regulated the release of beads (Gamble 2008). Nevertheless, the fact that they had such a source of power placed them in an economically advantageous position. The determination of when the tomol was first used in the Chumash region is fundamental to understanding the development of sociopolitical complexity. A systematic study of items associated with the construction, maintenance, and use of the plank canoe, including flaked canoe drills, asphaltum plugs, asphaltum caulking, and wooden planks, provides strong evidence that the plank canoe originated at least thirteen hundred to fifteen hundred years ago in southern California, approximately five hundred years earlier than previously proposed (Gamble 2002). This finding is significant because evidence of the plank canoe is several centuries earlier than Arnold proposed and therefore does not coincide with the timing of environmental degradation that she suggested (Arnold 1992).

Beads as a Proxy for Social Contexts of Power

Other researchers have proposed that environmental instability and resource scarcity were closely tied to Chumash conflict (Johnson 1988, 2007; Kennett 2005; Kennett and Kennett 2000; Lambert 1994). Although climatic volatility and resource stress are probably linked to conflict, I suspect that the reasons for warfare are much more complex and must be considered in the context of elaborate social processes (see Gamble 2005, 2008). We need to give credit to the people who lived in the region over a seven-thousand–year period and their abilities to innovate and find solutions to environmental stress. This was a population that shared cultural traits and adapted to changing climatic conditions such as ENSO events and drought conditions. In all probability, they chose not to rely on domesticated crops because of the inherent problems of doing so in such a setting, especially with the abundance of marine and terrestrial resources that could be stored and traded to minimize risks associated with these climatic threats. In other words, the Chumash had developed an oral tradition, a social memory of the dangers associated with their environment, and had, through intensification of resource acquisition and trade, worked out solutions that tended to serve the populations for thousands of years.

But why then was there conflict and how pronounced was it? Some of the best evidence of violence is a significant and impressive body of osteoarchaeological data from the Santa Barbara Channel region, where the skeletal remains of over seventeen hundred individuals from more than thirty sites on the mainland and islands have been analyzed for evidence of resource stress and violent conflict (Lambert 1994, 2002; Lambert and Walker 1991; Walker and Lambert 1989). The results of these extensive analyses indicate that there was some level of violence throughout time in the region. Lambert (1994, 2002:217–219) found that healed cranial vault fractures were present during all the time periods, but were more common between approximately 1500 BC and AD 1380. In contrast, lethal projectile wounds did not increase in frequency until approximately AD 580, at about the same time that the bow and arrow was introduced to the region. Between AD 580 and 1350, approximately 10 percent of the sample examined by Lambert exhibited evidence of projectile wounds, and many of these individuals were from the mainland, not the Channel Islands (Lambert 2002). After AD 1350, Lambert noted a decline in violence that she attributed to improving climatic conditions; however, the sample size for this period was small, making it a tentative conclusion (see Gamble 2008).

Evidence of violence is especially apparent on Mescalitan Island during the late Middle period (M4–M5c), where Lambert (1994:131–132) discovered particularly high numbers of victims with multiple projectile wounds in two cemeteries. She also noted that the frequency of projectile wounds in individuals from these cemeteries was greater than in samples from any time periods on the mainland or the islands. The mainland site of Mescalitan Island was situated on a small but prominent island in the middle of the Goleta Slough that could be reached only by boat. Mescalitan Island and the settlements surrounding the Goleta Slough were in the center of population and in the geographic center of the Chumash region. The high rate of projectile injuries in victims buried on Mescalitan Island is intriguing because of its naturally defensive location. If Mescalitan Island was as populated at this time as believed, then it would have been somewhat audacious to attack such a large, centrally located settlement. If resource stress was indeed an important cause of conflict, it is curious then that the level of violence was not more prominent on the islands than on the mainland during the late Middle and Late periods, where resource stress was reported to be more common (Arnold 1992, 2001a, 2001b; Kennett 2005; Kennett and Kennett 2000; Lambert 1994, 2002).

Recent approaches to the interpretation of warfare among hunter-gatherer societies may be too simplistic for explaining conflict among the inhabitants of the Santa Barbara Channel region. How do we account for conflict and warfare in the context of their heavy reliance on beads? I propose that they were protecting trade networks that were based, in part, on shell beads. Evidence suggests that the populations of the Channel area tried several strategies during their long trajectory in the region. They lived in smaller settlements situated in more defensive locations in the Early period. However, eventually, as their populations grew and maritime adaptation intensified, they occupied the best niches for their subsistence and exchange strategies. Because the Chumash relied on watercraft for exchange between the mainland and the islands, as well as for fishing, the south-facing beaches, on which most of the mainland towns were situated, served as excellent ports.

The islanders and the inhabitants of the interior, who were positioned in more peripheral areas, probably envied the strategic locations of these settlements for exchange, subsistence pursuits, and ceremonial gatherings. Because goods passing between the latter two regions were routed through the mainland coast, mainlanders had a distinct advantage over their neighbors on the islands and in the interior. Mainlanders also had a greater variety of subsistence resources than did those living in the interior or on the offshore islands. Once important locations were occupied, there was a concerted effort to maintain primary access to them. The early use of cemeteries in the region was one way that inhabitants could show ancestral claims to their settlements.

Alliances were established for many reasons among the Chumash, and they had great antiquity. The 'antap society, marriage practices, exchange networks, and other cultural traditions of the Chumash all required the formation of regional alliances. No doubt coalitions often shifted and included parallel and overlapping partnerships. Disagreements between individuals within these alliances had the potential of instigating a series of discordant reactions that could result in revenge or warfare. I propose that the Chumash fought over their network of alliances and the prime locations in the Santa Barbara Channel region. To some extent, everyone benefited politically, economically, and ideologically from cross-channel exchanges, ceremonial gatherings, redistributive efforts, and trade partnerships; however, not everyone benefited equally.

Beads as Social Memory

The most common archaeological context for shell beads throughout California, especially large quantities of beads, is with burials. Unlike effigies, deer-bone tibia whistles, and other artifacts, beads are seldom found in caches in the Santa Barbara Channel region. Although beads are often recovered in shell middens and other contexts, these are usually isolated beads. The association of beads and other artifacts with burials has been construed as an indicator of social rank among the Chumash (Gamble et al. 2001; King 1990). However, beads can also be interpreted in a broader context—as part of mortuary rituals that involve a "complex interplay of emotions, material culture, and social memories of the mourners and the deceased" (Chesson 2001:1). If we view beads as integral to the identity and memory of the deceased and the mortuary ritual itself, then beads serve as a material manifestation of the social memory of an individual and the ceremony honoring their life and journey to the afterworld. The preparation of the deceased and accompaniment of shell beads and ornaments served multiple purposes. The mourners honored the dead through the adornment of the body before, during, and after the mortuary ceremony. The identity of the deceased was re-created through the process of preparing the individual for the afterlife. The complex processes of mortuary ceremonies that include the adornment of the body ultimately demonstrate how people inscribe the deceased in the social memory of the living (Joyce 2001).

The presence of formal cemeteries, geographically separated from the living areas, occurred early in the Santa Barbara Channel area and, on the whole, continued throughout the history of the region. Shell beads were an important component in mortuary contexts for at least seven millennia in the Santa Barbara Channel region, with some individuals buried with hundreds or even thousands of beads, while others were interred without any beads at all. Although beads were associated with burials in the Early period, by the latter part of this period, larger quantities of beads were associated with the dead, a pattern that continued in the Middle period. In a comparison between a Middle period and Late period cemetery at Malibu, a continuity of burial practices was apparent (Gamble et al. 2001). For example, the Chumash buried the dead with their heads pointing in a west or southwest direction in both cemeteries. This same pattern was noted in other Chumash cemeteries, including the Medea Creek site (CA-LAN-243), the Calleguas Creek site (CA-VEN-110), and S'imomo (CA-VEN-24), suggesting that by the end of the Middle period, a persistent set of religious beliefs and concepts about certain aspects of the afterlife had developed in the region.

Archaeological mortuary evidence suggests that these beliefs were maintained well into the period of European colonization.

The creation of formal cemeteries, sanctified ceremonial grounds, and the adornment of the dead tend to reinforce the ancestral ties to the land and underscore the claims of the living to traditional sacred places and their descendants' rights to these claims. These actions served as a means of creating a social memory. It is significant that there were selectively few individuals buried with the majority of beads, a pattern that is particularly pronounced in the late Middle period and Late period. Funerals were community events in which beads were placed with the body of the deceased. The commemoration of the deceased at a public ceremony served to legitimize the power of the dead and record in the memory of all present the significance of this individual and their ancestral lineage both in life and in death.

Beads as Social Reproduction

Ethnographic sources are rife with accounts of feasting among the Chumash, who maintained a ritual calendar of ceremonial events. Many gatherings involved large public feasts where hundreds to thousands of people from a wide geographical range congregated for ritual events. Some of these events, such as the Winter Solstice Ceremony, lasted five to six days, and California Indians from areas outside the Chumash region attended, such as the Tulareños (Yokuts), the Gabrieleños, and other groups (Blackburn 1976; Hudson et al. 1981). Ceremonial redistribution of foods and goods was common at many of these events, and shell beads were integral to these transactions. Feasts were all inclusive, and people were in fact encouraged to attend and participate in these events. As indicated by one historic account, a failure to participate in important ritual events and to contribute to host chiefs could result in armed conflict (Geiger and Meighan 1976:122). As the following ethnographic account illustrates, some gatherings may have been quite profitable for the host. "According to Fernando [Fernando Librado, Ventureño consultant] visiting captains at a festival would make donations on their arrival so that the host would have enough for the festival and the rest of the year. There was a pecuniary interest in having a festival in Indian times, for the captain would save some of the offerings so that when his subjects were in distress he would have something with which to assist them" (King 1969:43). Undoubtedly many feasts were hosted at the large, centrally situated mainland settlements, locations that were used for ceremonial feasts for hundreds or thousands of years.

Gambling and trading also occurred at feasts, as they did outside the context of large ritual congregations. Shell beads served as a medium of exchange in all these transactions. The distribution of beads in the example of a regularly occurring feast created an opportunity for people to interact and maintain networks or forge new ones, whether they were playing *peon* (the traditional California Indian gambling game) or exchanging food and other items for beads. Shell beads were critical to these transactions as they provided a social vehicle for interaction that may have been more significant than the value of the bead itself.

Whether beads were exchanged between individuals or between chiefs at large ritual congregations, social reproduction, the processes that sustain or perpetuate beads in the hands of the elite, continued over generations. We also see this in the mortuary data, where large quantities of shell beads were buried with only a few individuals. In both contexts, groups of people, in this case the wealthy elite, reproduced their social identities over generations partly through the use of shell beads.

Discussion and Conclusions

Multilayered transformations in the types and quantities of beads, their symbolic meaning, and their distribution reveal a complex and not yet fully understood history. We know that shell beads were made and used in the Santa Barbara Channel region for at least seven thousand years. An increasing number and a greater variety of shell beads were produced and used over time, possibly reflecting greater complexity within Chumash society as well as the interactions between the Chumash and their neighbors. However, there was not a simple trajectory of greater complexity throughout time; instead perturbations in the symbolic meaning, distribution, and use of beads prevailed. We find that a wide range of people in California, the Great Basin, and the Southwest used the same types of beads during certain time periods and were linked to one another. These social ties crosscut genealogical, cultural, and linguistic boundaries to form a network of people who had a common interest in obtaining and using beads. The makers, distributors, and consumers of beads were connected in an elaborate web of overlapping and shifting networks of people and beads. Understanding these networks in the context of redistribution, gift giving, brokers, transportation, conveyance, demand, genealogical ties, and alliances allows a more nuanced understanding of the meaning of beads.

Archaeological evidence demonstrates that certain beads and ornaments were restricted to a limited set of the population within the Santa Barbara Channel region. These can be viewed as inalienable possessions, as described by Annette Weiner (1992). These types of items are imbued with inherent qualities that are irrevocably entwined with their owner—the types of possessions that are hoarded, inherited, and conserved (Weiner 1992:11). Among the Trobrianders, chiefs own rights to certain shells that are worn. These shells are ranked and define each lineage, but they do not circulate except within the kin group or as a loan to a man's children (Weiner 1992). They therefore reinforce the authority of their owners and their owners' ancestors. We can draw a parallel in the Chumash use of shell beads. The ostentatious clamshell ornaments with punctate designs, the large incised bone beads, and the large bone tubes with bead appliqué found in the early Middle period in the Chumash region may have been inalienable possessions used by individuals with recognized inherited power in life and death. These served as badges denoting position when buried with people.

Other types of beads, such as the large saucer beads that were exported from the Santa Barbara Channel region to the Bay area in the early Middle period, differed considerably from beads that were found in highly restricted contexts. These beads were part of a far-flung network of people who used them in social negotiations that encompassed people of different ranks and various cultures. They were intended for exchange and reflect the interactions of a wide variety of constituencies that formed alliances. These beads served very different purposes for the Chumash who produced and consumed them, as well as the groups outside of the region who used them. No doubt the symbolic meaning of beads changed as they passed through the hands of different agents. Shell beads may well have served as a passport of sorts, allowing foreigners to enter into regions where people spoke diverse languages and were from distinctive cultural backgrounds.

Multiple constituencies always existed in the production, distribution, and consumption of shell beads, which allowed multiple options for alliance through bead production, exchange, and use. Although chiefs may have had some control over the distribution of beads, especially in the context of redistribution, they could not control all aspects of this dynamic process. Instead, chiefs were constantly confronted by alternatives that would challenge their authority. The production, distribution, and use of shell beads were much more complicated than the economic benefits of bead use in the context of risk minimization. For example, when the inhabitants of the Bay Area suddenly stopped importing beads from the Santa Barbara Channel region and instead used locally made beads, what effect did this change have on the bead makers in the Chumash region, the many people involved in the conveyance of beads, the chiefs, and the Chumashan people as a whole? The permutations in the frequency and cultural meaning of beads are so complicated that ecological models cannot adequately explain all the variables that affect the people involved in the manufacture, distribution, and use of beads. In fact, the very system that functioned to alleviate risk in subsistence activities was highly vulnerable to manipulation, disruption, and intensification by any number of agents across the network. The maintenance of exchange networks operated within a context of shifting alliances, variable demands for shell beads from both within and outside the Chumash region, changes in the symbolic meaning of beads, and innovations in the production of beads.

Significant transformations in the use of shell beads took place over millennia within the region, with an increasing number of shell-bead types reflecting the growing complexity of Chumash society. In this chapter, I have focused on the long-term history of shell beads in their formal, spatial, and chronological variation, and how this reflects changes in their meaning, value, and power. The labor investments in the production of massive quantities of shell beads are enormous, yet the inhabitants of the Santa Barbara Channel chose to make this investment for economic and social reasons. The effort that was expended to produce shell beads and the network of alliances that was created through their distribution and use was of tremendous significance. Evidence of conflict among the Chumash at the large mainland settlements, which were prime locations for exchange and ritual congregations, is in part likely tied to vying groups who wanted to be in the centers of distribution.

In mortuary rituals, beads were used in the commemoration of the dead and were part of the social memory of the groups that participated in these rituals. Shell beads were critical components of large feasting events and served as a medium for social reproduction, reinforcing the rights of elite lineages to retain large quantities of beads, both in life and in death. Some beads served as markers for the elite and remained in the hands of high-ranked lineages, while others were intended for export and exchange. The importance of beads extended well beyond their economic value in that they provided a means for social interactions and integration; they also served as signifiers of power that was collectively reinforced through ancestral lineages. The systems of bead production, exchange, and use involved many thousands of individuals over a large part of western North America. Transformations in these networks may have had far greater impact on the political, economic, and social developments of groups than environmental changes and therefore deserve more attention from archaeologists. I have only briefly touched upon a few aspects of the long-term history of the inhabitants of the Santa Barbara Channel region and their use of shell beads. As we develop deep historical perspectives based on empirical knowledge of the many societies that were involved in these networks, we can better understand the cultural production of the past.

Acknowledgments

I am most grateful to Don Holly and Ken Sassaman for organizing the Society for American Archaeology symposium that brought this diverse group of scholars together for a highly focused session and then the following Amerind seminar. Both of them inspired me to expand my thinking on southern California bead economies to encompass the social and symbolic meanings of shell beads. Ken and I had significant discussions throughout the process of writing this chapter that gave me the confidence to go where I had not previously ventured. Don gently urged me to focus my ideas and provided support from the beginning. In particular, the Amerind experience offered an intellectual environment that was unencumbered with the daily distractions of life. I especially thank John Ware, the Director of the Amerind, for ensuring that the surroundings were ideal for scholarly reflection, but also for his active participation and practical advice. T. R. Kidder came up with the idea that beads served as "passports" and encouraged me to think about the "social economy of consumption," as did Brian Robinson, Ken, Asa Randall, and others. Anna Prentiss provided numerous examples of hunter-gatherers as "industrialists," as well as other cross-cultural comparisons. Kent Lightfoot and Kathleen Hull offered important insights into California archaeology and other advice. I especially thank Martin Wobst for suggesting that any disruptions in economic networks might cause regional-scale shifts that had nothing to do with the environment, as well as numerous other comments, and Laura Scheiber and Moira McCaffrey for their input and support. My chapter would look very different indeed without the thoughtful comments of everyone at the seminar. I also am indebted to several people who were not at the Amerind. Glenn Russell and Tom Blackburn read drafts of the chapter and provided important comments, and Chester King generously shared his depth of knowledge on beads and the Chumash. Of course, any weaknesses are solely my responsibility.

Epilogue
Foragers in Hindsight, or Theory and Method Meet History

H. Martin Wobst

At least since the Man the Hunter Symposium in 1966, we have known that of all the humans who have ever lived, the majority did so as foragers (Lee and DeVore 1968b:3). Foragers constitute the majority of the evidence for the ways in which humans have varied and the majority of the data about the human ability to vary. If science is an endeavor humans invented to deal with change and variation, then the historic and prehistoric data on foragers represent an immense reservoir against which our theories and methods need to be evaluated if we would like them to explain *humans*. To learn what causes human pain and suffering and what to do about it, we need to have a secure sense of all that change and variation as it is reflected in, has affected and has been affected by, humans in the past. We need to include that past human experience to better understand change and variation today and to more securely anticipate our futures.

The archaeological and historic past of foragers (and people obtaining their livelihood by agriculture and domestication) is not just in the past. It also preserves a near infinite number of futures, since each archaeological past is overlain by its actual futures. Whether for prehistoric North American foragers as discussed in this volume, or for any other slice of the past, these futures of the past constitute a unique resource for developing theory and for evaluating implications for change from our theories against the changes that actually occurred. This futuristic aspect of the archaeological past allows us to turn archaeological research into an experimental science (much like the behavioral sciences of the present), but without having to run experiments with living subjects. Our goal as anthropological archaeologists should be to develop theory that is dynamic, so that it encompasses, anticipates, and makes understood variation and variability through space and time. Admittedly, archaeologists have not yet made much use of this feature of the past, but one can find examples with North American "archaeological" foragers already in the early seventies (e.g., Thomas 1972).

What we know about forager populations today, in terms of change and variation, makes the consensus knowledge of only half a century ago, as fossilized in the Man the Hunter Symposium (Lee and DeVore 1968b) and the collections that followed it in the next decade (e.g., Bicchieri 1972; Damas 1969a) look a bit like the Flat Earth Society. On the other hand, the magnitude of change and variation across that forager universe has not yet penetrated the archaeological mainstream. There are a number of reasons for this failure to accept change and variation in the study of foragers. The original Man the Hunter model was developed as such a forceful system and machine that it was difficult to envision how one could ever change out of it—any potential deviation was seen as being counteracted by powerful systemic forces. Actually observed change and variation, not anticipated by the model, could thus more economically and safely be interpreted as error; that is, it would be corrected in the normal operation of the model through its powerful feedbacks or could be filed away and forgotten rather than constituting an interesting datum calling for publication and further analysis.

Adherence to the model had three effects. First, foragers in the past and present were overreported in the dimensions in which they fit the Man the Hunter consensus (keeping knowledge of variation and change down). Second, when really drastic change or difference was encountered, the groups concerned were placed into new categories, outside of the standard foragers, such as "tribes," "chiefdoms" (Grier et al. 2006), "incipient agriculturalists" (e.g., Bar-Yosef 2002), or "complex hunter-gatherers" (e.g., Koyama and Thomas 1981; Price and Brown 1985), and in that way served as construction material for equally forceful and compelling models and machines of greater cultural complexity. Their information did not get read as broadening the behavioral bandwidth of foragers, or as expanding the dynamism of the Man the Hunter model. Third, since change and variation among foragers were all accommodated in the same model and machine, one did not have to pay attention to history—history merely introduced noise or deviation to be controlled by the usual operation of the model (thus again, reducing the observable and actually observed variance).

Mindless archaeological methodology is another cause that keeps us from realizing that hunter-gatherers are significantly more varied and dynamic in time and space than our standard presentations allow them to be. This is caused by the archaeological habit to first generate order in one's data, before one poses questions of it. Archaeologists usually first sort their records through space into piles of likeness (with all categories and aspects that allow one them to do that), so that their data for further analysis are as internally homogeneous as possible. Then, questions are raised about difference and change and about the driving variables behind the "observed" (actually, generated) similarities. Even if archaeologists were sorting through perfect random numbers, they would report them first as sets of ones, twos, and threes, as being internally homogeneous but in sharp contrast among each other. That methodological step suppresses information on variation and change, increases the sense of internal homogeneity and cohesion, and "invisibilizes" (Bruchac 2007) both gradual change and more massive transformations. At every scale of analysis in space and time, that step overreports data categories that let themselves be sorted into piles of likeness (projectile points, typed pottery), and it underreports those that resist it or that are forever changing. Thus, again, that methodological step deflects from history and place and makes both appear fairly irrelevant, because something that is the same through time or space would not allow one to detect the specific signal of a given time or space in any case (cf. Wobst 2005).

The very category of foragers is generated through sorting on the basis of diet, as a number of contributors remind us. Such sorting arbitrarily distances people who exclusively subsist on foraged resources from those who interact with some of their foodstuffs like domesticators, even though we now know that "agriculture" and "domestication" are much more contingent than we used to think, and their absence in a given forager group is not that group's essential attribute but is contextually explainable (see, for example, Ames 2004, 2005b). Most so-called foragers, during the last 15,000 years, had domesticates (such as dogs), or domesticating interactions with plants and animals (as in the fire ecologies that Lightfoot et al. report in this vol.). Even those foragers who have served as the purest among the pure foragers, such as the !Kung San (e.g., Lee 1979) or the Hadza (e.g., Woodburn 1968), did not have foraging hardwired into their phenotype but may have had considerably more domesticating ways of interacting with "natural" resources in the past (and would again in the future, if their variability had not been foreshortened by our presence in their life; see, for example, Thorbahn 1979 or Wilmsen 1989).

Even where change through time has been the explicit goal of forager research, research often ends deflecting from forager variation. Particularly the more extreme behavioral or evolutionary ecology paradigms, in their forcing variables, run the risk of treating the culturally and historically constituted decision makers as black boxes. This effect is all the more likely, the more forceful the causal variables are assumed to have been. Local cultural understandings of driving variables and local socially constituted webs of decision making, in their historical context and diversity, are thus often mistaken as noise obscuring what is seen to really matter to the paradigm—that is, selective pressures as cause, and fitness-enhancing responses as effect. Without reasoning how such presumed stressful inputs would actually work themselves through the culturally constituted assessment of environmental variation and through culturally situated decision making, such "explanation" frequently does little more than establish an association, while the presumed cause and the presumed effect remain un-operationalized and causally unconnected. For the purposes of this volume, such an approach often deflects from sensitively reporting change and variation in context through time and space and, thus, downplays change and variation across the forager universe.

Much diachronic forager research is significantly simpler in its paradigm and working assumptions than behavioral ecology or evolutionary ecology. It is frequently driven by the search for "origins": since much of what has become important in history or prehistory had its first formal analogues in prehistoric forager contexts, the forager universe is a gold mine for origins research. Origins projects usually start with something impressive in the more recent past or present (bow and arrow, portable art, cave paintings, red ochre, etc.). This derived attribute is then taken to guide one's search through earlier archaeological records to its formal precedents. Ultimately, all likeness will disappear in the ever deeper past. Immediately following that point in time, the point of origin is located and widely publicized.

As caricatured, such origins research is anthropologically fairly vacuous. The data that it selectively exposes are determined by turning time backwards. Antecedents are recognized because of their likeness to the item at the more recent starting point of the search, but not because of any dynamics in the past that are hypothesized to generate futures. Ironically, as I have pointed out elsewhere (Wobst 1989), the data that origins research draws attention to are themselves similar through time. They are often that aspect of the past that is most similar to the present—meaning that origins research actually often deflects from visualizing and explaining change and variation and from understanding prehistoric contexts in their relation to that change and variation.

Where "evolution" is writ large in publications about foragers through time, that term is often simply used as a synonym for progress, that is, past data are assembled (from the present backwards) as if they had nothing better to do than to evolve into the present, in a logic very parallel to the origins research previously discussed. It makes *our* "present" look like it is driven by the evolutionary momentum of the ages, and it re-functions the past into being a less successful version of us. At the same time, it easily labels lack of directional motion, and particularly lack of directional motion in our direction, as failure, and variation, change, and deviation from this momentum of history, like all other aspects of history, have become irrelevant, and thus are underreported (cf. Conkey with Williams 1991).

In summary, while forager research has become more explicitly problem directed than it was only half a century ago and while we certainly have learned a great deal more about variation and change among foragers in the meantime, much of the day-to-day research has failed to appreciate the theoretical significance of change and variation across this significant part of the human experience. Instead, the most widely applied research designs have effectively downplayed variation and change in the world of foragers. Our histograms of variation among foragers, the bandwidth of forager decision making, the range of variation in structural poses that foragers are capable of under changing circumstances, and the dynamism of foraging as a set of social relations thus look significantly less impressive than they should.

The present volume is an explicit effort to extend that bandwidth of change and variation with the example of North America, the region of the world that has borne the brunt of archaeological research on foragers for the last century. In North America, this massive increase in forager research coincides first with the expansion of archaeology into academic departments, and then with the explosive growth of field work as a result of cultural resource management in North America (McGuire 2008; Trigger 2006). Our data now cover the forager universe much more systematically than heretofore, and much more comprehensively than in other parts of the world.

With this volume, we are encouraging archaeologists to give (even) hunter-gatherers more of an opportunity to enter history and to increase their ability to write that history. We want to observe how hunter-gatherers do their stuff that makes sense in their contexts, how they are similar to or different from us, and how, at times, they have changed in our direction and at times they have moved away from us. In that way, we want to use forager archaeology (like the archaeology of any part of humanity) to broaden our sense of human behavior. In many ways, we are thus culture historians. We are interested in how hunter-gatherers acted, given their cultural conditioned knowledges of the world, and how those actions helped to change or reproduce these cultural knowledges and the worlds around them. In that way, we want to use hunter-gatherers to contribute to our knowledge in the following areas: change and variation in human social behavior (and thus social theory); social evolution and history of humans; and historic process and processes, that is, what one can learn from historic instances about others and about the processes of history and culture.

In the direction of these goals, the participants expand our sense of the bandwidth of hunter-gatherer variation in many significant ways, from their North American vantage point. It often seemed that the range of variation within the category was as large or larger than between it and other categories, such as agriculturalists or even urban populations. On the one hand, this enlarged range on many different social axes makes foragers of the past, and thus humans, look significantly more dynamic and three-dimensional than they have appeared in much of the extant literature. Foragers mass produce, foragers have complex rituals, foragers can pile up huge amounts of dirt or shell, they may move things over long distances for reasons that to us look fairly arbitrary, they are capable of rapid cultural change, or they may manage

to clone heavily contrived and rule-bound behavior over long periods of
time and across large spaces.

On the other hand, the information from the different regions of the
participants in this volume helps to destabilize a number of analytical
dimensions that archaeologists often take for granted, such as function
and style, function and ritual, living and nonliving, nature and culture. They, thus, set in motion new ways of thinking about continuities,
changes, and variation in the past and present. It was interesting to us
that items of the forager cultural inventory that often serve as emblems
of utility and function and practical reason, such as projectile points,
may be rich keys into the hunter-gatherer world of meaning, and that
thinking may work well in some cases, but not in others. What might
be predicted from a gravity model takes on completely and complexly
new meaning if it is interpreted as a social intervention in a social context, such as migration as resistance. We learned that complex relationships of meaning may structure significant parts of the archaeologically
accessible inventories in some cases and not in others. Often, activities
that did not make sense in terms of their heavy energy expenditures
make perfect sense when their meaning context is probed. Meaning
contexts are enriched with the help of carefully probing local histories,
ethnohistories, and explorations of traditional knowledges, coupled
with cautious, problem-directed exploration of the archaeological find
contexts. Interestingly (and promisingly), the participants achieve these
results by means of new problem-directed field work and by approaching old museum collections with new ideas.

To capture the interplay between cultural context, social structure,
hunter-gatherer action, and change and diversity, many authors trace a
given region through the ages, carefully interpreting the given changes
in the changing meaning contexts in which they occurred, in this way
helping to understand both decision making by the human agents and
the changing web of knowledge that precedes that decision making and
is in part constituted by it. Contributors are surprised by the thickness
of historic description and understanding that could thus be generated
with archaeological records that other approaches had processed already
but had left looking fairly flat and culturally unengaging.

We appreciate that both time and space appeared significantly more
variable and in process than most extant forager publications allow

them to be. Most ethnographically observed foragers sport different time conceptions from ours (Fabian 1983). Thus the archaeological remains of foragers were most likely also generated in their own differing conceptions of time, rather than in ours, and these conceptions, like ours, were contested and in process. Our presently dominant conception keeps time in motion, with the help of a well-cognized and artifactually supported past, present, and future. If we want to problematize and expose our own progress-driven conception of time as being cultural and in process, and recognize its place in the pan-human distribution of conceptions of and discourses on time, we need to begin to take archaeological readings on it. Each time an archaeologist presents his or her foragers, uncritically, as living and acting within progressing time, he or she makes our own progressive time conception easier to swallow.

Space equally needs to be interpreted as being discursive, in process, and contested among hunter-gatherers. We appreciated the ability of hunter-gatherers over lengthy periods to engage in social process across significant amounts of space and to do so with the help of a number of varying material cultural dimensions. Spatial scale among North American hunter-gatherers is variable, and artifacts are used to generate, comment on, change, and evade it. What category of artifacts serves to accomplish that in the given case makes sense only with the detailed contextualized knowledge of what preceded it and what it interacts with on the other side of a social group, in other words, in a fine-grained, culturally sensitive reading of Native history.

The case studies in this volume provide powerful examples of artifacts as social devices, that is, as items that help to construct individuals, make social entities easier to imagine, and bring about social change. The crucial role of artifacts in helping to bring about cohesion and to make social fission more costly was exemplified in many North American foraging societies. Artifacts working that way help to weaken our stereotypes of them being predominantly functional devices (vis-à-vis environmental variables) and broaden our knowledge of materialities different from our own, introducing us to contexts in which even the most banal "utilitarian" artifacts assume their place as important and dynamic in constituting society and individuals.

All of the chapters in this volume are regional or interregional in their spatial focus. They point to North America as being an essentially unbounded population surface in which exchanges of energy, matter, and information in specific localities and at specific times on those scales significantly contributes to what happens at those places. These chapters make it apparent that the people from one end of the continent to the other do know what others are doing. So their doing something specific in a specific time and place is in part, if not to a significant degree, in reference to this interregional information surface. Some things form clinal distributions across the entire continent, unhindered by social boundaries, while others are neatly contained within boundaries or even generated easily observable boundaries. They exist in reference to these flows as much as those that plot as gradually changing clinal maps across the continent. The hunter-gatherer record of North America is richly informative about this process. It takes volumes such as this one to make that potential visible. Simply shaking the data in one's own small hole in the ground makes that potential often disappear.

We have learned over the last few decades that hunter-gatherers have been at the top of every food chain in the Americas. That must mean that the ecosystem structure is, to significant degrees, a human artifact. There is not a space in the Americas that is not (and has not been) indirectly or directly a human artifact. In this respect, foragers are no different from agriculturalists and urbanites: animal distributions and behaviors, such as those of deer and caribou, are in reference to human predation and thus human artifacts. Animal behavior, thus, should be treated almost like artifacts, as a response to its history of human predation and other interactions with humans. Behavioral ecology can easily become tautological without very complex bridging arguments that make clear why it does not simply establish that human behavior begets human behavior, rather than that variables in nature force human behavior.

The chapters of this volume powerfully alert us to the bandwidth of the human experience, in their observations on environmental variables that are not predicted from simplistic evolutionary expectations: for example, in the widespread evidence for landscape manipulation by foragers, be it by gracing it with mounds, or manipulating it with fire, or by otherwise artifactually modifying human visual scapes. Exposing the range of this artifactualizing of environmental variables by foragers is vital if we want to change human impacts on the environment in the present from irreversible to reversible, and if we want to convince humans that, where they suffer from environmental stress, they usually have nobody else to blame but themselves. This observation is a powerful reminder that ecosystems are flows of energy, matter, and information, and that usually energy and matter are foregrounded in the more biologizing approaches, while information receives the short shrift (a point made decades ago by Flannery [1972] in relation to the origins of states). Of course, we should retain interest in biological variables, but in terms of this volume, we gain by paying more attention to information, and how all three—energy, matter, and information flow—are embodied in and help to constitute human social actors and their social groupings.

Taking aim at foragers in the ways of the contributors of this volume is a good thing to happen to the cultural history of North American foragers, because it allows foragers to be human, to participate like all other humans in the human structure-action stream. They display an incredible amount of variation and change, they are multidimensional, and they are complex along many different directions. They must be given credit for their innovations, dynamism, and creativity. That they have that much variation and change needs to be put to work in future research designs, to probe it and to enlarge upon it. It should enrich the histories of the descendant populations in their battles to become recognized as being fully human. It needs to be taken into their history, so that we can feel our way to the processes that structure it. Finally, it needs to be taken into account in theory building about foragers and in more encompassing models that help to retrodict, predict, and understand human actions in the past and the present.

Acknowledgments

I would like to dedicate this chapter to my present and former students at the University of Massachusetts in Amherst and to my Indigenous friends who know me as "the rat chicken." Thanks are also due to the Amerind Foundation for its generosity, to the fellow participants in the seminar on whom these remarks reflect, and to the Native Americans on whose former lands the seminar took place. And deep respect is due to the seminar organizers, Ken and Don. I have learned so much from all of you. All of the errors in this chapter, though, are entirely my own.

Abel, Kerry

1993   *Drum Songs: Glimpses of Dene History.* McGill-Queen's University Press, Montreal.

Adams, Richard

2006   The Greater Yellowstone Ecosystem, Soapstone Bowls and the Mountain Shoshone. *World Archaeology* 38 (3): 528–546.

Administration Régionale Crie

1985   *La synthèse archéologique et ethnohistorique du Complexe La Grande.* Submitted to Société d'énergie de la Baie James, Montreal.

Ahler, Stanley, and Phil Geib

2000   Why Flute? Folsom Point Design and Adaptation. *Journal of Archaeological Science* 27:799–820.

Alexander, Lawrence

1983   *The Archaeology of the Emmett O'Neal Site (22 Ts954) in the Bay Springs Lake Segment of the Tennessee-Tombigbee Waterway, Tishomingo County, Mississippi.* Reports of Investigation 37. Office of Archaeological Research, University of Alabama, Tuscaloosa.

Alt, Susan

2006   The Power of Diversity: The Roles of Migration and Hybridity. In *Culture Change. In Leadership and Polity in Mississippian Society,* edited by B. M. Butler and P. D. Welch. Occasional Paper No. 33. Center for Archaeological Investigations, Southern Illinois University, Carbondale.

Ames, Kenneth

1985   Hierarchies, Stress, and Logistical Strategies among Hunter-Gatherers in Northwestern North America. In *Prehistoric Hunter-Gatherers: The Emergence of Cultural Complexity,* edited by T. D. Price and J. A. Brown, pp. 155–180. Academic Press, Orlando, Fla.

1995   Chiefly Power and Household Production on the Northwest Coast. In *Foundations of Social Inequality,* edited by T. Douglas Price and Gary M. Feinman, pp. 155–188. Plenum, New York.

1998   Economic Prehistory of the Northern British Columbia Coast. *Arctic Anthropology* 35:68–87.

2002   Going by Boat: The Forager-Collector Continuum at Sea. In *Beyond Foraging and Collecting: Evolutionary Change in Hunter-Gatherer Settlement Systems,* edited by B. Fitzhugh and J. Habu, pp. 19–52. Kluwer, New York.

2004   Supposing Hunter-Gatherer Variability (Book Review Essay). *American Antiquity* 69:364–374.

Ames, Kenneth

2005a   *The North Coast Prehistory Project Excavations in Prince Rupert Harbour, British Columbia: The Artifacts.* British Archaeological Reports, International Series 1342, Oxford, U.K.

2005b   Intensification of Food Production on the Northwest Coast and Elsewhere. In *Keeping It Living: Traditions of Plant Use and Cultivation on the Northwest Coast of North America,* edited by Douglas Duer and Nancy Turner, pp. 64–94. University of Washington Press, Seattle.

2006   Thinking about Household Archaeology on the Northwest Coast. In *Household Archaeology on the Northwest Coast,* edited by Elizabeth A. Sobel, D. Ann Trieu Gahr, and Kenneth M. Ames, pp. 16–36. International Monographs in Prehistory, Ann Arbor, Mich.

Ames, Kenneth M., and Herbert D. G. Maschner

1999   *Peoples of the Northwest Coast: Their Archaeology and History.* Thames and Hudson, London.

Ammerman, Albert J.

1989   Population Studies and the Archaeologist. *Norwegian Archaeological Review* 22 (2): 65–87.

Anderson, David G.

1990   The Paleoindian Colonization of Eastern North America: A View from the Southeastern United States. In *Early Paleoindian Economies of Eastern North America,* edited by K. Tankersley and B. Isaac, pp. 163–216. *Research in Economic Anthropology,* Suppl. no. 5.

1995   Paleoindian Interaction Networks in the Eastern Woodlands. In *Native American Interactions: Multiscalar Analysis and Interpretations in the Eastern Woodlands,* edited by Michael S. Nassaney and Kenneth E. Sassaman, pp. 3–26. University of Tennessee Press, Knoxville.

1996   Approaches to Modeling Regional Settlement in the Archaic Period Southeast. In *Archaeology of the Mid-Holocene Southeast,* edited by K. E. Sassaman and D. G. Anderson, pp. 157–176. University Press of Florida, Gainesville.

Anderson, James E., and James A. Tuck

1974   Osteology of the Dorset People. *Man in the Northeast* 8:89–97.

Anderson, M. Kat

2005   *Tending the Wild: Native American Knowledge and the Management of California's Natural Resources.* University of California Press, Berkeley.

Archéotec Inc.

1985   *Réservoir de LG 4. Synthèse de l'occupation amérindienne: 3 500 ans de sobriété.* Submitted to Société d'énergie de la Baie James, Montreal.

1992   *Complexe Grande Baleine. Interventions archéologiques 1991 sur le réservoir de GB 1 et le réservoir de Bienville. Analyse et synthèse.* 3 vols. Submitted to Vice-présidence Environnement, Hydro-Québec, Montreal.

2009   *Suivi environnemental du complexe La Grande. Synthèse des données archéologiques.* Submitted to Vice-présidence, Exploitation des équipements de production, Barrages et environnement, Hydro-Québec, Montreal.

Archer, David J. W.

2001   Village Patterns and the Emergence of Rank Society in the Prince Rupert Area. In *Perspectives on Northern Northwest Coast Prehistory,* edited by J. S. Cybulski, pp. 203–222. Mercury Series. Archaeological Survey of Canada Paper No. 160. Canadian Museum of Civilization, Ottawa.

Armitage, Peter

2004   Romancing Labrador: the Social Contruction of Wilderness and the Labrador Frontier. In *Every Grain of Sand: Canadian Perspectives on Ecology and Environment,* edited by J. Andrew Wainwright, pp. 151–171. Wilfred Laurier University Press, Waterloo.

Arnold, Jeanne E.

1987   *Craft Specialization in the Prehistoric Channel Islands, California.* University of California Publications in Anthropology, vol. 18. University of California Press, Berkeley.

1992   Complex Hunter-Gatherer-Fishers of Prehistoric California: Chiefs, Specialists, and Maritime Adaptations of the Channel Islands. *American Antiquity* 57:60–84.

1993   Labor and the Rise of Complex Hunter-Gatherers. *Journal of Anthropological Archaeology* 12:75–119.

1995   Social Inequality, Marginalization, and Economic Process. In *Foundations of Social Inequality,* edited by T. Douglas Price and Gary M. Feinman, pp. 87–103. Plenum Press, New York.

2001a   Social Evolution and the Political Economy in the Northern Channel Islands. In *The Origins of a Pacific Coast Chiefdom: The Chumash of the Channel Islands,* edited by J. E. Arnold, pp. 287–296. University of Utah Press, Salt Lake City.

2001b   The Chumash in World and Regional Perspectives. In *The Origins of a Pacific Coast Chiefdom: The Chumash of the Channel Islands,* edited by J. E. Arnold, pp. 1–19. University of Utah Press, Salt Lake City.

Arnold, J. E., and A. Munns

1994   Independent of Attached Specialization: The Organization of Shell Bead Production in California. *Journal of Field Archaeology* 21:473–489.

Arnold, J. E., and B. Tissot

1993   Measurement of Significant Marine Paleotemperature Variation Using Black Abalone Shells from Prehistoric Middens. *Quaternary Research* 39:390–394.

Aron, Stephen

2006   *American Confluence: The Missouri Frontier from Borderland to Border State.* Indiana University Press, Bloomington.

Asselin, Hugo, and Serge Payette

2005　Late Holocene Opening of the Forest Tundra Landscape in Northern Québec, Canada. *Global Ecology and Biogeography* 14:307–313.

Aten, Lawrence E.

1999　Middle Archaic Ceremonialism at Tick Island, Florida: Ripley P. Bullen's 1961 Excavations at the Harris Creek Site. *Florida Anthropologist* 52:131–200.

Baer, John Leonard

1921　A Preliminary Report on the So-Called "Bannerstones." *American Anthropologist* 23:445–459.

Bamforth, Douglas B.

2002　High Tech Foragers? Folsom and Later Paleoindian Technology on the Great Plains. *Journal of World Prehistory* 16:55–98.

Bamforth, Douglas B., and Keri Hicks

2008　Production Skill and Paleoindian Workgroup Organization in the Medicine Creek Drainage, Southwestern Nebraska. *Journal of Archaeological Method and Theory* 15:132–153.

Barabási, Albert-László

2003　*Linked: How Everything Is Connected to Everything Else and What It Means for Business, Science, and Everyday Life*. Plume, New York.

Barnard, Alan

2004a　Hunter-Gatherers in History, Archaeology, and Anthropology: An Introductory Essay. In *Hunter-Gatherers in History, Archaeology, and Anthropology*, edited by A. Barnard, pp. 1–13. Berg, Oxford, U.K.

2004b　Hunting-and-Gathering Society: An Eighteenth-Century Scottish Invention. In *Hunter-Gatherers in History, Archaeology, and Anthropology*, edited by A. Barnard, pp. 31–13. Berg, Oxford, U.K.

Barrett, John C.

1999　The Mythical Landscapes of the British Iron Age. In *Archaeologies of Landscape: Contemporary Perspectives*, edited by W. Ashmore and A. B. Knapp, pp. 253–265. Blackwell, Malden, Mass.

Barrett, John C., Richard Bradley, and Martin Green

1991　*Landscapes, Monuments and Society: The Prehistory of Cranborne Chase*. Cambridge University Press, Cambridge.

Bar-Yosef, Ofer

1998　The Natufian Culture in the Levant, Threshold to the Origins of Agriculture. *Evolutionary Anthropology* 6:159–177.

2002　The Natufian: A Complex Society of Foragers. In *Beyond Foraging and Collecting: Evolutionary Change in Hunter-Gatherer Settlement*, edited by Ben Fitzhugh and Junko Habu, pp. 91–152. Plenum Press, New York.

Bar-Yosef, O., and R. Meadow

1995　Origins of Agriculture in the Near East. In *Last Hunters, First Farmers*, edited by T. Douglas Price and Anne B. Gebauer, pp. 39–94. School of American Research Press, Santa Fe, N.M.

Basso, Keith H.
1996 Wisdom Sits in Places: Notes on a Western Apache Landscape. In *Senses of Place*, edited by S. Feld and K. H. Basso, pp. 53–90. School of American Research Press, Santa Fe, N.M.

Beals, L., M. Goss, and S. Harrell
2000 Diversity Indices: Shannon's H and E. http://www.tiem.utk.edu/~mbeals/shannonDI.html.

Bean, Lowell John
1976 Social Organization in Native California. In *Native Californians: A Theoretical Retrospective*, edited by Lowell J. Bean and Thomas C. Blackburn, pp. 99–123. Ballena Press, Menlo Park, Calif.

Bean, Lowell John, and Harry Lawton
1976 Some Explanations for the Rise of Cultural Complexity in Native California with Comments on Proto-Agriculture and Agriculture. In *Native Californians: A Theoretical Retrospective*, edited by Lowell J. Bean and Thomas C. Blackburn, pp. 19–48. Ballena Press, Menlo Park, Calif.

Bell, Catherine
1997 *Ritual: Perspectives and Dimensions*. Oxford University Press, New York.

Bell, Trevor, and M.A.P. Renouf
2008 The Domino Effect: Culture Change and Environmental Change in Newfoundland, 1500–1100 cal BP. *The Northern Review* 28 (Winter): 72–94.

Bennyhoff, James A., and Richard E. Hughes
1987 Shell Bead and Ornament Exchange Networks between California and the Western Great Basin. *Anthropological Papers of the American Museum of Natural History* 64:2.

Bense, Judith A.
1987 *The Midden Mound Project: Final Report*. Reports of Investigation 6. Office of Cultural and Archaeological Research, University of West Florida, Pensacola.

Bentley, R. Alexander, Matthew W. Hahn, and Stephen J. Shennan
2004 Random Drift and Culture Change. *Proceedings of the Royal Society of London B* 271:1443–1450.

Bentley, R. Alexander, and Herbert D. G. Maschner (editors)
2003 *Complex Systems in Archaeology: Empirical and Theoretical Applications*. University of Utah Press, Salt Lake City.

Bentley, R. Alexander, and Herbert D. G. Maschner
2008 Complexity Theory. In *Handbook of Archaeological Theories*, edited by R. A. Bentley, H. D. G. Maschner, and C. Chippindale, pp. 245–270. AltaMira Press, Lanham, Md.

Benton, Tim G., Stewart J. Plaistow, and Tim N. Coulson
2006 Complex Population Dynamics and Complex Causation: Devils, Details and Demography. *Proceedings of the Royal Society B* 273:1173–1181.

Bernardini, Wesley

2004   Hopewell Geometric Earthworks: A Case Study in the Referential and Experiential Meaning of Monuments. *Journal of Anthropological Archaeology* 23:331–356.

Berndt, Catherine H.

1994   Mythology. In *The Encyclopaedia of Aboriginal Australia: Aboriginal and Torres Strait Islander History, Society and Culture*, edited by D. Horton. Aboriginal Studies Press, Australian Institute of Aboriginal and Torres Strait Islander Studies, Canberra.

Bessire, Lucas

2005   Isolated Ayoreo: Will History Repeat Itself in the Gran Chaco? *Before Farming* 2:1–4.

Bettinger, Robert L.

1991   *Hunter-Gatherers: Archaeological and Evolutionary Theory*. Interdisciplinary Contributions to Archaeology. Plenum Press, New York.

1999   What Happened in the Medithermal? In *Models for the Millenium: Great Basin Anthropology Today*, edited by C. Beck, pp. 62–74. University of Utah Press, Salt Lake City.

2009   Macroevolutionary Theory and Archaeology. In *Macroevolution and Human Prehistory: Evolutionary Theory and Processual Archaeology*, edited by Anna M. Prentiss, Ian Kuijt, and James C. Chatters, pp. 275–296. Springer, New York.

Bicchieri, Michael G. (editor)

1972   *Hunters and Gatherers Today*. Holt, Rinehart and Winston, New York.

Binford, Lewis R.

1968   Post-Pleistocene Adaptations. In *New Perspectives in Archaeology*, edited by S. R. Binford and L. R. Binford, pp. 313–341. Aldine, Chicago.

1979   Organization and Formation Processes: Looking at Curated Technologies. *Journal of Anthropological Research* 35 (3): 255–273.

1980   Willow Smoke and Dog's Tails: Hunter-Gatherer Settlement Systems and Archaeological Site Formation. *American Antiquity* 45:4–20.

1990   Mobility, Housing, and Environment: A Comparative Study. *Journal of Anthropological Research* 46:119–152.

1991   A Corporate Caribou Hunt. *Expedition* 33 (1): 33–43.

2001   *Constructing Frames of Reference: An Analytical Method for Archaeological Theory Building Using Hunter-Gatherer and Environmental Data Sets*. University of California Press, Berkeley.

Bintliff, John

2008   History and Continental Approaches. In *Handbook of Archaeological Theories*, edited by R. A. Bentley, H.D.G. Maschner, and C. Chippindale, pp. 147–164. AltaMira Press, Lanham, Md.

Bird, Douglas W., and James F. O'Connell

2006 Behavioral Ecology and Archaeology. *Journal of Archaeological Research* 14:143–188.

Bird-David, Nurit

1990 The Giving Environment: Another Perspective on the Economic System of Gatherer-Hunters. *Current Anthropology* 31:189–196.

Birkett, Tyson C.

1991 *Origin of the Lower Proterozoic Fleming Chert-Breccia, Newfoundland, Labrador-Quebec.* Paper No. 91–12. Geological Survey of Canada, Ottawa.

Blackburn, Thomas C.

1975 *December's Child: A Book of Chumash Oral Narratives.* University of California Press, Berkeley.

1976 Ceremonial Integration and Social Interaction in Aboriginal California. In *Native Californians: A Theoretical Retrospective*, edited by Lowell J. Bean and Thomas C. Blackburn, pp. 225–244. Ballena Press, Ramona, Calif.

Blitz, John H.

1993 Locust Beads and Archaic Mounds. *Mississippi Archaeology* 28 (1): 20–43.

Blitz, John H., and Karl G. Lorenz

2006 *The Chattahoochee Chiefdoms.* University of Alabama Press, Tuscaloosa.

Bloch, Maurice

1977 The Past and the Present in the Present. *Man* 12:278–292.

Bochart, Jessica

2005 Interpreting the Past through Faunal Analysis at the Bridge River Site, British Columbia, Canada. Master's thesis, University of Montana, Missoula.

Boone, James L.

1992 Competition, Conflict, and the Development of Social Hierarchies. In *Evolutionary Ecology and Human Behavior*, edited by Eric A. Smith and Bruce Winterhalder, pp. 301–338. Aldine De Gruyter, New York.

Boserup, Ester

1965 *Conditions of Agricultural Growth.* Aldine, Chicago.

Bourdieu, Pierre

1977 *Outline of a Theory of Practice.* Stanford University Press, Stanford, Calif.

1990 *The Logic of Practice.* Polity Press, Cambridge, U.K.

Bourque, Bruce J.

1989 Ethnicity on the Maritime Peninsula, 1600–1759. *Ethnohistory* 36:257–284.

1992 *Prehistory of the Central Maine Coast.* Garland, New York.

1995 *Diversity and Complexity in Prehistoric Maritime Societies: A Gulf of Maine Perspective.* Plenum Press, New York.

Bowdler, Sandra

2002　Hunters and Traders in Northern Australia. In *Forager-Traders in South and Southeast Asia*, edited by Kathleen D. Morrison and Laura L. Junker, pp. 167–184. Cambridge University Press, Cambridge.

Bowen, Jonathan E.

1994　*The Distribution of Five Late Archaic Time Period Artifact Types in Ohio: Notched Butterfly Bannerstones, Bar-Type Birdstones, Marine Shell Sandal Sole Gorgets, Plummets, and Ashtabula Bifaces.* Sandusky Valley Chapter, Archaeological Society of Ohio.

Boyd, Robert, Monique B. Mulder, William H. Durham, and Peter J. Richerson

1997　Are Cultural Phylogenies Possible? In *Human by Nature: Between Biology and the Social Sciences*, edited by P. Weingart, S. D. Mitchell, P. J. Richerson, and S. Maasen, pp. 355–384. Lawrence Erlbaum, Mahwah, N.J.

Boyd, Robert, and Peter J. Richerson

1985　*Culture and the Evolutionary Process.* University of Chicago Press, Chicago.

1996　Why Culture Is Common, but Cultural Evolution Is Rare. *Proceedings of the British Academy* 88:77–93.

Bradley, Bruce A.

1991　Flaked Stone Technology in the Northern High Plains. In *Prehistoric Hunters of the High Plains*, 2nd ed., edited by George C. Frison, pp. 369–395. Academic Press, New York.

Bradley, Richard

1998　*The Significance of Monuments: On the Shaping of Human Experience in Neolithic and Bronze Age Europe.* Routledge, London.

2000　*An Archaeology of Natural Places.* Routledge, London.

2003　The Translation of Time. In *Archaeologies of Memory*, edited by R. M. Van Dyke and S. E. Alcock, pp. 221–227. Blackwell, Malden, Mass.

2005　*Ritual and Domestic Life in Prehistoric Europe.* Routledge, London.

Braidwood, Robert J.

1960　The Agricultural Revolution. *Scientific American* 230:130–148.

Braudel, Fernand

1996　*The Mediterranean and Mediterranean World in the Age of Philip II.* Vol. 1. University of California Press, Berkeley.

Brody, Hugh

2000　*The Other Side of Eden: Hunters, Farmers and the Shaping of the World.* Douglas & McIntyre, Vancouver.

Brown, Stuart C.

1988　Archaeological Investigations at Crow Head Cave and the Gargamelle Rockshelter in the Port au Choix National Historic Park, Newfoundland. MS. Provincial Archaeology Office, Department of Tourism, Culture and Recreation, Government of Newfoundland and Labrador.

Broyles, Bettye

    1971   *Second Preliminary Report: The St. Albans Site, Kanawha County, West Virginia*. Report of Archaeological Investigations 3. West Virginia Geological and Economic Survey, Morgantown.

Bruchac, Margaret M.

    2007   *Historical Erasure and Cultural Recoverey: Indigenous People in the Connecticut River Valley*. PhD diss., University of Massachusetts, Amherst.

Brumfiel, Elizabeth M.

    1992   Breaking and Entering the Ecosystem—Gender, Class, and Faction Steal the Show. *American Anthropologist* 94:551–567.

Brumfiel, Elizabeth M., and Timothy K. Earle

    1987   Specialization, Exchange, and Complex Societies: An Introduction. In *Specialization, Exchange, and Complex Societies*, edited by Elizabeth M. Brumfiel and Timothy K. Earle, pp. 1–9. Cambridge University Press, Cambridge.

Buckland, P. C., T. Amorosi, L. K. Barlow, A. J. Dugmore, P. A. Mayewski, T. H. McGovern, A.E.J. Ogilvie, J. P. Sadler, and P. Skidmore

    1996   Bioarchaeological and Climatological Evidence for the Fate of Norse Farmers in Medieval Greenland. *Antiquity* 70:88–96.

Buikstra, Jane E., and Douglas K. Charles

    1999   Centering the Ancestors: Cemeteries, Mounds, and Sacred Landscapes of the Ancient North American Midcontinent. In *Archaeologies of Landscape: Contemporary Perspectives*, edited by W. Ashmore and A. B. Knapp, pp. 201–228. Blackwell, Oxford, U.K.

Burchell, Meghan

    2006   Gender, Grave Goods and Status in British Columbia Burials. *Canadian Journal of Archaeology* 30:251–271.

Burdin, Richard

    2004   *Interaction, Exchange, and Social Organization among Hunter-Gatherers in the Midcontinent—Evidence from the Lower Ohio River Valley: Bannerstone Use from 6500 to 3000 BP*. Master's thesis, University of Kentucky, Lexington.

Burley, David, and Christopher Knusel

    1989   Burial Patterns and Archaeological Interpretation: Problems in the Recognition of Ranked Society in the Coast Salish Region. In *Development of Hunting-Fishing-Gathering Maritime Societies along the Gulf Coast of North America*, edited by Blukas Onat. Reprint Proceedings of the Circum-Pacific Prehistory Conference, Vol. 3C, Seattle, Wash. Washington State University Press, Pullman.

Bushnell, David I., Jr.

    1910   Myths of the Louisiana Choctaw. *American Anthropologist* 12:526–535.

Butler, Robert B.

    1978   *A Guide to Understanding Idaho Archaeology: The Upper Snake and Salmon River Country*. 3rd ed. Idaho State Historic Preservation Office, Boise.

Byers, Douglas

    1954   Bull Brook—A Fluted Point Site in Ipswich, Massachusetts. *American Antiquity* 19:343–351.

    1955   Additional Information on the Bull Brook Site, Massachusetts. *American Antiquity* 20:274–276.

    1956   Ipswich BC. *Essex Institute Historical Collections* 92:252–64.

    1959   Radiocarbon Dates for the Bull Brook Site, Massachusetts. *American Antiquity* 24:427–429.

Cameron, Catherine M., and Andrew I. Duff

    2008   History and Process in Village Formation: Context and Contrasts from the Northern Southwest. *American Antiquity* 73:29–57.

Cannon, Michael D., and Jack M. Broughton

    2010   Evolutionary Ecology and Archaeology: An Introduction. In *Evolutionary Ecology and Archaeology: Applications to Problems in Human Evolution and Prehistory*, edited by Jack M. Broughton and Michael D. Cannon, pp. 1–12. University of Utah Press, Salt Lake City.

Carle, David

    2008   *Introduction to Fire in California*. University of California Press, Berkeley.

Carleton, Kenneth

    1996   Nanih Waiya: Mother Mound of the Choctaw. *Common Ground: Archeology and Ethnography in the Public Interest* 1 (1). http://www.nps.gov/history/archeology/cg/vo11_num1/mother.htm.

Carlson, Roy L.

    1994   Trade and Exchange in Prehistoric British Columbia. In *Prehistoric Exchange Systems in North America*, edited by Timothy Baugh and Jonathan Ericson, pp. 307–361. Plenum Press, New York.

Carr, Philip J., and Lee H. Stewart

    2004   Poverty Point Chipped-Stone Tool Raw Materials: Inferring Social and Economic Strategies. In *Signs of Power: The Rise of Complexity in the Southeast*, edited by J. L. Gibson and P. J. Carr, pp. 129–145. University of Alabama Press, Tuscaloosa.

Catton, W. R., Jr.

    1998   Darwin, Durkheim, and Mutualism. *Advances in Human Ecology* 7:89–138.

Cérane Inc.

    1983a   *Analyse des données archéologiques du reservoir LG-3*. Submitted to Société d'énergie de la Baie James, Montreal.

    1983b   *Analyses des données archéologiques du réservoir LG-3. Deuxième partie. Analyse du matériel lithique et céramique*. Submitted to Société d'énergie de la Baie James, Montreal.

    1984   *Occupations préhistoriques, historiques et contemporaines de la région de Washadimi, réservoir LG-2, Baie James. Deux millénaires d'archives archéologiques.* Submitted to Direction régionale du Nouveau-Québec, Ministère des Affaires culturelles, Quebec.

1995 *Contribution à l'histoire des Cris de l'Est: La région de Laforge-1. Rapport synthèse.* 3 vols. Submitted to Société d'énergie de la Baie James, Montreal.

Chandler, F. W.

1988 *The Early Proterozoic Richmond Gulf Graben, East Coast of Hudson Bay, Quebec.* Bulletin 362. Geological Survey of Canada, Ottawa.

Chapman, Robert

2000 *Fragmentation in Archaeology: People, Places and Broken Objects in the Prehistory of South Eastern Europe.* Routledge, London.

Charles, Douglas K., and Jane E. Buikstra

1983 Archaic Mortuary Sites in the Central Mississippi Drainage: Distribution, Structure, and Behavioral Implications. In *Archaic Hunters and Gatherers in the American Midwest,* edited by J. L. Phillips and J. A. Brown, pp. 117–145. Academic Press, New York.

Charles, D. K., J. E. Buikstra, and L. W. Konigsberg

1986 Behavioral Implications of Terminal Archaic and Early Woodland Mortuary Practices in the Lower Illinois Valley. In *Early Woodland Archaeology,* edited by K. B. Farnsworth and T. E. Emerson, pp. 458–474. Kampsville Seminars in Archeology, Vol. 2. Center for American Archeology Press, Kampsville, Ill.

Charles, Douglas K., Julieann Van Nest, and Jane E. Buikstra

2004 From the Earth: Minerals and Meaning in the Hopewellian World. In *Soils, Stones, and Symbols: Cultural Perceptions of the Mineral World,* edited by N. Boivin and M. A. Owoc, pp. 43–70. University College London Press, U.K.

Chatters, James C.

1995 Population Growth, Climatic Cooling, and the Development of Collector Strategies on the Southern Plateau, Western North America. *Journal of World Prehistory* 9:341–400.

2009 A Macroevolutionary Perspective on the Archaeological Record of North America. In *Macroevolution and Human Prehistory: Evolutionary Theory and Processual Archaeology,* edited by Anna M. Prentiss, Ian Kuijt, and James C. Chatters, pp. 213–234. Springer, New York.

Chatters, James C., Virginia L. Butler, Michael J. Scott, David M. Anderson, and Duane A. Neitzel

1995 A Paleoscience Approach to Estimating the Effects of Climatic Warming on Salmonid Fisheries of the Columbia Basin. *Canadian Special Publication in Fisheries and Aquatic Sciences* 21:489–496.

Chatters, James C., and William C. Prentiss

2005 A Darwinian Macro-Evolutionary Perspective on the Development of Hunter-Gatherer Systems in Northwestern North America. *World Archaeology* 37:45–65.

Chesson, Meredith S.

2001   Social Memory, Identity, and Death: An Introduction. *Archeological Papers of the American Anthropological Association* 10:1–10.

Chevrier, Daniel

1986   GaFf-1: Un atelier de taille du quartz en Jamésie orientale. *Recherches amérindiennes au Québec* 16 (2–3): 57–72.

Chisholm, James S.

1993   Death, Hope, and Sex: Life-history Theory and the Development of Reproductive Strategies. *Current Anthropology* 34:1–24.

Christensen, Tina, and Jim Stafford

2005   Raised Beach Archaeology in Northern Haida Gwaii: Preliminary Results from the Cohoe Creek Site. In *Haida Gwaii: Human History and Environment from the Time of the Loon to the Time of the Iron People*, edited by D. W. Fedje and R. W. Mathewes, pp. 245–273. University of British Columbia Press, Vancouver.

Claassen, Cheryl

1992   Shell Mounds as Burial Mounds: A Revision of the Shell Mound Archaic. In *Current Archaeological Research in Kentucky*, Vol. 2, edited by D. Pollack and A. G. Henderson, pp. 1–12. Kentucky Heritage Council, Frankfort.

1996   A Consideration of the Social Organization of the Shell Mound Archaic. In *Archaeology of the Mid-Holocene Southeast*, edited by K. E. Sassaman and D. G. Anderson, pp. 235–258. University Press of Florida, Gainesville.

Clark, Jeffery J., J. Brett Hill, and Deborah Huntley

2008   *Communities in Crisis: Kayenta Diaspora and Salado Coalescence in Southwestern New Mexico.* National Science Foundation Proposal No. 0819657. Cited with permission of the authors.

Clark, John E.

2004   Surrounding the Sacred: Geometry and Design of Early Mound Groups as Meaning and Function. In *Signs of Power: The Rise of Complexity in the Southeast*, edited by J. L. Gibson and P. J. Carr, pp. 162–213. University of Alabama Press, Tuscaloosa.

Clark, John E., and Michael Blake

1989   The Emergence of Rank Societies on the Pacific Coasts of Chiapas, Mexico. Paper presented at the Circum-Pacific Prehistory Conference, Seattle, Wash.

1994   The Power of Prestige: Competitive Generosity and the Emergence of Rank Societies in Lowland Mesoamerica. In *Factional Competition and Political Development in the New World*, edited by E. Brumfiel and J. Fox, pp. 17–30. Cambridge University Press, Cambridge.

Clarke, David

1978   *Analytical Archaeology.* 2nd ed. Revised by Bob Chapman. Methuen, London.

Clayton, A.G.

1926   A Brief History of the Washakie National Forest and the Duties and Some Experiences of a Ranger. *Annals of Wyoming* 4 (2): 277–295.

Cobb, Charles R. (editor)

2003   *Stone Tool Traditions in the Contact Era.* University of Alabama Press, Tuscaloosa.

Cobb, Charles R.

2005   Archaeology and the "Savage Slot": Displacement and Emplacement in the Premodern World. *American Anthropologist* 107:563–574.

Cobb, Charles R., and Eric Drake

2008   The Colour of Time: Head Pots and Temporal Convergences. *Cambridge Journal of Archaeology* 18:85–93.

Cobb, Charles R., and Adam King

2005   Re-Inventing Mississippian Tradition at Etowah, Georgia. *Journal of Archaeological Method and Theory* 12:167–192.

Coe, Joffre L.

1964   The Formative Cultures of the Carolina Piedmont. *Transactions of the American Philosophical Society* 54 (5): 1–130.

Cohen, Mark Nathan

1977   *The Food Crisis in Prehistory.* Yale University Press, New Haven, Conn.

Conkey, Margaret W.

2001   Hunting for Images, Gathering Up Meanings: Art for Life in Hunting-Gathering Societies. In *Hunter-Gatherers: An Interdisciplinary Perspective*, edited by Catherine Panter-Brick, Robert H. Layton, and Peter Rowley-Conwy, pp. 267–292. Cambridge University Press, New York.

Conkey, Margaret W., with Sarah Williams

1991   Original Narratives: The Political Economy of Gender in Archaeology. In *Gender at the Crossroads of Knowledge: Feminist Anthropology in the Postmodern Era*, edited by Micaela di Leonardi, pp. 102–139. University of California Press, Berkeley.

Connerton, Paul

1989   *How Societies Remember.* Cambridge University Press, Cambridge.

Connolly, Robert P.

2002   The 1980–1982 Excavations on the Northwest Ridge 1 at the Poverty Point Site. *Louisiana Archaeology* 25:1–92.

2006   An Assessment of Radiocarbon Age Results from the Poverty Point Site. *Louisiana Archaeology* 27:1–14.

Cook, Sherburne F.

1976   *The Population of the California Indians 1769–1770.* University of California Press, Berkeley.

Corbett, Ray
    1999   Chumash Bone Whistles: The Development and Elaboration of Ritual Activity and Ceremonial Integration in Chumash Society. Master's thesis, University of California, Los Angeles.

Costin, Cathy Lynne
    2001   Craft Production Systems. In *Archaeology at the Millenium: A Sourcebook*, edited by Gary M. Feinman and T. Douglas Price, pp. 273–327. Kluwer/Plenum, New York.

Coupland, Gary
    1988   *Prehistoric Cultural Change at Kitselas Canyon*. Mercury Series. Archaeological Survey of Canada Paper No. 138. Canadian Museum of Civilization, Ottawa.

Coupland, Gary, and Edward B. Banning (editors)
    1996   *People Who Lived in Big Houses: Archaeological Perspectives on Large Domestic Structures*. Prehistory Press, Madison, Wisc.

Cresswell, Tim
    1993   Mobility as Resistance: A Geographic Reading of Kerouac's 'On the Road.' *Transactions of the Institute of British Geographers* 18 (2): 249–262.

Cross, John R.
    1999   "By Any Other Name …": A Reconsideration of Middle Archaic Lithic Technology and Typology in the Northeast. In *The Archaeological Northeast*, edited by Mary Ann Levine, Kenneth E. Sassaman, and Michael S. Nassaney, pp. 57–73. Bergin & Garvey, Westport, Conn.

Crothers, George M.
    1999   *Prehistoric Hunters and Gatherers, and the Archaic Period Green River Shell Middens of Western Kentucky*. PhD diss., Washington University, St. Louis.
    2004   The Green River in Comparison to the Lower Mississippi Valley during the Archaic: To Build Mounds or Not to Build Mounds. In *Signs of Power: The Rise of Complexity in the Southeast*, edited by J. L. Gibson and P. J. Carr, pp. 86–96. University of Alabama Press, Tuscaloosa.

Crusoe, Donald L., and Chester B. DePratter
    1976   A New Look at the Georgia Coastal Shellmound Archaic. *Florida Anthropologist* 29:1–23.

Curran, Mary Lou
    1984   The Whipple Site and Paleoindian Tool Assemblage Variation: A Comparison of Intrasite Structuring. *Archaeology of Eastern North America* 12:5–40.
    1999   Exploration, Colonization, and Settling In: The Bull Brook Phase, Antecedents, and Descendants. In *The Archaeological Northeast*, edited by Mary Ann Levine, Kenneth. E. Sassaman, and Michael S. Nassaney, pp. 3–24. Bergin & Garvey, Westport, Conn.

Cusick, James G. (editor)

1998   *Studies in Culture Contact: Interaction, Culture Change, and Archaeology*. Occasional Paper No. 25. Center for Archaeological Investigations, Southern Illinois University, Carbondale.

2000   Creolization and the Borderlands. *Historical Archaeology* 34 (3): 46–55.

Damas, David (editor)

1969a   *Contributions to Anthropology: Band Societies*. Bulletin 228. National Museums of Canada, Ottawa.

1969b   *Contributions to Anthropology: Ecological Essays*. Bulletin 230. National Museums of Canada, Ottawa.

Dawson, Kenneth C. A.

1977   An Application of the Direct Historical Approach to the Algonkians of Northern Ontario. *Canadian Journal of Archaeology* 1:151–181.

1982   The Northern Ojibwa of Ontario. In *Approaches to Algonquian Archaeology*, edited by Margaret G. Hanna and Brian Kooyman, pp. 81–96. Proceedings of the Thirteenth Annual Conference, Archaeology Association of the University of Calgary.

1983   Prehistory of the Interior Forest of Northern Ontario. In *Boreal Forest Adaptations*, edited by A. T. Steegmann Jr., pp. 55–84. Plenum Press, New York.

1987   Northwestern Ontario and the Early Contact Period: The Northern Ojibwa from 1615–1715. *Canadian Journal of Archaeology* 11:143–180.

Deagan, Kathleen A.

1990   Accommodation and Resistance: The Process and Impact of Spanish Colonization in the Southeast. In *Archaeological and Historical Perspectives on the Spanish Borderlands East*, Vol. 2, edited by David H. Thomas, pp. 297–314. Smithsonian Institution Press, Washington, D.C.

Dean, Jeffrey S., George J. Gumerman, Joshua M. Epstein, Robert L. Axtell, Alan C. Swedlund, Miles T. Parker, and Stephen McCarroll

2000   Understanding Anasazi Culture Change through Agent-based Modeling. In *Dynamics of Human and Primate Societies: Agent-based Modeling of Social and Spatial Process*, edited by Timothy A. Kohler and George J. Gumerman, pp. 179–206. Oxford University Press, New York.

DeAtley, Suzanne P., and Frank J. Findlow (editors)

1984   *Exploring the Limits: Frontiers and Boundaries in Prehistory*. British Archaeological Reports, International Series 223, Oxford, U.K.

De Block, Andreas, and Siegfried Dewitte

2007   Mating Games: Cultural Evolution and Sexual Selection. *Biology and Philosophy* 22:475–491.

DeBoer, Warren R.

2005   Colors for a North American Past. *World Archaeology* 37:66–91.

de Certeau, Michel
  1984   *The Practice of Everyday Life.* Translated by S. Rendell. University of California Press, Berkeley.
  1988   *The Writing of History.* Columbia University Press, New York.
Deller, Brian D., and Christopher Ellis
  1984   Crowfield: A Preliminary Report on a Probable Paleo-Indian Cremation in Southwestern Ontario. *Archaeology of Eastern North America* 12:41–71.
  2001   Evidence for Late Paleoindian Ritual from the Carodoc Site (AfHj–104), Southwestern Ontario, Canada. *American Antiquity* 66 (2): 267–284.
Denbow, James
  1984   Prehistoric Herders and Foragers of the Kalahari: The Evidence for 1500 Years of Interaction. In *Past and Present in Hunter-Gatherer Studies*, edited by Carmel Schrire, pp. 175–193. Academic Press, Orlando, Fla.
Denton, David
  1988   Long Term Land Use Patterns in the Caniapiscau Area, Nouveau-Québec. In *Boreal Forest and Sub-arctic Archaeology*, edited by C. S. "Paddy" Reid, pp. 146–156. Occasional Publication 6. London Chapter, Ontario Archaeological Society, London.
  1989   La période préhistorique récente dans la région de Caniapiscau. *Recherches amérindiennes au Québec* 19 (2–3): 59–75.
  1998   From the Source, to the Margins and Back: Notes on Mistassini Quartzite and Archaeology in the Area of the Colline Blanche. In *L'éveilleur et l'ambassadeur: Essais archéologiques et ethnohistoriques en homage à Charles A. Martijn*, edited by Roland Tremblay, pp. 17–32. Paléo-Québec, 27. Recherches amérindiennes au Québec, Montreal.
Denton, David, and Moira T. McCaffrey
  1988   A Preliminary Statement on the Prehistoric Utilization of Chert Deposits Near Schefferville, Nouveau-Québec. *Canadian Journal of Archaeology* 12:137–152.
Denton, David, Moira T. McCaffrey, and Pierre Desrosiers
  1984   *Analyse des collections archéologiques de la région du réservoir Caniapiscau (Phase I).* Submitted to Société d'énergie de la Baie James, Montreal.
Desrosiers, Pierre M., and Noura Rahmani
  2007   Essai sur l'exploitation des matières premières lithiques au Nunavik durant le Paléoesquimau. In *Des Tuniit aux Inuits: Patrimoines archéologique et historique au Nunavik*, edited by D. Arsenault and D. Gendron, pp. 95–124. Nunavik Archaeological Monograph Series, No. 2. Cahiers d'archéologie CÉLAT, Université Laval, Québec, and Avataq Cultural Institute, Montreal.
Deter-Wolf, Aaron
  2004   The Ensworth School Site (40DV184): A Middle Archaic Benton Occupation along the Harpeth River Drainage in Middle Tennessee. *Tennessee Archaeology* 1:18–35.

Diamond, Jared

2005   *Collapse: How Societies Choose to Fail or Succeed.* Viking, New York.

Diamond, Stanley

1974   *In Search of the Primitive: A Critique of Civilization.* Transaction, Brunswick, N.J.

Dincauze, Dena F.

1968   *Cremation Cemeteries in Eastern Massachusetts.* Peabody Museum of Archaeology and Ethnology, Harvard University, Cambridge, Mass.

1976   *The Neville Site: 8000 Years at Amoskeag.* Peabody Museum Monographs, No. 4. Harvard University, Cambridge, Mass.

1993   Pioneering in the Pleistocene: Large Paleoindian Sites in the Northeast. In *Archaeology of Eastern North America: Papers in Honor of Stephen Williams,* edited by James B. Stoltman, pp. 43–60. Archaeological Report No. 25. Mississippi Department of Archives and History, Jackson.

Dincauze, Dena F., and Mitchell Mulholland

1977   Early and Middle Archaic Site Distributions and Habitats in Southern New England. In *Amerinds and Their Paleoenvironments in Northeastern North America,* edited by W. Newman and B. Salwen, pp. 439–456. *Annals of the New York Academy of Sciences* 288.

Dobres, Marcia-Anne, and Christopher R. Hoffman

1999   Introduction: A Context for the Present and Future of Technological Studies. In *The Social Dynamics of Technology: Practice, Politics and World Views,* edited by Marcia-Anne Dobres and Christopher R. Hoffman, pp. 1–19. Smithsonian Institution Press, Washington, D.C.

Dominick, David

1964   The Sheepeaters. *Annals of Wyoming* 36 (2): 131–168.

Donnan, Hastings, and Thomas M. Wilson

1994   An Anthropology of Frontiers. In *Border Approaches: Anthropological Perspectives on Frontiers,* edited by Hastings Donnan and Thomas M. Wilson, pp. 1–14. University Press of America, Lanham, Md.

Doran, Glen H.

2002   *Windover: Multidisciplinary Investigations of an Early Archaic Florida Cemetery.* University Press of Florida, Gainesville.

Dowd, John T.

1989   *The Anderson Site: Middle Archaic Adaptation in Tennessee's Central Basin.* Miscellaneous Papers, No. 13. Tennessee Anthropological Association, Knoxville.

Dugmore, Andrew J., Christian Keller, and Thomas McGovern

2007   Norse Greenland Settlement: Reflections on Climate Change, Trade, and the Contrasting Fates of Human Settlements in the North Atlantic Islands. *Arctic Anthropology* 44:12–36.

Durham, William H.

    1979   Toward a Coevolutionary Theory of Human Biology and Culture. In *Evolutionary Biology and Human Social Behavior: An Anthropological Perspective*, edited by N. A. Chagnon and W. Irons, pp. 39–59. Duxbury Press, North Scituate, Mass.

    1990   *Coevolution: Genes, Culture, and Human Diversity.* Stanford University Press, Stanford, Calif.

Dye, David H.

    1996   Riverine Adaptation in the Midsouth. In *Of Caves and Shellmounds*, edited by K. C. Carstens and P. J. Watson, pp. 140–158. University of Alabama Press, Tuscaloosa.

Dyke, B.

    1981   Computer Simulation in Anthropology. *Annual Review of Anthropology* 10:193–207.

Edinborough, Kevan

    2009   Population History and the Evolution of Mesolithic Arrowhead Technology in South Scandinavia. In *Pattern and Process in Cultural Evolution*, edited by Stephen Shennan, pp. 191–202. University of California Press, Berkeley.

Eerkens, Jelmer W.

    2003   Residential Mobility and Pottery Use in the Western Great Basin. *Current Anthropology* 44 (5): 728–738.

Eerkens, Jelmer W., Gregory S. Herbert, Jeffrey S. Rosenthal, and Howard J. Spero

    2005   Provenance Analysis of *Olivella biplicata* Shell Beads from the California and Oregon Coast by Stable Isotope Fingerprinting. *Journal of Archaeological Science* 32:1501–1514.

Eerkens, Jelmer W., Amy M. Spurling, and Michelle A. Gras

    2008   Measuring Prehistoric Mobility Strategies Based on Obsidian Geochemical and Technological Signatures in the Owens Valley, California. *Journal of Archaeological Science* 35:668–680.

Eldredge, Niles

    1985   *Unfinished Synthesis: Biological Hierarchies and Modern Evolutionary Thought.* Oxford University Press, New York.

    1995   *Reinventing Darwin.* Wylie, New York.

    2008   Hierarchies and the Sloshing Bucket: Toward the Unification of Evolutionary Biology. *Evolution: Education and Outreach* 1:10–15.

    2009   Material Cultural Macroevolution. In *Macroevolution and Human Prehistory: Evolutionary Theory and Processual Archaeology*, edited by Anna M. Prentiss, Ian Kuijt, and James C. Chatters, pp. 297–316. Springer, New York.

Ellis, Christopher J.

    1997   Factors Influencing the Use of Stone Projectile Tips: An Ethnographic Perspective. In *Projectile Point Technology*, edited by Heidi Knecht, pp. 37–78. Plenum Press, New York.

Ellis, Christopher J., and D. Brian Deller

2000   *An Early Paleoindian Site Near Parkhill, Ontario.* Mercury Series. Archaeological Survey of Canada Paper No. 159. Canadian Museum of Civilization, Hull.

Elmendorf, William W.

1965   Linguistic and Geographic Relations in the Northern Plateau Area. *Southwestern Journal of Anthropology* 21:63–78.

Emerson, Thomas E., and Dale L. McElrath

2001   Interpreting Discontinuity and Historical Process in Midcontinental Late Archaic and Early Woodland Societies. In *The Archaeology of Tradition: Agency and History before and after Columbus,* edited by T. R. Pauketat, pp. 195–217. University Press of Florida, Gainesville.

Endicott, Kirk

1983   The Effects of Slave Raiding on the Aborigines of the Malay Peninsula. In *Slavery, Bondage, and Dependency in Southeast Asia,* edited by Anthony Reid, pp. 216–245. St. Martin's Press, New York.

1999   Introduction: Southeast Asia. In *The Cambridge Encyclopedia of Hunters and Gatherers,* edited by Richard Lee and Robert Daly, pp. 275–283. Cambridge University Press, Cambridge.

Endonino, Jon C.

2003   Pre-Ceramic Archaic Burial Mounds along the St. Johns River, Florida. Paper presented at the Fifty-ninth Annual Southeastern Archaeological Conference, Charlotte, N.C.

2008   The Thornhill Lake Archaeological Research Project: 2005–2008. *The Florida Anthropologist* 61 (3–4): 149–165.

Erasmus, Charles

1965   Monument Building: Some Field Experiments. *Southwestern Journal of Anthropology* 21:277–301.

Erlandson, Jon M.

1994   *Early Hunter-Gatherers of the California Coast.* Plenum Press, New York.

Erwin, John C.

2001   *A Prehistoric Soapstone Quarry in Fleur de Lys, Newfoundland.* PhD diss., University of Calgary, Alberta.

2003   Dorset Palaeoeskimo Settlement Patterns in White Bay, Newfoundland. *Northeast Anthropology* 66 (Fall): 5–14.

Erwin, John C., Donald H. Holly Jr., Stephen H. Hull, and Timothy L. Rast

2005   Form and Function of Projectile Points and the Trajectory of Newfoundland Prehistory. *Canadian Journal of Archaeology* 29:46–67.

Estioko-Griffin, Agnes, and P. Bion Griffin

1981   Woman the Hunter: The Agta. In *Woman the Gatherer,* edited by Frances Dahlberg, pp. 121–151. Yale University Press, New Haven, Conn.

Ethnoscop
    1995   *Projets La Grande 1 et La Grande 2A. La Grande Rivière, de LG2 à la baie James: Synthèse archéologique.* 3 vols. Submitted to Société d'énergie de la Baie James, Montreal.

Fabian, Johannes
    1983   *Time and the Other: How Anthropology Makes Its Object.* Columbia University Press, New York.

Fagan, Brian
    2008   *The Great Warming: Climate Change and the Rise and Fall of Civilizations.* Bloomsbury Press, New York.

Faught, Michael K.
    2002   Submerged Paleoindian and Archaic Sites of the Big Bend, Florida. *Journal of Field Archaeology* 29: 273–290.

Fedje, Daryl W., and Quentin Mackie
    2005   Overview of Culture History. In *Haida Gwaii: Human History and Environment from the Time of the Loon to the Time of the Iron People,* edited by D. W. Fedje and R. W. Mathewes, pp. 154–162. University of British Columbia Press, Vancouver.

Feit, Harvey A.
    1973   The Ethno-Ecology of the Waswanipi Cree: Or How Hunters Can Manage Their Resources. In *Cultural Ecology: Readings on the Canadian Indians and Eskimos,* edited by Bruce Cox, pp. 115–125. McClelland and Stewart, Toronto.

    1995   Hunting and the Quest for Power: The James Bay Cree and Whitemen in the Twentieth Century. In *Native Peoples: The Canadian Experience,* 3rd ed., edited by R. Bruce Morrison and C. Roderick Wilson, pp. 181–223. McClelland and Stewart.

Ferguson, Jeffrey R., and Michael D. Glascock
    2007   Instrumental Neutron Activation Analysis of Intermountain Ware from Four Sites in Northwestern Wyoming. Report on file, Archaeometry Laboratory, Research Reactor Center, University of Missouri, Columbia.

Ferguson, Leland
    1991   Struggling with Pots in Colonial South Carolina. In *The Archaeology of Inequality,* edited by Randall H. McGuire and Robert Paynter, pp. 28–39. Blackwell, Oxford, U.K.

    1992   *Uncommon Ground: Archaeology and Early African America, 1650–1800.* Smithsonian Institution Press, Washington, D.C.

Finney, Bruce P., Irene Gregory-Eaves, Marianne S. V. Douglas, and John P. Smol
    2002   Fisheries Productivity in the Northeastern Pacific Ocean over the Past 2,200 Years. *Nature* 416:729–733.

Fitzgerald, Richard T., Terry L. Jones, and Adella Schroth
    2005   Ancient Long-Distance Trade in Western North America: New AMS Radiocarbon Dates from Southern California. *Journal of Archaeological Science* 32:423–434.

Fitzhugh, Ben

    2001   Risk and Invention in Human Technological Evolution. *Journal of Anthropological Archaeology* 20:125–167.

Fitzhugh, William

    1972a   *Environmental Archaeology and Cultural Systems in Hamilton Inlet, Labrador.* Smithsonian Contributions to Anthropology 16. Smithsonian Institution Press, Washington, D.C.

    1972b   The Eastern Archaic: Commentary and Northern Perspective. *Pennsylvania Archaeologist* 42 (4): 1–19.

    1973   Environmental Approaches to the Prehistory of the North. *Journal of the Washington Academy of Sciences* 63 (2): 39–53.

    2006   Settlement, Social and Ceremonial Change in the Labrador Maritime Archaic. In *The Archaic of the Far Northeast*, edited by David Sanger and M.A.P. Renouf, pp. 47–81. The University of Maine Press, Orono.

Flannery, Kent V.

    1972   The Cultural Evolution of Civilizations. *Annual Review of Ecology and Systematics* 3:399–426.

    2001   The Origins of the Village Revisited: From Nuclear to Extended Households. *American Antiquity* 67:417–434.

Fogelin, Lars

    2007   The Archaeology of Religious Ritual. *Annual Review of Anthropology* 36:55–71.

Ford, James A.

    1969   *A Comparison of Formative Cultures in the Americas: Diffusion or the Psychic Unity of Man.* Smithsonian Contributions to Anthropology 11. Smithsonian Institution, Washington, D.C.

Ford, James A., and Clarence H. Webb

    1956   *Poverty Point, a Late Archaic Site in Louisiana.* Anthropological Papers, Vol. 46, Pt. 1. American Museum of Natural History, New York.

Forrest, Daniel

    1999   Beyond Presence and Absence: Establishing Diversity in Connecticut's Early Holocene Archaeological Record. *Bulletin of the Connecticut Archaeological Society* 62:79–100.

Foster, Mary LeCron

    1990   Introduction. In *The Life of Symbols*, edited by Mary LeCron Foster and Lucy Jayne Botscharow, pp. 1–8. Westview Press, Boulder.

Foster, Stephen William

    1988   *The Past Is Another Country: Representation, Historical Consciousness, and Resistance in the Blue Ridge.* University of California Press, Berkeley.

Fox, Richard G.

    1969   Professional Primitives: Hunters and Gatherers of Nuclear South Asia. *Man in India* 49:139–160.

Francis, Daniel, and Toby Morantz
1983   *Partners in Furs: A History of the Fur Trade in Eastern James Bay 1600–
        1870.* McGill-Queen's University Press, Montreal.
Francis, Julie E., and Lawrence L. Loendorf
2002   *Ancient Visions: Petroglyphs and Pictographs from the Wind River and Bighorn
        Country, Wyoming and Montana.* University of Utah Press, Salt Lake City.
Fredrickson, David
1974   Social Change in Prehistory: A Central California Example. In *?Antap:
        California Indian Political and Economic Organization,* edited by Lowell J.
        Bean and Thomas F. King, pp. 55–73. Ballena Press, Ramona, Calif.
Fricke, Tom
1997   Culture Theory and Demographic Process: Toward a Thicker Demog-
        raphy. In *Anthropological Demography: Toward a New Synthesis,* edited
        by David I. Kertzer and Tom Fricke, pp. 248–278. University of Chi-
        cago Press, Chicago.
Fried, Morton H.
1960   On the Evolution of Social Stratification and the State. In *Culture in
        History,* edited by Stanley Diamond, pp. 713–731. Columbia University
        Press, New York.
Frink, Lisa
2005   Gender and the Hide Production Process in Colonial Western Alaska.
        In *Gender and Hide Production,* edited by Lisa Frink and Kathryn
        Weedman, pp. 89–103. AltaMira, Lanham, Md.
Frison, George C.
1987   Prehistoric, Plains-Mountain, Large-Mammal, Communal Hunting
        Strategies. In *The Evolution of Human Hunting,* edited by Matthew H.
        Nitecki and Doris V. Nitecki, pp. 177–211. Plenum Press, New York.
1991   *Prehistoric Hunters of the High Plains.* 2nd ed. Academic Press, New York.
Frison, George C., Charles A. Reher, and Danny N. Walker
1990   Prehistoric Mountain Sheep Hunting in the Central Rocky Mountains
        of North America. In *Hunters of the Recent Past,* edited by Leslie B.
        Davis and Brian O. K. Reeves, pp. 208–240. Unwin-Hyman, London.
Fundaburke, Emma Lila, and Mary Douglas Fundaburke Foreman
1957   *Sun Circles and Human Hands: The Southeastern Indians Art and Indus-
        tries.* Author, Laverne, Ala.
Gaines, Sylvia W., and Warren M. Gaines
1997   Simulating Success or Failure: Another Look at Small-Population
        Dynamics. *American Antiquity* 62:683–697.
Galaty, Michael L.
1996   Labor, Population, and Social Complexity. *Chicago Anthropology Exchange*
        22:33–49.
Galloway, Patricia
1998   *Choctaw Genesis, 1500–1700.* University of Nebraska Press, Lincoln.

Gamble, Clive

1996   *Timewalkers: A Prehistory of Human Global Colonization.* Harvard University Press, Cambridge.

Gamble, Lynn H.

2002   Archaeological Evidence for the Origin of the Plank Canoe in North America. *American Antiquity* 67:301–315.

2005   Culture and Climate: Reconsidering the Effect of Paleoclimatic Variability among Southern California Hunter-Gatherer Societies. *World Archaeology* 37:92–108.

2008   *The Chumash World at European Contact: Power, Trade, and Feasting among Complex Hunter-Gatherers.* University of California Press, Berkeley.

Gamble, Lynn H., Phillip L. Walker, and Glenn S. Russell

2001   An Integrative Approach to Mortuary Analysis: Social and Symbolic Dimensions of Chumash Burial Practices. *American Antiquity* 66:185–212.

Gamble, Lynn H., and Irma Carmen Zepeda

2002   Social Differentiation and Exchange during the Historic Period among the Kumeyaay. *Historical Archaeology* 36:71–91.

Gaudreau, Denise C.

1988   The Distribution of Late Quaternary Forest Regions in the Northeast: Pollen Data, Physiography, and the Prehistoric Record. In *Holocene Human Ecology in Northeastern North America*, edited by George P. Nicholas, pp. 215–256. Plenum Press, New York.

Geiger, Maynard, and Clement W. Meighan

1976   *As the Padres Saw Them: California Indian Life and Customs as Reported by the Franciscan Missionaries, 1813–1815.* Santa Barbara Mission Library, Santa Barbara, Calif.

Georgekish, Fred

1979   Traditional Cree Structural Forms: Their Variety, Function and Construction Procedures. MS. Service Patrimoine Autochtone, Direction générale du Patrimoine, Ministère des Affaires culturelles, Québec.

Gero, Joan M

1991   Genderlithics: Women's Roles in Stone Tool Production. In *Engendering Archaeology: Women and Prehistory*, edited by Joan M. Gero and Margaret W. Conkey. Blackwell, Oxford. U.K.

Gibson, Jon L.

1974   Poverty Point: The First North American Chiefdom. *Archaeology* 27:96–105.

1987a   *The Ground Truth about Poverty Point: The Second Season, 1985.* Report No. 7. Center for Archaeological Studies, University of Southwestern Louisiana, Lafayette.

1987b   The Poverty Point Earthworks Reconsidered. *Mississippi Archaeology* 22 (2): 14–31.

Gibson, Jon L.

1994a   Empirical Characterization of Exchange Systems in Lower Mississippi
        Valley Prehistory. In *Prehistoric Exchange Systems in North America*, edited
        by T. G. Baugh and J. E. Ericson, pp. 127–175. Plenum Press, New York.

1994b   Lower Mississippi Valley Exchange at 1100 BC. In *Exchange in the
        Lower Mississippi Valley and Contiguous Areas at 1100 BC*, edited by
        J. L. Gibson, pp. 1–11. Louisiana Archaeology 17. Louisiana Archaeo-
        logical Society, Lafayette, La.

1994c   Over the Mountain and Across the Sea: Regional Poverty Point
        Exchange. In *Exchange in the Lower Mississippi Valley and Contiguous
        Areas at 1100 BC*, edited by J. L. Gibson, pp. 251–299. Louisiana Archae-
        ology 17. Louisiana Archaeological Society, Lafayette, La.

1998a   Broken Circles, Owl Monsters, and Black Earth Midden: Separating
        the Sacred and Secular at Poverty Point. In *Ancient Earthen Enclosures
        of the Eastern Woodlands*, edited by R. C. Mainfort Jr. and L. P. Sullivan,
        pp. 17–30. University Press of Florida, Gainesville.

1998b   Elements and Organization of Poverty Point Political Economy: High-
        Water Fish, Exotic Rocks, and Sacred Earth. *Research in Economic
        Anthropology* 19:291–340.

2000   *The Ancient Mounds of Poverty Point: Place of Rings*. University Press of
        Florida, Gainesville.

2004   The Power of Beneficent Obligation in First Mound-Building Societ-
        ies. In *Signs of Power: The Rise of Complexity in the Southeast*, edited by
        J. L. Gibson and P. J. Carr, pp. 255–269. University of Alabama Press,
        Tuscaloosa.

2006   Navel of the Earth: Sedentism at Poverty Point. *World Archaeology*
        38:311–329.

2007   "Formed from the Earth of That Place": The Material Side of Com-
        munity at Poverty Point. *American Antiquity* 72:509–523.

Glassow, Michael A.

1993   Introduction: A Status Report on the Northern Channel Islands
        Archaeological Research. In *Archaeology of the Northern Channel Islands
        of California*, pp. 1–17. Archives of California Prehistory 34. Coyote
        Press, Salinas, Calif.

Glassow, Michael A., Lynn H. Gamble, Jennifer E. Perry, and Glenn S. Russell

2007   Prehistory of the Northern California Bight and Adjacent Transverse
        Ranges. In *California Prehistory: Colonization, Culture, and Complexity*,
        edited by Terry L. Jones and Kathryn A. Klar, pp. 191–213. AltaMira
        Press, Lanham, Md.

Goggin, John M.

1952   *Space and Time Perspectives in Northern St. Johns Archaeology, Florida*.
        Yale University Publications in Anthropology 47. Yale University Press,
        New Haven, Conn.

Gomez-Pompa, A., H. L. Morales, E. J. Avila, and J. J. Avila
  1982   Experiences in Traditional Hydraulic Agriculture. In *Maya Subsistence: Studies in Memory of Dennis E. Puleston*, edited by K. Flannery, pp. 327–342. Academic Press, London.

Goodale, Nathan B., Ian Kuijt, and Anna M. Prentiss
  2008   The Demography of Prehistoric Fishing/Hunting People: A Case Study of the Upper Columbia Area. In *Recent Advances in Paleodemography*, edited by J. P. Bocquet-Appel, pp. 179–207. Springer, New York.

Goodale, Nathan B., William C. Prentiss, and Ian Kuijt
  2004   Cultural Complexity: A New Chronology of the Upper Columbia Drainage Area. In *Complex Hunter-Gatherers: Evolution and Organization of Prehistoric Communities on the Plateau of Northwestern North America*, edited by W. C. Prentiss and I. Kuijt, pp. 36–48. University of Utah Press, Salt Lake City.

Goodyear, Albert C.
  1979   *A Hypothesis for the Use of Cryptocrystalline Raw Materials among Paleoindian Groups of North America*. Research Manuscript Series 156. Institute of Archaeology and Anthropology, University of South Carolina, Columbia.

Gosden, Chris
  1994   *Social Being and Time*. Blackwell, Oxford, U.K.
  2001   Making Sense: Archaeology and Aesthetics. *World Archaeology* 33 (2): 163–167.
  2005   What Do Objects Want? *Journal of Archaeological Method and Theory* 12:193–211.

Gosden, Chris, and Gary Lock
  1998   Prehistoric Histories. *World Archaeology* 30:2–12.

Gosden, Chris, and Yvonne Marshall
  1999   The Cultural Biography of Objects. *World Archaeology* 31:169–178.

Gould, Richard A.
  1980   *Living Archaeology*. Cambridge University Press, Cambridge.
  1982   To Have and Have Not: The Ecology of Sharing among Hunters and Gatherers. In *Resource Managers: North American and Australian Hunter-Gatherers*, edited by Nancy M. William and Eugene S. Hunn, pp. 69–91. Westview Press, Boulder, Colo.

Gould, Richard A., and Sherry Saggers
  1985   Lithic Procurement in Central Australia: a Closer Look at Binford's Idea of Embeddedness in Archaeology. *American Antiquity* 50 (1): 117–136.

Gould, Stephen J.
  2002   *The Structure of Evolutionary Theory*. Belknap Press, Cambridge, Mass.

Gould, Stephen J., and Richard C. Lewontin
  1979   The Spandrels of San Marco and the Panglossian Paradigm: A Critique of the Panglossian Programme. *Proceedings of the Royal Society of London B* 205: 581–598.

Gould, Stephen J., and Elizabeth S. Vrba

    1982   Exaptation—A Missing Term in the Science of Form. *Paleobiology* 8:4–15.

Grantham, Bill

    2002   *Creation Myths and Legends of the Creek Indians*. University Press of Florida, Gainesville.

Green, Stanton W., and Stephen M. Perlman (editors)

    1985   *The Archaeology of Frontiers and Boundaries*. Academic Press, New York.

Greenhalgh, Susan

    1995   Anthropology Theorizes Reproduction: Integrating Practice, Political Economic, and Feminist Perspectives. In *Situating Fertility: Anthropology and Demographic Inquiry*, edited by Susan Greenhalgh, pp. 3–28. Cambridge University Press, Cambridge.

Grier, Colin, Kim Jangsuk, and Junzo Uchiyama (editors)

    2006   *Beyond Affluent Foragers: Rethinking Hunter-Gatherer Complexity*. Oxbow, Oxford, U.K.

Griffin, James B.

    1964   The Northeast Woodlands Area. In *Prehistoric Man in the New World*, edited by Jesse D. Jennings and Edward Norbeck, pp. 223–258. University of Chicago Press, Chicago.

Grimes, John R.

    1979   A New Look at Bull Brook. *Anthropology* 3:109–130.

Grinker, Roy Richard

    1994   *Houses in the Rainforest: Ethnicity and Inequality among Farmers and Foragers in Central Africa*. University of California Press, Berkeley.

Guenther, Mathias

    1999   From Totemism to Shamanism: Hunter-Gatherer Contributions to World Mythology and Spirituality. In *The Cambridge Encyclopedia of Hunters and Gatherers*, edited by R. B. Lee and R. Daly, pp. 426–433. Cambridge University Press, Cambridge.

Guthrie, Dale

    1983   Osseous Projectile Points: Biological Considerations Affecting Raw Material Selection and Design among Paleolithic and Paleoindian Peoples. In *Animals and Archaeology I: Hunters and Their Prey*, edited by Juliet Clutton-Brock and Caroline Grigson, pp. 273–294. British Archaeological Reports, International Series 163, Oxford, U.K.

Haag, William G.

    1990   Excavations at the Poverty Point Site: 1972–1975. *Louisiana Archaeology* 13:1–36.

Hall, Robert L.

    1997   *An Archaeology of the Soul: North American Indian Belief and Ritual*. University of Illinois Press, Urbana.

Halperin, Rhoda H.
  1980   Ecology and Mode of Production: Seasonal Variation and the Division
          of Labor by Sex among Hunter-Gatherers. *Journal of Anthropological
          Research* 36:379–399.
Halstead, Paul, and John O'Shea
  1989   Introduction: Cultural Responses to Risk and Uncertainty. In *Bad
          Year Economics: Cultural Responses to Risk and Uncertainty*, edited by
          Paul Halstead and John O'Shea, pp. 1–7. Cambridge University Press,
          Cambridge.
Hamilton, Fran E.
  1999   Southeastern Archaic Mounds: Examples of Elaboration in a Tempo-
          rally Fluctuating Environment? *Journal of Anthropological Archaeology*
          18:344–355.
Hammel, Eugene A.
  1990   A Theory of Culture for Demography. *Population and Development
          Review* 16:455–486.
  2005a   Demographic Dynamics and Kinship in Anthropological Populations.
          Proceedings of the National Academy of Science 102:2248–2252.
  2005b   Kinship-based Politics and the Optimal Size of Kin Groups. *Proceedings
          of the National Academy of Science* 102:11951–11956
Hammel, Eugene A., and Nancy Howell
  1987   Research in Population and Culture: An Evolutionary Framework.
          Current Anthropology 28:141–160.
Harp, Elmer Jr.
  1969–1970 Late Dorset Eskimo Art from Newfoundland. *Folk* 11–12:109–124.
  1976   Dorset Settlement Patterns in Newfoundland and Southeastern Hud-
          son Bay. In *Eastern Arctic Prehistory: Paleoeskimo Problems*, edited by
          Moreau S. Maxwell, pp. 119–138. Memoirs for the Society for American
          Archaeology 31.
Harrington, John P.
  1942   Culture Element Distributions: XIX, Central California Coast. *Univer-
          sity of California Anthropological Records* 7 (1). Berkeley.
Harrison, Rodney
  2002   Archaeology and the Colonial Encounter: Kimberley Spear Points,
          Cultural Identity and Masculinity in the North of Australia. *Journal of
          Social Archaeology* 2 (3): 352–377.
Harrison, Rodney, and Christine Williamson (editors)
  2004   *After Captain Cook: The Archaeology of the Recent Indigenous Past in Aus-
          tralia*. AltaMira, Walnut Creek, Calif.
Haspel, Howard
  1984   Study of Shoshonean Ceramics of Wyoming: the Bugas-Holding
          Ceramic Assemblage. *The Wyoming Archaeologist* 27 (3–4): 25–40.

Hassan, Fekri A.

  1978   Demographic Archaeology. In *Advances in Archaeological Method and Theory*, Vol. 1, edited by Michael B. Schiffer, pp. 49–105. Academic Press, New York.

  1979   Demography and Archaeology. *Annual Review of Anthropology* 8:137–160.

  1981   *Demographic Archaeology*. Academic Press, New York.

Hassen, Harold, and Kenneth B. Farnsworth

  1987   *The Bullseye Site: A Floodplain Archaic Mortuary Site in the Lower Illinois River Valley*. Reports of Investigation 42. Illinois State Museum, Springfield.

Hawkes, Kristen, James F. O'Connell, and Nicholas G. Blurton Jones

  1997   Hadza Women's Time Allocation, Offspring Provisioning, and the Evolution of Long Postmenopausal Life Spans. *Current Anthropology* 38:551–577.

Hay, Murrey B., Audrey Dallimore, Richard E. Thomson, Stephen E. Calvert, and Reinhard Pienitz

  2007   Siliceous Microfossil Record of Late Holocene Oceanography and Climate along the West Coast of Vancouver Island, British Columbia (Canada). *Quaternary Research* 67:33–49.

Hayden, Brian (editor)

  1992   *A Complex Culture of the British Columbia Plateau*. University of British Columbia Press, Vancouver.

Hayden, Brian

  1994   Competition, Labor, and Complex Hunter-Gatherers. In *Key Issues in Hunter-Gatherer Research*, edited by E. S. Burch and L. J. Ellana, pp. 223–239. Berg, Oxford, U.K.

  1995   Pathways to Power: Principles for Creating Socioeconomic Inequalities. In *Foundations of Social Inequality*, edited by T. D. Price and G. M. Feinman, pp. 15–86. Plenum Press, New York.

Hayden, Brian, and Aubrey Cannon

  1982   Corporate Group as an Archaeological Unit. *Journal of Anthropological Archaeology* 1:132–158.

Hayden, Brian, and June Ryder

  1991   Prehistoric Cultural Collapse in the Lillooet Area. *American Antiquity* 56:50–65.

Headland, Thomas N., and Lawrence A. Reid

  1989   Hunter-Gatherers and Their Neighbors from Prehistory to the Present. *Current Anthropology* 30 (1): 43–66.

Hegmon, Michelle, Matthew A. Peeples, Ana P. Kinzig, Stephanie Kulow, Cathryn M. Meegan, and Margaret C. Nelson

  2008   Social Transformation and Its Human Costs in the Prehispanic U.S. Southwest. *American Anthropologist* 110:313–324.

Heizer, Robert F.

1958   Prehistoric Central California: A Problem in Historical-Developmental Classification. *University of California Archaeological Survey Reports* 41:19–26.

Helm, June

1968   Does Hunting Bring Happiness? In *Man the Hunter*, edited by Richard B. Lee and Irven DeVore, pp. 89–92. Aldine De Gruyter, New York.

Henrich, Joseph

2004   Demography and Cultural Evolution: How Adaptive Cultural Processes Can Produce Maladaptive Losses—The Tasmanian Case. *American Antiquity* 69:197–214.

Henriksen, Georg

1973   *Hunters in the Barrens. The Naskapi on the Edge of the White Man's World.* Institute of Social and Economic Research. Memorial University of Newfoundland, St. John's, Newfoundland.

2009   *I Dreamed the Animals. Kaniuekutat: The Life of an Innu Hunter.* Berghahn Books: New York.

Hensley, Christine

1994   *The Archaic Settlement System of the Middle Green River Valley.* PhD diss., Washington University, St. Louis.

Hickerson, Harold

1966   The Genesis of Bilaterality among Two Divisions of Chippewa. *American Anthropologist* 68:1–26.

Hicks, Brent A., Maury Morgenstein, and Steven Hamilton (editors)

2006   *Archeological Test and Data Recovery Excavations of Seven Sites in East Yosemite Valley, Yosemite National Park.* Entrix, Inc. Submitted to USDI National Park Service, Yosemite National Park, Calif.

Hill, J. Brett, Jeffery J. Clark, William H. Doelle, Patrick D. Lyons

2004   Prehistoric Demography in the Southwest: Migration, Coalescence, and Hohokam Population Decline. *American Antiquity* 69:689–716.

Hill, Kim, and A. Magdalena Hurtado

1996   *Ache Life History: The Ecology and Demography of a Foraging People.* Aldine De Gruyter, New York.

Hodder, Ian

2002   Two Approaches to an Archaeology of the Social. *American Anthropologist* 104 (1): 320–324.

Hodgetts, Lisa M., M.A.P. Renouf, Maribeth S. Murray, Darlene McCuaig-Balkwill, and Lesley Howse

2003   Changing Subsistence Practices at the Dorset Paleoeskimo Site of Phillip's Garden, Newfoundland. *Arctic Anthropology* 40:106–120.

Hoffman, Carl L.

1984   Punan Foragers in the Trading Networks of Southeast Asia. In *Past and Present in Hunter-Gatherer Studies*, edited by Carmel Schrire, pp. 123–149. Academic Press, Orlando, Fla.

Hofman, Jack L.

1986   *Hunter-Gatherer Mortuary Variability: Toward an Explanatory Model.*
        PhD diss., University of Tennessee, Knoxville.

Holden, Claire J., and Stephen Shennan

2005   Introduction to Part 1: How Tree-like Is Cultural Evolution? In *The
        Evolution of Cultural Diversity: A Phylogenetic Approach*, edited by
        R. Mace, C. J. Holden, and S. Shennan, pp. 11–29. University College
        London Press, U.K.

Holly, Donald H., Jr.

2002a   Subarctic "Prehistory" in the Anthropological Imagination. *Arctic Anthro-
        pology* 39 (1–2): 10–26.

2002b   *From Space to Place: An Archaeology and Historical Geography of the
        Recent Indian Period in Newfoundland.* PhD diss., Brown University,
        Providence, R.I.

2005   The Place of "Others" in Hunter-Gatherer Intensification. *American
        Anthropologist* 107:207–220.

2008   Social Aspects and Implications of "Running to the Hills": The Case of
        the Beothuk Indians of Newfoundland. *Journal of Island and Coastal
        Archaeology* 3:170–190.

Holmer, Richard N.

1994   In Search of Ancestral Northern Shoshone. In *Across the West: Human
        Population Movement and the Expansion of the Numa*, edited by David B.
        Madsen and David Rhode, pp. 179–187. University of Utah Press, Salt
        Lake City.

Howell, Nancy

1986   Demographic Anthropology. *Annual Review of Anthropology* 15:219–246.

Hudson, Travis, and Thomas C. Blackburn

1986   Ceremonial Paraphernalia, Games, and Amusements. *The Material
        Culture of the Chumash Interaction Sphere*, Vol. 4, Ballena Press Anthro-
        pological Papers, No. 25, edited by Thomas C. Blackburn. Ballena Press,
        Los Altos, Calif./Santa Barbara Museum of Natural History, Santa
        Barbara, Calif.

Hudson, Travis, Thomas Blackburn, Rosario Curletti, and Janice Timbrook

1981   *The Eye of the Flute: Chumash Traditional History and Ritual as Told
        by Fernando Librado Kitsepawit to John P. Harrington.* Santa Barbara
        Museum of Natural History, Santa Barbara, Calif.

Hudson, Travis, Janice Timbrook, and Melissa Rempe (editors)

1978   *Tomol: Chumash Watercraft as Described in the Ethnographic Notes of
        John P. Harrington.* Ballena Press Anthropological Papers, No. 9. Bal-
        lena Press, Socorro, N.M.

Hudson, Travis, and Ernest Underhay

1978   *Crystals in the Sky: An Intellectual Odyssey Involving Chumash Astronomy,
        Cosmology and Rock Art.* Ballena Press, Socorro, N.M.

Hughes, Richard E., and Randall Milliken
  2007   Prehistoric Material Conveyance. In *California Prehistory: Colonization, Culture, and Complexity*, edited by Terry L. Jones and Kathryn A. Klar, pp. 259–271. AltaMira Press, Lanham, Md.

Hughes, Susan S.
  2000   The Sheepeater Myth of Northwestern Wyoming. *Plains Anthropologist* 45 (171): 63–83.

Hull, Kathleen L.
  2001   Reasserting the Utility of Obsidian Hydration Dating: A Temperature-Dependent Empirical Approach to Practical Temporal Resolution with Archaeological Obsidians. *Journal of Archaeological Science* 28:1025–1040.

  2002   *Culture Contact in Context: A Multiscalar View of Catastrophic Depopulation and Culture Change in Yosemite Valley, California.* PhD diss., University of California, Berkeley.

  2005   Process, Perception, and Practice: Time Perspectivism in Yosemite Native Demography. *Journal of Anthropological Archaeology* 24:354–377.

  2007   The Sierra Nevada: Archaeology in the Range of Light. In *California Prehistory: Colonization, Culture, and Complexity*, edited by Terry Jones and Kathryn Klar, pp. 177–190. AltaMira, Walnut Creek, Calif.

  2008   Archaeological Time on a Human Scale. Paper presented at the Sixth World Archaeological Congress (WAC-6), Dublin, Ireland.

  2009   *Pestilence and Persistence: Yosemite Indian Demography and Culture in Colonial California.* University of California Press, Berkeley.

Hull, Kathleen L., and Michael J. Moratto
  1999   *Archeological Synthesis and Research Design, Yosemite National Park, California.* Yosemite Research Center Publications in Anthropology 21. USDI National Park Service, Yosemite National Park, Calif.

Hultkrantz, Åke
  1957   The Indians in Yellowstone Park. *Annals of Wyoming* 29 (2): 125–149.

  1961   The Shoshones in the Rocky Mountain Region. *Annals of Wyoming* 33 (1): 19–40.

  1979   The Fear of Geysers among Indians of the Yellowstone Park Area. In *Lifeways of Intermontane and Plains Montana Indians*, edited by Leslie B. Davis, pp. 33–42. Occasional Paper No.1. Museum of the Rockies, Bozeman, Mont.

Husted, Wilfred M.
  1995   The Western Macrotradition Twenty-Seven Years Later. *Archaeology in Montana* 36 (1): 37–92.

Ingold, Tim
  1993   The Temporality of the Landscape. *World Archaeology* 25:152–174.

  1999   On the Social Relations of the Hunter-Gatherer Band. In *The Cambridge Encyclopedia of Hunters and Gatherers*, edited by R. B. Lee and R. Daly, pp. 399–410. Cambridge University Press, Cambridge.

Ingold, Tim

 2000 *The Perception of the Environment: Essays in Livelihood, Dwelling, and Skill.* Routledge, London.

Ingold, Tim, David Riches, and James Woodburn (editors)

 1991 *Hunters and Gatherers.* Vol. 1: *History, Evolution and Social Change.* Berg, New York.

Irving, Washington

 1837 *The Adventures of Captain Bonneville, USA.* J. B. Miller, New York.

 1910 *Astoria.* Century, New York.

Jackson, H. Edwin

 1986 *Sedentism and Hunter-Gatherer Adaptations in the Lower Mississippi Valley: Subsistence Strategies during the Poverty Point Period.* PhD diss., University of Michigan, Ann Arbor.

 1991 The Trade Fair in Hunter-Gatherer Interaction: The Role of Intersocietal Trade in the Evolution of Poverty Point Culture. In *Between Bands and States,* edited by S. A. Gregg, pp. 265–286. Occasional Papers, No. 9. Center for Archaeological Investigations, Southern Illinois University, Carbondale.

Jackson, Robert H., and Edward Castillo

 1995 *Indians, Franciscans, and Spanish Colonization: The Impact of the Mission System on California Indians.* University of New Mexico, Albuquerque.

Janssen, Marco A., Timothy A. Kohler, and Marten Scheffer

 2003 Sunk-Cost Effects and Vulnerability to Collapse in Ancient Societies. *Current Anthropology* 44:722–728.

Jarvenpa, Robert

 2004 *Silot'ine*: An Insurance Perspective on Northern Dene Kinship Networks in Recent History. *Journal of Anthropological Research* 60:153–178.

Jefferies, Richard W.

 1996 The Emergence of Long-Distance Exchange Networks in the Southeastern United States. In *Archaeology of the Mid-Holocene Southeast,* edited by K. E. Sassaman and D. G. Anderson, pp. 222–234. University Press of Florida, Gainsville.

 1997 Middle Archaic Bone Pins: Evidence of Mid-Holocene Regional-Scale Social Groups in the Southern Midwest. *American Antiquity* 62:464–487.

Jefferies, Richard W., and Brian M. Butler (editors)

 1982 *The Carrier Mills Archaeological project: Human Adaptation in the Saline Valley, Illinois.* Research Paper No. 33. Center for Archaeological Investigations, Southern Illinois University, Carbondale.

Jernigan, E. Wesley

 1978 *Jewelry of the Prehistoric Southwest.* School of American Research Press, Santa Fe, N.M./University of New Mexico Press, Albuquerque.

Johnson, Douglas H.

1994   *Nuer Prophets: A History of Prophecy from the Upper Nile in the Nine-
        teenth and Twentieth Centuries*. Clarendon Press, Oxford, U.K.

Johnson, Jay K., and Samuel O. Brookes

1989   Benton Points, Turkey Tails, and Cache Blades: Middle Archaic Exchange
        in the Midsouth. *Southeastern Archaeology* 8:134–145.

Johnson, John R.

1988   *Chumash Social Organization: An Ethnohistoric Perspective*. PhD diss.,
        University of California, Santa Barbara.

1998   Foreword: A Bibliographic History of Chumash Sites. In *The Chumash
        and Their Predecessors, An Annotated Bibliography*. Compiled by Marie S.
        Holmes and John R. Johnson, pp. i–xi. Santa Barbara Museum of Nat-
        ural History, Santa Barbara, Calif.

2007   Ethnohistoric Descriptions of Chumash Warfare. In *North American
        Indigenous Warfare*, edited by Richard Chacon and Ruben Mendoza,
        pp. 74–113. University of Arizona Press, Tucson.

Johnson, John R., and Joseph G. Lorenz

2006   Genetics, Linguistics, and Prehistoric Migrations: An Analysis of Cali-
        fornia Indian Mitochondrial DNA Lineages. *Journal of California and
        Great Basin Anthropology* 26:31–62.

Johnson, Steven

2002   *Emergence: The Connected Lives of Ants, Brains, Cities, and Software*.
        Simon and Shuster, New York.

Jordan, Douglas F.

1960   *The Bull Brook Site in Relation to "Fluted Point" Manifestations in East-
        ern North America*. PhD diss., Harvard University, Cambridge, Mass.

Jordan, Peter

2003   *Material Culture and Sacred Landscape: The Anthropology of the Siberian
        Khanty*. AltaMira Press, Walnut Creek, Calif.

2008   Hunters and Gatherers. In *Handbook of Archaeological Theories*, edited
        by R. A. Bentley, H.D.G. Maschner, and C. Chippindale, pp. 447–465.
        AltaMira Press, Lanham, Md.

Jordan, Peter, and Thomas Mace

2006   Tracking Culture-Historical Lineages: Can "Descent with Modifica-
        tion" Be Linked to "Association by Descent"? In *Mapping Our Ances-
        tors: Phylogenetic Approaches in Anthropology and Prehistory*, edited by
        C. L. Lipo, M. J. O'Brien, M. Collard, and S. J. Shennan, pp. 149–168.
        Aldine Transaction, New Brunswick, N.J.

Joyce, Rosemary

2001   Burying the Dead at Tlatilco: Social Memory and Social Identities.
        Archeological Papers of the American Anthropological Association 10:12–26.

2004   Unintended Consequences? Monumentality as a Novel Experience in For-
        mative Mesoamerica. *Journal of Archaeological Method and Theory* 11:5–29.

Julig, Patrick J.
  1988   Prehistoric Site Survey in the Western James Bay Lowlands. In *Boreal Forest and Sub-Arctic Archaeology*, edited by C. S. "Paddy" Reid, pp. 121–145. Occasional Publication 6. London Chapter, Ontario Archaeological Society, London.
  1994   *The Sourcing of Chert Artifacts by INAA: Some Examples from the Great Lakes Region.* http://wings.buffalo.edu/anthropology/research/anthrogis/JWA/V1N2/julig-pap.html.

Julig, Patrick J., L. A. Pavlish, C. Clark, and R. G. V. Hancock
  1992   Chemical Characterization and Sourcing of Upper Great Lakes Cherts by INAA. *Ontario Archaeology* 54:37–50.

Junker, Laura L.
  2002   Introduction: Southeast Asia. In *Forager-Traders in South and Southeast Asia*, edited by Kathleen D. Morrison and Laura L. Junker, pp. 131–166. Cambridge University Press, Cambridge.

Kahn, Miriam
  1990   Stone-Faced Ancestors: The Spatial Anchoring of Myth in Wamira, Papua New Guinea. *Ethnology* 29:51–66.
  1996   Your Place and Mine: Sharing Emotional Landscapes in Wamira, Papua New Guinea. In *Senses of Place*, edited by S. Feld and K. H. Basso, pp. 167–196. School of American Research Press, Santa Fe, N.M.

Kaplan, David
  2000   The Darker Side of the "Original Affluent Society." *Journal of Anthropological Research* 56:301–324.

Kaplan, Susan
  1985   European Goods and Socio-Economic Change in Early Labrador Inuit Society. In *Cultures in Contact: The Impact of European Contacts on Native Cultural Institutions AD 1000–1800*, edited by William Fitzhugh, pp. 45–69. Smithsonian Institution Press, Washington, D.C.

Kauffman, Stuart
  1995   *At Home in the Universe: The Search for Laws of Self-Organization and Complexity.* Oxford University Press, Oxford, U.K.

Keefe, Susan E.
  2000   Mountain Identity and the Global Society in a Rural Appalachian County. Paper presented at the Center for Ethnicity and Gender in Appalachia, Huntington, W.Va. www.marshall.edu/csega/research.

Keeley, Jon E.
  2002   Native American Impacts on Fire Regimes of the California Coastal Ranges. *Journal of Biogeography* 29:303–320.

Keen, Ian
  2006   Constraints on the Development of Enduring Inequalities in Late Holocene Australia. *Current Anthropology* 47:7–38.

Kelly, Robert L.

1995   *The Foraging Spectrum: Diversity in Hunter-Gatherer Lifeways.* Smithsonian Institution Press, Washington, D.C.

Kennett, Douglas J.

2005   *The Island Chumash: Behavioral Ecology of a Maritime Society.* University of California Press, Berkeley.

Kennett, D. J., and J. P. Kennett

2000   Competitive and Cooperative Responses to Climatic Instability in Coastal Southern California. *American Antiquity* 65:379–395.

Kertzer, David I.

1995   Political-economic and Cultural Explanations of Demographic Behavior. In *Situating Fertility*, edited by Susan Greenhalgh, pp. 29–52. Cambridge University Press, Cambridge.

Kertzer, David I., and Tom Fricke

1997   Toward an Anthropological Demography. In *Anthropological Demography: Toward a New Synthesis*, edited by David I. Kertzer and Tom Fricke, pp. 1–35. University of Chicago Press, Chicago.

Kidder, Tristram R.

1991   New Directions in Poverty Point Settlement Archaeology: An Example from Northeast Louisiana. In *Poverty Point Culture: Its Local Manifestations, Subsistence Practices, and Trade Networks*, edited by K. Byrd, pp. 27–53. Geoscience and Man 29. Geoscience Publications, Department of Geography and Anthropology, Louisiana State University, Baton Rouge.

2002   Mapping Poverty Point. *American Antiquity* 67:89–101.

2006   Climate Change and the Archaic to Woodland Transition (3000–2500 cal BP) in the Mississippi River Basin. *American Antiquity* 71:195–231.

Kidder, Tristram R., Katherine A. Adelsberger, Lee J. Arco, and Timothy M. Schilling

2008   Basin Scale Reconstruction of the Geological Context of Human Settlement: An Example from Northeast Louisiana, USA. *Quaternary Science Reviews* 27:1255–1270.

Kidder, Tristram R., Lee J. Arco, Anthony L. Ortmann, T. M. Schilling, C. Boeke, R. Bielitz, T. Heet, and K. A. Adelsberger

2009   *Poverty Point Mound A: Final Report of the 2005 and 2006 Field Seasons.* Louisiana Division of Archaeology and the Louisiana Archaeological Survey and Antiquities Commission, Baton Rouge.

Kidder, Tristram R., Anthony L. Ortmann, and Thurman Allen

2004   Mounds B and E at Poverty Point. *Southeastern Archaeology* 23:98–113.

Kidder, Tristram R., and Kenneth E. Sassaman

2009   The View from the Southeast. In *Archaic Societies: Diversity and Complexity across the Midcontinent*, edited by T. Emerson, D. McElrath, and A. Fortier, pp. 667–696. State University of New York Press, Albany.

Kim, Jangsuk, and Colin Grier
  2006   Beyond Affluent Foragers. In *Beyond Affluent Foragers: Rethinking Hunter-Gatherer Complexity*, edited by Colin Grier, Jangsuk Kim, and Junzo Uchiyama, pp. 192–200. Oxbow, Oxford, U.K.

King, Chester D.
  1976   Chumash Intervillage Economic Exchange. In *Native Californians: A Theoretical Retrospective*, edited by Lowell J. Bean and Thomas C. Blackburn, pp. 289–318. Ballena Press, Ramona.

  1990   *Evolution of Chumash Society: A Comparative Study of Artifacts Used for Social System Maintenance in the Santa Barbara Channel Region before AD 1804.* The Evolution of North American Indians, edited by David Hurst Thomas. Garland, New York.

King, Chester D., and Lynn H. Gamble
  2008   Beads from Anza Borrego State Park, San Diego County, California, Report submitted to California Department of Parks and Recreation, Sacramento.

King, Linda
  1969   The Medea Creek Cemetery (LAn–243): An Investigation of Social Organization from Mortuary Practices. *UCLA Archaeological Survey Annual Review* 11:23–58.

  1982   *Medea Creek Cemetery: Late, Inland Chumash Patterns of Social Organization, Exchange and Warfare.* PhD diss., University of California, Los Angeles.

King, Thomas F.
  1970   *The Dead at Tiburon.* Occasional Paper No. 2. Northwestern California Archaeological Society, Petaluma, Calif.

  1974   The Evolution of Status Ascription around San Francisco Bay. In *?Antap: California Indian Political and Economic Organization*, edited by Lowell J. Bean and Thomas F. King, pp. 35–54. Ballena Press, Ramona, Calif.

  1978   Don't That Beat the Band? Nonegalitarian Political Organization in Prehistoric Central California. In *Social Archaeology: Beyond Subsistence and Dating*, edited by C. E. Redman, M. J. Berman, E. V. Curtain, W. T. Langhome Jr., N. M. Versaggi, and J. C. Wanser, pp. 225–248. Academic Press, New York.

Klein, Kerwin L.
  1997   *Frontiers of Historical Imagination: Narrating the European Conquest of Native America, 1890–1990.* University of California Press, Berkeley.

Knecht, Heidi
  1997   Projectile Points of Bone, Antler, and Stone: Experimental Explorations of Manufacture and Use. In *Projectile Point Technology*, edited by Heidi Knecht, pp. 191–212. Plenum Press, New York.

Knight, Vernon J., Jr.
  1986   The Institutional Organization of Mississippian Religion. *American Antiquity* 51:675–687.

2006   Symbolism of Mississippian Mounds. In *Powhatan's Mantle: Indians in the Colonial Southeast*, rev. ed., edited by P. H. Wood, G. A. Waselkov and M. T. Hatley, pp. 421–434. University of Nebraska Press, Lincoln.

Kohl, Philip L.

2008   Shared Social Fields: Evolutionary Convergence in Prehistory and Contemporary Practice. *American Anthropologist* 110:495–506.

Kohler, Timothy A., and George J. Gumerman

2000   *Dynamics of Human and Primate Societies: Agent-based Modeling of Social and Spatial Process*. Santa Fe Institute, N.M.

Kohler, Timothy A., and Sander E. Van der Leeuw

2007   *The Model-based Archaeology of Socionatural Systems*. School for Advanced Research Press, Santa Fe, N.M.

Koldehoff, Brad, and John A. Walthall

2004   Settling In: Hunter-Gatherer Mobility during Pleistocene-Holocene Transition in the Central Mississippi Valley. In *Aboriginal Ritual and Economy in the Eastern Woodlands: Essays in Honor of Howard D. Winters*, edited by A. Cantwell and L. Conrad. Illinois State Museum, Springfield.

2009   Dalton and the Early Holocene Midcontinent: Setting the Stage. In *Archaic Societies: Diversity and Complexity across the Midcontinent*, edited by T. E. Emerson, D. L. McElrath, and A. C. Fortier, pp. 137–151. State University of New York Press, Albany.

Kosse, Krisztina

1990   Group Size and Societal Complexity: Thresholds in the Long-term Memory. *Journal of Anthropological Archaeology* 9:275–303.

1994   The Evolution of Large, Complex Groups: A Hypothesis. *Journal of Anthropological Archaeology* 13:35–50.

Kowalewski, Stephen A.

1995   Large-Scale Ecology in Aboriginal Eastern North America. In *Native American Interactions, Multiscalar Analyses and Interpretations in the Eastern Woodlands*, edited by Michael S. Nassaney and Kenneth E. Sassaman, pp. 148–173. University of Tennessee Press, Knoxville.

Koyama, Shuzo, and David Hurst Thomas (editors)

1981   *Affluent Foragers: Pacific Coasts East and West*. Senri Ethnological Studies 9. National Museum of Ethnology, Osaka.

Koyama, Shuzo, and Junzo Uchiyama

2006   Why "Beyond Affluent Foragers"?: Looking Back at the Original Affluent Foragers Concept. In *Beyond Affluent Foragers: Rethinking Hunter-Gatherer Complexity*, edited by Colin Grier, Jangsuk Kim, and Junzo Uchiyama, pp. 1–3. Oxbow, Oxford, U.K.

Kreager, Philip

1997   Population and Identity. In *Anthropological Demography: Toward a New Synthesis*, edited by David I. Kertzer and Tom Fricke, pp. 139–174. University of Chicago Press, Chicago.

Kroeber, Alfred L.

1927   Disposal of the Dead. *American Anthropologist* 29: 308–315.

1935   History and Science in Anthropology. *American Anthropologist* 37:539–569.

1936   Prospects in California Prehistory. *American Antiquity* 2:108–116.

1948   *Anthropology*. Harcourt Brace, New York.

1952   *The Nature of Culture*. University of Chicago Press, Chicago.

1955   Nature of the Land-holding Group. *Ethnohistory* 2:303–314.

Küchler, Susanne

1993   Landscape as Memory: The Mapping of Process and Its Representation in a Melanesian Society. In *Landscape: Politics and Perspectives*, edited by B. Bender, pp. 85–106. Berg, Oxford, U.K.

Kuijt, Ian, and William C. Prentiss

2004   Villages on the Edge: Pithouses, Cultural Change, and the Abandonment of Aggregate Pithouse Villages. In *Complex Hunter-Gatherers: Evolution and Organization of Prehistoric Communities on the Plateau of Northwestern North America*, edited by W. C. Prentiss and I. Kuijt, pp. 155–170. University of Utah Press, Salt Lake City.

Kuper, Adam

1988   *The Invention of Primitive Society: Transformations of an Illusion*. Routledge, London.

Kyriakidis, Evangelos

2007a   Archaeologies of Ritual. In *The Archaeology of Ritual*, edited by Evangelos Kyriakidis, pp. 289–308. Costen Advanced Seminars 3. Costen Institute of Archaeology, Los Angeles.

2007b   In Search of Ritual. In *The Archaeology of Ritual*, edited by Evangelos Kyriakidis, pp. 1–8. Costen Advanced Seminars 3. Costen Institute of Archaeology, Los Angeles.

Lambert, Patricia M.

1994   *War and Peace on the Western Front: A Study of Violent Conflict and Its Correlates in Prehistoric Hunter-Gatherer Societies of Coastal Southern California*. PhD diss., University of California, Santa Barbara.

2002   The Archaeology of War: A North American Perspective. *Journal of Archaeological Research* 10:207–241.

Lambert, Patricia M., and Phillip L. Walker

1991   The Physical Anthropological Evidence for the Evolution of Social Complexity in Coastal Southern California. *Antiquity* 65:963–973.

Lankford, George E., III

1987   *Native American Legends: Southeastern Legends—Tales from the Natchez, Caddo, Biloxi, Chickasaw, and Other Nations*. August House, Little Rock.

Lansing, J. Stephen

2003   Complex Adaptive Systems. *Annual Review of Anthropology* 32:183–204.

Larson, Mary Lou, and Marcel Kornfeld

1994　Betwixt and Between the Basin and the Plains: The Limits of Numic Expansion. In *Across the West: Human Population Movement and the Expansion of the Numa*, edited by David B. Madsen and David Rhode, pp. 200–210. University of Utah Press, Salt Lake City.

Layton, Robert H.

2001　Hunter-Gatherers, Their Neighbours and the Nation State. In *Hunter-Gatherers: An Interdisciplinary Perspective*, edited by Catherine Panter-Brick, Robert H. Layton, and Peter Rowley-Conwy, pp. 292–321. Cambridge University Press, New York.

Le Baron, J. Francis

1884　Prehistoric Remains in Florida. In *Annual Report of the Smithsonian Institution*, pp. 771–790. Government Printing Office, Washington, D.C.

Lechtman, Heather

1977　Style in Technology—Some Early Thoughts. In *Material Culture: Styles, Organization, and Dynamics of Technology*, edited by Heather Lechtman and Robert Merrill, pp. 3–20. West, St. Paul.

Lee, Richard B.

1972　!Kung Spatial Organization: An Ecological and Historical Perspective. *Human Ecology* 1:125–147.

1979　*The !Kung San: Men, Women and Work in a Foraging Society*. Cambridge University Press, Cambridge.

2006　Commonalities and Diversities in Contemporary Hunter-Gatherers: From Settlement Archaeology to Development Ethnography. *Archeological Papers of the American Anthropological Association* 16 (1): 157–169.

Lee, Richard B., and Richard Daly

1999a　Introduction: Foragers and Others. In *The Cambridge Encyclopedia of Hunters and Gatherers*, edited by Richard B. Lee and Richard Daly, pp. 1–22. Cambridge University Press, New York.

Lee, Richard B., and Richard Daly (editors)

1999b　*The Cambridge Encyclopedia of Hunters and Gatherers*. Cambridge University Press, Cambridge.

Lee, Richard B., and Irven DeVore (editors)

1968a　*Man the Hunter*. Aldine, Chicago.

Lee, Richard B., and Irven DeVore

1968b　Problems in the Study of Hunters and Gatherers. In *Man the Hunter*, edited by Richard B. Lee and Irven DeVore, pp. 3–12. Aldine, Chicago.

Lee, Ronald Demos

1974　The Formal Dynamics of Controlled Populations and the Echo, the Boom, and the Bust. *Demography* 11:563–585.

1986　Malthus and Boserup: A Dynamic Synthesis. In *The State of Population Theory: Forward from Malthus*, edited by David Coleman and Roger Schofield, pp. 96–130. Blackwell, Oxford, U.K.

Lekson, Stephen H.

    1995   The Abandonment of Chaco Canyon, the Mesa Verde Migrations, and
            the Reorganization of the Pueblo World. *Journal of Anthropological
            Archaeology* 14:184–202.

Lenert, Michael P.

    2007   *Coast Salish Household and Community Organization at Sxwoxwiymelh:
            An Ancient Sto:lo Village in the Upper Fraser Valley, British Columbia.* PhD
            diss., University of California, Los Angeles.

Lepofsky, Dana, Michael Blake, Douglas Brown, Sandra Morrison, Nicole Oakes,
and Natasha Lyons

    2000   The Archaeology of the Scowlitz Site, SW British Columbia. *Journal of
            Field Archaeology* 27:391–416.

Lepofsky, Dana, Ken Lertzman, Douglas Hallett, and Rolf Mathewes

    2005   Climate Change and Culture Change on the Southern Coast of Brit-
            ish Columbia 2400–1200 cal. BP: An Hypothesis. *American Antiquity*
            70:267–294.

Lepofsky, Dana, and Natasha Lyons

    2003   Modeling Ancient Plant Use on the Northwest Coast: Towards an
            Understanding of Mobility and Settlement. *Journal of Archaeological
            Science* 30:1357–1371.

Lepofsky, Dana, David M. Schaepe, Anthony P. Graesch, Michael Lenert, Patricia
Ormerod, Keith Thor Carlson, Jeanne E. Arnold, Michael Blake, Patrick Moore,
and John J. Clague

    2009   Exploring Sto:Lo-Coast Salish Interaction and Identity in Ancient
            Houses and Settlements in the Fraser Valley, British Columbia. *Ameri-
            can Antiquity* 74:595–626.

Leventhal, Alan

    1993   *A Reinterpretation of Some Bay Area Shellmound Sites: A View from the
            Mortuary Complex from CA-ALA-329, the Ryan Mound.* Master's thesis,
            San Jose State University. Calif.

Lightfoot, Kent G.

    1995   Culture Contact Studies: Redefining the Relationship between Prehis-
            toric and Historical Archaeology. *American Antiquity* 60:199–217.

    1997   Cultural Construction of Coastal Landscapes: A Middle Holocene Per-
            spective from San Francisco Bay. In *Archaeology of the California Coast
            during the Middle Holocene*, edited by Jon M. Erlandson and Michael
            Glassow, pp. 129–141. UCLA Institute of Archaeology, Los Angeles.

    2005   *Indians, Missionaries, and Merchants: The Legacy of Colonial Encounters
            on the California Frontier.* University of California Press, Berkeley.

Lightfoot, Kent G., and Edward M. Luby

    2002   Late Holocene in the Greater San Francisco Bay Area: Temporal Trends
            in the Use and Abandonment of Shell Mounds in the East Bay. *In Cata-
            lysts to Complexity: The Late Holocene on the California Coast*, edited by

Jon M. Erlandson and Terry Jones, pp. 263–281. Costen Institute of Archaeology, University of California, Los Angeles.

Lightfoot, Kent G., and Antoinette Martinez
  1995   Frontiers and Boundaries in Archaeological Perspective. *Annual Review of Anthropology* 24:471–492.

Lightfoot, Kent G., and Otis Parrish
  2009   *California Indians and Their Environment: An Introduction.* University of California Press, Berkeley.

Lipo, C. P., M. J. O'Brien, M. Collard, and S. Shennan (editors)
  2006   *Mapping Our Ancestors: Phylogenetic Approaches in Anthropology and Prehistory.* Aldine De Gruyter, New York.

Loendorf, Lawrence, and Nancy Medaris Stone
  2006   *Mountain Spirit: The Sheep Eater Indians of Yellowstone.* University of Utah Press, Salt Lake City.

Lohse, Ernest S., and Dorothy Sammons-Lohse
  1986   Sedentism on the Columbia Plateau: A Matter of Degree Related to Easy and Efficient Procurement of Resources. *Northwest Anthropological Research Notes* 20:115–136.

Long, Darrel G. F., Brenda Silveira, and Pat Julig
  2001   Chert Analysis by Infrared Spectroscopy. In *A Collection of Papers Presented at the Thirty-third Annual Meeting of the Canadian Archaeological Association*, edited by Jean-Luc Pilon, Michael W. Kirby, and Caroline Thériault, pp. 256–267. Ontario Archaeological Society, Toronto.

Loring, Stephen
  1992   *Princes and Princesses of Ragged Fame: Innu Archaeology and Ethnohistory in Labrador.* PhD diss., University of Massachusetts, Amherst.
  1997   On the Trail to the Caribou House: Some Reflections on Innu Caribou Hunters in Northern Ntessinan (Labrador). In *Caribou and Reindeer Hunters of the Northern Hemisphere*, edited by Lawrence J. Jackson and Paul T. Thacker, pp. 185–220. Avebury, Hong Kong.
  2002   "And They Took Away Stones from Ramah": Lithic Raw Material Sourcing and Eastern Arctic Archaeology. In *Honoring Our Elders: A History of Eastern Arctic Archaeology*, edited by William W. Fitzhugh, Stephen Loring, and Daniel Odess, pp. 163–85. Arctic Studies Center, National Museum of Natural History, Smithsonian Institution, Washington, D.C.

Love, J. D., and A. C. Christiansen
  1985   Geological Map of Wyoming. U.S. Geological Survey.

Lovis, William A.
  2009   Hunter-Gatherer Adaptations and Alternative Perspectives on the Michigan Archaic: Research Problems in Context. In *Archaic Societies: Diversity and Complexity across the Midcontinent*, edited by T. E. Emerson, D. L. McElrath, and A. C. Fortier, pp. 725–754. State University of New York Press, Albany.

Luby, Edward M.
  2004   Shell Mound and Mortuary Behavior in the San Francisco Bay Area.
          North American Archaeologist 25:1–33.
Luby, Edward M., Clayton D. Drescher, and Kent G. Lightfoot
  2006   Shell Mounds and Mounded Landscapes in the San Francisco Bay
          Area: An Integrated Approach. *Journal of Island and Coastal Archaeol-
          ogy* 1:191–214.
Luby, Edward M., and Mark F. Gruber
  1999   The Dead Must Be Fed: Symbolic Meanings of the Shellmounds of the
          San Francisco Bay Area. *Cambridge Archaeological Journal* 9:95–108.
Lyman, R. Lee
  1991   *Prehistory of the Oregon Coast: The Effects of Excavation Strategies and
          Assemblage Size on Archaeological Inquiry.* Academic Press, San Diego.
Lyons, Claire L., and John K. Papadopoulos (editors)
  2002   *The Archaeology of Colonialism.* Getty Research Institute, Los Angeles.
Lyons, William H., Scott P. Thomas, and Craig E. Skinner
  2001   Changing Obsidian Sources at the Lost Dune and McCoy Creek Sites,
          Blitzen Valley, Southeast Oregon. *Journal of California and Great Basin
          Anthropology* 23:273–296.
Lytwyn, Victor P.
  2002   *Muskekowuck Athinuwick: The Original People of the Great Swampy
          Land.* University of Manitoba Press, Winnipeg.
MacDonald, Douglas H.
  1998   Subsistence, Sex, and Cultural Transmission in Folsom Culture. *Journal
          of Anthropological Archaeology* 17:217–239.
MacDonald, George F.
  1968   *Debert: A Paleo-Indian Site in Central Nova Scotia.* Anthropological
          Papers, No. 16. National Museums of Canada, Ottawa.
Mace, Ruth, and Clare J. Holden
  2005   A Phylogenetic Approach to Cultural Evolution. *Trends in Ecology and
          Evolution* 20:116–121.
Mace, Ruth, Clare J. Holden, and Stephen Shennan (editors)
  2005   *The Evolution of Cultural Diversity: A Phylogenetic Approach.* Routledge
          Cavendish, London.
Mackie, Quentin, and Steven Acheson
  2005   The Graham Tradition. In *Haida Gwaii: Human History and Environ-
          ment from the Time of the Loon to the Time of the Iron People,* edited by
          D. W. Fedje and R. W. Mathewes, pp. 274–302. University of British
          Columbia Press, Vancouver.
Mailhot, José
  1997   *The People of Sheshatshit: In the Land of the Innu.* Social and Economic
          Studies, No. 58. Institute for Social and Economic Research, Memorial
          University of Newfoundland, St. John's, Newfoundland.

Malinowski, Bronislaw

    1922   *Argonauts of the Western Pacific: An Account of Native Enterprise and Adventure in the Archipelagoes of Melanesian New Guinea*. Routledge, New York.

Malthus, Thomas R.

    1976   *An Essay on the Principle of Population as It Affects the Future Improvement*
    [1798]   *of Society*. Johnson, London.

Marceau, T. E.

    1982   Steatite, Intermountain Pottery and the Shoshone: Some Preliminary Considerations. *Wyoming Archaeologist* 25 (1–2): 11–32.

Marquardt, William H.

    1985   Complexity and Scale in the Study of Fisher-Gatherer-Hunters: An Example from the Eastern United States. In *Prehistoric Hunter-Gatherers: The Emergence of Cultural Complexity*, edited by T. D. Price and J. A. Brown, pp. 59–98. Academic Press, Orlando, Fla.

Marquardt, William H., and Patty Jo Watson

    1983   The Shell Mound Archaic of Western Kentucky. In *Archaic Hunter-Gatherers in the American Midwest*, edited by J. L. Phillips and J. A. Brown, pp. 323–339. Academic Press, New York.

Marquardt, William H., and Patty Jo Watson (editors)

    2005   *Archaeology of the Middle Green River Region, Kentucky*. Monograph No. 5. Institute of Archaeology and Palaeoenvironmental Studies, University Press of Florida, Gainesville.

Marshall, Ingeborg

    1996   *A History and Ethnography of the Beothuk*. McGill-Queen's University Press, Montreal.

Martijn, Charles A.

    1990   The Iroquoian Presence in the Estuary and Gulf of St. Lawrence River Valley: a Reevaluation. *Man in the Northeast* 40:45–63.

Martijn, Charles A., and Edward S. Rogers

    1969   *Mistassini-Albanel: Contributions to the Prehistory of Quebec*. Travaux Divers 25. Centres d'etudes nordiques, Université Laval, Quebec.

Marx, K., and F. Engels

    1963   *The Eighteenth Brumaire of Louis Napoleon*. International, New York.

Maschner, Herbert D. G., and John Q. Patton

    1996   Kin Selection and the Origins of Hereditary Social Inequality: A Case Study from the Northern Northwest Coast. In *Darwinian Archaeologies*, edited by H.D.G. Maschner, pp. 89–108. Plenum Press, New York.

Mason, R.J., and C. Irwin

    1960   An Eden-Scottsbluff Burial in Northeastern Wisconsin. *American Antiquity* 26:43–57.

Matson, R. G.

    1983   Intensification and the Development of Cultural Complexity: The Northwest versus Northeast Coast. In *The Evolution of Maritime*

Cultures on the Northeast and Northwest Coasts, edited by Ronald Nash,
pp. 125–148. Publication No. 11. Department of Archaeology, Simon
Fraser University, Burnaby.

Matson, R. G., and Gary Coupland
    1995   *The Prehistory of the Northwest Coast*. Academic Press, San Diego.

Maxwell, Moreau S.
    1980   Archaeology of the Arctic and Subarctic Zones. *Annual Review of
          Anthropology* 9:161–185.

Mayewski, Paul A., Eelco E. Rohling, J. Curt Stager, Wibjörn Karlén, Kirk A.
Maasch, L. David Meeker, Eric A. Meyerson, Francoise Gasse, Shirley van Kreveld,
Karin Holmgren, Julia Lee-Thorp, Gunhild Rosqvist, Frank Rack, Michael Staub-
wasser, Ralph R. Schneider, and Eric J. Steig
    2004   Holocene Climate Variability. *Quaternary Research* 62:243–255.

McCaffrey, Moira T.
    1983   Lithic Analysis and the Interpretation of Two Prehistoric Sites from the
          Caniapiscau Region of Nouveau-Quebec. Master's thesis, McGill Univer-
          sity, Montreal.
    1989a   L'acquisition et l'échange des matières lithiques durant la préhistoire
          récente: Un regard vers la fosse du Labrador. *Recherches amérindiennes
          au Québec* 19 (2–3): 95–107.
    1989b   Archaeology in Western Labrador. In *Archaeology in Newfound-
          land and Labrador 1986*, edited J. S. Thomson and C. Thomson,
          pp. 72–113, Annual Report No. 7. Historic Resources Division, St. John's,
          Newfoundland.
    2006   Archaic Period Occupation in Subarctic Quebec: A Review of the Evi-
          dence. In *The Archaic of the Far Northeast*, edited by David Sanger and
          M.A.P. Renouf, pp. 161–190. University of Maine Press, Orono.

McCaffrey, Moira, and Pierre Dumais (editors)
    1989   En marche entre deux mondes: Préhistoire récente au Québec, au
          Labrador et à Terre-Neuve. *Recherches amérindiennes au Québec* 19 (2–3).

McElrath, Dale L., and Thomas E. Emerson
    2000   Toward an "Intrinsic Characteristics" Approach to Chert Raw Material
          Classification: An American Bottom Example. *Midcontinental Journal
          of Archaeology* 25 (2): 215–244.

McElrath, Dale L., Andrew C. Fortier, Brad Koldehoff, and Thomas E. Emerson
    2009   The American Bottom: An Archaic Cultural Crossroads. In *Archaic
          Societies: Diversity and Complexity across the Midcontinent*, edited by
          T. E. Emerson, D. L. McElrath, and A. C. Fortier, pp. 317–375. State
          University of New York Press, Albany.

McGee, Ray M., and Ryan J. Wheeler
    1994   Stratigraphic Excavations at Groves' Orange Midden, Lake Monroe,
          Volusia County, Florida: Methodology and Results. *Florida Anthropolo-
          gist* 47:333–349.

McGhee, Robert

   1977   Ivory for the Sea Woman: The Symbolic Attributes of a Prehistoric Technology. *Canadian Journal of Archaeology* 1:141–149.

McGovern, Thomas

   1985   Contributions to the Paleoeconomy of Norse Greenland. *Acta Archaeologia* 54:73–122.

   1994   Management for Extinction in Norse Greenland. In *Historical Ecology: Cultural Knowledge and Changing Landscapes*, edited by Carole L. Crumley, pp. 127–154. School for American Research Press, Santa Fe, N.M.

McGuire, Randall H.

   2008   *Archaeology as Political Action.* University of California Press, Berkeley.

McMahon, Janet S.

   1990   *The Biophysical Regions of Maine: Patterns in the Landscape and Vegetation.* Master's thesis. University of Maine, Orono.

McMillan, Alan

   2003   Reviewing the Wakashan Migration Hypothesis. In *Emerging from the Mist: Studies in Northwest Coast Culture History*, edited by R. G. Matson, G. Coupland, and Q. Mackie, pp. 244–259. University of British Columbia Press, Vancouver.

Mead, James I., and David J. Meltzer (editors)

   1985   *Environments and Extinctions: Man in Late Glacial North America.* Center for the Study of Early Man, University of Maine, Orono.

Meltzer, David J.

   1999   Human Responses to Middle Holocene (Altithermal) Climates on the North American Great Plains. *Quaternary Research* 52:404–416.

Menzel, E. J.

   2001   *The Poverty Point Site: A Technological Assessment of a Sample of Chipped Stone Materials from the Type-Site in Northeast Louisiana.* Master's thesis, University of Tulsa, Okla.

Meskell, Lynn

   2003   Memory's Materiality: Ancestral Presence, Commemorative Practice and Disjunctive Locales. In *Archaeologies of Memory*, edited by R. M. van Dyke and S. E. Alcock, pp. 34–55. Blackwell, Oxford, U.K.

Milanich, Jerald T.

   1994   *Archaeology of Precolumbian Florida.* University Press of Florida, Gainesville.

Miller, James J.

   1998   *An Environmental History of Northeast Florida.* University Press of Florida, Gainesville.

Miller, John H., and Scott E. Page

   2007   *Complex Adaptive Systems: An Introduction to Computational Models of Social Life.* Princeton University Press, Princeton, N.J.

Milliken, Randall, Richard T. Fitzgerald, Mark G. Hylkema, Randy G. Groza, Tom
Origer, David G. Bieling, Alan Leventhal, Randy S. Wiberg, Andrew Gottsfield,
Donna Gillette, Viviana Bellifemine, Eric Strother, Robert Cartier, and David A.
Fredrickson
    2007   Punctuated Culture Change in the San Francisco Bay Area. In *Cali-
fornia Prehistory: Colonization, Culture, and Complexity*, edited by
Terry L. Jones and Kathryn A. Klar, pp. 99–123. AltaMira, Walnut
Creek, Calif.

Mills, Barbara
    2002   Acts of Resistance: Zuni Ceramics, Social Identity, and the Pueblo
Revolt. In *Archaeologies of the Pueblo Revolt: Identity, Meaning, and
Renewal in the Pueblo World*, edited by Robert W. Preucel, pp. 85–98.
University of New Mexico Press, Albuquerque.
    2008   How the Pueblos Became Global: Colonial Appropriations, Resis-
tance, and Diversity in the North American Southwest. *Archaeologies*
4:218–232.

Milner, George R.
    2004   Old Mounds, Ancient Hunter-Gatherers, and Modern Archaeologists.
In *Signs of Power: The Rise of Complexity in the Southeast*, edited by
J. L. Gibson and P. J. Carr, pp. 300–315. University of Alabama Press,
Tuscaloosa.

Milner, George R., and Richard W. Jefferies
    1998   The Read Archaic Shell Midden in Kentucky. *Southeastern Archaeology*
17:119–132.

Miracle, Preston T., and Lynn E. Fisher
    1991   Introduction: Hunter-Gatherers and their Ethnography. In *Foragers
in Context: Long-Term, Regional and Historical Perspectives in Hunter-
Gatherer Studies*, edited by Preston T. Miracle, Lynn E. Fisher, and Jody
Brown, pp. 1–8. Michigan Discussions in Anthropology 10. University
of Michigan, Ann Arbor.

Mitchell, Mark D., and Laura L. Scheiber
    2010   Crossing Divides: Archaeology as Long-Term History. In *Across a Great
Divide: Change and Continuity in Native North America, 1400–1900*,
edited by Laura L. Scheiber and Mark D. Mitchell, pp. 1–22. University
of Arizona Press, Tucson.

Moore, Clarence B.
    1999   *The East Florida Expeditions of Clarence Bloomfield Moore*. Classics in
Southeastern Archaeology. University of Alabama Press, Tuscaloosa.

Moore, John H.
    1994   Putting Anthropology Back Together Again: The Ethnogenetic Cri-
tique of Cladistic Theory. *American Anthropologist* 96:925–948.

Moore, Omar
    1957   Divination—A New Perspective. *American Anthropologist* 59:69–74.

Moorehead, Warren K.
  1922   *A Report on the Archaeology of Maine.* Department of Anthropology,
          Phillips Academy, Andover.
Morphy, Howard
  1995   Landscape and the Reproduction of the Ancestral Past. In *The
          Anthropology of Landscape: Perspectives on Place and Space,* edited
          by E. Hirsch and M. O'Hanlon, pp. 184–209. Clarendon Press,
          Oxford, U.K.
Morrison, Kathleen D.
  2002a   Introduction: South Asia. In *Forager-Traders in South and Southeast
          Asia,* edited by Kathleen D. Morrison and Laura L. Junker, pp. 21–40.
          Cambridge University Press, Cambridge.
  2002b   Pepper in the Hills: Upland-Lowland Exchange and the Intensifica-
          tion of the Spice Trade. In *Forager-Traders in South and Southeast Asia,*
          edited by Kathleen D. Morrison and Laura L. Junker, pp. 105–128.
          Cambridge University Press, Cambridge.
Morrow, Juliet E., and Toby A. Morrow
  1999   Geographic Variation in Fluted Projectile Points: A Hemispheric Per-
          spective. *American Antiquity* 64:215–230.
Morse, Dan F.
  1997   *Sloan: A Paleoindian Dalton Cemetery in Arkansas.* Smithsonian Institu-
          tion Press, Washington, D.C.
Morse, Dan F., and Phyllis A. Morse
  1983   *Archaeology of the Central Mississippi Valley.* Academic Press, New York.
Muller, Jon
  1997   *Mississippian Political Economy.* Plenum Press, New York.
Munn, Nancy D.
  1996   Excluded Spaces: The Figure in the Australian Aboriginal Landscape.
          Critical Inquiry 22:446–465.
Murray, Tim (editor)
  2004   *The Archaeology of Contact in Settler Societies.* Cambridge University
          Press, New York.
Nabokov, Peter
  2002   *A Forest of Time: American Indian Ways of History.* Cambridge Univer-
          sity Press, Cambridge.
Nabokov, Peter, and Lawrence L. Loendorf
  2004   *Restoring a Presence: American Indians and Yellowstone National Park.*
          University of Oklahoma Press, Norman.
Nagel, Joane
  1998   Constructing Ethnicity: Creating and Recreating Ethnic Identity
          and Culture. In *New Tribalism: The Resurgence of Race and Ethnicity,*
          edited by Michael Hughey, pp. 237–272. New York University Press,
          New York.

Nicholson, Christopher, Laura L. Scheiber, Judson Byrd Finley, and Maureen P. Boyle
2008   Developing a Predictive GIS Model of Bighorn Sheep Traps in Northwest Wyoming. Paper presented at the 2008 Environmental Science Research Institute Southwest Users Group Conference, Laramie, Wyo., October.

Niels, Lynnerup, Jørgen Meldgaard, Jan Jakobsen, Martin Appelt, Anders Koch, and Bruno Frøhlich
2003   Human Dorset Remains from Igloolik, Canada. *Arctic* 56:349–358.

Norris, P. W.
1881   *Report upon the Yellowstone National Park, to the Secretary of the Interior, for the Year 1880.* Government Printing Office, Washington, D.C.

O'Brien, Michael J., and R. Lee Lyman
2000   *Applying Evolutionary Archaeology.* Kluwer/Plenum, New York.
2003   *Cladistics and Archaeology.* University of Utah Press, Salt Lake City.

Ormerod, Paul, and Bridget Rosewell
2009   Validation and Verification of Agent-Based Models in the Social Sciences. *Lecture Notes in Artificial Intelligence* 5466:130–140.

Ortmann, Anthony L.
2007   *The Poverty Point Mounds: Analysis of the Chronology, Construction History, and Function of North America's Largest Hunter-Gatherer Monuments.* PhD diss., Tulane University, New Orleans.

Outram, Alan K.
1999   A Comparison of Paleo-Eskimo and Medieval Norse Bone Fat Exploitation in Western Greenland. *Arctic Anthropology* 36 (1–2): 103–117.

Oyama, S., P. E. Griffiths, and R. D. Gray (editors)
2001   *Cycles of Contingency: Developmental Systems and Evolution.* Massachusetts Institute of Technology Press, Cambridge, Mass.

Oyuela-Caycedo, Augusto
2004   The Ecology of a Masked Dance: Negotiating at the Frontier of Identity in the Northwest Amazon. *Baessler-Archiv* 52:55–74.

Paine, Richard R.
1997a   The Need for a Multidisciplinary Approach to Prehistoric Demography. In *Integrating Archaeological Demography: Multidisciplinary Approaches to Prehistoric Population,* edited by Richard R. Paine, pp. 1–20. Occasional Paper No. 24. Center for Archaeological Investigations, Southern Illinois University, Carbondale.

Paine, Richard R. (editor)
1997b   *Integrating Archaeological Demography: Multidisciplinary Approaches to Prehistoric Population.* Occasional Paper No. 24. Center for Archaeological Investigations, Southern Illinois University, Carbondale.

Parker, Malcolm
1974   *The Owl Creek People, 6660 BC: The Hart Site at Nashville, Tennessee. 1972–1974.* MS on file. Tennessee Department of Environment and Conservation, Division of Archaeology, Nashville.

Pastore, Ralph T.
  1986   The Spatial Distribution of Late Palaeo-Eskimo Sites on the Island of
          Newfoundland. In *Palaeo-Eskimo Cultures in Newfoundland, Labrador
          and Ungava*, pp. 125–133. Memorial University Reports in Archaeology 1.
          Memorial University of Newfoundland, St. John's.

Paterson, Alistair G.
  2008   *The Lost Legions: Culture Contact in Colonial Australia*. AltaMira, Wal-
          nut Creek, Calif.

Patterson, R. Timothy, Andreas Prokoph, Arun Kumar, Alice S. Chang, and
Helen M. Roe
  2003   Late Holocene Variability in Pelagic Fish Scales and Dinoflagellate
          Cysts along the West Coast of Vancouver Island, NE Pacific Ocean.
          Marine Micropaleontology 55:183–204.

Pauketat, Timothy R.
  2001a   Practice and History in Archaeology: An Emerging Paradigm. *Anthro-
          pological Theory* 1:73–98.

  2001b   A New Tradition in Archaeology. In *The Archaeology of Tradition:
          Agency and History before and after Columbus*, edited by T. R. Pauketat,
          pp. 1–16. University Press of Florida, Gainesville.

  2004   *Ancient Cahokia and the Mississippians*. Cambridge University Press,
          Cambridge.

  2007   *Chiefdoms and Other Archaeological Delusions*. AltaMira, Walnut Creek,
          Calif.

  2008   Of Leaders and Legacies in Native North America. MS.

Pauketat, Timothy R., and Susan M. Alt
  2003   Mounds, Memory, and Contested Mississippian History. In *Archae-
          ologies of Memory*, edited by R. Van Dyke and S. Alcock, pp. 151–179.
          Blackwell, Malden, Mass.

  2004   The Making and Meaning of a Mississippian Axe-head Cache. *Antiq-
          uity* 78:779–797.

  2005   Agency in a Postmold? Physicality and the Archaeology of Culture-
          Making. *Journal of Archaeological Method and Theory* 12:213–236.

Paynter, Robert, and Randall H. McGuire
  1991   Archaeology of Inequality: Material Culture, Domination, and Resis-
          tance. In *Archaeology of Inequality*, edited by Randall H. McGuire and
          Robert Paynter, pp. 1–27. Basil, Oxford, U.K.

Peebles, Christopher S., and Susan M. Kus
  1977   Some Archaeological Correlates of Ranked Societies. *American Antiq-
          uity* 42:421–448.

Pelletier, Bertrand G., and Brian S. Robinson
  2005   Tundra, Ice and a Pleistocene Cape on the Gulf of Maine: A Case
          of Paleoindian Transhumance. *Archaeology of Eastern North America*
          33:163–176.

Petersen, James B., and David E. Putnam
  1992   Early Holocene Occupation in the Central Gulf of Maine Region. In
          Early Holocene Occupation in Northern New England, edited by Brian S.
          Robinson, James B. Petersen, and Ann K. Robinson, pp. 13–61. Occa-
          sional Publications in Maine Archaeology 9. Maine Historic Preserva-
          tion Commission, Augusta.
Petersen, William
  1975   A Demographer's View of Prehistoric Demography. *Current Anthropol-
          ogy* 16:227–246.
Piatek, Bruce John
  1994   The Tomoka Mound Complex in Northeast Florida. *Southeastern
          Archaeology* 13:109–118.
Piddocke, Stuart
  1965   The Potlatch System of the Southern Kwakiutl: A New Perspective. *South-
          western Journal of Anthropology* 21:244–264.
Pilon, Jean-Luc
  1990   Historic Native Archaeology along the Lower Severn River, Ontario.
          Canadian Journal of Archaeology 14:123–141.
Pintal, Jean-Yves
  1989   Contributions à la préhistoire récente de Blanc-Sablon. *Recherches amérin-
          diennes au Québec* 19 (2–3): 33–44.
  1998   *Aux frontières de la mer: La préhistoire de Blanc-Sablon*. Municipalité de
          Blanc-Sablon, Collection Patrimoines, Dossiers No. 102, Les Publica-
          tions du Québec.
  2003   Préhistoire de la chasse au phoque dans le détroit de Belle-Isle. *Recherches
          amérindiennes au Québec* 33 (1): 35–44.
Pleger, Thomas C.
  2000   Old Copper and Red Ocher Social Complexity, *Midcontinental Journal
          of Archaeology* 25: 169–190.
Pluciennik, Mark
  2002   The Invention of Hunter-Gatherers in Seventeenth-Century Europe.
          Archaeological Dialogues 9:98–118.
  2004   The Meaning of "Hunter-Gatherers" and Modes of Subsistence: A
          Comparative Historical Perspective. In *Hunter-Gatherers in History,
          Archaeology and Anthropology*, edited by A. Barnard, pp. 17–29. Berg,
          Oxford, U.K.
Pollard, Joshua
  2001   The Aesthetics of Depositional Practice. *World Archaeology* 33:315–333.
Pollock, Stephen G., Nathan D. Hamilton, and Richard A. Boisvert
  2008   Prehistoric Utilization of Spherulitic and Flow Banded Rhyolites
          from Northern New Hampshire. *Archaeology of Eastern North America*
          36:91–118.

Povinelli, Elizabeth A.

2002   *The Cunning of Recognition: Indigenous Alteries and the Making of Australian Multiculturalism.* Duke University Press, Durham, N.C.

Prentiss, Anna Marie

2009   The Emergence of New Socio-Economic Strategies in the Middle and Late Holocene Pacific Northwest Region. In *Macroevolution and Human Prehistory: Evolutionary Theory and Processual Archaeology,* edited by Anna M. Prentiss, Ian Kuijt, and James C. Chatters, pp. 111–132. Springer, New York.

Prentiss, Anna Marie, Eric Carlson, Nicole Crossland, Hannah Schremser, and Lee Reininghaus

2009   Report of the 2008 University of Montana Investigations at the Bridge River Site (EeRl4). Report on file at the National Science Foundation and Bridge River Band Office, Lillooet, British Columbia.

Prentiss, Anna Marie, Guy Cross, Thomas Foor, Mathew Hogan, Dirk Markle, and David S. Clarke

2008   Evolution of a Late Prehistoric Winter Village on the Interior Plateau of British Columbia: Geophysical Investigations, Radiocarbon Dating, and Spatial Analysis of the Bridge River Site. *American Antiquity* 73:59–81.

Prentiss, Anna Marie, Natasha Lyons, Lucille E. Harris, Melisse R. P. Burns, and Terence M. Godin

2007   The Emergence of Status Inequality in Intermediate Scale Societies: A Demographic and Socio-Economic History of the Keatley Creek Site, British Columbia. *Journal of Anthropological Archaeology* 26:299–327.

Prentiss, William C., and James C. Chatters

2003a   Cultural Diversification and Decimation in the Prehistoric Record. *Current Anthropology* 44: 33–58.

2003b   The Evolution of Collector Systems in the Pacific Northwest Region of North America. *Senri Ethnological Studies* 63:49–82.

Prentiss, William C., James C. Chatters, Michael Lenert, David S. Clarke, and Robert C. O'Boyle

2005   The Archaeology of the Plateau of Northwestern North America during the Late Prehistoric Period (3500–200 BP): Evolution of Hunting and Gathering Societies. *Journal of World Prehistory* 19:47–118.

Prentiss, William C., and Ian Kuijt (editors)

2004   *Complex Hunter-Gatherers: Evolution and Organization of Prehistoric Communities on the Plateau of Northwestern North America.* University of Utah Press, Salt Lake City.

Prentiss, William C., Michael Lenert, Thomas A. Foor, Nathan B. Goodale, and Trinity Schlegel

2003   Calibrated Radiocarbon Dating at Keatley Creek: The Chronology of Occupation at a Complex Hunter-Gatherer Community. *American Antiquity* 68:719–735.

Price, T. Douglas, and James Brown (editors)
  1985   *Prehistoric Hunter-Gatherers: The Emergence of Cultural Complexity.*
          Academic Press, Orlando.

Prince, Paul
  2002   Cultural Coherency and Resistance in Historic-Period Northwest
          Coast Mortuary Practices at Kimsquit. *Historical Archaeology* 36 (4):
          50–65.

Randall, Asa R.
  2007   *St. Johns Archaeological Field School 2005: Hontoon Island State Park.*
          Technical Report No. 7. Laboratory of Southeastern Archaeology,
          Department of Anthropology, University of Florida, Gainesville.

  2010   *Remapping Histories: Archaic Period Community Construction along the
          St. Johns River, Florida.* PhD diss., University of Florida, Gainesville.

Randall, Asa R., and Kenneth E. Sassaman
  2005   *St. Johns Archaeological Field School 2003–2004: Hontoon Island State
          Park.* Technical Report No. 6. Laboratory of Southeastern Archaeology,
          Department of Anthropology, University of Florida, Gainesville.

  2010   (E)Mergent Complexities during the Archaic in Northeast Florida.
          In *Confounding Categories and Conceptualizing Complexities,* edited by
          S. M. Alt. University of Utah Press, Salt Lake City (in press).

Rast, Tim, M.A.P. Renouf, and Trevor Bell
  2004   Patterns in Precontact Site Location on the Southwest Coast of New-
          foundland. *Northeast Newfoundland* 68 (Fall): 41–55.

Ray, Arthur J.
  1974   *Indians in the Fur Trade: Their Role as Trappers, Hunters and Middlemen
          in the Lands Southwest of Hudson Bay 1660–1870.* University of Toronto
          Press, Toronto.

Ray, K.
  2004   Axes, Kula, and Things That Were 'Good to Think' in the Neolithic
          of the Irish Sea Region. In *The Neolithic of the Irish Sea: Material-
          ity and Traditions of Practice,* edited by V. Cummings and C. Fowler,
          pp. 160–173. Oxbow, Oxford, U.K.

Read, Dwight W.
  2003   Emergent Properties in Small-Scale Societies. *Artificial Life* 9:419–434.

Read, Dwight W., and Steven A. LeBlanc
  2003   Population Growth, Carrying Capacity, and Conflict. *Current Anthro-
          pology* 44:59–83.

Reedy-Maschner, Katherine L., and Herbert D. G. Maschner
  1999   Marauding Middlemen: Western Expansion and Violent Conflict in
          the Subarctic. *Ethnohistory* 46:703–743.

Reiger, John F.
  2001   *American Sportsmen and the Origins of Conservation.* 3rd ed. Oregon
          State University Press, Corvallis.

Renfrew, Colin

1977   Alternative Models for Exchange and Spatial Distribution. In *Exchange Systems in Prehistory*, edited by T. K. Earle and J. E. Ericson, pp. 71–90. Academic Press, New York.

1997   Setting the Scene: Stonehenge in the Round. In *Science and Stonehenge*, edited by B. Cunliff and C. Renfrew, pp. 3–14. Proceedings of the British Academy 92. Published for the British Academy by Oxford University Press, Oxford, U.K.

Renouf, M.A.P.

1993   Palaeoeskimo Seal Hunters at Port au Choix, Northwestern Newfoundland. *Newfoundland Studies* 9:185–212.

1999a   Prehistory of Newfoundland Hunter-Gatherers: Extinctions or Adaptations? *World Archaeology* 30:403–420.

1999b   *Ancient Cultures, Bountiful Seas: The Story of Port au Choix*. Historic Sites Association of Newfoundland and Labrador, St. John's.

2000   Symbolism and Subsistence: Seals and Caribou at Port au Choix, Northwestern Newfoundland. In *Animal Bones, Human Societies*, edited by Peter Rowley-Conwy, pp. 65–73. Oxbow, Oxford, U.K.

2003   Hunter-Gatherer Interactions: Mutualism and Resource Partitioning on the Island of Newfoundland. *Before Farming* 1 (4): 1–16.

Renouf, M.A.P., and Trevor Bell

2009   Contraction and Expansion in Newfoundland Prehistory, AD 900–1500. In *The Northern World AD 900–1400*, edited by Herbert Maschner, Owen Mason, and Robert McGhee, pp. 263–278. University of Utah Press, Salt Lake City.

Renouf, M.A.P., Trevor Bell, and Michael Teal

2000   Making Contact: Recent Indians and PalaeoEskimos on the Island of Newfoundland. In *Identities and Culture Contacts in the Arctic*, edited by Martin Appelt, Joel Berglund, and Hans-Christian Gulløv, pp. 106–119. Danish National Museum and Danish Polar Centre, Copenhagen.

Rice, Prudence M.

1998   Context of Contact and Change: Peripheries, Frontiers, and Boundaries. In *Studies in Culture Contact: Interaction, Culture Change, and Archaeology*, edited by James G. Cusick. Occasional Paper No. 25. Center for Archaeological Investigations, Southern Illinois University, Carbondale.

Richards, Colin

2004   Labouring with Monuments: Constructing the Dolmen at Carreg Samson, South-West Wales. In *The Neolithic of the Irish Sea: Materiality and Traditions of Practice*, edited by V. Cummings and C. Fowler, pp. 72–80. Oxbow, Oxford, U.K.

Richards, Colin, and Julian Thomas

1984   Ritual Activity and Structured Deposition in Later Neolithic Wessex. In *Neolithic Studies: A Review of Some Current Research*, edited by

R. Bradley and J. Gardiner, pp. 189–218. British Archaeological Reports, British Series 133, Oxford, U.K.

Richerson, Peter J., and Robert Boyd

2005   *Not by Genes Alone.* University of Chicago Press, Chicago.

Richerson, Peter J., Robert Boyd, and Robert L. Bettinger

2001   Agriculture Impossible during the Pleistocene but Mandatory during the Holocene? A Climate Change Hypothesis. *American Antiquity* 66:387–412.

Riede, Felix, and R. Alex Bentley

2008   Increasing the Relevance of Mathematical Approaches to Demographic History. *Quality and Quantity* 42:275–281.

Rindos, David

1984   *The Origins of Agriculture: An Evolutionary Perspective.* Academic Press, New York.

Ritchie, William A.

1969   *The Archaeology of New York State.* Rev. ed. Natural History Press, Garden City, N.Y.

Rival, Laura M.

2002   *Trekking through History: The Huaorani of Amazonian Ecuador.* Columbia University Press, New York.

Robbins, Maurice

1968   *An Archaic Ceremonial Complex at Assawompsett.* Massachusetts Archaeological Society, Attleboro.

Robinson, Brian S.

1992   Early and Middle Archaic Period Occupation in the Gulf of Maine Region: Mortuary and Technological Patterning. In *Early Holocene Occupation in Northern New England,* edited by Brian S. Robinson, James B. Petersen, and Ann K. Robinson, pp. 63–116. Occasional Publications in Maine Archaeology 9. Maine Historic Preservation Commission, Augusta.

1996   A Regional Analysis of the Moorehead Burial Tradition: 8500–3700 BP. *Archaeology of Eastern North America* 24:95–148.

2001   *Burial Ritual: Groups and Boundaries on the Gulf of Maine: 8600–3800 BP.* PhD diss., Brown University, Providence, R.I.

2006   Burial Ritual, Technology, and Cultural Landscape in the Far Northeast: 8600–3700 BP. In *The Archaic of the Far Northeast,* edited by David Sanger and M.A.P. Renouf, pp. 341–381. University of Maine Press, Orono.

Robinson, Brian S., and William E. Eldridge

2005   Debating Bull Brook, 1965–1972. *Bulletin of the Massachusetts Archaeological Society* 66 (2): 67–75.

Robinson, Brian S., Jennifer C. Ort, William A. Eldridge, Adrian L. Burke, and Bertrand G. Pelletier

2009   Paleoindian Aggregation and Social Context at Bull Brook. *American Antiquity* 74:423–447.

Rodman, Margaret C.

1992   Empowering Place: Multilocality and Multivocality. *American Ethnologist* 94:640–56.

Rodríguez-Alegría, Enrique

2008   Narratives of Conquest, Colonialism, and Cutting-Edge Technology. *American Anthropologist* 110:33–43.

Rogers, Edward S.

1967   *The Material Culture of the Mistassini.* Bulletin 218. National Museums of Canada, Ottawa.

Rose, H., and S. Rose

2000   *Alas Poor Darwin: Arguments against Evolutionary Psychology.* Harmony, New York.

Rosenberg, Michael

1990   The Mother of Invention: Evolutionary Theory, Territoriality, and the Origins of Agriculture. *American Anthropologist* 92:399–415.

1994   Pattern, Process, and Hierarchy in the Evolution of Culture. *Journal of Anthropological Archaeology* 13:307–340.

1998   Cheating at Musical Chairs: Territoriality and Sedentism in an Evolutionary Context. *Current Anthropology* 39:653–681.

2009   Proximate Causation, Group Selection, and the Evolution of Hierarchical Human Societies: System, Process, and Pattern. In *Macroevolution and Human Prehistory: Evolutionary Theory and Processual Archaeology,* edited by Anna M. Prentiss, Ian Kuijt, and James C. Chatters, pp. 23–50. Springer, New York.

Rousseau, Gilles

2007   L'archéologie de l'Eastmain-1: Deux sites associés à des paléosols enfouis dans des alluvions. *Archéologiques* 20:1–15.

Rumsey, Alan

1994   The Dreaming, Human Agency and Inscriptive Practice. *Oceania* 65:116–130.

Russell, Osborne

1955   *Journal of a Trapper.* University of Nebraska Press, Lincoln.
[1914]

Ruyle, Eugene E.

1973   Slavery, Surplus, and Stratification on the Northwest Coast: The Ethnoenergetics of an Incipient Stratification System. *Current Anthropology* 14:603–631.

Sahlins, Marshall

1968   Notes on the Original Affluent Society. In *Man the Hunter,* edited by Richard B. Lee and Irven DeVore, pp. 85–89. Aldine De Gruyter, New York.

1972   *Stone Age Economics.* Aldine De Gruyter, New York.

1981   *Historical Metaphors and Mythical Realities: Structure in the Early History of the Sandwich Islands Kingdom.* University of Michigan Press, Ann Arbor.

1985   *Islands of History.* University of Chicago Press, Chicago.

1995   *How "Natives" Think: About Captain Cook, for Example.* University of Chicago Press, Chicago.

Samson, Gilles

1975   *Contributions to the Study of the Mushuau Innuts and Their Territory, Nouveau-Quebec.* Master's thesis, Laval University, Quebec.

Sanger, David

1973   *Cow Point: An Archaic Cemetery in New Brunswick.* Archaeological Survey of Canada Paper No. 12. National Museum of Man, Ottawa.

1996   Gilman Falls Site: Implications for the Early and Middle Archaic of the Maritime Peninsula. *Canadian Journal of Archaeology* 20:7–28.

2003   Who Lived in Pre-European Maine? A Cosmology Approach to Social Patterning on the Landscape. *Northeast Anthropology* 66:29–39.

2006   An Introduction to the Archaic of the Maritime Peninsula: The View from Central Maine. In *The Archaic of the Far Northeast,* edited by D. Sanger and M.A.P. Renouf, pp. 221–252. University of Maine Press, Orono.

Sanger, David, Heather Almquist, and Ann Dieffenbacher-Krall

2007   Mid-Holocene Cultural Adaptations to Central Maine. In *Climate Change and Cultural Dynamics: A Global Perspective on Mid-Holocene Transition.* edited by D. G. Anderson, K. A. Maasch, and D. H. Sandweiss, pp. 435–456. Academic Press, New York.

Sassaman, Kenneth E.

1995   The Cultural Diversity of Interactions among Mid-Holocene Societies of the American Southwest. In *Native American Interactions,* edited by M. S. Nassaney and K. E. Sassaman, pp. 174–204. University of Tennessee Press, Knoxville.

1996   Technological Innovations in Economic and Social Contexts. In *Archaeology of the Mid-Holocene Southeast,* edited by K. E. Sassaman and D. G. Anderson, pp. 57–74. University Press of Florida, Gainesville.

2001   Hunter-Gatherers and Traditions of Resistance. In *The Archaeology of Tradition: Agency and History before and after Columbus,* edited by T. Pauketat, pp. 218–236. University Press of Florida, Gainesville.

2003a   New AMS Dates on Orange Fiber-Tempered Pottery from the Middle St. Johns Valley and Their Implications for Culture History in Northeast Florida. *Florida Anthropologist* 56:5–14.

2003b   *St. Johns Archaeological Field School 2000–2001: Blue Spring and Hontoon Island State Parks.* Technical Report No. 4. Laboratory of Southeastern Archaeology, Department of Anthropology, University of Florida, Gainesville.

2004a   Complex Hunter-Gatherers in Evolution and History: A North American Perspective. *Journal of Archaeological Research* 12:227–280.

2004b   Common Origins and Divergent Histories in the Early Pottery Traditions of the American Southeast. In *Early Pottery: Technology, Function, Style and Interaction in the Lower Southeast*, edited by R. Saunders and C. T. Hays, pp. 23–39. University of Alabama Press, Tuscaloosa.

2005a   Poverty Point as Structure, Event, Process. *Journal of Archaeological Method and Theory* 12:335–364.

2005b   Hontoon Dead Creek Mound (8VO214). In *St. Johns Archaeological Field School 2003–2004: Hontoon Island State Park*, edited by A. R. Randall and K. E. Sassaman, pp. 83–106. Technical Report No. 6. Laboratory of Southeastern Archaeology, Department of Anthropology, University of Florida, Gainesville.

2006   *People of the Shoals: Stallings Culture of the Savannah River Valley.* University Press of Florida, Gainesville.

2010   *The Eastern Archaic, Historicized.* AltaMira, Walnut Creek, Calif.

Sassaman, Kenneth E., and Michael J. Heckenberger

2004   Crossing the Symbolic Rubicon in the Southeast. In *Signs of Power: The Rise of Complexity in the Southeast*, edited by J. L. Gibson and P. J. Carr, pp. 214–233. University of Alabama Press, Tuscaloosa.

Sassaman, Kenneth E., and Asa R. Randall

2007   The Culture History of Bannerstones in the Savannah River Valley. *Southeastern Archaeology* 26:196–211.

Saunders, Joe W.

2004   Are We Fixing to Make the Same Mistakes Again? In *Signs of Power: The Rise of Complexity in the Southeast*, edited by J. L. Gibson and P. J. Carr, pp. 146–161. University of Alabama Press, Tuscaloosa.

Saunders, Joe W., Thurman Allen, Dennis LaBatt, Reca Jones, and David Griffing

2001   An Assessment of the Antiquity of the Lower Jackson Mound. *Southeastern Archaeology* 20:67–77.

Saunders, Nicholas J.

1999   Biographies of Brilliance: Pearls, Transformations of Matter and Being, c. AD 1492. *World Archaeology* 31 (2): 243–257.

Saunders, Rebecca

2004   Spatial Variation in Orange Culture Pottery: Interaction and Function. In *Early Pottery: Technology, Function, Style and Interaction in the Lower Southeast*, edited by R. Saunders and C. T. Hays, pp. 40–62. University of Alabama Press, Tuscaloosa.

Savelle, James M.

2002   Logistical Organization, Social Complexity, and the Collapse of Prehistoric Thule Whaling Societies in the Central Canadian Arctic. In *Beyond Foraging and Collecting: Evolutionary Change in Hunter-Gatherer Settlement Systems*, edited by B. Fitzhugh and J. Habu, pp. 73–90. Kluwer/Plenum, New York.

Schaepe, David M.

 1998   *Recycling Archaeology: Analysis of Material from the 1973 Excavation of an
         Ancient House at the Maurer Site.* Master's thesis, Simon Fraser Univer-
         sity, Burnaby, British Columbia.

Scham, Sandra Arnold

 2001   The Archaeology of the Disenfranchised. *Journal of Archaeological
         Method and Theory* 8 (2): 183–213.

Schauffler, Molly, and George L. Jacobson

 2002   Persistence of Coastal Spruce Refugia during the Holocene in North-
         ern New England, USA, Detected by Stand-Scale Pollen Stratigraphies.
         Journal of Ecology 90:235–250.

Scheiber, Laura L., and Judson Byrd Finley

 2010   Mountain Shoshone Technological Transitions across the Great Divide.
         In *Across a Great Divide: Change and Continuity in Native North Amer-
         ica, 1400–1900,* edited by Laura L. Scheiber and Mark D. Mitchell,
         pp. 128–148. University of Arizona Press, Tucson.

 2011   Obsidian Source Use in the Greater Yellowstone Area, Wyoming Basin,
         and Central Rocky Mountains. *American Antiquity,* forthcoming.

Scheiber, Laura L., and Mark D. Mitchell (editors)

 2010   *Across a Great Divide: Change and Continuity in Native North America,
         1400–1900.* University of Arizona Press, Tucson.

Schlanger, Sarah H.

 1988   Patterns of Population Movement and Long-Term Population Growth
         in Southwestern Colorado. *American Antiquity* 53:773–793.

Schlesinger, Roger, and Arthur P. Stabler

 1986   *André Thevet's North America. A Sixteenth Century View.* McGill-Queen's
         University Press, Kingston.

Schmidt, Christopher W., Rachel L. Sharkey, Christopher Newman, Anna Ser-
rano, Melissa Zolneirz, A. Plunkett, and Anne Bader

 2010   Skeletal Evidence of Cultural Variation: Mutilation Related to Warfare.
         In *Human Variation in the Americas: The Integration of Archaeology and
         Biological Anthropology,* edited by B. Auerbach. Center for Archaeologi-
         cal Investigations, Southern Illinois University, Carbondale.

Schmidt, Christopher W., Curtis Tomak, Rachel A. Lockhart, Tammy R. Greene,
and Gregory A. Reinhardt

 2008   Early Archaic Cremations from Southern Indiana. In *The Analysis of
         Burned Human Remains,* edited by C. W. Schmidt and S. A. Symes,
         pp. 227–237. Academic Press, London.

Schrire, Carmel

 1980   An Inquiry into the Evolutionary Status and Apparent Identity of San
         Hunter-Gatherers. *Human Ecology* 8 (1): 9–32.

 1995   *Digging through Darkness: Chronicles of an Archaeologist.* University
         Press of Virginia, Charlottesville.

Schulting, Rick J.

    1995   *Mortuary Variability and Status Differentiation on the Columbia-Fraser Plateau.* Archaeology Press, Burnaby.

Schwarz, Frederick A.

    1994   Paleo-Eskimo and Recent Indian Subsistence and Settlement Patterns on the Island of Newfoundland. *Northeast Anthropology* 47 (Spring): 55–70.

Sears, William H.

    1960   The Bluffton Burial Mound. *Florida Anthropologist* 13:55–60.

Secoy, Frank Raymond

    1953   *Changing Military Patterns on the Great Plains (17th Century through Early 19th Century).* Monographs of the American Ethnological Society, No. 21. University of Washington Press, Seattle.

Service, Elman R.

    1962   *Primitive Social Organization: An Evolutionary Perspective.* Random House, New York.

Shennan, Stephen

    1993   Settlement and Society in Central Europe 3500–1500 BC. *Journal of World Prehistory* 7: 121–161.

    2000   Population, Culture History, and the Dynamics of Culture Change. *Current Anthropology* 41:811–835.

    2003   *Genes, Memes and Human History: Darwinian Archaeology and Cultural Evolution.* Thames and Hudson, London.

Sheridan, P. H.

    1882   *Report of an Exploration of Parks of Wyoming, Idaho, and Montana in August and September, 1882.* Government Printing Office, Washington D.C.

Shimkin, Demitri B.

    1947   Wind River Shoshone Ethnogeography. *Anthropological Records of the University of California* 5 (4): 245–288.

    1986   Eastern Shoshone. In *The Great Basin*, edited by William C. Sturtevant and Warren L. D'Azevedo, pp. 308–335. Vol. 11 of *Handbook of North American Indians*, edited by William C. Sturtevant. Smithsonian Institution, Washington, D.C.

Shott, Michael

    1999   The Early Archaic: Life after the Glaciers. In *Retrieving Michigan's Buried Past: The Archaeology of the Great Lakes State*, edited by J. R. Halsey, pp. 71–82. Bulletin 64. Cranbrook Institute of Science, Bloomfield Hills, Michigan.

Sidell, Nancy Asch

    1999   Prehistoric Plant Use in Maine: Paleoindian to Contact Period. In *Current Northeast Paleoethnobotany*, edited by John P. Hart, pp. 191–223. Bulletin 494. New York State Museum.

Silliman, Stephen

    2003   Using a Rock in a Hard Place: Native-American Lithic Practices in Colonial California. In *Stone Tool Traditions in the Contact Era*, edited by Charles R. Cobb, pp. 127–150. University of Alabama Press, Tuscaloosa.

    2005   Obsidian Studies and the Archaeology of 19th-Century California. *Journal of Field Archaeology* 30:75–94.

    2009   Change and Continuity, Practice and Memory: Native American Persistence in Colonial New England. *American Antiquity* 74:211–230.

Skinner, B. F.

    1981   Selection by Consequences. *Science* 213:501–504.

Smith, Bruce

    2001   Low-Level Food Production. *Journal of Archaeological Research* 9:1–43.

Smith, Maria O.

    1996   Biocultural Inquiry into Archaic Period Populations of the Southeast: Trauma and Occupational Stress. In *Archaeology of the Mid-Holocene Southeast*, edited by K. E. Sassaman and D. G. Anderson, pp. 134–154. University Press of Florida, Gainesville.

Snoek, Jan A. M.

    2006   Defining 'Rituals.' In *Theorizing Rituals: Issues, Topics, Approaches, Concepts*, edited by J. Kreinath, J. Snoek, and M. Stausberg, pp. 3–14. Brill, Leiden.

Snow, Dean R.

    1980   *The Archaeology of New England*. Academic Press, New York.

Spaulding, Albert C.

    1946   Northeastern Archaeology and General Trends in the Northern Forest Zone. In *Man in Northeastern North America*, edited by Frederick Johnson, pp. 143–167. Papers of the Robert S. Peabody Foundation for Archaeology, No. 3. Phillips Academy, Andover.

Speck, Frank G.

    1931   Montagnais-Naskapi Bands and Early Eskimo Distribution in the Labrador Peninsula. *American Anthropologist* 33 (4): 557–600.

    1935   *Naskapi: The Savage Hunters of the Labrador Peninsula*. University of Oklahoma Press, Norman.

Spencer, Charles S.

    1997   Evolutionary Approaches in Archaeology. *Journal of Archaeological Research* 5:209–264.

    2009   Testing the Morphogenesist Model of Primary State Formation: The Zapotec Case. In *Macroevolution and Human Prehistory: Evolutionary Theory and Processual Archaeology*, edited by Anna M. Prentiss, Ian Kuijt, and James C. Chatters, pp. 133–156. Springer, New York.

Spielmann, Katherine A., and James F. Eder

    1994   Hunters and Farmers: Then and Now. *Annual Review of Anthropology* 23 (1): 303–323.

Spiess, Arthur E.

1979   *Reindeer and Caribou Hunters: An Archaeological Study*. Academic Press, New York.

1984   Arctic Garbage and New England Paleo-Indians: The Single Occupation Option. *Archaeology of Eastern North America* 12:280–285.

1992   Archaic Period Subsistence in New England and the Atlantic Provinces. In *Early Holocene Occupation in Northern New England*, edited by Brian S. Robinson, James B. Petersen, and Ann K. Robinson, pp. 163–185. Occasional Publications in Maine Archaeology 9. Maine Historic Preservation Commission, Augusta.

Spiess, Arthur E., and Robert Lewis

2001   *The Turner Farm Fauna: 5000 Years of Hunting and Fishing in Penobscot Bay, Maine*. Occasional Publications in Maine Archaeology 11. Maine State Museum, Maine Historic Preservation Commission, and Maine Archaeological Society, Augusta.

Spiess, Arthur E., and John Mosher

2006   Archaic Period Hunting and Fishing around the Gulf of Maine. In *The Archaic of the Far Northeast*, edited by David Sanger and M.A.P. Renouf, pp. 383–408. University of Maine Press, Orono.

Spiess, Arthur E., Deborah Wilson, and James W. Bradley

1998   Paleoindian Occupation in the New England-Maritimes Region: Beyond Cultural Ecology. *Archaeology of Eastern North America* 26:201–264.

Stamm, Henry E., IV

1999   *People of the Wind River: The Eastern Shoshones 1825–1900*. University of Oklahoma Press, Norman.

Staski, Edward

2004   Change and Inertia on the Frontier: Archaeology at the Paraje de San Diego, Camino Real, in Southern New Mexico. *International Journal of Historical Archaeology* 2:21–44.

Stearman, Allyn MacLean

1984   The Yuquí Connection: Another Look at Sirionó Deculturation. *American Anthropologist* 86:630–650.

Steegman, A. Theodore Jr.

1983   Boreal Forest Hazards and Adaptations: The Past. In *Boreal Forest Adaptations: the Northern Algonkians*, edited by A. Theodore Steegman Jr., pp. 243–267. Plenum, New York.

Steele, James

2009   Human Dispersals: Mathematical Models and the Archaeological Record. *Human Biology* 81 (2–3): 121–140.

Steele, James, Jonathan Adams, and Tim Sluckin

1998   Modeling Paleoindian Dispersals. *World Archaeology* 30:286–305.

Stein, Gil (editor)

    2005   *The Archaeology of Colonial Encounters: Comparative Perspectives*. School of American Research Press, Santa Fe, N.M.

Stephens, Scott L., and Danny L. Fry

    2005   Fire History in Coast Redwood Stands in the Northeastern Santa Cruz Mountains, California. *Fire Ecology* 1:2–19.

Stephens, Scott L., Robert E. Martin, and Nicholas E. Clinton

    2007   Prehistoric Fire Area and Emissions from California's Forests, Woodlands, Shrublands, and Grasslands. *Forest Ecology and Management* 251:205–216.

Steward, Julian H.

    1938   *Basin-Plateau Aboriginal Sociopolitical Groups*. Bulletin No. 20. Bureau of American Ethnology, Smithsonian Institution, Washington, D.C.

Stockwell, C. H., J. C. McGlynn, R. F. Emslie, B. V. Sanford, A. W. Norris, J. A. Donaldson, W. F. Fahig, and K. L. Currie

    1970   Geology of the Canadian Shield. In *Geology and Economic Minerals of Canada*, edited by R.J.W. Douglas, pp. 43–150. Geological Survey of Canada, Ottawa.

Stopp, Marianne P.

    2002   Ethnohistoric Analogues for Storage as an Adaptive Strategy in Northeastern Subarctic Prehistory. *Journal of Anthropological Archaeology* 21:301–328.

    2008   FbAx-01: A Daniel Rattle Hearth in Southern Labrador. *Canadian Journal of Archaeology* 32:96–127.

Strassburg, Jimmy

    2003   Rituals at the Meso 2000 Conference and the Mesolithic-Neolithic Terminological Breakdown. In *Mesolithic on the Move: Papers Presented at the Sixth International Conference on the Mesolithic in Europe, Stockholm 2000*, edited by L. Larsson, H. Kindgren, K. Knutsson, D. Loeffler, and A. Åkerlund, pp. 542–546. Oxbow, Oxford, U.K.

Sugihara, Neil G., Jan W. van Wagtendonk, Kevin E. Shaffer, Joann Fites-Kaufman, Adrea E. Thode (editors)

    2006   *Fires in California's Ecosystems*. University of California Press, Berkeley.

Surovell, Todd A.

    2000   Early Paleoindian Women, Children, Mobility, and Fertility. *American Antiquity* 65:493–508.

Surovell, Todd A., and P. Jeffrey Brantingham

    2007   A Note on the Use of Temporal Frequency Distributions in Studies of Prehistoric Demography. *Journal of Archaeological Science* 34:1868–1877.

Surovell, Todd A., Judson Byrd Finley, Geoffrey M. Smith, P. Jeffrey Brantingham, and Robert Kelly

    2009   Correcting Temporal Frequency Distributions for Taphonomic Bias. *Journal of Archaeological Science* 36:1715–1724.

Swanson, Earl H., Jr., and Alan Lyle Bryan

1964   *Birch Creek Papers No. 1: An Archaeological Reconnaissance in the Birch Creek Valley of Eastern Idaho*. Occasional Papers of the Idaho State University Museum, No. 13. Idaho State University, Pocatello.

Swanton, John R.

1907   Mythology of the Indians of Louisiana and the Texas Coast. *Journal of American Folklore* 1907:285–289.

1917   Chitimacha Myths and Beliefs. *Journal of American Folklore* 30:474–478.

1929   *Myths and Tales of the Southeastern Indians*. Bulletin 88. Bureau of American Ethnology, Smithsonian Institution, Washington, D.C.

1931   *Source Material for the Social and Ceremonial Life of the Choctaw Indians*. Bulletin 103. Bureau of American Ethnology, Smithsonian Institution, Washington, D.C.

Taçon, Paul S. C.

1999   Identifying Ancient Sacred Landscapes in Australia: From Physical to Social. In *Archaeologies of Landscape: Contemporary Perspectives*, edited by W. Ashmore and A. B. Knapp, pp. 33–57. Blackwell, Malden, Mass.

Tanner, Adrian

1979   *Bringing Home Animals. Religious Ideology and Mode of Production of the Mistassini Cree Hunters*. Social and Economic Studies, No. 23. Institute of Social and Economic Research, Memorial University of Newfoundland, St. John's.

Taussig, Michael

1993   *Mimesis and Alterity: A Particular History of the Senses*. Routledge, New York.

Teit, James

1909   *The Shuswap*. Memoirs of the American Museum of Natural History 4 (Part 7). American Museum of Natural History, New York.

Thomas, David Hurst

1972   A Computer Simulation Model of Great Basin Shoshonean Subsistence and Settlement Pattern. In *Models in Archaeology*, edited by David L. Clarke, pp. 671–704. Methuen, London.

Thomas, Julian

1993   The Politics of Vision and the Archaeologies of Landscape. In *Landscape: Politics and Perspectives*, edited by B. Bender, pp. 19–48. Berg, Oxford, U.K.

Thomas, Nicholas

1989   *Out of Time: History and Evolution in Anthropological Discourse*. University of Michigan Press, Ann Arbor.

Thompson, Laurence C., and M. Dale Kinkade

1990   Languages. In *Northwest Coast*, edited by W. Suttles, pp. 30–51. Vol. 7 of *Handbook of North American Indians*, edited by William C. Sturtevant. Smithsonian Institution Press, Washington, D.C.

Thoms, Alston V.

1989   *The Northern Roots of Hunter-Gatherer Intensification: Camas and the Pacific Northwest.* PhD diss., Washington State University, Pullman.

Thorbahn, Peter F.

1979   *The Precolonial Ivory Trade of East Africa: Reconstruction of a Human-Elephant Ecosystem.* PhD diss., University of Massachusetts, Amherst.

Thwaites, Reuben Gold (editor)

1896–   *The Jesuit Relations and Allied Documents.* 73 vols. Burrows Brothers,
1901   Cleveland, Ohio.

Tilley, Christopher

1997   *A Phenomenology of Landscape: Places, Paths and Monuments.* Berg, Oxford, U.K.

Timbrook, Jan, John R. Johnson, and David D. Earle

1982   Vegetation Burning by the Chumash. *Journal of California and Great Basin Anthropology* 4:163–186.

Tomak, Curtis H.

1979   Jerger: An Early Archaic Mortuary Site in Southwest Indiana. *Proceedings of the Indiana Academy of Science* 85:62–69.

Torrence, Robin

1989   Tools as Optimal Solutions. In *Time, Energy and Stone Tools*, edited by Robin Torrence, pp. 1–6. Cambridge University Press, London.

Trenholm, Virginia Cole, and Maurine Carley

1964   *The Shoshonis: Sentinels of the Rockies.* University of Oklahoma Press, Norman.

Trigger, Bruce G.

1991   Distinguished Lecture in Archaeology: Constraint and Freedom—a New Synthesis for Archaeological Explanation. *American Anthropologist* 93 (3): 551–569.

1998   Archaeology and Epistomology: Dialoguing across the Darwinian Chasm. *American Journal of Archaeology* 102 (1): 1–34.

2006   *A History of Archaeological Thought.* 2nd ed. Cambridge University Press, New York.

Trigger, David S.

1999   Hunter-Gatherer Peoples and Nation-States. In *The Cambridge Encyclopedia of Hunters and Gatherers*, edited by R. B. Lee and R. Daly, pp. 473–479. Cambridge University Press, Cambridge.

Tuck, James A.

1976   *Ancient People of Port au Choix: The Excavation of an Archaic Indian Cemetery in Newfoundland.* Social and Economic Studies, No. 17. Institute of Social and Economic Research, Memorial University of Newfoundland, St. John's.

1978   Regional Cultural Development, 3000–300 BC. In *Northeast*, edited by Bruce G. Trigger, pp. 28–43. Vol. 15 of *Handbook of North American*

Indians, edited by William C. Sturtevant. Smithsonian Institution, Washington, D.C.

Tuck, James A., and Ralph T. Pastore

1985   A Nice Place to Visit, but . . . Prehistoric Human Extinctions on the Island of Newfoundland. *Canadian Journal of Archaeology* 9:69–80.

Tucker, Bram

2003   Mikea Origins: Relicts or Refugees? *Michigan Discussions in Anthropology* 14:193–215.

Tucker, Bryan D.

2009   *Piercing the Seasonal Round: Isotopic Investigations of Archaic Period Subsistence and Settlement in the St. Johns River Drainage, Florida.* PhD diss., University of Florida, Gainesville.

Tunnicliffe, V., J. M. O'Connell, and M. R. McQuoid

2001   A Holocene Record of Marine Fish Remains from the Northeastern Pacific. *Marine Geology* 174: 197–210.

Turnbull, Colin

1968   *The Forest People.* Simon and Schuster, New York.

Turner, Frederick J.

1962   *The Frontier in American History.* Holt, Rinehart, and Winston,
[1920]   New York.

Turner, Lucien M.

1894   *Ethnology of the Ungava District, Hudson Bay Territory. Indians and Eskimos in the Quebec-Labrador Peninsula.* Annual Report 11:159–350. U.S. Bureau of Ethnology, Smithsonian Institution, Washington, D.C.

Tuzin, Donald

2001   *Social Complexity in the Making: A Case Study among the Arapesh of New Guinea.* Routledge, London.

Usman, Aribidesi A.

2004   On the Frontier of Empire: Understanding the Enclosed Walls in Northern Yoruba, Nigeria. *Journal of Anthropological Archaeology* 23:119–132.

Van Dyke, Ruth M., and Susan Alcock (editors)

2003   *Archaeologies of Memory.* Blackwell, Oxford, U.K.

Van Nest, Julieann

2006   Rediscovering This Earth: Some Ethnogeological Aspects of the Illinois Hopewell Mounds. In *Recreating Hopewell*, edited by D. K. Charles and J. E. Buikstra, pp. 402–426. University Press of Florida, Gainesville.

VanStone, James W.

1982   *The Speck Collection of Montagnais Material Culture from the Lower St. Lawrence Drainage, Quebec.* Fieldiana Anthropology 5. Field Museum of Natural History, Chicago.

1985   *Material Culture of the Davis Inlet and Barren Ground Naskapi: The William Duncan Strong Collection.* Fieldiana Anthropology 7. Field Museum of Natural History, Chicago.

Vayda, Andrew P.
    2001   The Turn to Causal Histories of Events. Paper presented at the One Hundredth Annual Meeting of the American Anthropological Association, Washington, D.C.

Waguespack, Nicole M.
    2005   The Organization of Male and Female Labor in Foraging Societies: Implications for Early Paleoindian Archaeology. *American Anthropologist* 107:666–676.

Walker, Phillip L., and Patricia M. Lambert
    1989   Skeletal Evidence for Stress during a Period of Cultural Change in Prehistoric California. In *Advances in Paleopathology, Journal of Paleopathology*, edited by L. Capasso, pp. 207–212. Monographic Publication 1. Marino Solfanelli, Chieti, Italy.

Walker, William H., and Lisa J. Lucero
    2001   The Depositional History of Ritual and Power. In *Agency in Archaeology*, edited by M.-A. Dobres and J. E. Robb, pp. 130–147. Routledge, New York.

Walthall, John A.
    1998   Rockshelters and Hunter-Gatherer Adaptation to the Pleistocene/Holocene Transition. *American Antiquity* 63:223–238.

Walthall, John A., and Brad Koldehoff
    1998   Hunter-Gatherer Interaction and Alliance Formation: The Cult of the Long Blade. *Plains Anthropologist* 43:257–273.

Waters, Michael R., and Thomas W. Stafford Jr.
    2007   Redefining the Age of Clovis: Implications for the Peopling of the Americas. *Science* 315:1122–1126.

Watts, Douglas J.
    2003   *Six Degrees: The Science of a Connected Age.* Norton, New York.

Webb, Clarence H.
    1970   Intrasite Distribution of Artifacts at the Poverty Point Site, with Special Reference to Women's and Men's Activities. *Southeastern Archaeological Conference Bulletin* 12:21–34.
    1982   *The Poverty Point Culture.* 2nd ed. Geoscience and Man No. 17. Geoscience Publications, Department of Geography and Anthropology, Louisiana State University, Baton Rouge.

Webb, Clarence H., James A. Ford, and Sherwood M. Gagliano
    1963   Poverty Point and the American Formative. MS. on file, Poverty Point State Historic Site, Epps, La.

Webb, William S.
    1939   *An Archaeological Survey of Wheeler Basin on the Tennessee River of Northern Alabama.* Bulletin 122. Bureau of American Ethnology, Smithsonian Institution, Washington, D.C.
    1974   *Indian Knoll.* University of Tennessee Press, Knoxville.

Webb, William S., and David L. DeJarnette

1942   *An Archaeological Survey of Pickwick Basin in the Adjacent Portions of the States of Alabama, Mississippi, and Tennessee.* Bulletin 129. Bureau of American Ethnology, Smithsonian Institution, Washington, D.C.

Weiner, Annette

1992   *Inalienable Possessions: The Paradox of Keeping-While-Giving.* University of California Press, Berkeley.

Wendrich, Willeke, and Hans Barnard

2008   The Archaeology of Mobility: Definitions and Research Approaches. In *The Archaeology of Mobility: Old World and New World Nomadism,* edited by Hans Barnard and Willeke Wendrich, pp. 1–21. Cotsen Advanced Seminars 4. Cotsen Institute of Archaeology, University of California, Los Angeles.

Whallon, Robert

2006   Social Networks and Information: Non-"Utilitarian" Mobility among Hunter-Gatherers. *Journal of Anthropological Archaeology* 25 (2): 259–270.

Wheeler, Ryan J., Christine L. Newman, and Ray M. McGee

2000   A New Look at the Mount Taylor and Bluffton Sites, Volusia County, with an Outline of the Mount Taylor Culture. *Florida Anthropologist* 53:133–157.

White, Leslie

1949   *The Science of Culture.* Grove Press, New York.

Whitelaw, Todd M.

1983   People and Space in Hunter-Gatherer Camps: A Generalising Approach in Ethnoarchaeology. *Archaeological Review from Cambridge* 2:48–65.

1991   Some Dimensions of Variability in the Social Organisation of Community Space among Foragers. In *Ethnoarchaeological Approaches to Mobile Campsites: Hunter-Gatherer and Pastoralist Case Studies,* edited by Clive Gamble and William A. Boismer, pp. 139–188. International Monographs in Prehistory, Ann Arbor, Mich..

Wiessner, Polly

1996   Leveling the Hunter: Constraints on the Status Quest in Foraging Societies. In *Food and the Status Quest,* edited by Polly Wiessner and Wulf Schiefenhövel, pp. 171–191. Berghahn Books, Providence, R.I.

Willey, Gordon R., and Philip Phillips

1958   *Method and Theory in American Archaeology.* University of Chicago Press, Chicago.

Wilmsen, Edwin N.

1989   *Land Filled with Flies: A Political Economy of the Kalahari.* University of Chicago Press, Chicago.

Wilson, Samuel M.

1993   Structure and History: Combining Archaeology and Ethnohistory in the Contact Period Caribbean. In *Ethnohistory and Archaeology: Approaches to Postcontact Change in the Americas*, edited by J. Daniel Rogers and Samuel Wilson, pp. 19–30. Plenum Press, New York.

Winters, Howard D.

1968   Value Systems and Trade Cycles of the Late Archaic in the Midwest. In *New Directions in Archaeology*, edited by S. R. Binford and L. R. Binford, pp. 175–221. Aldine, Chicago.

1969   *The Riverton Culture.* Reports of Investigation 13. Illinois State Museum, Springfield.

Wobst, H. Martin

1974   Boundary Conditions for Paleolithic Social Systems: A Simulation Approach. *American Antiquity* 39:147–178.

1978   The Archaeo-Ethnology of Hunter-Gatherers or the Tyranny of the Ethnographic Record in Archaeology. *American Antiquity* 43:303–309.

1989   The Origination of *Homo Sapiens*, or the Invention, Control and Manipulation of Modern Human Nature. In *Critical Approaches in Archaeology: Material Life, Meaning and Power.* International Symposium in Portugal, sponsored by the Wenner Gren Foundation for Anthropological Research, New York.

2000   Agency in (Spite of) Material Culture. In *Agency in Archaeology*, edited by M.-A. Dobres and J. E. Robb, pp. 40–50. Routledge, London.

2005   Power to the (Indigenous) Past or Present! Or: The Theory behind Archaeological Theory and Method. In *Indigenous Archaeologies: Decolonising Theory and Practice*, edited by Claire Smith and H. Martin Wobst, pp. 17–32. Routledge, London.

Wolf, Eric R.

1982   *Europe and the People without History.* University of California Press, Berkeley.

1984   Culture: Panacea or Problem? *American Antiquity* 49:393–400.

Wood, James W.

1998   A Theory of Preindustrial Population Dynamics. *Current Anthropology* 39 (1): 99–121.

Wood, Raymond W., and Thomas D. Thiessen

1985   *Early Fur Trade on the Northern Plains: Canadian Traders among the Mandan and Hidatsa Indians, 1738–1818.* University of Oklahoma Press, Norman.

Woodburn, James

1968   An Introduction to Hadza Ecology. In *Man the Hunter*, edited by Richard B. Lee and Irven DeVore, pp. 49–55. Aldine, Chicago.

Wright, Gary A.

1978   The Shoshonean Migration Problem. *Plains Anthropologist* 23 (80): 113–137.

Wright, Henry T.

2000   Agent-based Modeling of Small-scale Societies: State of the Art and Future Prospects. In *Dynamics in Human and Primate Societies: Agent-based*

Modeling of Social and Spatial Processes, edited by Timothy Kohler and George J. Gumerman, pp. 373–385. Santa Fe Institute Studies in the Sciences of Complexity. Oxford University Press, New York.

Wright, James V.
1972   *The Shield Archaic.* Publications in Archaeology, No. 3. National Museums of Canada, Ottawa.

Wright, Sewall
1932   Roles of Mutation, Inbreeding, Crossbreeding and Selection in Evolution. *Proceedings of the Sixth International Congress of Genetics* 1:356–366.

Wylie, Alison
1993   Invented Lands/Discovered Pasts: The Westward Expansion of Myth and History. *Historical Archaeology* 27 (4): 1–19.

Wyman, Jeffries
1875   Fresh-Water Shell Mounds of the St. John's River, Florida. *Memoirs of the Peabody Academy of Science* 1 (4).

Yatsko, Andrew
2000   *Late Holocene Paleoclimatic Stress and Prehistoric Human Occupation on San Clemente Island.* PhD diss., University of California, Los Angeles.

Yen, D. E.
1989   The Domestication of Environment. In *Foraging and Farming: The Evolution of Plant Exploitation*, edited by David R. Harris and Gordon C. Hillman, pp. 55–75. Unwin Hyman, Boston.

Yengoyan, Aram A.
2004   Anthropological History and the Study of Hunters and Gatherers: Cultural and Non-Cultural. In *Hunter-Gatherers in History, Archaeology, and Anthropology*, edited by A. Barnard, pp. 57–66. Berg, Oxford, U.K.

Zeder, Melinda A.
2009a   Neolithic Macro-(R)evolution: Macroevolutionary Theory and the Study of Culture Change. *Journal of Archaeological Research* 17:1–63.

2009b   Evolutionary Biology and the Emergence of Agriculture: The Value of Co-opted Models of Evolution in the Study of Culture Change. In *Macroevolution and Human Prehistory: Evolutionary Theory and Processual Archaeology*, edited by Anna M. Prentiss, Ian Kuijt, and James C. Chatters, pp. 157–212. Springer, New York.

Ziegler, A. C.
1968   Quasi-Agriculture in North-Central California and Its Effect on Aboriginal Social Structure. *Kroeber Anthropological Society Papers* 38:52–67.

Zvelebil, Marek
1998   What's in a Name: The Mesolithic, the Neolithic, and Social Change at the Mesolithic-Neolithic Transition. In *Understanding the Neolithic of North-Western Europe*, edited by Mark Edmonds and Colin Richards, pp. 1–36. Cruithne Press, Glasgow.

JUDSON BYRD FINLEY earned his PhD in 2008 from Washington State University and is Assistant Professor of Earth Sciences at the University of Memphis. His research focuses on Wyoming's natural and cultural history. He is currently investigating rockshelter formation processes and the associated environmental history of the Bighorn Mountains, as well as exploring social landscapes, culture contact, and colonialism in the Rocky Mountains through the recent archaeological history of the Crow and the Shoshone peoples in northwestern Wyoming. Dr. Finley is also an adjunct faculty at Northwest College in Powell, Wyoming, and regularly teaches archaeological field schools involving local students and community members in his research. He has published articles in *Antiquity, Plains Anthropologist, Journal of Archaeological Science, Current Research in the Pleistocene,* and *The American Surveyor,* as well as several book chapters.

LYNN H. GAMBLE is Professor of Anthropology at the University of California, Santa Barbara, where she received her PhD in 1991. Her research focuses on emergent sociopolitical complexity among hunter-gatherer societies in southern California through the examination of exchange systems, religious organization, hierarchy, and cultural landscapes. Her recent book, *The Chumash World at European Contact: Power, Trade, and Feasting among Complex Hunter-Gatherers* (University of California Press), draws on archaeology, historical documents, ethnography, and ecology to reconstruct daily life in the large mainland settlements of the Santa Barbara Channel region. She has also published widely on Chumash mortuary practices, watercraft, architecture, long-term change in the Santa Barbara Channel region, the effects of paleoclimatic variability among southern California hunter-gatherer societies, and social differentiation and exchange among the Kumeyaay Indians during the historic period. She currently is Editor of the *Journal of California and Great Basin Anthropology,* a position she has held since 2005.

DONALD H. HOLLY JR. earned his BA from Penn State University in 1995 and his PhD from Brown University in 2002. He is Assistant Professor of Anthropology at Eastern Illinois University. His research focuses on the Beothuk Indians of the island of Newfoundland, the archaeology of the Eastern Subarctic, and the history of hunter-gatherer studies. His publications include "The Place of Others in Hunter-Gatherer Intensification" (*American Anthropologist*), "Subarctic Prehistory in the Anthropological Imagination" (*Arctic Anthropology*), and "Social Aspects and Implications of 'Running to the Hills': The Case of the Beothuk Indians of Newfoundland (*Journal of Island and Coastal Archaeology*).

KATHLEEN L. HULL received her PhD from the University of California, Berkeley. She is Assistant Professor of Anthropology and faculty affiliate of the Sierra Nevada Research Institute at the University of California, Merced. Her research addresses demography, ethnogenesis, and identity in small-scale societies of the American West, including analysis of the impacts of European colonialism on indigenous communities. She has explored the latter topic at length in her book *Pestilence and Persistence: Yosemite Indian Demography and Culture in Colonial California*, while she has also published on a variety of topics in professional journals including the *Journal of Anthropological Archaeology, Journal of Archaeological Science*, and *American Antiquity*.

TRISTRAM R. KIDDER received his PhD from Harvard University in 1988 and is Professor and Chair in the Department of Anthropology at Washington University in St. Louis. He has been conducting archaeological research in the Mississippi Valley for over twenty years and has excavated numerous sites, notably Poverty Point, where he and his students have been working for the last ten years. In addition to studying Archaic complex hunter-gatherers, his research focuses on the use of geoarchaeological methods for studying Holocene human adaptations to climate change in large river valleys. His most recent projects include reexcavation of the Jaketown site in west-central Mississippi and geoarchaeological study of deeply buried Han Dynasty farming communities in the Yellow River Valley, China. He has published in *Science, American Antiquity, Southeastern Archaeology*, and other journals and has authored a number of book chapters.

KENT G. LIGHTFOOT is Professor of Anthropology at the University of California, Berkeley. He received his BA from Stanford University and MA and PhD from Arizona State University. Since joining the Berkeley faculty in 1987, Lightfoot has been involved in developing a local archaeology program in northern California, the purpose of which is to generate a better understanding of the precolonial and colonial history of the greater San Francisco Bay Area and to provide educational and research opportunities for UC Berkeley students and community members. Much of this recent work involves collaboration with contemporary Native people in projects that examine the creation of shell mounds, the development of pyrodiversity economies, and the implications of their past encounters with European explorers and settlers. Although most of this research has taken place in the greater San Francisco Bay Area, Kent and his students have traced various historical connections back to Alaska, Hawaii, and Baja California. He is the author of *Indians, Missionaries, and Merchants* and co-author (with Otis Parrish) of *California Indians and Their Environment*, both published by the University of California Press.

EDWARD M. LUBY received his BA (biology and anthropology) from the University of Rochester and his PhD (anthropological sciences) from the State University of New York, Stony Brook. He is Associate Professor of Museum Studies at San Francisco State University and formerly served as Associate Director of the Berkeley Natural History Museums at the University of California, Berkeley. Dr. Luby's recent research involves two main areas: collections-based museum research into the large shell mounds of the San Francisco Bay Area, and understanding and developing best practices for museums concerning their interactions with community or descent groups. He has published in the *Journal of Island and Coastal Archaeology, North American Archaeologist,* and *Cambridge Archaeological Journal,* as well as in *Collections: A Journal for Museum and Archives Professionals, Museum Management and Curatorship,* and *American Indian Culture and Research Journal.*

MOIRA MCCAFFREY is Vice-President of Research and Collections at the Canadian Museum of Civilization in Gatineau, Quebec. She holds an MA in archaeology from McGill University and is completing a PhD at McGill on prehistoric exchange networks in the Eastern Subarctic. McCaffrey has directed archaeological projects in northern Quebec, in western Labrador, and on the Îles-de-la-Madeleine in the Gulf of St. Lawrence. She has published papers and has edited two volumes on the archaeology of the Northeast, ethnology, and museology. McCaffrey has served on numerous advisory committees including the Cultural Properties Commission of Quebec. Her research interests include hunter-gatherer archaeology in the Eastern Subarctic, lithic exchange networks, archaeological applications of complexity theory, museology, and the history of ethnographic collections.

JENNIFER C. ORT began working on Paleoindian sites with the State Conservation and Rescue Archaeology Program in New Hampshire in 1996. She received her BA from Roger Williams University followed by cultural resource management work around New England. Her MS research at the University of Maine (Climate Change Institute) involved a major cataloging project and spatial analysis of the Bull Brook Paleoindian site as part of a National Science Foundation–funded project, including four months spent in the basement of the Peabody Essex Museum. She is currently completing her thesis while working for John Milner and Associates.

LISA PESNICHAK received her BA in anthropology from Indiana University in 2000 and her MA in anthropology from San Francisco State University in 2009. Most of her professional archaeological career has taken place in the San Francisco Bay Area working for several cultural resource management firms. In addition, she has been a part of several archaeological projects in Belize (Belize Valley Archaeological Reconnaissance and Maya Research Program). Most of her work has focused on prehistoric archaeological sites, specifically in the San Francisco Bay Area, with particular emphasis on GIS analysis of spatial organization. Pesnichak has worked with Kent Lightfoot and Ed Luby on the Shell Mound Project as a GIS specialist since 2005. She is an independent contractor in the Lake Tahoe area.

ANNA MARIE PRENTISS received her PhD from Simon Fraser University in 1993 and is Professor of Archaeology in the Department of

Anthropology at the University of Montana. She is interested in evolutionary theory, lithic technology, complex hunter-gatherers, and the archaeology of the greater Pacific Northwest and North Pacific Rim. She directed excavations at the Keatley Creek and Bridge River sites in south-central British Columbia from 1999 to 2009. Her recent publications include an edited book (*Macroevolution in Human Prehistory*, Springer, 2009) and articles in *American Antiquity*, *Journal of Anthropological Archaeology*, and *Journal of World Prehistory*.

ASA R. RANDALL is the Senior Archaeologist of the Laboratory of Southeastern Archaeology, Department of Anthropology, University of Florida, where he earned his PhD in 2010. His research focuses on the social and ecological conditions surrounding the emergence of Archaic period complex hunter-gatherer communities of the southeastern United States. Since 2003 Randall has examined the construction histories of monumental shell mounds along the St. Johns River in northeast Florida. In tandem with fieldwork, Randall uses historic records and contemporary remote sensing data to reconstruct the location, structure, and sequence of Archaic inhabitation. Prior to his work along the St. Johns, Randall investigated changing patterns of technological organization and social interaction at several localities in the Southeast, including Dust Cave, Alabama, and Stallings Island, Georgia.

BRIAN S. ROBINSON received a BA at the University of New Hampshire and a PhD in anthropology from Brown University. He had the good fortune to work on regional-scale projects with a large number of sites, in Alaska and in the Northeast, in which spatial patterning on the landscape was an important focus. Having grown up academically in volatile times when theoretical positions were often expressed polemically, he has found the constant interplay of general and particular processes a source of salvation, with many domains to explore. Past positions include a decade of cultural resource management archaeology in the Northeast and research on the Tangle Lakes project in Alaska. He is an Associate Professor in the Anthropology Department and the Climate Change Institute at the University of Maine, where Northeast culture history, ritual practices, working with Maine's Native communities, and climate change are among ongoing pursuits.

KENNETH E. SASSAMAN earned his PhD in anthropology from the University of Massachusetts, Amherst, in 1991. He is the Hyatt and Cici Brown Professor of Florida Archaeology, Department of Anthropology, University of Florida. Before joining the faculty at UF in 1998, Sassaman worked for eleven years with the Savannah River Archaeological Research Program of the South Carolina Institute of Archaeology and Anthropology, University of South Carolina. His field research in Florida has centered on the mid-Holocene hunter-gatherers of the middle St. Johns River valley, notably on the circumstances surrounding the construction of some of the oldest shell mounds in North America. In 2009, Sassaman launched the Lower Suwannee Archaeological Survey to develop data on coastal living pertinent to the challenges of sea-level rise today. He is the author or editor of eight books and over ninety articles, chapters, and monographs.

LAURA L. SCHEIBER is Assistant Professor of Anthropology and Director of the William R. Adams Zooarchaeology Laboratory at Indiana University. She received her PhD in anthropology from the University of California at Berkeley in 2001. Her research interests include hunter-gatherers, culture contact and colonialism, household production, interactions between foragers and farmers, food practices as markers of cultural identity, and long-term social dynamics on the western North American Plains and Rocky Mountains. She is the co-director of Exploring Social and Historical Landscapes of the Greater Yellowstone Ecosystem, which is a collaborative project involving Indiana University, Northwest College (Powell, Wyoming), Little Big Horn College (Crow Agency, Montana), St. Cloud State University, the National Park Service, and the U.S. Forest Service. She is co-editor of *Archaeological Landscapes on the High Plains* (University of Colorado Press, 2008) and *Across a Great Divide* (University of Arizona, 2010). She has also published articles in *Antiquity*, *Journal of Field Archaeology*, *Plains Anthropologist*, and *The American Surveyor*, as well as numerous book chapters.

H. MARTIN WOBST is Professor of Anthropology at the University of Massachusetts, Amherst, where he has taught since earning his PhD in anthropology from the University of Michigan in 1971. His research and writing center on archaeological method and theory, the ecology and demography of egalitarian societies, Old World prehistory, and postcolonial indigenous archaeologies. His most recent publications include the co-edited volumes *Indigenous Archaeologies: Decolonizing Theory and Practice* (Routledge, 2005) and *Indigenous Archaeologies: A Reader on Decolonization* (Left Coast Press, 2010).